PROPHECY AND PAPACY

F. Lamennais

PROPHECY AND PAPACY

A STUDY OF LAMENNAIS
THE CHURCH AND
THE REVOLUTION

The Birkbeck Lectures
1952-1953

ALEC R. VIDLER

Mon unique désir est de vivre et de mourir
en défendant la grande cause de l'Église et
de la société.   LAMENNAIS, 1826

SCM PRESS LTD
56 BLOOMSBURY STREET
LONDON

First published 1954

Made and printed in Great Britain by
William Clowes and Sons, Limited, London and Beccles

To
NORMAN SYKES

CONTENTS

ABBREVIATIONS

*For further details and for other abbreviations
see bibliography, pp. 288–292 infra*

A.A.	Articles de l'*Avenir*.
A.R.	Lamennais, *Affaires de Rome*.
Ahrens	Ahrens, *Lamennais und Deutschland*.
Blaize	*Œuvres inédites de F. Lamennais*. Ed. Blaize.
Boutard	Boutard, *Lamennais: sa vie et ses doctrines*.
Confidences	*Confidences de La Mennais*. Ed. de la Villerabel.
Cottu	*Lettres de Lamennais à la baronne Cottu*. Ed. d'Haussonville.
Debidour	Debidour, *Histoire des rapports de l'Église et l'État en France de 1789 à 1870*.
De Courcy	*Lettres de La Mennais à Mgr Bruté*. Ed. de Courcy.
Dispute	Maréchal, *La Dispute de l'Essai sur l'indifférence*.
Duine	Duine, *La Mennais: sa vie, ses idées, ses ouvrages*.
Essai	Lamennais, *Essai sur l'indifférence en matière de religion*.
Famille	Maréchal, *La Famille de La Mennais*.
Feugère	Feugère, *Lamennais avant l'Essai sur l'indifférence*.
Forgues	*Lamennais: Correspondance*. Ed. E. D. Forgues.
Haag	Haag, *Les Origines du Catholicisme libéral en Belgique*.
Jeunesse	Maréchal, *La Jeunesse de La Mennais*.
L. à M.	*Lettres de Lamennais à Montalembert*. Ed. E. Forgues.
Lamennais inconnu	*Lettres de Lamennais à Benoît d'Azy*. Ed. Laveille.
M. à L.	*Lettres de Montalembert à La Mennais*. Ed. Goyau and Lallemand.

9

O.C.	Lamennais, *Œuvres complètes*.
P.C.	Lamennais, *Paroles d'un Croyant*.
Portefeuille	*Le Portefeuille de Lamennais*. Ed. Goyau.
Réflexions	Lamennais, *Réflexions sur l'état de l'Église de France*.
Sainte-Beuve	Sainte-Beuve, *Les Grands Écrivains Français*. Ed. Allem.
Schmidlin	Schmidlin, *Histoire des Papes de l'époque contemporaine 1800–1846*.
Tradition	Lamennais, *Tradition de l'Église sur l'institution des évêques*.
Trannoy	Trannoy, *Le Romantisme politique de Montalembert*.
Vitrolles	*Correspondance entre Lamennais et le baron de Vitrolles*. Ed. E. Forgues.

INTRODUCTION

THIS BOOK contains a much expanded and an annotated version of six Birkbeck lectures which I delivered in Cambridge during the May term, 1953. For some years I had been intending and preparing to write a book about Lamennais, when I was honoured with an invitation from the Council of Trinity College to become Birkbeck Lecturer in the College for the academical year 1952–1953; and the Council was good enough to approve of the subject that I proposed.

I can best introduce the subject by making some remarks about the three terms in my sub-title, reserving the title itself for comment in the epilogue. The *revolution* includes here both the original French revolution, i.e. what took place between 1789 and 1799—to which I will refer when necessary as the 'great' revolution—and also the whole body of ideas and the course and sway of events stemming from and associated with the great revolution, which marked and moved the history of Europe during at least the first half of the nineteenth century. It so happens that Lamennais was born under the *ancien régime*, and lived through the great revolution, through the Consulate, the Empire, the Bourbon Restoration, the July Monarchy, the Second Republic, and on into the Second Empire. This book will not proceed so far as that, because it is concerned with ecclesiastical history, and in 1836, when the publication of *Affaires de Rome* sealed his rupture with catholicism, Lamennais ceased to be a significant figure in the history of the church.

The *church* means here primarily the Church of France, but also the Church of Rome, and in particular the papacy. It may be, however, that in the history of the Church of France during this period there can be seen a paradigm of what other national churches have done or left undone, in one way or another, at one time or another—and especially a paradigm of their shifting experiences during the last century and a half. If so, this piece of history should have a widespread and living, if somewhat melancholy, interest. The Church of France in our period was first a church privileged but far gone in decadence; then, a church persecuted, divided, and almost extirpated; then, a church restored but patronized and exploited; and finally, a church which, given new and great opportunities, can hardly be said to have risen to them. All that we shall be considering does in fact bear upon those new relations between church and state, and between church and society, which were made necessary by the crumbling of the *ancien régime*, and which nowhere yet seem to have reached a conspicuously satisfactory resettlement. But my aim is not to point out what it is fashionable to call the 'contemporary relevance' of my subject; it can be left to do that of itself. My aim is to unfold as faithfully and as fairly as I can the story of what actually happened in France and at Rome.

I am not trying, however, to produce another general introduction to the history of the Church of France during the period under review, such as was admirably done by the late Dr C. S. Phillips in *The Church in France 1789–1848* (1929). It is true that there are some minor inaccuracies in his book, and eventually it will need to be done again, in the light of the fuller knowledge that is constantly accumulating. But it is doubtful whether the time for that has yet come.

My own purpose is to illustrate in some detail and with as little generalization as possible those aspects of the church history of the period which impose themselves on the attention of anyone who studies the career and the writings of Lamennais. But why choose *Lamennais*?

First, because he always stood, though he never stood still for long, on the frontiers where church and state, church and society, meet and interact. It might be said of him that he represents the antithesis of the religion of the sacristy, and so the most important, though not the most cultivated, of the church's spheres of interest.

Secondly, different phases of his career and of his teaching appear to represent almost diametrically opposite ways in which the church could respond, and did respond or failed to respond, to the revolution in the broadest sense. Indeed it has been said that the life of Lamennais is a drama in which the history of a whole century is concentrated.[1] And there is the testimony of Sainte-Beuve: 'The story of M. de La Mennais is, more or less, the story of each one of us in these days: what he went through in his astonishing vicissitudes . . . is typical of what any number of us have been fated to experience.'[2]

[1] See Boutard, I, vii.
[2] See Sainte-Beuve, II, 290. Cp. H. J. Laski, *Authority in the Modern State*, p. 189: 'There is a sense . . . in which his (Lamennais's) career is little less than the

Thirdly, apart from this representative character, Lamennais is, in his personality and accomplishments, one of the most remarkable men that have ever lived. Renan, who was well qualified to judge in this matter, said that Lamennais had written the fifty finest pages of the century, so far as style went. But he was much more than a master of literary style. He was the founder, if anyone was, of modern ultramontanism, and of liberal catholicism, and perhaps of christian socialism,[3] while he was pronounced to be an heresiarch and apostate by a church that has since appeared to adopt many of his ideas. An Irish writer lately spoke of Lamennais as 'the greatest individual loss which the Church has sustained for four hundred years'.[4]

Lastly, though there is an immense literature about Lamennais in French, only one book has been written about him in English, namely *The Abbé de Lamennais and the Liberal Catholic Movement in France* by the Hon. W. Gibson (afterwards Lord Ashbourne), published in 1896. Since then many additional sources of information have become available. Our encyclopedias are not always reliable; the two-column entry about Lamennais in the 1945 edition of the *Encyclopædia Britannica* contains at least sixteen mistakes.[5] The only considerable essays on Lamennais in English that have appeared in this century are one by a political theorist, the late Professor H. J. Laski, in his book *Authority in the Modern State* (1919), and the other by an international historian, Professor E. L. Woodward, in his *Three Studies in European Conservatism* (1929). It would appear to be time that an ecclesiastical historian recounted and reassessed a story which both Laski and Woodward, from

mirror of his age. For the course of his life represents not merely the reaction of Catholicism from the destructive assault of the French Revolution, but also the dawning perception in the minds of able men that when due rejection of its errors has been achieved, it still embodied political truth which is fundamental to the creative understanding of modern life.' Also Claude Carcopino, *Les doctrines sociales de Lamennais*, p. 197: 'Lamennais concentre en lui et les résume en quelque sorte toutes les passions romantiques de son siècle. . . . Les questions qu'il se posait à lui-même étaient dans l'esprit de tous, les réponses qu'il y faisait correspondaient aux désirs latents de beaucoup.'

3 As regards the sense in which Lamennais may be described as a socialist, see Duine, pp. 275, 277. See also G. D. H. Cole, *Socialist Thought; the forerunners 1789–1850* (1953), which contains a chapter on Lamennais; Carcopino, *op. cit.*, part III, chap. I. 'Lamennais fut-il socialiste?'

4 W. J. Hegarty in *The Irish Ecclesiastical Record*, February 1953, p. 92.

5 The shorter entry in the *Schaff-Herzog Encyclopaedia of Religious Knowledge* (3rd edition, 1894), II, 1271, is proportionately as inaccurate.

their respective points of view, deemed to be of great and present interest.

I add a few words about sources. In 1923 abbé Duine published a Bibliography of Lamennais[6] which comprised 1,300 items, and there would be many additions he could make to it now, if he were still alive.[7] The most important sources are of course Lamennais's own published books and articles, and not least his correspondence[8] which began to be published soon after his death and has gone on being published ever since. He was an indefatigable and brilliant letter writer. His letters have made their appearance not only at sundry times, but in dozens of different books and periodicals, many of which are not at all easy of access. I have been able to lay hands on these and other rare and important sources principally through the kindness of the Frères de l'Instruction Chrétienne de Ploërmel, who most hospitably allowed me to utilize the splendid collection of mennaisian[9] literature and manuscripts in their Archives at Maison Saint-Joseph, Highlands, Jersey, C.I. I wish to take this opportunity of thanking them very warmly, especially the librarian, Brother Donat, and his assistant, Brother Libert.

Much that has been written about Lamennais has been unreliable, romantic, vitiated by controversial animus, and uncontrolled by reference to primary sources. There is no adequately documented biography even in French—as distinguished from special studies of sections of the subject matter.[10] The two best complete biographies are those by abbé Boutard, *Lamennais: sa vie et ses doctrines* (three volumes, 1905–1913), and by abbé Duine, *La Mennais: sa vie, ses idées, ses ouvrages* (one volume, 1922). Both are on the whole thoroughly reliable in matters of fact as well as strikingly sympa-

---

[6] *Essai de Bibliographie de Félicité Robert de La Mennais.*

[7] Many subsequent items are listed by H. Talvart and J. Place in their *Bibliographie des auteurs modernes de langue française* (1952), xi, 167–229.

[8] For a collection of testimonies to the importance of Lamennais's correspondence, see Versluys, pp. 4 f.

[9] The epithet 'mennaisian' is commonly and conveniently used to mean 'of or relating to Lamennais'. There has been a difference of opinion about how this word should be spelt in French: see Duine, *Bibliographie*, p. ii.

[10] Three well-documented volumes by Christian Maréchal go far to cover Lamennais's life up to and including the *Essai sur l'indifférence*, namely *La Famille de La Mennais* (1913), *La Jeunesse de La Mennais* (1913), and *La Mennais: la Dispute de l'Essai sur l'indifférence* (1925). These volumes should be consulted where other references are not given in the first three chapters of the present work.

thetic in interpretation; but Boutard's documentation is incomplete and lacking in precision, whereas Duine gives no references at all, though as the author of the afore-mentioned bibliography and of many pieces of original mennaisian research no one was in a better position to do so. I hope the present book may be found to be a useful contribution towards remedying this absence of adequate documentation.

When quoting from the French, I have done what I did in my book *The Modernist Movement in the Roman Church* and *as a rule* have translated passages appearing in the text while leaving untranslated quotations in the footnotes.

I have not succeeded in achieving complete consistency in the use of initial capital letters. So far as the titles of books are concerned, this is partly accounted for by the fact that French authors and publishers do not follow a consistent rule in the matter. Generally speaking, I prefer to dispense with initial capitals, when there is an option.

Chapter One

A BRETON FAMILY
AND THE REVOLUTION
1782–1801

HUGUES-FÉLICITÉ ROBERT DE LA MENNAIS was born
on 19[1] June 1782 at St Malo, within a stone's throw of the
house where Chateaubriand had been born fourteen years
before. He was a diminutive and delicate child, and was baptized at
home on the day following his birth.[2] His father was head of a
prosperous firm of merchants and shipowners. Félicité was the
fourth[3] son in a family of five brothers and one sister; their mother,
who was a cultured and devout woman, died in 1787, when Félicité
was five years old. Only one of his brothers played an important
part in his life, namely Jean-Marie (1780–1860), whom I shall call
Jean or, later, *abbé Jean*.[4] Their father, Pierre-Louis Robert de La
Mennais (1743–1828), I shall call *M. de La Mennais*; and his brother
and partner in the family business, Denys-François Robert des Saudrais (1744–1829), I shall call *des Saudrais*. Félicité de La Mennais I
shall call simply *Lamennais*, or *Féli* as he was known to his family.

A few words in explanation of the family's somewhat curious
nomenclature may be added. The surname or patronymic of this
family was Robert. It was Féli's grandfather, Louis-François Robert
(1717–1804), who added to it the title 'de La Mennais' from a small
farm which he had bought. ('Mennais' is derived from a celtic word
menez which means mountain.) It was the fashion at the time for
members of the upper bourgeoisie to take such titles. Des Saudrais,
being a second son, left 'de La Mennais' to his elder brother, and

---

[1] Not 'June 29', as C. S. Phillips says: *The Church in France 1789–1848*, p. 216.
[2] He was received into the church by the Bishop of St Malo (des Laurents) on
26 October 1782. For this and all other details mentioned here, except where
other references are given, see Maréchal, *Famille*, which supersedes and corrects
the information supplied in earlier books.
[3] Not 'the youngest son' as Phillips says, *ibid*.
[4] See Laveille, *Jean-Marie de La Mennais* (2 vols, 1903); also Ropartz, *La Vie et les
Œuvres de M. Jean-Marie Robert de La Mennais* (1874).

made use of another old family title. During the first part of his life
Féli signed himself 'F. de La Mennais', but after he had completely
aligned himself with the democratic movement[5] he signed himself
'F. Lamennais', which is the form of his name that has become usual.

The attitude of this Breton family to the great revolution is of
interest for two reasons. First, because it illustrates what was the
attitude of the French bourgeoisie generally, and particularly in
Brittany, to the revolution, not least in its ecclesiastical aspects.
Secondly, because it can hardly be doubted that Féli's outlook on
society and on the church was permanently influenced by the bias
of his family and by the experience of the revolution as it developed
at St Malo.[6]

In an article on 'The Role of the Breton Bourgeoisie on the eve
of the Revolution', published in 1921 in the *Annales de Bretagne*,
M. Henri Sée pointed out that the preponderant part played by the
bourgeoisie in preparing for and initiating the revolution was especially conspicuous in Brittany.[7] They had, he observed, as a class an
interest in seeking a new and more efficient system of government,
and in getting the privileges of the nobility and clergy abolished and
civil equality recognized. Moreover, they felt themselves to be quite
capable of taking over the business of government. But it was not
only their interests and their ambitions that pushed them in this
direction. The bourgeoisie was also deeply impregnated with the
liberal philosophical ideas of the eighteenth century, so that it was
idealism or ideology as well as self-interest that made them promote
and welcome the revolution.[8] M. Sée's observations are exactly
borne out by what we know about the La Mennais family.

[5] Likewise Robespierre's name had been 'Derobespierre'. See Morley, *Biographical Studies*, p. 194.

[6] I think M. Christian Maréchal, who investigated the family history more fully
than anyone had done before, was inclined to exaggerate the extent of these
early influences on Féli. But his two books, *La Famille de Lamennais* and *La
Jeunesse de La Mennais*, both published in 1913, are invaluable because of the
documents which they made available. They are freely drawn on in the present
chapter, and where no other references are given they contain the evidence for
what is said.

[7] *Op. cit.*, p. 405. Cp. Chateaubriand's remark: 'Mes compatriotes ont souvent
pris l'initiative dans nos dernières révolutions; il y a dans les têtes bretonnes
quelque chose des vents qui tourmentent les rivages de notre péninsule':
Mémoires d'outre-tombe, v, 172 f.

[8] *Ibid.*, pp. 428 f. For a classification of the ideas that were in the air, see Jacques
Godechot, *Les institutions de la France sous la Révolution et l'Empire* (1951),
book I, chap. 1, 'Les idées nouvelles à la fin du XVIIIᵉ siècle'.

Two months after Féli's birth in 1782, M. de La Mennais was appointed Sub-delegate, that is local representative, for St Malo and district of the Intendant of Brittany. Under the *ancien régime* the Intendants controlled the administration in the provinces on behalf of the king, and they wielded great authority.[9] The correspondence between the Intendant of Brittany and his Sub-delegate at St Malo has survived in the Archives of the department of Ille-et-Vilaine, the department in which St Malo is situated. It bears witness, amongst other things, to the benevolent paternalism and high standards of responsibility that were characteristic of the royal government in the years before 1789, particularly in the provinces.[10] Any government officer or civil servant in any age, who carried out the instructions which the Intendant of Brittany had printed and circulated to his Sub-delegates in 1788,[11] would have nothing with which to reproach himself. It was not lack of concern or goodwill on the part of the king and his representatives that made the revolution inevitable, but the obsoleteness of the traditional machinery of government and of the privileges of the aristocracy and the church, which no longer bore any relation to the services they rendered to the common-wealth. These privileges, however, were so firmly and deeply entrenched that they could not be shifted without an explosion.

The Intendant of Brittany and his Sub-delegate at St Malo carried out their duties most conscientiously. For instance, whenever there was a threatened shortage of food whether for human consumption or for cattle, or of raw materials for the local industries, they at once consulted about precautionary measures and measures of relief. But there arose an interesting difference between them. Whereas the Intendant was inclined to depend on direct government regulations and provisions, M. de La Mennais advocated free trade and private enterprise. He was a disciple of Turgot and the physio-crats. His liberal economic principles were no doubt in accordance with his business interests, but it is also clear that he sincerely believed that the needs of the people would be better met by dependence on local initiative and responsibility than by the provision of relief by central government regulation.

9 See Funck-Brentano, *The Old Regime in France* (1929), p. 107; Morley, *Bio-graphical Studies*, p. 37.

10 Pasquier in his *Mémoires* (I, 41) said of the years that preceded 1789: 'Si l'État n'avait pas eu de grands ministres, les provinces avaient eu des intendants fort éclairés et très habiles.'

11 See *Famille*, pp. 59–63.

M. de La Mennais combined with a sturdy independence of
character a self-sacrificing humanitarianism. In times of scarcity he
sold goods at cost price on a large scale, and incurred substantial
financial losses. He also took a leading part in initiating charitable
undertakings. The church he valued chiefly as a bulwark of morality.
He was proud of the tradition of tough austerity and moral earnest-
ness that was characteristic of St Malo. 'There are few towns in the
kingdom', he wrote to the Intendant in 1785, 'that have preserved
such pure morals as ours especially in the upper class of the inhabitants. To that no doubt is due the spiritual energy which maintains
a sense of patriotism and honour, that has unhappily been too much
enfeebled in the large cities.'[12]

St Malo certainly had a distinct character that marked successive
generations of its citizens. Despite the fact that most of its old buildings were destroyed by bombardment in 1944,[13] it is still easy for a
visitor to imagine how, in the days before modern means of communication and transport were invented, the peculiar geographical
situation of this seaport must have affected the character of its inhabitants. Built on a circle of rock, hemmed in by huge walls of
granite, its lofty houses were crowded one against another and
separated only by narrow streets. It had the intimacy of a shelter,
especially when in stormy weather furious waves hurled themselves
against the ramparts; but the inhabitants were also enclosed in a
prison, from which in order to subsist they had to break out and to
venture far afield. This was for long a home of corsairs. It nourished
strong men who were drawn ineluctably to strange and daring
adventures.

The high standard of morality that M. de La Mennais claimed for
St Malo was no doubt a consequence of the fact that the traditional
catholic piety was still a living force there. Earlier in the eighteenth
century St Malo had been a stronghold of jansenism, and although
after much controversy the 'heresy' had been officially suppressed it
had left a puritan imprint on the place; its tradition was sober,
severe, and even sombre. A meditation on the Psalm, *De profundis*,
by Mme de La Mennais, Féli's mother, exists in manuscript;[14] this
betrays a spiritual scrupulousness and anxiety, which may be attributed to jansenism, and which may account for certain features of
Féli's own spiritual experience.

[12] See *Famille*, p. 5.   [13] See Paul Aubry, *L'Agonie de Saint-Malo* (1945).
[14] See *Famille*, chap. 6.

As regards M. de La Mennais, Maréchal summed up his attitude to the church as follows: 'M. de La Mennais was fond of his bishop . . . and of his curé . . . he held them in great respect. We must not however suppose that he was a very rigid catholic; at this time, so far as one can judge, he was a christian according to the style of the upper bourgeoisie towards the end of the eighteenth century. He professed indifference to dogma and, so far as the practice of religion went, he was lukewarm. A good bishop, a good curé, were for him, as for his brother des Saudrais and for most of their contemporaries, models of virtue, apostles of charity . . . masters and examples of morality.'[15]

Industry, benevolence, and broadmindedness were the virtues that he esteemed. One of the first things he tried to do as Sub-delegate was to get the mendicant orders prohibited from coming from elsewhere to beg in St Malo, and in this he had the support of the local clergy. He told the Intendant that he would prefer to see the money given to hospitals and schools, where it would do much more good.[16] Monastic orders which were dependent on alms he regarded as out of date, and not suited au siècle présent. He would like to have seen them abolished.[17] He urged his views on the Intendant, who in fact shared them but pointed out that it was not within their power to institute such a reform. 'What you say is certainly well-founded,' he wrote. 'But it would not be feasible to put a stop to the abuse in question (i.e. mendicants' asking for alms) except by suppressing the various monasteries for men and women which are not endowed and which by their constitution are obliged to live by alms. All these establishments, no doubt very pious in themselves, do not appear to me to be in harmony with conditions in the present century, but so long as the government considers it must let them continue, the persons who have embraced this state of poverty must necessarily be given permission to seek alms for themselves. . . .'[18]

This is an instance of the way in which M. de La Mennais's experience as Sub-delegate revealed the difficulty of securing reforms that he regarded as necessary, and prepared him to welcome the revolution.

Another experience, in which he had a keen personal interest— at any rate until his wife's death in 1787[19]—must have told in the

[15] Famille, p. 76.   [16] Famille, pp. 78 f.
[17] Famille, p. 80.   [18] Famille, p. 81.
[19] After which he does not seem to have cared so much about it. See Famille, pp. 196 f., 202.

same direction.[20] In recognition of his services as Sub-delegate
and of the notable sacrifices he had made for the public good, the
Intendant proposed that he should be raised to the nobility. But
the aristocracy was at this time very jealous of the admission to its
ranks of more members of the third estate, and although there could
be no question of M. de La Mennais's deserts there were unaccount-
able delays and obstacles, and in the end it was only by a direct
approach to the king that the honour was granted. It is said that
M. de La Mennais was the last man to be ennobled before the
revolution.[21]

But what may have made him despair of the *ancien régime* even
more than the delay in the honourable recognition of his public
services was the refusal of the authorities to comply with the request,
which the Intendant made on his behalf, that he should be excused
from making the payment that was required in order that his en-
noblement should be registered. The request was made on the very
reasonable ground that he had already given a large amount of
money for the public benefit. There were again exasperating delays
and mysterious refusals, and the matter was not settled when the
revolution broke out and put it out of the question,[22] with the result
that his title was never formally registered. Oddly enough, this
misfortune served him in good stead later on at a time of extreme
jacobin ascendancy, when he was being attacked as an aristocrat, for
he was able to produce a certificate to say that he never had been
ennobled.[23]

With the revolution M. de La Mennais's office as Sub-delegate
came to an end, and he decided to devote himself chiefly to the
conduct of his business. But fortunately just about the same time his
brother, des Saudrais, entered public life as (what we should call) a
town councillor, and the Archives of the commune of St Malo
enable us to trace his support of the new régime, including its
ecclesiastical measures. There is every reason to suppose that the
two brothers saw eye to eye though des Saudrais, as we shall see
later, was much more a man of ideas and of letters. He undoubtedly
regarded his municipal office (he not infrequently deputized for the

[20] Cp. *Famille*, p. 228.
[21] See E. Spuller, *Lamennais*, p. 18. Blaize, *Essai biographique*, pp. 16–20, prints the
full text of 'Lettres de noblesse en faveur du Sieur Pierre-Louis Robert de La
Mennais, négociant armateur à Saint-Malo'.
[22] See *Famille*, p. 201. The refusal was probably determined by the precarious
state of the public finances.
[23] See *Famille*, pp. 330 ff.

mayor[24]) as an opportunity of putting into practice the ideas that he had imbibed from his favourite philosophers, and especially from Rousseau.

In March 1790 des Saudrais joined in supporting those monks in St Malo who took advantage of the decrees of the National Assembly that authorized them to abandon the cloister. The municipal council heard with approval a denunciation of 'monastic slavery' as the most formidable of tyrannies, from which the revolution was providing a way of deliverance.[25]

In May 1790 the council prefaced new regulations that it was making for the local police with some general observations in the spirit of Rousseau and in the style of the time:

> To believe that man may be the sole judge of his actions would be an error destructive of all society; therefore the National Assembly, in decreeing the rights of man, equality and liberty, has been no less occupied with the drawing up of laws, which alone can assure to him the enjoyment of these precious advantages. . . .
>
> If each man were arbitrarily to determine his own conduct, no order would reign in society. The passions of men, without guide or check, would at once upset the order and harmony of the body corporate.
>
> There must then be a public order on which depend the safety and tranquillity of each man, and this public order cannot exist without the law.
>
> What then is the law? It is the expression of the general will about matters of common interest, put into action by those members of society to whom it entrusts its execution.[26]

The police regulations, that were introduced with this rhetoric, secured protection for the national religion—the catholic church serving the purpose of Rousseau's state religion. Consequently, the council expected the ministers of the church to submit themselves to the general will and to act as public functionaries. The curé of St Malo, however, when he was directed to read from the pulpit

[24] For the municipal organization of St Malo at this time, see E. Herpin, *Saint-Malo sous la Révolution 1789–1800* (1931). It is regrettable that this book, which contains much interesting information, is not as precisely documented as it ought to be.

[25] See *Famille*, pp. 235–238.

[26] *Famille*, pp. 239 f. The last sentence, as Maréchal points out, is directly dependent on Rousseau's *Social Contract*.

the decrees of the National Assembly that dealt with the treatment of religious who abandoned the cloister, refused to do so. Among the reasons he gave was that the reading of the decrees would have a disturbing effect on the people. The council indignantly rejected this idea, asserting that the curé's suggestion was an insult to the town of St Malo, since it would give the impression that 'the people of this town were still unhappily enthralled by that fanaticism and superstition which the sensible philosophy of the eighteenth century had surely banished for ever from the French empire'.[27]

Likewise, the communal assembly of St Malo welcomed the decrees of the National Assembly that deprived the church of its property. Here is an extract from the report of its meeting on 25 May 1790:

> The National Assembly, on the one hand by restoring to the nation the ownership of the property which several centuries of abuse had unfortunately concentrated in the hands of the clergy and of the religious houses, and on the other hand by accepting responsibility for the expenses of public worship and for the payment of its ministers, has found in these two acts the means of saving the state, and of bringing back the clergy to its proper functions. . . .
>
> The whole of France has applauded this great operation; the clergy itself, at least that numerous and worthy part of it which bears practically the whole burden of the ministry. . . .[28]

The parish clergy were generally popular in contrast to the hierarchy and the religious orders. It is to be remembered that 'the value of the land and buildings belonging to the church was variously estimated at between a fifth and a half of all such property in the country', and that the church's 'annual income might be anything from fifty to a hundred millions sterling'.[29]

The decrees about the civil constitution of the clergy, which had been passed by the National Assembly on 12 July 1790 and promulgated by the king on 24 August, reached St Malo on 14 October. They were welcomed by the municipal authorities who required that they be put into effect. The civil constitution of the clergy[30]

[27] *Famille*, p. 244.   [28] *Famille*, p. 245.
[29] J. M. Thompson, *The French Revolution*, p. 142.
[30] See Debidour, chap. 2; de la Gorce, *Histoire religieuse de la Révolution française*, I, book iv; de Bourgogne and de Barthélemy, *La Révolution en Bretagne*, pp. 212–216; A. Latreille, *L'Église catholique et la Révolution française*, I, 87–104.

reconstructed the diocesan boundaries of the French Church so that they became co-terminous with the civil departments. Fifty-seven dioceses were suppressed, including that of St Malo, which has never since been revived.[31] Archbishoprics were abolished, but there were sees with metropolitan status, of which Rennes was one. The Bishop of Rome ceased to have any authority over the Church of France, though this was said to be 'without prejudice to the unity of faith and the communion which will be maintained with the visible head of the universal church'. Each bishop was to be curé of his cathedral church; cathedral chapters and other dignitaries were abolished. But the bishop was to have a staff which would be his diocesan council and without which he could not act in matters of jurisdiction. Bishops were to be elected by the civil electorate of the department: before the election the electors were to hear mass and to take an oath that they would consider only the interests of religion. The bishop-elect would seek confirmation from the metropolitan or senior bishop, but not from the pope. He would merely inform the pope that he had been elected. Curés would be elected in a similar manner.[32]

On 27 November 1790 the National Assembly passed a law by which all bishops and curés then in office had to take an oath accepting the civil constitution; otherwise they could not continue in office. This law was sanctioned by the king on 26 December, though with the utmost reluctance. The civil constitution was formally condemned by the pope in briefs of 10 March and 13 April 1791. The most probable estimate is that over the country as a whole about fifty per cent of the clergy affected took the oath and about fifty per cent refused to take it.[33]

At St Malo the bishop (Cortois de Pressigny, 1745–1823) had left the town in October 1790,[34] and in the following year he emigrated. The curé had consented to continue his ministrations only under

31 It would have been revived by the Concordat of 1817, if that had ever come into force. See Roussel, *Correspondants*, p. 101.
32 The aim of those who drew up the civil constitution was to return to what they regarded as the practice of the primitive church. 'Les philosophes étaient séduits par ce retour à l'âge d'or du christianisme, les gallicans par la perspective d'une Église à peu près indépendante du pape, les jansénistes par l'espoir d'une vie religieuse plus austère.' Godechot, *Les Institutions de la France sous la Révolution et l'Empire* (1951), p. 224.
33 J. M. Thompson, *op. cit.*, p. 237; cp. A. Latreille, *op. cit.*, I, 95.
34 See art. by E. Herpin on 'La Fin d'un Évêché' in *Revue de Bretagne*, June 1909, pp. 281–292.

protest. More trouble arose when the oath arrived in January 1791. The municipal authorities deplored the refusal of some of the clergy to take the oath and the controversy to which it gave rise. The municipality declared that it 'was very sorry to see that an oath of fidelity to the constitution, which is the first duty of every citizen who holds any public office in the state, should become the pretext, insiduously used by fanaticism and ill-will, to mislead the people, to raise the spirit of revolt, and to set in motion, if it were possible, in the eighteenth century, a war of religion'.[35] At the same time, it was liberal enough to issue orders that both the clergy who took the oath and those who refused were equally to be protected from interference and insult.

There is no doubt, however, that the municipal authorities were all in favour of the introduction of the civil constitution of the clergy. As the curé (Le Saout) had refused to take the oath and also to proclaim from the pulpit the instructions of the National Assembly about the new ecclesiastical constitution, they arranged for a municipal officer to read it in his stead (13 February 1791).[36] Likewise, the election of Claude Le Coz (1740–1815) as metropolitan bishop of the North-West with his seat at Rennes was proclaimed at St Malo with a *Te Deum*, sung by a hospital chaplain (Chedeville) who had accepted the constitution, and who was subsequently elected constitutional curé of the neighbouring parish of St Servan.

Des Saudrais participated in all these acts, and also in the acquisition by the town of the episcopal palace which was turned over to municipal offices, and in the election of a new conforming curé of St Malo[37] which was celebrated with enthusiasm on 23 June 1791. On 8 July the new bishop visited the town and des Saudrais joined in the elaborate ceremonial and acclamations with which he was received. A little later two non-juring priests who were trying to turn one of the churches in St Malo into a cave of Adullam were ordered by the municipality to leave the town.

As time went on, the municipal authorities at St Malo were pressed by the directory of the district to take more drastic measures against the non-jurors and the religious orders, but at first they complied

[35] *Famille*, p. 249; Herpin, *Saint-Malo sous la Révolution*, pp. 63 f.

[36] For the dispersion of the non-juring clergy of St Malo, see Herpin, *op. cit.*, pp. 66 f., 102–105.

[37] Alexandre-René Duhamel, 'Docteur en théologie de l'université d'Angers'. See Herpin, *op. cit.*, p. 100. In 1794 Duhamel abandoned the priesthood and married. He was then appointed municipal librarian. *Ibid.*, p. 204.

with some reluctance. There was, however, serious trouble over the first communion at St Malo in April 1792,[38] the non-jurors refusing to hand over some of the properties that were needed for the ceremony and causing disturbances during the proceedings. Des Saudrais took a prominent part in handling this matter, and it seems to have led him and his colleagues to adopt a severer attitude to the non-jurors; sterner measures against them and against the religious orders were adopted shortly after this.[39] At the end of September 1792 with the rest of the municipality he accepted the abolition of royalty and the proclamation of the Republic.

Des Saudrais ceased to be a town councillor about the end of 1792. It is evident that M. de La Mennais had so far shared his brother's attitude to the revolution. He had contributed handsomely from his purse to public funds and had performed various public duties. On 25 February 1792 he had been elected president of the chamber of commerce. Everything suggests that until 1793 the two brothers were regarded as advanced revolutionaries. There is a report, which was never contradicted, that they fitted out a warship, called Le Révolutionnaire, which was adorned with the figure of a sansculotte holding a dagger in one hand and the head of a tyrant in the other.[40] We cannot however be sure at what stage their support of revolutionary measures ceased to be sincere, and became merely tactical, that is, gestures that would keep them in the good graces of the extreme jacobins.

M. de La Mennais and his brother were genuine liberals and, when a tyranny began to be installed under the cloak of revolutionary liberty, their enthusiasm began to cool. They had welcomed and supported the revolution because it had abolished archaic privileges, had introduced a more rational system of government, and had ushered in, as they supposed, a happier era, not least for themselves. It was the Terror, which was a brutal experience for the inhabitants of St Malo, that shook them and led them to revise their ideas about the relation between order and liberty and about the church.

Towards the end of 1793 the port of St Malo appeared to be exposed to a double threat. On the one side, there was the threat of attack by the English fleet, for England and France were now at war.

38 Cp. Herpin, op. cit., p. 101.
39 For details see Herpin, op. cit., pp. 205–229.
40 Famille, p. 310. This was recorded in a newspaper entitled L'Écho de l'Ouest in 1819, and presumably would have been denied by Féli or his brother, if it could have been.

On the other side, the royalist armies of the Vendée were making formidable incursions into Brittany and Normandy, and were likely to try to capture this strategic port. The revolutionary government in Paris, that is the Committee of Public Safety to which the Convention had delegated its powers, was therefore anxious to make sure of the defence of St Malo, especially as there were reports that the loyalty of the local authorities could not be depended upon. The government's way of dealing with problems of this kind was to send representatives on mission. Some of these representatives had had little experience of exercising political authority, were easily corrupted by the semi-dictatorial powers assigned to them, and became notorious for the brutality of their administration. Such was Jean-Baptiste Le Carpentier (1759–1829), about whom an interesting and well-documented biography was published in 1912.[41]

He arrived in St Malo on 15 December 1793, and for the next eight months conducted an increasingly ferocious reign of terror in the town and surrounding district. The prisons were packed and the guillotine constantly in motion. Local officials were replaced. 'Aristocrats' and non-juring priests[42] were the first objects of Le Carpentier's purging operations. To the clergy of the Constitutional Church he was, to begin with, more indulgent, but before long he set about the entire suppression of the traditional religion and its ministers. He ordered the strict observance of the new kalendar which had been introduced in October 1793,[43] and so of the *décadi* instead of Sunday. The curious revolutionary rites of this period were established.[44] Denunciation of priests, except those who had married, was encouraged, so that they could be imprisoned. The churches were despoiled of their ornaments, and transformed into temples of Reason or of the Supreme Being in accordance with the changes in the object of the official cultus.

[41] Le Vicomte de Brachet, *Le Conventionnel J.-B. Le Carpentier d'après de nouveaux documents.*

[42] The free-masons were also suppressed on the ground that secret societies cannot be tolerated in a republican régime, 'où la liberté est devenu un bien commun, dont la jouissance n'a pas besoin des ombres du mystère, et d'ailleurs toute réunion d'individus qui se dérobent à la vigilance publique ne peut qu'exciter la suspicion dans un temps où les actions doivent être soumis à la surveillance du gouvernement'. See Herpin, *op. cit.*, p. 187.

[43] Details of the new kalendar will be found in de Bourgogne and de Barthélemy, *La Révolution en Bretagne*, p. 53.

[44] For a description, based on contemporary records, of the colourful rites that were celebrated at St Malo, see Herpin, *op. cit.*, pp. 189–204.

Not until the thermidorian reaction which followed the fall of Robespierre (27 July 1794) was a measure of tranquillity restored to St Malo, for then Le Carpentier was recalled. M. de La Mennais and his brother escaped victimization at this time, but only because they continued to offer prudent proofs of their patriotism.[45] For example, when in February 1794 Le Carpentier ordered the expulsion of the religious from the hospital and its secularization, M. de La Mennais accepted election as its treasurer; even so he was forced to resign after two months as a result of a denunciation, and was reinstalled only when he had secured 'un certificat de civisme'. Le Carpentier, before he left, extorted vast sums of money from the rich merchants of St Malo, threatening them with the guillotine as an alternative,[46] and the de La Mennais family business was in consequence three parts ruined.

These experiences under the Terror, which are said to have caused the death of Mme des Saudrais,[47] opened the eyes of the whole family to what was involved in jacobinism. This was not at all what they had bargained for, when they had welcomed 1789. There are not sufficient data to enable us to follow in detail the change of outlook that came over M. de La Mennais and his brother during the next few years. It is not suggested that they underwent anything in the nature of a sudden conversion. But we shall not be surprised to learn that upon the advent of Napoleon 'Papa Mennais', as Féli's grandfather was called in the family, hastened to buy a bust of the first consul which he put on his mantelpiece,[48] nor that the restoration of the Church of France in 1802 met with the warm approval of this, as of many other, bourgeois families.

These events formed the background of Féli's upbringing. They cannot have failed to make a deep impression upon his imagination. They go far to account for his life-long preoccupation with the quest for a form of social order in which liberty would be secure from arbitrary interference. Moreover, the discovery that liberalism was deeply rooted in the tradition of his family means that Lamennais was faithful to his origins when the love of liberty and the hatred of tyranny became his ruling passions. They were manifestly so in the end, and perhaps were fundamentally so all along, even in the most authoritarian phases of his evolution.

[45] See *Famille*, pp. 311–319.   [46] For details, see *ibid.*, pp. 323 ff.
[47] See Blaize, I, 11.
[48] See Roussel, *Revue des questions historiques*, April 1908, p. 576.

How much reliable information about his childhood do we possess? A variety of anecdotes has been collected and handed down and embroidered in the process. In later life Lamennais himself seldom spoke about his early life, and I do not feel that much reliance can be placed on the stories that biographies have contained. Anyhow, there are only two that I propose to mention here.

One is the story, which Ange Blaize (1811–1871), Féli's nephew and one of his earliest biographers, says that he had from Féli himself,[49] to the effect that, when Jean was thirteen (i.e. in 1793), a non-juring priest used to celebrate clandestine masses in an attic in the de La Mennais's house in the centre of St Malo. This story has been taken as evidence that the family's sympathies throughout the revolution were with the non-juring clergy and that Féli was brought up not only 'in the catholic religion' but also to regard 'the revolution with horror'.[50] But in view of what we now know of the family's attitude to the revolution and to the Constitutional Church until 1793, that inference from the story cannot be warranted. It may have been a recollection of something that took place at a later date.

The other story, which Blaize also says he had from his uncle, and which would be scarcely credible about any one except Lamennais, tells that when he was eight years old he was walking one day on the ramparts of St Malo with his nurse, while a heavy sea was raging. After watching it for a time, as other people were doing near by, the child exclaimed: 'They are looking at what I am looking at, but they do not see what I see.' Blaize says that whenever in his old age Lamennais recalled this incident he used to say that so conceited a notion in a child of eight still made him shudder.[51] If it never happened, it is a marvellously apt piece of proleptic mythology.

He was certainly a strange child. The contradictions that marked his character in its maturity were already present. He was self-willed and intractable, constantly going off on wild expeditions by himself, yet eager for affection and docile to surrounding influences so long as they were not forced upon him. Since his mother had died when he was five,[52] and his father was preoccupied with his business and

---

[49] See Blaize, I, 10, and also his *Essai biographique*, pp. 17 ff.

[50] See Blaize, *Essai biographique*, p. 14. Cp. Forgues, I, 6; Spuller, *Lamennais*, p. 35; de Courcy, p. xii; L. de Villefosse, *Lamennais ou l'occasion manquée*, pp. 16 f.; E. Dowden, *Studies in Literature 1789–1877* (1878), p. 315.

[51] See Blaize, I, 8.

[52] In 1787, not 1797. E. L. Woodward was mistaken when he wrote: 'Her death in 1797 was an irreparable loss to a lovable and sensitive boy of sixteen.'— *Three Studies in European Conservatism*, p. 250.

with public affairs, the boy was left a good deal to his own devices, and attempts to provide him with a tutor did not meet with much success.

At length, his uncle des Saudrais took his education in hand. Des Saudrais had no children of his own, he was a man of keen intellectual interests and of literary tastes and accomplishments, and he knew how to handle his difficult nephew. For he knew his Rousseau. Rousseau is the father of what are called 'free' methods of education, of education by means of self-expression, the method of letting children do what they want. Whatever may be thought of this method as a general rule, it was marvellously suited to a boy like Féli. No habits were to be imposed on children, according to Rousseau; in everything they were to be encouraged to be masters of themselves and to do what they wanted.[53]

Des Saudrais adopted this method,[54] and allowed Féli to follow his own inclinations, discreetly guiding them into what he regarded as desirable directions.[55] Charmed by the methods of his new instructor Féli became a consuming, if undisciplined, reader and student. He read widely in all kinds of literature, and in the coming years he taught himself several languages—English, Spanish, German, and Italian as well as Latin and Greek, and later Hebrew.[56]

He was for a time apprenticed to the family business, but he was hardly likely to settle for long at an accountant's desk. From now onwards much of his time, at any rate in the summer, seems to have been spent at La Chesnaie, a country house near Dinan, which became the property of Jean and himself on their maternal grandfather's death in 1799. Thirty years later, La Chesnaie will be famous as the home and headquarters of the whole movement which Lamennais inspired. It stands in the history of the Church of France for at least as much as, say, Oriel and Littlemore do in the history of the Church of England. As this is the first occasion of its mention, it may at once be briefly introduced.

La Chesnaie is much the same today as it was 150 years ago, and

---

53 See Rousseau, *Émile* (Ed. F. and P. Richard), e.g. p. 42.

54 His library is known to have contained a brochure entitled *Mon élève, ou Émile instituteur, nouvelle éducation nationale* (1791). See Maréchal, *Jeunesse*, p. 16.

55 It is probably in this sense that the often repeated story should be understood about des Saudrais shutting Féli in his library as a punishment. He was wise enough to tell the boy not to read the books he specially wanted him to read! Cp. *Jeunesse*, pp. 15 ff.

56 See Blaize, I, 14. It is interesting to note that Maistre also 'unaided . . . taught himself five languages'. See Morley, *Biographical Studies*, p. 138.

anyone entering Brittany by St Malo will find that it is well worth a visit. The house has often been described as a château; Lamennais once, when he was expecting some distinguished visitors, described it as a cottage.[57] It is neither one nor the other, but a small country house, which you are surprised to hear accommodated in its heyday quite a dozen persons. The house derives its charms from its deep seclusion amid woods on the edge of a forest, and from a beautiful lake that lies beside it—a lake about which I noted, when I was last there, that nowhere had I seen kingfishers flying in such profusion and with such an absence of timidity.

Many who have experienced the fascination of La Chesnaie have attempted to describe it in words. Here is what the poet Maurice de Guérin (1810–1839) wrote in a letter when he first arrived at La Chesnaie in December 1832 as a young mennaisian recruit:

> La Chesnaie is a sort of oasis in the heart of the steppes of Brittany. In front of the house stretches a spacious garden broken by a terrace planted with lime trees, and at the bottom there is a tiny chapel. I am very fond of this little oratory where one breathes two kinds of peace, the peace of solitude and the peace of the Lord. In the spring we shall go to our prayers between two lines of flowers. To the east and a few paces from the house, there sleeps a little lake between two woods that are full of birds in the dry season; and then to the right and to the left, on every side, are woods, woods, everywhere woods. It is melancholy now that everything is bare, and the forests are rust-coloured, with the Breton sky always overcast and so low that it seems to want to crush you; but, with the return of spring, the sky clears, the woods come to life again, and everything will be enchanting.[58]

The principal difference between what de Guérin describes and what may be seen now is the absence of the chapel in the garden, which was built by Lamennais in 1812, but was demolished before the end of the century. But of course it had not yet been built at the time with which we are now concerned, and classical culture was more in evidence at La Chesnaie than the catholic cultus.

Des Saudrais was an amateur of style as well as of ideas. *Multa in*

---

[57] *L. à M.* (3 June 1833), p. 141.
[58] Maurice de Guérin, *Correspondance* (Ed. Bernard d'Harcourt), pp. 66 f.; cp. *ibid.*, p. 58. See also C. Latreille on 'Lamennais à La Chesnaie' in *Mercure de France*, 15 April 1907; C. Sainte-Foi, *Souvenirs de Jeunesse*, pp. 87 ff.; Boutard, II, 85 ff.; Laveille, *J.-M. de La Mennais*, I, 59 ff.

paucis was his literary motto. He set great store on the virtues of lucidity, precision, and conciseness as well as of depth and vigour. At La Chesnaie Féli learned to develop the art of writing as well as the powers of his mind. Jean, who seems always to have been destined for the priesthood, was often there too, and we know something of the discussions that went on between uncle and nephews, since notes and compositions, which sprang out of them, have survived in manuscript. Des Saudrais never treated his nephews *de haut en bas*, but took it for granted that they were all three on an equal footing. Perhaps for this reason Féli seems to have followed closely in the wake of his uncle's mind.

Féli, like his uncle, seems first to have fallen under the spell of Rousseau and perhaps of the more sceptical eighteenth-century philosophers. But des Saudrais was now beginning to wonder whether they were such oracles of wisdom as he had been accustomed to suppose, and Féli was soon wondering too. Des Saudrais found himself returning to Montaigne and Horace,[59] and relishing their good sense, their discrimination, and their freedom from excess. Then both uncle and nephews were much struck by the conversion of La Harpe (1738–1803), which was announced in 1797.[60] La Harpe had been a friend of Voltaire, one of the most violent of *les philosophes*, and an outspoken atheist. He was converted to catholicism as a result of his experiences during the revolution, and he became an apostle of that kind of reaction that was to be variously developed by Chateaubriand, Bonald, and Maistre—as is indicated by the title of one of his brochures: *Du fanatisme dans la langue révolutionnaire ou de la persécution suscitée par les barbares du dix-huitième siècle contre la religion chrétienne et ses ministres.*[61]

Between 1798 and 1802 des Saudrais himself, stimulated and assisted by his nephews, tried his hand at composing a small treatise which pointed the same way. The manuscript, which has survived, was copied in the handwriting of Féli, with a preface copied by Jean.[62] It was entitled *Les Philosophes*, and is introduced thus. 'Once upon a time all the Philosophers of the Earth, convinced at last that they would never agree among themselves, unless they met together

---

[59] The only book that des Saudrais published was *Vingt odes d'Horace, traduit en française par un de ses amis* (1905). See Duine, p. 17.

[60] See Duine on 'Influence de La Harpe sur La Mennais' in *Annales de Bretagne*, January 1913, pp. 198–202. Chateaubriand has a good deal to say about La Harpe in his *Mémoires d'outre-tombe*, see II, 217, 236 ff., 409–412.

[61] See Duine, p. 13.   [62] See *Jeunesse*, p. 19.

in a corner of the world where with complete liberty of speech they could canvass, study, and decide the great and important questions which concern the human race, arranged to carry out this fine project, as you are going to hear.'[63] The two principal questions discussed are the existence of God and the immortality of the soul, and in each case various types of philosophical negation are first presented with vivacity and irony, and then the case for belief is stated in more serious manner. Here, while des Saudrais still draws largely on Rousseau, it is significant that it is chiefly upon Pascal that he depends to clinch the argument.[64]

There was a deeper note now in his reflections on religion. Before long, he was translating the book of Job and the book of Wisdom.[65] As for Féli, he is now—at the turn of the century—already adept at arguing on the christian side, but his faith is not yet engaged and he is not yet a practising catholic. Sainte-Beuve, who was fairly intimate with him thirty years later, and whom Lamennais may have taken into his confidence about this period of his life, summed up his position thus: 'Christianity had become for the hot-headed young man a very probable opinion which he would defend in the world, which he would produce in conversation, but which no longer ruled his heart or his life.'[66]

In 1799 Volney's *Leçons d'histoire* was published, and there is in manuscript a refutation of this sceptical work which Féli appears to have helped Jean in composing.[67] It shows in what direction the wind was blowing at La Chesnaie and the change of outlook that had come over this Breton family since 1789. Here is a passage directed against *les philosophes*:

> Ah! it is from them that all the tyrants, who have brought desolation to France and covered it with blood, learned their lessons: they have done no more than draw the conclusions from their false principles; and the appalling disorders of which we have been the unhappy witnesses are the necessary result of the absence of all religious belief, and the outcome of all the wild systems of these insane philosophers who persuade themselves that they can govern men while speaking to them only of *liberty* and *reason*—of liberty, to which they have erected altars, while the

---

[63] *Ibid.*, p. 22.

[64] As regards the influence of Pascal on Lamennais from this time onwards, see Duine on 'La Mennais et Pascal' in *Annales de Bretagne*, 1923, pp. 568–577.

[65] See *Jeunesse*, pp. 31–34.   [66] Sainte-Beuve, II, 13.

[67] See Duine, pp. 21 f.

whole nation was groaning under the most cruel slavery; of reason, to which they opened temples, while they were outraging it at every moment both by their words and their deeds. Oh! why do they not listen to, and follow the example of, all the great law-givers who were before them, and who found that 'it was easier to build a city in the air than to give it a government and security without religion . . . ?' (Plutarch). Wretched philosophy! all our evils are your work; when you came among us you brought with you every kind of crime; you have known only how to destroy and to corrupt; misery, ignorance, egoism, licentiousness—these are the gifts you bring, these are the benefits you confer![68]

Jean already knew that he wanted to be a priest. But Féli was as yet quite uncertain about his future. In 1800 at the age of eighteen he was restless and unsettled and was seriously thinking of emi-grating.[69] It was not the last time he would think of doing that,[70] for he was never to settle down, nor to rest anywhere for long. In that respect, if in no other, Lamennais was certainly a child of the revolution.

[68] See Duine, pp. 22 f.   [69] See Blaize, I, 19.   [70] Cp. Versluys, p. 66.

Chapter Two

REACTING TO NAPOLEON
1802-1816

LORD MORLEY described Chateaubriand's book, *Le Génie du Christianisme*, as 'the most superb rainbow that ever rose in a storm-beaten sky'.[1] The metaphor is as apt as it is colourful. This book is the classical exposition of the romantic case for christianity. Its appeal is based on the view that christianity is beautiful, rather than on the ground that it is true. Chateaubriand has been described as *Doctor sensibilis*.[2] Considered as a rational apology for the truth of christianity, the book was no doubt as unsubstantial as a rainbow. But after the darkness, the disturbances, and the desolation of the revolutionary storms—which had begun, continued, and ended with the invocation of Reason—men were ready to be carried away by what was colourful and pleasing to the emotions, without asking too closely whether it was true. And even if Chateaubriand's superb rainbow was unsubstantial, it was accompanied by a quite substantial transformation of the social scene.

Le Génie du Christianisme was published on 14 April 1802. Four days later, on Easter day, the concordat[3] which Napoleon had negotiated with the pope was solemnly promulgated in Paris. On the same day Napoleon ratified the Peace of Amiens which brought to an end the state of war with England. With imposing ceremony

[1] Morley, *Recollections*, I, 170. With this image there may be compared Bonald's description of *Le Génie du Christianisme*: 'La vérité dans les ouvrages de raisonnement est un roi à la tête de son armée au jour de combat; dans l'ouvrage de M. de Chateaubriand, elle est comme une reine au jour de son couronnement, au milieu de la pompe des fêtes, de l'éclat de sa cour, des acclamations des peuples, des décorations et des parfums.' Quoted by Mouliné, *De Bonald*, p. 53.

[2] Poulet, *Histoire de l'Église de France: époque contemporaine*, p. 118.

[3] For an account of the negotiations and for the full text of the concordat, see Constant, *L'Église de France sous le consulat et l'empire*. H. H. Walsh, *The Concordat of 1801: a study of the problem of nationalism in the relations of church and state* (New York, 1933), contributes little or nothing to our knowledge about the concordat itself. But see also Debidour, chap. 6.

the leaders of the Republic went to the cathedral of Notre Dame, where a few years before the goddess Reason had been enthroned. The cathedral's great bell, which had not been heard for ten years, sounded again. Mass was celebrated by the cardinal legate, a sermon was preached by an archbishop who had preached at the coronation of Louis XVI, and a *Te Deum* was sung.[4]

It must not however be supposed that the restoration of the church was easily brought about, or that the concordat was the consequence of an irresistible tide of religious reaction. Far from it. It was the consequence of Napoleon's own determination. He had to overcome powerful opposition in the government and in his own entourage. 'Tout ce qui entoure Bonaparte est mal disposé,' M. Emery had written to the Bishop of Alais in February 1801.[5] Bonaparte had to reconcile to his project the deeply divided factions in the Church of France.[6] He had to break down the reluctance of the papacy to agree to the terms which he regarded as indispensable. What were his motives? His own attachment to the religion of his childhood may have counted for something, though this cannot be rated very highly.[7] But he certainly regarded religion as the necessary foundation of morality and social stability.

'There is only one way of securing morality,' he said in 1800, 'and that is to re-establish religion. Society cannot exist without inequality of possessions, and inequality of possessions cannot subsist without religion. When a man is dying of hunger alongside another who is bloated, it is impossible for him to accept this contrast unless there is an authority there which says to him: God wills it to be so; there must be the poor and the rich in this world; but afterwards and during eternity things will be shared out differently.'[8] And in the proclamation in which he promulgated the concordat (April 1802) he said: 'It was an insane policy that tried to bury religious dissensions beneath the débris of the altars, beneath the ruins of religion itself. . . . Passions were unfettered, morality was without support, misery was without a future hope, everything combined to bring

---

[4] See Constant, *op. cit.*, pp. 199 f., 364 ff.

[5] See J. Leflon, *Monsieur Emery*, ii, 70. On Talleyrand's attitude see Comte de Saint Aulaire, *Talleyrand*, E. T., pp. 128 ff.

[6] There was not only the schism between the Constitutional Church and the non-jurors, but among the non-jurors a number of fierce feuds had been occasioned by the question whether the various oaths imposed on priests by the different revolutionary governments might rightly be taken. The non-jurors also differed in their attitude to royalism.

[7] See Constant, *op. cit.*, pp. 40 ff.   [8] *Ibid.*, pp. 42 f.

disorder into society. To stop this disorder, it was necessary to restore religion.'[9]

It was perhaps more to the point that, in order to secure his own power and to forward his long-term designs, Napoleon needed at this time to give the French people peace at home as well as abroad. The Peace of Amiens provided peace abroad—or at any rate a welcome breathing-space. The chief obstacle to peace at home was the revolution's legacy of religious dissension, schism, and persecution. It was because he meant the restoration of religion to be a means of bringing cohesion to the nation that he insisted that the concordat should weld together the constitutionals with the non-jurors. Thus it was he who insisted that all the bishops, both constitutional and non-juring, should hand in their resignations or, failing that, have their sees declared vacant by the pope,[10] and also that in the reconstructed church the constitutionals should be given a fair share of the new appointments. These were bitter pills for Rome to swallow, but the restoration of catholicism in France seemed such a magnificent prize that in the end the necessary concessions were made.

It was however some consolation to the Roman Curia that the deposition by the pope of those bishops who refused to resign was about as flagrant a break with the boasted liberties and privileges of the Gallican Church as could be imagined. There could not be a plainer assertion and acknowledgment of the rights of the holy see.[11] But Napoleon at once made it clear that, so far as he was concerned, this particular stroke of ultramontanism was purely opportunist and created no precedent. For with the concordat he promulgated the 'Organic Articles',[12] of which the pope and the papal negotiators had had no notice in advance, and which reasserted in the most

---

[9] Ibid., p. 43.

[10] ' "Je veux un épiscopat vierge", avait dit Bonaparte à Martiniana: par quoi il entendait qu'il fût aussi lié au régime nouveau que libre par rapport à l'ancien. Une virginité de vestale, commandée et surveillée, sous peine de mort!'—Poulet, op. cit., p. 136.

[11] This was perceived, and regarded as a recompense for the concessions Rome had to make, by Cardinal Antonelli who had grave misgivings about the terms of the concordat. In his votum he wrote: 'C'est un grand coup donné aux libertés gallicanes. Chacun sait combien les Français sont jaloux de ce que la cause de leurs évêques ne soit pas examinée et jugée à Rome en vertu de leurs prétendus privilèges. Or, le Pape, par sa suprême autorité, dépose cinquante ou soixante évêques de leur siège, et ne donne d'autre raison que le bien de l'Église. Cet acte de suprême autorité est sanctionné par le gouvernement lui-même; on en fait un article exprès du Concordat.' See Leflon, Monsieur Emery, II, III.

[12] For the full text, see Constant, op. cit., pp. 349–359.

concrete manner all the gallican liberties. This meant that Napoleon intended to wield the same authority in and over the Church of France as Louis XIV had done.

The French catholics, with few exceptions,[13] were however so enchanted by the restoration of the church[14] that they cheerfully took the appearance of Napoleon's goodwill at its face value, especially after the pope had set his seal to it by visiting Paris to crown him as emperor. Lamennais himself, a few years later (in 1809), after describing the state of ruin to which the revolution had reduced the Church of France, summed up the effect of the concordat thus: 'Suddenly the storm ceased. A powerful stream of energy in a moment restored life to all these ruins. The churches revived, public worship blossomed forth, and with it the sentiments which christianity inspires and nourishes. Feuds and animosities were stilled, and a multitude of innocent victims of a disastrous revolution forgot their sufferings now that they could weep at the foot of the altars of the God who consoles.'[15]

This sense of relief or of revival was reflected in the de La Mennais family. MM. de La Mennais and des Saudrais, Féli's father and uncle, had by now repented of the support which they had given to the Constitutional Church. In 1801 when the concordat was being prepared, they had both taken a leading part on behalf of the citizens of St Malo in trying to get their former bishop restored to his see.[16] We have already seen the way in which des Saudrais's mind had been moving, from the direction of his reading and writing.[17] He was soon to be remarking upon the absence of eagerness displayed by the people of St Malo in erecting *reposoirs* (i.e. temporary altars) for the Corpus Christi procession.[18] He was also gratified to see Napoleon call catholicism 'our holy religion', and he deplored the fact that nine-tenths of the French nation were 'atheists or absolutely without religion'.[19]

---

13 The opposition, which was as much political as religious, centred in the group of royalist émigré bishops who had refused to resign their sees. It found expression in France itself in 'La Petite Église', which has lasted on a tiny scale to our own time. See J. P. Martin, *La Nonciature de Paris*, pp. 53 f.

14 For evidence of the increase of Napoleon's popularity with the clergy in Ille-et-Vilaine, see Godechot, *Les Institutions de la France sous la Révolution et l'Empire*, pp. 494, 500.

15 *O.C.*, VI, 72.   16 See Ropartz, *J.-M. de La Mennais*, pp. 24 ff.

17 See pp. 33 ff, *supra*.

18 See Roussel, 'Lamennais d'après ses correspondants inconnus' in *Revue des questions historiques*, July 1908, p. 226.   19 *Ibid.*, October 1908, pp. 616 f.

As regards M. de La Mennais, an interesting series of letters exists
in the Mennaisian Archives at Highlands, Jersey, that he wrote to his
family during a business visit to Spain, which he made when the
Peace of Amiens had opened the way to the resumption of his
commercial relations there. They show him to be the same practical,
moralistic christian that he always had been, with a keen sense of
what was proper. Describing a holy week procession that he wit-
nessed in Spain, he wrote: 'Nothing could be less edifying. . . .
There was nothing to inspire devotion. The priests and the students
were talking and laughing, nobody seemed to be affected, or
interested in what was going on. The streets were full of women
laughing and talking and displaying themselves in their Sunday
finery. I did not see anyone praying to God; in short, nothing was
less like a religious ceremony.'[20]

In another letter M. de La Mennais reflected (no doubt having
himself in mind) that the causes of the constitutional schism had
been more political than religious. 'Some of the constitutional
clergy', he wrote, 'were corrupted by the modern philosophy, others
were really clerical jacobins, who wanted to be able to establish in
the church a democratic government.'[21] At the same time, Napoleon
had made their reconciliation possible and he hoped that they would
be treated indulgently. The enduring liberality of M. de La Mennais's religious outlook is shown in what he wrote about the constitutional curé of St Pierre de Plesguen, the village nearest to La
Chesnaie.

> I want to hear that M. Norjau . . . has made his peace; he is
> really an honest man, and of pure morals. I hardly suppose that
> he is in a condition to be given a parochial charge . . . but he is a
> man who must be got for our parish of St Malo. He ought to be
> given the office of succentor. A little remuneration added to what
> he receives in mass fees will enable him to live, and that is all he
> wants. I should be very sorry if Rennes cathedral were to steal
> him away from us. Tell M. le Curé, M. Norjau alone will keep
> up the choir better than all the rest of our cantors, and it is not a
> matter of indifference that the service should be marked by
> dignity. . . . However, it may be that at the moment I am letting

[20] Letter of 5 April 1803. See *Jeunesse*, p. 53. In *Famille*, pp. 8 f., where this letter
is quoted more fully, Maréchal gives its date as 3 April 1803. In the MS. it
appears to be undated but to form part of a letter begun on 1 April.
[21] MS. letter undated, but attributed by Maréchal (*Jeunesse*, p. 54) to September
1802.

myself be carried away by my taste for music and fine voices, since I heard those of the cathedral of Paris.[23]

But of more consequence for the future of the Church of France were the reactions at this time of Féli and his brother Jean. Jean, as I have said, seems always to have been destined for the priesthood. One of the last acts of the last Bishop of St Malo, before he had to acknowledge that he no longer had a title to the see, was to confer minor orders on him in Paris (December 1801).[24] Jean's temperament was quite different from that of Féli. Equable and serene, he never knew the pangs of uncertainty and doubt which tormented his brother, nor the moods of melancholy. A man of robust action and abounding in good works, he infected others with his zeal for the propagation of the faith, for the renewal of the church, and for the education of the young.[25] His interest in ideas and in learning, which was considerable, was subordinate to these purposes.[26]

Jean was the dominant influence in Féli's life from now until 1814, and the two brothers were together for most of this period—in St Malo, where Jean taught theology and Féli mathematics in a church college that had been founded there in 1802[27]—or at La Chesnaie, where they spent vacations and also long periods for the sake of their health—or in Paris, which they visited together for about six months in 1806.[28]

Jean had, by the beginning of this period, recognized the brilliant

[23] *Ibid.* M. de La Mennais had spent some weeks in Paris before going to Spain. What happened to M. Norjau we do not know, but there is a reference to him in a letter from Féli to Jean of 25 February 1815 (Blaize, I, 200), which appears to imply that he had been domestic chaplain to a family in the neighbourhood.

[24] Laveille, *J.-M. de La Mennais*, I, 36.

[25] The Frères de l'Instruction Chrétienne de Ploërmel, which he founded, now number 2,000, and they are working in many different countries.

[26] Cp. Charles Sainte-Foi, *Souvenirs de Jeunesse*, p. 70: 'L'abbé Jean était . . . un homme tout pratique, peu exercé dans les matières qui faisaient le sujet habituel des méditations de son frère, et pour qui les plus hautes spéculations ne valaient pas une bonne œuvre. Il s'entendait mieux à faire le bien qu'à en définir la nature. . . . L'abbé Jean avait passé de l'innocence de l'enfant à celle du saint. Son âme était calme, comme toutes les âmes qui n'ont point ressenti le choc des passions.' Charles Sainte-Foi (Éloi Jourdain, 1805–1861) did not come to know abbé Jean till 1828, and was not aware how closely he shared Féli's interest in speculation from 1800–1810.

[27] For the history of the College of St Malo from its foundation in 1802, see E. Herpin, *Histoire du Collège de Saint-Malo* (Ploërmel, 1902).

[28] This was not Féli's first visit to Paris, for he had been there with his father in 1795 or 1796. See *Jeunesse*, pp. 35 f.; Forgues, I, 5 f.; *Annales de Bretagne*, January 1914, p. 211; April 1914, pp. 464–469.

gifts which Féli might bring as an apologist to the service of the church, and he longed first for his complete conversion, and then for his acceptance of a vocation to the priesthood. The first of these hopes was realized in May 1804, shortly after Jean himself had been ordained priest.[29] Féli made his confession, and received the communion—for the first time, so it is said.[30] We know little about this conversion apart from its consequences, and in view of the final issue some[31] have doubted its genuineness or completeness, as they have doubted still more the reality of Féli's vocation to the priesthood. All we can say is that after his conversion Féli gave himself to the ardent and persevering cultivation of a devout life, and if he was not during the next thirty years a converted christian it is not easy to see what conversion can mean. His vocation to the priesthood is another matter, about which I shall have something to say later.

The two brothers were already seeing visions and dreaming

[29] Jean was ordained priest on 25 February 1804 (see Laveille, op. cit., I, 46), not in March, as Maréchal says in Jeunesse, p. 85.

[30] It has been generally said that Féli never received the first communion as a child or that he refused to do so after arguments with the priest who was preparing him. This may however be a legend that was developed to cover up the fact (which would later on have become a source of embarrassment) that he had received the first communion in the Constitutional Church. Cp. Maréchal, Famille, p. 280, who says that it was then the custom for children to receive the first communion at ten years of age. Duine (p. 5), on the other hand, says that the customary age was twelve. If so, Féli would not have reached the appropriate age till 1794 when there would have been no opportunity for a first communion on account of the Terror. It has also been suggested that he received the first communion in private from a non-juring priest, and that the first communion of 1804 was in public or after confirmation: see Roussel, Revue du monde catholique, 15 August 1900, p. 413; Correspondants, pp. 9 f. See also Feugère, pp. 26 f.; Laveille, op. cit., I, 47; Sainte-Beuve, p. 12; Victor Giraud, Revue des deux mondes, 1 March 1919, p. 120. Unless further information comes to light, no firm conclusion about this matter can be reached. I note that in a letter on 22 January 1827 Lamennais mentions someone who made two first communions during the revolution: Forgues, I, 296.

[31] E.g. Maréchal, who seems to have been obsessed with the idea that the fundamental influence in Lamennais's life must always have been that of Rousseau. Henri Bremond (Pour le romantisme, p. 49) protested against this idea: 'De toute son érudition qui est immense, de tout son esprit tenace, M. Maréchal s'est acharné à rendre à Rousseau ce qui appartient au Christ, je veux dire la jeunesse de Lamennais. Rousseau par ci, Rousseau par là, ce nom revient à toutes les pages du livre (Jeunesse), mais sans que jamais un document limpide ou une preuve convaincante justifie cette obsession monotone.'

dreams of what they might do together for the renaissance of the Church of France, now that the concordat had made a renaissance of catholicism possible. They were absorbed in reading and discussing whatever literature would be useful to them in meeting and vanquishing the anti-christian philosophy of the eighteenth century. It is true that Féli no more than Jean received a formal theological education or went through an ecclesiastical seminary,[32] but it is obtuse to say, as has been said,[33] that he was for that reason a poor theologian. As abbé Boutard remarked, Lamennais's learning in the ecclesiastical sciences by the time of his first ordination was much more extensive than that of most young priests who emerge from seminaries in the twentieth century.[34]

During these years, under the supervision and at the impulse of abbé Jean, he studied the Bible, in which he became very deeply versed, the Fathers, the schoolmen, the standard divines of the Gallican Church, especially Bossuet, Fénelon, Malebranche, and Nicolle, as well as contemporary catholic writers such as Chateaubriand and Bonald. Concerning the advantages of studying the works of the old theologians, he wrote in 1809: 'One should be careful not to set aside the ancient theologians, and the scholastics who are today so disparaged; only ignorance is contemptuous, and real science makes use of everything. These writers who are called barbaric because their style is dry and tedious are sometimes full of good sense; moreover, how is one to constitute the chain of tradition if one cuts out the scholastics who by themselves cover several centuries?'[35]

The independence and range of Lamennais's reading put him in a position to perceive the triviality and utter insufficiency of the conventional seminary training in theology. In 1814 he was to criticize its shortcomings in no uncertain terms. Professors, he says, instead of making their pupils penetrate for themselves into the heart of christianity, by sending them to Holy Scripture and Tradition so that they may grasp the wholeness of the faith, put into their hands booklets that settle the largest and most delicate questions with a few proof-texts torn from their context and in accordance with the

---

32 *Schaff-Herzog Encyclopaedia of Religious Knowledge* (1894), II, 1271, is mistaken in saying that Lamennais 'entered the seminary of St Malo in 1811'. Renan also made the mistake of assuming that he had been through a seminary: see *Revue des deux mondes*, 15 August 1857, p. 768.

33 E.g. by E. Spuller, *Lamennais*, p. 101.   34 Boutard, I, 67.

35 *O.C.*, VI, 108.

prejudices of a party. This narrow, barren method stifles the possibility of theological growth even in those priests who come to realize the sterile way in which they have been taught.[36]

The fact that circumstances forced Jean and Féli to get their own grounding in theology and set them free to go to original sources for themselves can hardly be regarded as a handicap. Their arduous and extensive reading and their constant conversations bore fruit in two books: *Réflexions sur l'état de l'Église en France pendant le xviii*^e *siècle, et sur sa situation actuelle* (1809) and *Tradition de l'Église sur l'institution des évêques* (1814). I shall refer to the former as *Réflexions* and to the latter as *Tradition*. Féli has usually been credited with the authorship of these books, but it is certain that Jean did a great deal of the spade work, and particularly that he amassed much of the material for *Tradition*. He also sketched some of the cardinal ideas.[37] But no one realized better than he that Féli was the more gifted writer and should be entrusted with the task of putting the results of their joint labours into literary shape. Féli included *Réflexions* in his *Œuvres complètes* (1836–1837 and 1844 editions), but not *Tradition*, and this may indicate that he regarded himself as the principal author of the one and Jean as the principal author of the other.[38] But it will be convenient here to refer to Féli as the author of both.

Réflexions is of interest both because it is a good illustration of the catholic reaction and hopes of a revival at the beginning of the nineteenth century—indeed, it is a prospectus for such a revival—and also because it is a first annunciation of the doctrines and program which Lamennais was later to develop in a variety of ways.[39] It is a manifesto, addressed primarily to the clergy—'Ministres de Jésus Christ, c'est à vous surtout que je m'adresse'[40]—

---

[36] *Tradition*, I, xviii f. On the intellectual deficiencies of the French clergy early in the nineteenth century, see Leflon, *La crise révolutionnaire*, pp. 362 f.

[37] E.g. see the MS. entitled 'Torrent d'idées vagues' (13 November 1807) which is in the Mennaisian Archives at Highlands College, Jersey, and is quoted by Maréchal, *Jeunesse*, pp. 204–208.

[38] H. J. Laski (*Authority in the Modern State*, p. 195) is mistaken in saying that Lamennais refused *Réflexions* 'a place in his collected works'. We have Jean's own statement that Féli had the principal part in the authorship of *Réflexions* (see his letter to Bruté of 22 June 1809 in de Courcy, p. 66, where *Réflexions* is certainly referred to, despite what the editor says). On the other hand, when Féli wrote to Bruté on 25 April 1815 that *Tradition* was as a matter of fact his work (de Courcy, p. 95), he had a motive for wanting to clear Jean of responsibility for it: cp. p. 61, *infra*. See also Ropartz, *op. cit.*, p. 141; Maréchal, *Jeunesse*, pp. 495 f.; Feugère, pp. 149 ff.

[39] Cp. Duine, p. 29.   [40] *O.C.*, VI, 114.

and designed to arouse in them a high sense of their mission in the circumstances of the time. It aims at exposing the evils from which the church was suffering and at indicating the means by which they could best be remedied. But the book also appears to have been intended to serve as an 'apology' (in the early christian sense) to the emperor, showing that, so far from his having any reason to fear a free and vigorous revival of catholicism, it would make for the moral health and social stability of the empire.[41] In this connexion the book contained some passages of extremely lavish compliment to the emperor, extolling his military exploits, the beneficence of his government, and his concern for the restoration of religion.[42] These compliments may have been sincere, for it appears that Lamennais and his family still shared the enthusiasm of the French people for Bonaparte.[43]

I will quote only one of these passages, by no means the most lavish, but one that combines flattery with the clear insinuation of Lamennais's apologetic aim.

One of the wisest pontiffs who have governed the church (*sc.* Pius VII) combined with one of the greatest monarchs who have ruled over France (*sc.* Napoleon) to re-establish the Gallican Church in its ancient splendour. The time had gone when seditious assemblies . . . arrogated to themselves a jurisdiction which could in no way belong to them. Instructed by experience and guided by other views, the civil government, far from being frightened of the parallel exercise of ecclesiastical authority, on the contrary engaged it to use its power to the greatest possible extent.[44]

The first and longer part of *Réflexions* begins with a rapid survey of the history of the church, calculated to show that it has always been the way of God to bring good out of evil; this leads up to a general characterization of the evils of the eighteenth century and an indictment of *les philosophes*. The errors of eighteenth-century philosophy and of the revolution are treated as the inevitable consequence of the reformation. 'The reformers of the sixteenth century undermined at the same time the foundations of religious order and of social order. They established the principle of anarchy in the

---

[41] E.g. see *O.C.*, VI, 94 f., 103.

[42] Feugère, pp. 90–99, prints the relevant passages (which were removed from all editions after the first); cp. p. 51, *infra.* See also Maréchal, *Jeunesse,* pp. 217–221.

[43] See Duine in *Annales de Bretagne,* January 1913, p. 181.

[44] See Feugère, pp. 92 f.

church and in the state, by attributing sovereignty to the people and
the right of private judgment in matters of belief to each individual.
Thus the final consequence of their maxims has been the most complete destruction of religion and the most fearful disruption of
society.'[45] This first part of *Réflexions* might be described as a first
rough draft of the *Essai sur l'indifférence*, which will be the subject of
the next chapter; I will therefore do no more than quote two or
three typical extracts that illustrate its somewhat adolescent vitality.

The famous *Encyclopedia* of the eighteenth century was, according
to Lamennais, 'a monstrous chaos of all opinions; a building without
an architect, to which each builder brought his stone and placed it
where he liked; a veritable Babel of philosophy—in the delirium of
its pride it was permitted to present to the world a second time the
spectacle of the confusion of languages, as though to prove for ever
the incurable weakness of human reason'.[46] And here is his description of the Terror: 'Then were realized in their full measure the
designs and hopes of *la philosophie*. Now that worship and God and
monarchy had been abolished, society was free at last; it was in the
name of liberty that twenty-five million men groaned in the most
abject slavery. Wealth, birth, talents, virtues, became titles of pro-
scription: everything was a crime, except crime itself; and during
two years terror and death stalked in silence from one end of France
to the other.'[47]

[45] *O.C.*, VI, 6. It is to be feared that Lamennais did not carry out with regard to
the reformers his own excellent precepts about the way to study catholic
theology. There is no evidence, for instance, that he ever read Luther for himself. He seems to have been content to depend on and to repeat the stock-in-
trade of catholic anti-protestant apologetics. There was no work by Luther in
his library, though there were two copies of Calvin's Institutes: see *Catalogue
de la Bibliothèque de M. F. de La Mennais* (Daubrée, Paris, 1836), pp. 34–37. It is
to be remembered that French protestantism at the beginning of the nineteenth
century was hardly a faithful reflection of the thought of the original reformers.
Cp. de Ladoue, who writes: 'Le protestantisme doctrinal n'existait plus en
France au commencement de ce siècle. Il y avait encore un certain nombre de
protestants qui se distinguaient même les uns des autres par les titres de Luthér-
iens et de Calvinistes, mais un corps de doctrine avoué, reconnu, il n'en existait
plus.'—*Vie de Mgr Gerbet* (1872), I, 102. If we are to believe Professor Marcel
Simon, 'the average Frenchman, unless he is himself a Protestant, or lives
among Protestants, hardly knows anything about Protestantism': see *Modern
Churchman*, September 1951, p. 218.
   Lamennais also failed to distinguish between the effects of the reformation
and the renaissance. Cp. Feugère, p. 83.

[46] *O.C.*, VI, 44.
[47] *O.C.*, VI, 68.

The ineffectiveness of the church's answers to its critics and assailants is acknowledged, and excused or explained as follows:

> The French clergy, despite the defection of some of its members, fought courageously against infidelity. It met the productions of the philosophers with numerous apologies for religion; but, it must be confessed, most of these works, excellent as they were as regards their substance, were too deficient in literary appeal, and in those adornments which an austere reason may despise, but which nevertheless it ought sometimes to allow itself, and even to require itself, to employ in order to make the truth more attractive to sick souls. In this case, especially, these adventitious aids were all the more called for, since error was surrounding itself with all the magical qualities of style and with all the seductions of eloquence.[48]

Lamennais did not intend that *his* apologies for the faith should be deficient in this respect, and he was qualified to meet the literary magicians with their own spells.

The confession of the ineffectiveness of the church in the eighteenth century prepares the way for the second part of *Réflexions* in which practical proposals for a revival of the church are outlined. These proposals may seem rather commonplace now, but they were not so then.[49] Most of them came to be accepted as items in the program of church revival in the nineteenth century, in other countries as well as in France, but it would seem that to Lamennais and his brother belongs the credit, such as it is, of having first framed a general policy on these lines.

First, in order to set forward the realization of unity and the reformation of discipline in the Church of France, there ought to be regular meetings of the whole body of bishops in a national council or synod.[50] Lamennais judiciously quotes an address that the bishops

[48] O.C., VI, 50 f.

[49] Some of course were revivals of what had fallen into disuse, but the trouble Lamennais takes to show that he is not demanding innovations is a measure of the extent to which he was doing so. Some of his proposals had behind them the authority of the Council of Trent, but they had not been acted upon. Cp. P. Broutin on 'Un Aspect de l'Œuvre menaisienne' in *Nouvelle Revue Théologique*, November 1937, pp. 969–985.

[50] In point of fact, the only meetings of the whole body of French bishops that were held prior to 1951 were in 1811 and in 1906–1907. See D. F. Vandenbroucke on 'Le Nouveau Directoire français des Sacrements' in *Les Questions Liturgiques et Paroissiales*, November–December 1951, p. 260. Only the cardinals and archbishops meet regularly.

had made to Louis XIV in 1670 in favour of such assemblies, in the course of which they had cited the example of Charlemagne who, they said, was remembered much less for his political and military achievements than for his services to the church. It must be remembered that Napoleon regarded himself as a second Charlemagne.[51]

Secondly, Lamennais urges the value of local synods of the clergy. The scarcity of priests in the country meant that they were mostly isolated and lonely, and needed opportunities of supporting, encouraging, and consulting with, one another. For the same reason he advocates the revival of the office of rural dean. Rural deans would exercise a pastoral care over the clergy in their district, which on account of the size of dioceses the bishops and their vicars-general could not do unless they were to be incessantly peripatetic. Still more valuable would be the holding of retreats and conferences on doctrine (i.e. what are nowadays called 'clergy schools')—the latter being 'one of the most powerful means of preserving and reviving the taste for study among ecclesiastics'.[52] 'Let no one object', Lamennais says, 'that the time of the clergy is already too fully occupied by the demands of their ministry; that would be like dispensing doctors from studying medicine on the ground that there were too many sick people.'[53]

Next, Lamennais suggests the value of community life for the clergy in large parishes. Such parochial communities (companies of mission priests, one might say) would in several respects take the place of the older religious orders 'in offering to a corrupt age the spectacle of some men practising in all their purity the evangelical precepts and counsels'.[54]

He then turns to the need for recruiting more priests. The need was very grave; the towns were producing few vocations, and the wealthy classes practically none. It was in the rural parishes that recruits must now be sought. 'It is fishermen, shepherds, labourers, that Providence is today calling into the sanctuary; it is they who are destined to renew the faith which they have known how to keep.'[55] The country clergy ought therefore to do everything possible to foster vocations. There was also need for more religious congregations like that of St Sulpice which would make themselves responsible for the conduct of seminaries. Lamennais observes that the shortage of priests would make people want to shorten the period of their training, and he issues a warning against doing that. It is

[51] Cp. Leflon, *La crise révolutionnaire*, pp. 237 f.   [52] *O.C.*, VI, 98.
[53] *O.C.*, VI, 99.   [54] *O.C.*, VI, 101 f.   [55] *O.C.*, VI, 104.

not so much priests that are needed as priests who are thoroughly zealous and enlightened. He goes on to deplore the state of almost complete neglect into which the higher theological studies had fallen in France, and the need for cultivating them afresh. Otherwise catholics will find that they are being out-thought all along the line.

As regards the renewal of christian faith and life among the laity, Lamennais advocated the founding of christian schools in which the children of the poor could learn the elements of religion and morality; parochial missions which would bring the gospel vividly home to the people; guilds and associations which would bind the converts together in christian practice and devotion; and a more exalted standard of piety for all.

The familiarity now of most of the ideas put forward in the second part of *Réflexions* should not be allowed to obscure their remarkable originality and novelty in 1809.[56]

Réflexions was unfortunate in the time of its first appearance in the world. While it was passing through the press, events were taking place which the author could hardly have foreseen.

The manuscript was completed by 18 February 1809.[57] It was then, with abbé Simon Bruté (1779–1839)[58] as intermediary, submitted to M. Emery, the Superior of St Sulpice,[59] who approved of it, though he suggested that there were passages which might encounter unfavourable notice from the government, and Lamennais consequently introduced a few modifications.[60] The book was printed during April and May, and published in the latter part of June. It bore the date '1808', which was the date of its composition, and this has often been given as the year of publication; there is however no doubt that it was published in June 1809. If '1808' was inserted at the last minute, it was a measure of prudence since, for

56 Cp. Boutard, I, 55: 'La plupart des idées exposées dans la seconde partie des *Réflexions* sont devenues aujourd'hui des lieux communs. Elles étaient, quand elles furent exprimées, neuves et originales, car bien peu d'hommes avaient alors l'intelligence des besoins des temps nouveaux. On peut même s'étonner qu'un écrivain dont la conversion était encore si récente ait pu concevoir tout d'un coup un plan à la fois si vaste, si précis et si détaillé. Mais il ne faut pas oublier que cet écrivain avait un collaborateur, l'abbé Jean, doué aussi d'une vive intelligence, et déjà très au courant des choses ecclésiastiques.'

57 See Maréchal, *Jeunesse*, p. 244.

58 On Bruté, see *Simon Bruté de Rémur* by Sister Mary Salesia Godecker (St Meinrad, Indiana, 1931).

59 See de Courcy, pp. 30 f. For M. Emery's reply to Bruté, see Leflon, *Monsieur Emery*, II, 396 f.   60 See de Courcy, p. 49.

reasons about to be noticed, its appearance in 1808 would have been less provocative than it was in 1809.[61]

For it was during the very months when *Réflexions* was passing through the press and being published that the rupture between Napoleon and Pius VII came to a head. Their relations had been deteriorating ever since the pope's visit to Paris in December 1804 for the coronation.[62] Disillusion about Napoleon's good faith had been deepening at Rome, while a series of incidents had driven him to more and more drastic measures against the papal pretensions to independence in matters temporal as well as spiritual. The fundamental causes of the rupture were Napoleon's ambition to be a new Charlemagne and the pope's resolute determination not to accept a position of vassalage.

By 1808 the papal states were occupied by French troops, and the pope was virtually a prisoner in the Quirinal. On 17 May 1809 Napoleon signed the decree by which he annexed ('reunited') the papal states to the French Empire, proposing to allow the pope an annuity of two million francs with the possession of his palace and other properties which would enjoy a special immunity. On 10 June the tricolour was hoisted in Rome, and on 11 June the pope replied by issuing the bull of excommunication against Napoleon[63] and his accomplices which he had previously prepared for such an eventuality. On the night of 5–6 July the Quirinal was invested by French troops and forcibly entered. Pius VII was arrested and made to leave Rome at once for captivity in France. He reached Savona, a small town on the gulf of Genoa, early in August. He was to be kept there till 1812.

The French newspapers were forbidden to report these events, and some time elapsed before knowledge of them became common property. M. Emery however had secret sources of information,[64]

---

61 See Maréchal, *Jeunesse*, p. 246.

62 For what follows see Constant, chap. 8; C. S. Phillips, *The Church in France 1789–1848*, chap. 6.

63 Napoleon was not mentioned by name in the bull, so that he would not be technically *vitandus*, which would have been extremely embarrassing for all catholics who had business with him. See Constant, p. 296.

64 See Leflon, *Monsieur Emery*, II, 398. For instance, a copy of the papal bull excommunicating Napoleon was secretly transmitted to M. Emery, who made himself responsible for getting its authentic text known to the French clergy. When at the end of September Jean and Bruté returned from Paris to Brittany they were entrusted with a copy of the bull, which they secreted in Bruté's hat. See *ibid.*, II, 397.

and it seems to me probable that a visit to Paris, which abbé Jean paid in August and September 1809, and which his biographer attributes to the state of his health,[65] was really the result of a warning from St Sulpice about the dangerous character that the publication of *Réflexions* had assumed.

For I have not mentioned that the book contained the following account of the imprisonment of Pope Pius VI under the Directory, and it will at once be apparent that, in view of the similar treatment that had just been meted out to Pius VII, it would now read like a bitter and offensive piece of irony:

> The christian had to groan under the horrible outrage that was committed against the head of the church, the immortal Pius VI. Arrested in his capital city, loaded with insults and infamous treatment, dragged from prison to prison like a vile criminal, this venerable pontiff, whose conduct called forth the respect and admiration even of his tormentors, upheld with a magnificent courage until the end the glory of the tiara and the dignity of his character, and crowned his saintly life with a martyr's death. We must be thankful to the government which has made honourable reparation for this monstrous scandal, and has cleared France, in the eyes of Europe and of posterity, of a heinous crime for which she was not at all responsible.[66]

The imperial government was not likely to tolerate a book which contained a passage like that, appearing at such a pointed moment.[67] But what exactly happened is something of a mystery. In the preface to the 1819 and subsequent editions of *Réflexions*[68] Lamennais stated (i) that the book had been first published in 1808, (ii) that it had been immediately seized by Bonaparte's police, and (iii) that nothing had been added (*sc.* to the text in subsequent editions). The first of these statements was incorrect, for the book was published in 1809, as we have seen; the third was disingenuous, for omissions and alterations were made in the second and following editions.[69] Maréchal,

65 The visit to Paris was urged upon Jean by Bruté; see his letter in Laveille, *J.-M. de La Mennais*, I, 118. But the letter says nothing about ill-health, and is more consistent with the suggestion made in the text. Cp. *Jeunesse*, p. 250.

66 See *Jeunesse*, p. 249; Feugère, pp. 90 f.

67 For the rigorous supervision of books under the Empire, see Godechot, *op. cit.*, pp. 658 f.

68 As regards the preface to the 1814 edition, see Feugère, pp. 89 f.

69 For details of this equivocal proceeding and of Lamennais's attempted defence of it, when his opponents called attention to it in 1821–1822, see Feugère, pp. 90–103. Cp. Maréchal, *Dispute*, pp. 158 ff.

therefore, writing in 1913,[70] might have been justified in question-
ing the veracity of the second statement, and in doubting whether
Réflexions ever had been seized by the police. He had however over-
looked the fact that Père Dudon in 1907 had quoted in *Études*[71] a note
written by Pierre Dubois, the Prefect of Police in 1809, which refers
to the seizure of *Réflexions*. It is certain then that there was a seizure by
the police. Pasquier, who succeeded Dubois as Prefect of Police, assures
us in his *Mémoires*[72] that books seized for political purposes were
always pulped immediately. What then is the explanation of the fact
that for the second edition of *Réflexions*, published in 1814 after the
fall of Napoleon, sheets of the first edition were used, with a new title-
page and some substituted pages in the text?[73] I would suggest that
abbé Jean during his visit to Paris in August-September 1809 took care
to arrange for as many as possible of the printed sheets of the book
to be hidden away before they could be seized by the police, and that
the police were deceived when they supposed that they had got all
that remained of the edition.[74] A letter from Féli to Jean, written on
29 June 1814, shows that plans were made to take a similar precaution
with regard to copies of *Tradition*.[75]

The eyes of both brothers were now wide open to the way in
which the church was being imperilled by Napoleon's despotism.
It was in this year—1809—that Féli took his first two steps towards
the priesthood, encouraged, if not pushed, by Jean.[76] He received
the tonsure on 16 March and minor orders on 23 December, in both
cases at Rennes and after making a retreat. It was also in this year
that Lamennais published *Le Guide spirituel ou le Miroir des âmes
religieuses*,[77] a translation of a sixteenth-century book of an ascetic
and mystical character by Louis de Blois (d. 1566), a child of a noble
family, who left the court of Charles V to become a benedictine

---

[70] *Jeunesse*, p. 250.
[71] *Études*, 20 April 1907, p. 274. For the full text of the Prefect's note, see *Études*,
5 December 1913, p. 728, where Dudon transcribes it from the *Archives
nationales*.
[72] I, 452.
[73] See *Jeunesse*, pp. 473–478, where the alterations are noted in detail; they are
remarkable not only for the omission of favourable allusions to Napoleon (cp.
p. 45, *supra*) but also for the strongly ultramontane tone of the new insertions.
[74] See *Études*, 5 December 1913, p. 728.
[75] See Blaize, I, 143.
[76] See MS. letter no. 7524 (Jean to Bruté) in the Archives at Highlands, Jersey.
[77] There were subsequent editions in 1820 and 1828, and it was republished in
1915. See Duine, *Bibliographie*, p. 2.

monk. It should not be forgotten that in addition to his apologetic and polemical writings Lamennais published a number of works of piety which are significant of the fact that the mennaisian movement stood for an exalted standard of devotion as well as for intellectual enterprise and ecclesiastical reform.[78]

It was now apparent that the struggle between Napoleon and the pope would hinge on the institution of bishops. Under the terms of the concordat of 1801 the First Consul had the right of nominating to vacant episcopal sees, and the pope undertook to confer canonical institution in accordance with the forms that had been followed before the revolution.[79] Of all the means that the papacy had employed in the middle ages to subdue insubordinate rulers and intractable nations, the only practicable one left was the refusal of institution to the nominees of civil governments. Pius VII, even in his imprisonment, still had this instrument of resistance at his disposal. Long-suffering as he was, and strangely susceptible to Napoleon's charms,[80] there were limits to his willingness to smooth the tyrant's way, and he was now resolved to use the only weapon that remained to him.

A deadlock was therefore inevitable, and Napoleon's ecclesiastical policy was henceforth directed to discovering a resource by which he could overcome it without causing a schism in the church. However much he might threaten, he was determined to avoid repeating the fiasco of the Constitutional Church. There were then, from his point of view, only two possible solutions. Either he might bring influence or pressure to bear on the pope so that he would give way or, failing that, the Church of France with its gallican traditions might be persuaded to proceed with the institution of bishops without having recourse to the pope. We cannot follow here the protracted series of negotiations, intrigues, and artifices by means of which Napoleon sought in vain from 1809 to 1813 to overcome or circumvent the resistance of Pius VII.[81] Could the pope be persuaded

---

[78] For Lamennais's interest in the republication of devotional classics, see Paul Dudon on 'Bibliothèque des dames chrétiennes publiée sous la direction de Lamennais (1820–1826)' in Études, 5 July 1923, pp. 39–57.

[79] I.e. according to the concordat of 1516 between Leo X and Francis I, which had abrogated the Pragmatic Sanction of Charles VII. See Constant, pp. 329 f. There was a similar clause in the Italian Concordat of 1803 to that in the French Concordat of 1801. See Leflon, La crise révolutionnaire, pp. 196 f.

[80] See d'Haussonville, L'Église romaine et le Premier Empire, 1800–1814 (1868) II, 11 f.

[81] See Constant, pp. 293–328; Leflon, La crise révolutionnaire, pp. 254–273; Leflon, Monsieur Emery, II, chaps. 13, 16, and 17; C. S. Phillips, op. cit., chaps. 7 and 8.

that, if he failed to confer institution, it would be in order, after a delay of six months, for the metropolitan to do so, or was it impossible for a bishop to exercise jurisdiction canonically without direct institution by the pope? While there were moments when Pius VII, sorely pressed, seemed prepared to concede the essential point, notably on the occasion of the so-called 'Concordat of Fontainebleau' (January 1813), he immediately withdrew his concessions, and it is fair to say that in the end he alone consistently withstood the emperor's will to dominate the church.

It is this fact more than anything else that accounts for the complete conversion of Lamennais to ultramontanism. If the church had depended on the cardinals and bishops, not to mention the inferior clergy, it would have succumbed to Napoleon, as was shown by the way in which his agents succeeded in manœuvring the National Council of 1811 into compliance with his desires. This council, consisting of six cardinals, eight archbishops, and eighty-one bishops, began with a fine show of loyalty to the holy see but, after it had been dealt with, it adopted by eighty votes to thirteen the decree that the emperor imposed upon its members. The final surrender of the church to an unscrupulous tyrant was thus demonstrably prevented only by the superhuman steadfastness of the vicar of Christ—imprisoned, solitary, aged, and infirm as he was. What more conclusive evidence could there be for the divinely ordained dependence of the church on the papacy?

Still, he was not the man to be content with a single piece of evidence nor with a pragmatic basis for his faith; he must needs work out a complete system to justify it. So it was convenient that when abbé Jean had been in Paris in 1809 M. Emery of St Sulpice, who until his death in 1811 was the moral leader and arbiter of the French clergy, had asked him to investigate the history of the institution of bishops,[82] with a view to showing what the traditional role of the papacy had been. To do this it was necessary to examine all the relevant historical material from the New Testament onwards. It was a very large undertaking, and it provided employment for both Jean and Féli for several years. The outcome was their second and much more ambitious—three-volume—book, *Tradition*. By the time it was finished, Féli believed he had elaborated a complete historical vindication of the ultramontane position.

[82] In fact, Jean had already started work on the subject before he received M. Emery's request, though not with a view to publication. See *Jeunesse*, pp. 301–305.

The book had no direct effect on the struggle between Napoleon and Pius VII, because it was not published till after the fall of the Empire. Its long-term importance lay in the challenge it offered to the accepted gallican teaching about the authority of the papacy. The moderate gallican position,[83] for which St Sulpice stood, was that until the thirteenth century institution of bishops by metropolitans had been the normal practice of the church, and that the subsequent requirement of papal bulls of institution was a matter only of ecclesiastical discipline which the church could alter if it wanted to do so. In other words, the right of instituting bishops was not an essential prerogative of the pope but a concession which the church had made to him since the thirteenth century, so that the church could withdraw the right from him and invest metropolitans with it again. A national church could not do this, only the universal church could; but the universal church had not done so, and therefore the Church of France was not at liberty to accept Napoleon's demands.

Resistance to an oppressor of the church would however be much more firmly grounded if the papal prerogative to institute bishops could be shown to rest not merely on ecclesiastical law but on divine right, and this is what Lamennais confidently claimed to show. He traversed the whole history of the church, and provided an ultramontane interpretation of all the evidences. There can be no question here of going over the ground, of contrasting the gallican and ultramontane handling of the material, and of deciding in each case who had the better of argument: that could by itself form the subject of more than one course of Birkbeck Lectures![84] There are

---

83 For the moderate gallican position see the lectures on the doctrine of the Church of M. Boyer of St Sulpice which have survived in manuscript. They are summarized and the most important passages transcribed in *Jeunesse*, pp. 309–317. Boyer was a moderate gallican compared with Tabaraud, who published in 1811 his *Essai historique et critique sur l'institution canonique des évêques*. See Maréchal, *ibid.*, pp. 350–355. Lamennais gave an ironical account of Tabaraud's book in a letter of 21 August 1811 to Bruté, see Blaize, I, 105 f.; cp. de Courcy, pp. 82 f.

84 Cp. what Maréchal says in *Jeunesse*, p. 392: 'Il ne saurait entrer dans le plan de cet ouvrage d'en (*sc.* de *Tradition*) apprécier la valeur historique et critique. Ce n'est pas que cet examen n'offre en lui-même un intérêt considérable: mais il faudrait qu'il fît l'objet d'un travail spécial et fort étendu.' For the reasons why so little reference was made to *Tradition* by subsequent writers on the papal question, see Feugère, pp. 173 ff. *Dictionnaire de théologie catholique*, VIII, col. 2501, says that Turmel, *Histoire de la théologie du concile de Trente au concile du Vatican* (1906), pp. 340–359, should be consulted.

however one or two remarks that may be made about this daring book.

The scientific historian, accustomed to weighing evidences as objectively as possible and never pressing them beyond what they warrant, will doubtless regard the working out of Lamennais's thesis as a *tour de force*—though he may be willing to admit that it is skilfully contrived with a fine array of learning, and that an argument that might have been extremely tedious is enlivened with many passages of eloquence, irony, and invective. But it was an axiom with Lamennais that to understand history objectively or to write history without a prejudice is impossible, and this is an axiom that seems to be much favoured in theological circles today, though it is of course appealed to in the interest of many different beliefs.

For example, Father A. G. Hebert, defending the thesis of *The Apostolic Ministry*[85] and referring to 'the criticism, which several people have made, that the book starts from a preconceived idea and proceeds to find reasons for it', writes: 'But the actual meaning of the criticism is that our critic does not, as we do, regard the episcopal ministry as of divine ordinance. Let me explain. Faith is our response to divine revelation; and in matters of faith all Christians start with some preconceived idea and reach a fuller understanding of it afterwards. This is the *credo ut intelligam*.'[86] Perhaps Lamennais was pressing the same axiom to its logical conclusion and conceiving it more romantically when he wrote in *Tradition*:

> The history of the church and its discipline is only a chaos of contradictions, a formless accumulation of incoherent facts, an obscure labyrinth in which the greatest scholars soon get lost if they have not from the outset seized with a firm hand the torch which should lighten their way in the darkness, that is to say, if they have not understood, or have understood only imperfectly, the general principles of the government of the church. These principles provide the key to all difficulties, and are the best commentary on the monuments of the past, because being neither arbitrary nor variable they must always be and have in fact always been the basis of ecclesiastical administration in its progressive

[85] Edited by K. E. Kirk, 1946.

[86] See *Theology*, December 1951, p. 460. It may be also noted that Edward Carpenter, reviewing *The Reformation in England* by Philip Hughes in the *Church of England Newspaper*, 4 January 1952, p. 5, wrote: 'Objective history, we all know, cannot be written. There must be some principle of interpretation, some insight around which the writer groups his facts and indeed selects them.'

developments and in the necessary changes which it has had to undergo as the centuries have passed. Put these great maxims at the head of history, and everything becomes clear, everything falls into place: the facts, hitherto scattered and unconnected, arrange themselves around this common centre in an order as simple as it is magnificent; knotty details which baffle an unimaginative criticism, and the apparent contradictions which distress it, vanish; and in this majestic concert of diverse events, of conflicts, of triumphs, and sometimes of terrible catastrophes, one recognizes the work of God which advances gloriously across the ages. . . .[87]

A feature of *Tradition* that is significant in view of later developments in Lamennais's teaching is his clear recognition of the distinction between the temporal and the spiritual spheres. Thoroughgoing as was his ultramontanism, he rejected the notion that the pope had any authority, direct or indirect, over kings in temporal matters.[88] He admitted that there had been a time when the popes had tried to exercise such authority, adding that in the circumstances then existing it had been happy for Europe that they did so; perhaps it was the unique instance of an error doing good. 'It is a fine thing to issue orders to kings when one does so in favour of peoples.'[89] But that was not the divinely ordained relation between the ecclesiastical and the civil authorities.

In the political as in the religious society, the church teaches us to reverence a power which comes from God, and which commands in the name of God; a power . . . which is responsible solely to the all-powerful Being whom it represents and who instituted it. She shows us two heads (*chefs*), one civil and the other spiritual, who, in two different and perfectly distinct orders, have an equal right to our obedience, in so far as they do not plainly offend against the natural and divine law. Let them remain sincerely united, without seeking to invade one another's authority.[90]

The qualifications should be noticed. If either the prince or the pope should be found to encroach on the other's authority and sphere of responsibility or if either should plainly offend against the natural or divine law, he must expect to forfeit Lamennais's support.

[87] *Tradition*, II, 93 f.
[88] See *ibid.*, I, lxxii.
[89] *Ibid.*, I, lxxvi.
[90] *Ibid.*, I, cxv.

Lamennais was putting the final touches to a manuscript that had been much redrafted and revised, when on 31 March 1814 the Allies entered Paris.[91] At first sight, it seemed a happy coincidence, for the book could hardly have been published while Napoleon was still in power, and now the way was open. Lamennais was in Paris before the end of April to see it through the press.[92] *Tradition* was actually published early in August. But it neither caused the sensation nor had the success for which the author had hoped. For *Tradition* was not much happier in the time of its appearance than *Réflexions* had been.

In the first place, the immediate state of affairs out of which the book originated and which it envisaged had ceased to exist. Napoleon had fallen, the pope was safely back in Rome, and the institution of bishops was no longer a matter of acute controversy. Secondly, while there had been a marked trend towards ultramontanism among the younger French clergy during the latter years of the Empire, it had been no more than a temporary reaction against Napoleon's tyrannical oppression of the pope and the church.[93] That was now removed, the Bourbons were back, and the enthusiasm of the hour was for the return of the *ancien régime* in which ultramontanism had seemed unnecessary and out of place.[94] Thirdly, the exiled bishops had just returned to France, and they were as gallican as they had always been.[95] An ultramontane manifesto at this moment, so far from evoking enthusiasm, did not even appear to be a serious menace. So for the time being the book fell flat.[96]

Whatever may be thought of the ultramontane thesis, it may be agreed that Lamennais's reaction to Napoleon was not only more persistent but also more far-sighted than that of the French clergy. He perceived that Napoleon's tyranny and his attempted exploitation of the church were not a peculiar and passing phenomenon, a kind of historical freak, but a foretaste of what was in future to be expected of civil governments when they had cast off the traditional faith of Christendom and were no longer checked by its restraints. Lamennais's reaction to Napoleon was to dedicate himself and all his talents to the struggle, which he felt had only just begun, for the integrity and liberty of the church, upon which, he believed, the

[91] See Blaize, I, 134; Maréchal, *Jeunesse*, pp. 424-434.
[92] See de Courcy, pp. 88, 90.   [93] E.g. see Blaize, I, 162, 177.
[94] Cp. Hocedez, *Histoire de la Théologie au XIXe siècle*, I, 96 f.
[95] Cp. de Courcy, pp. 92 f.
[96] See Blaize, I, 181. So few copies of the first edition were sold that after the success of the *Essai sur l'indifférence* the remainder was available for publication as the second edition (1818) with only a new title-page; see *Jeunesse*, p. 434.

regeneration of society in Europe depended. Perhaps this was the fundamental, if unconscious, motive at the bottom of his willingness at last—in 1816—to proceed to the priesthood. But we have not arrived there yet, and other motives also were at work.

For one thing, it became apparent that for the first time in his life Lamennais had got to find a way of earning a living. The Napoleonic wars, and in particular the continental blockade, had proved fatal to the family business, which had depended chiefly on foreign trade.[97] In 1813 M. de La Mennais and his brother had had to admit that they were bankrupt, and the younger members of the family had to shoulder the responsibility of supporting them in their old age.[98] Abbé Jean, despite pressing appeals from Féli to continue their life together and their literary collaboration, accepted early in 1814 the position of domestic chaplain to the Bishop of St Brieuc, and henceforth was taken up with ecclesiastical administration and the founding and care of those religious institutions which would have given him a pre-eminent place in the history of the Church of France, if the fame of his brother had not eclipsed his own honourable reputation.

How was Féli to contribute to his own and the family exchequer? Journalism was the obvious answer, and while he was in Paris seeing *Tradition* through the press he was also busily canvassing the idea of starting a journal—perhaps a daily, perhaps a fortnightly—that would be the organ of the church revival for which the times cried out and of course thoroughly ultramontane.[99] But the project was impracticable owing to lack of capital. However, he found other ways of wielding his pen in the cause he had at heart.

Thus he published in the form of a brochure[100] a violent attack on the University, the Napoleonic institution by which all secondary and higher education throughout France had been centralized and brought under the direct control of the state. It was owing to this institution that the church college at St Malo had had to close down in 1812. Lamennais never forgave the Restoration government for taking over and maintaining the University. The opening paragraph of this brochure is typical of his pamphleteering style.

[97] See Laveille, *J.-M. de La Mennais*, I, 136.

[98] Jean, Féli, and Ange Blaize, their brother-in-law, each undertook a third of the responsibility. See *Jeunesse*, pp. 439, 443.

[99] See Blaize, I, 136 f., 146, 148, 152, 163 ff., 167–170, 172. On the great outburst of journalistic activity which followed the fall of Napoleon, see R. Burnand, *La vie quotidienne en France en 1830* (1943), p. 187.

[100] It is reprinted in *O.C.*, VI, 308–328.

I have no hesitation in saying that, of all Bonaparte's conceptions, the most appalling to every considering man, the most
profoundly anti-social, in a word the most characteristic of its
author, is the University. When the tyrant thought he had made
sure by so many horrible laws of the misery of the present
generation, he raised this monstrous edifice as a monument of his
hatred for future generations; it was as though he wanted to rob
the human race even of hope.[101]

In this his first attack on the University, Lamennais advocated its
complete abolition and the establishment of unrestricted liberty
for the foundation of new schools and colleges; the emulation between them would be the best guarantee of their quality. His perception of the dangers of a state monopoly of education is another
instance of his far-sightedness; it is also a striking anticipation of his
later political liberalism, though he little dreamed at present where
his concern for liberty would carry him at last.

His concern for the liberty and independence of the church *vis-à-
vis* the state is illustrated by another of his journalistic essays in 1814.
Unable to start a periodical of his own, Lamennais at the instigation
of his St Sulpice friend abbé Teysseyrre[102] contributed at this time
some articles to *L'Ami de la Religion et du Roi*, an organ of moderate
gallicanism,[103] and he was furious when he found that the editor
blue-pencilled them without consulting him. Among them was an
article on 'Endowment of the Clergy'.[104] In this Lamennais argued
against the provision of the concordat of 1801, according to which
the clergy were paid salaries by the state, and in favour of the
restoration of endowments that would secure the independence of
the church and proper respect for its ministry. He granted that it
would be impossible to restore to the church all the property that
it had possessed before the revolution, but there was nothing to
prevent the return of that portion of its ancient possessions that had
become public property.

Lamennais was quickly disillusioned by the policy and proceedings
of the Restoration government. So far from securing to the church
its independence, it showed no signs in this respect, any more than

[101] *O.C.*, VI, 308.

[102] See Paguelle de Follenay, *Monsieur Teysseyrre* (1882); Maréchal, *Jeunesse*,
pp. 595 ff.

[103] On the attitude of this journal to gallicanism and ultramontanism, see *Dispute*,
pp. 151 f.

[104] 'Dotation du Clergé', included in *O.C.*, VI, 187–193.

in the case of the University, of reversing the work of the Empire. It maintained the University, the concordat, and the censorship, but in weaker hands. In a letter to Jean of 7 July 1814 he said that it looked as though all France had got was a weak despotism instead of a strong one.[105]

When in March 1815 the return of Napoleon from Elba was announced, Lamennais was back at La Chesnaie, where he had just been predicting that some awful calamity was impending.[106] His own course was to go at once into exile. The Hundred Days began on 20 March, when Napoleon reached Paris. His intentions towards those who were opposed to him were indicated by the fact that, a week before, he had decreed the banishment from his territory of the émigrés who had returned to France since 1 April 1814.[107] Lamennais would find himself gravely compromised under the new régime both by certain virulent passages about Napoleon in *Tradition* and still more by his brochure on the University, though he may have magnified the dangers to which he was exposed.[108] But he had a better motive than concern for his own safety. Féli seems to have thought that, if he left the country, he would clear Jean of responsibility for the publication of *Tradition*,[109] and Jean was needed at his post at this moment, since he had recently been appointed vicar capitular of the diocese of St Brieuc after the death of the bishop.

In letters written to relatives in France at the time of his departure Féli said that he was going to the colonies.[110] In point of fact, he

---

[105] See Blaize, I, 150. Cp. what Féli wrote to Bruté on 25 April 1815: 'Le pauvre Roi a fait tout ce qu'il est possible de faire pour amener sa chute. Nul fermeté, point de gouvernement, toutes les idées révolutionnaires, oppression de l'Église, etc., etc.'—De Courcy, p. 97.

[106] See Roussel, *Documents*, I, 63 f.; cp. Blaize, I, 199. It may be that Lamennais's faculty for predicting impending calamities has been exaggerated. He was constantly predicting them throughout his life, so that some predictions were bound to seem remarkable. Cp. Sevrin, *Dom Guéranger et La Mennais*, p. 87.

[107] See Duine, p. 50.

[108] As regards his motives, see Versluys, pp. 129 f.

[109] On 25 April 1815 Féli wrote to Bruté from London: 'Mon départ, sous plusieurs rapports, est un gage de sûreté pour Jean, et c'est ce qui m'a décidé. Cela lui donne le moyen de désavouer la *Tradition*, qui est en effet mon ouvrage, l'ayant fait en entier sur les textes qu'il avoit recueillis.'—De Courcy, p. 95.

[110] Maréchal (*Jeunesse*, pp. 494 f.) and Duine (pp. 50 f.) think that this really was his intention when he left France, but Forgues (I, 11) may be right in suggesting that he said this with a view to misleading the imperial police who might open his letters. Maréchal and Duine conjecture that abbé Carron dissuaded him from proceeding to the colonies.

went first to Guernsey,[111] where he remained only a week or two,[112] and then went on to London. He assumed the name 'Patrick Robertson',[113] though it does not appear why this should have been necessary.[114] Arrived in London, he had to find some way of maintaining himself. He got into touch with abbé Carron, a devoted priest, who was acting as unofficial chaplain and welfare officer to the émigré community, and who did more for Lamennais than put him in the way of employment.

Guy Carron (1760–1821)[115] was himself a Breton. He had been arrested during the revolution for refusing to take the constitutional oath, and was subsequently deported. He was instrumental in getting Lamennais a post as teacher in a school in Kensington. Lamennais does not appear to have made any serious attempt to understand the religious or political institutions and ideas of the English, for whom indeed at no time did he evince admiration.[116] Finding himself surrounded by protestants, whose beliefs he was confident he could easily refute, he set himself the task of making some converts to catholicism. So far as we know, he was successful only in the case of a boy of thirteen.[117] But he made a determined onset on the headmaster of the school in which he was teaching—Mr Morton, an Irish protestant—with whom his relations seem to have been very

[111] See Blaize, I, 207 f.

[112] Not 'several months' as Forgues (I, 12) says, since by 25 April he was writing from London to Bruté, see n. 109, *supra*.

[113] Robertson because 'Robert' was his patronymic, and Patrick presumably because he had Irish ancestors on his mother's side. Over this signature he wrote carefully disguised letters to his relations in France. See Blaize, I, 207–210.

[114] Boutard (I, 100) says that Lamennais was persuaded that the imperial police might pursue him even in England, but this hardly seems likely. Perhaps he thought it would be safer to communicate with his relations and friends in France under an assumed name.

[115] See *Vie de l'abbé Carron* par un bénédictin de la Congrégation de France (Dom Jausions) (1866).

[116] 'Je n'ai pas besoin de t'assurer que je m'ennuie et me déplais furieusement dans ce pays-ci,' wrote Féli to Jean on 12 September 1815: Blaize, I, 223. Cp. Boutard, I, 103, who assigns Lamennais's dislike of England partly to 'la répugnance que lui causait l'utilitarisme outré, qui est le trait distinctif du caractère anglais.' But we may be sure that both his anti-protestant animus and the traditional hostility of the inhabitants of St Malo to the English were contributory factors. See also Forgues, I, 183, 403; de Courcy, p. 158; *Essai*, I, 55–60; Maréchal, *La Mennais au Drapeau Blanc*, p. 54; *Béranger et Lamennais*, p. 106.

[117] Henry Moorman. See Blaize, I, 222 f., 229, 275, 337, 341, 385 f.

cordial. Two long letters have survived in which he sought to convince Morton of the truth of catholicism.[118]

It may be that the spectacle of English protestantism, and the apostolic zeal that it evoked in him, had something to do with the reawakening in Lamennais of a sense of vocation to the priesthood, which had been dormant, if not abandoned, for some years. Anyhow, he revealed to abbé Carron his uncertainty about his vocation. Carron was greatly attracted to Lamennais, for whom he conceived a warm affection. He was struck by his apologetic ardour, and quickly appreciated his talents as a writer and the services he might render to the church if he became a priest.[119] Lamennais, on his side, gratefully accepted Carron as the guide and master whom God had provided for him, now that he was deprived of the direction of abbé Jean. Carron advised him to make a long retreat at the end of which he undertook to tell him what he ought to do.[120] And so the fateful decision was at last taken. On 27 August 1815 Féli wrote to his brother from London:

> Here I am now irrevocably decided, thanks to my good and tender father [i.e. Carron]. By myself I should never have got out of my eternal irresolution; but God had prepared for me in this country the succour that I needed; his Providence, by a wonderful sequence of graces, has led me to the goal where it was waiting for me.[121]

---

[118] 'Lettres à un Anglais sur le protestantisme', see Blaize, II, 271–286. Maréchal (*Jeunesse*, p. 497) is undoubtedly right in saying that these letters were intended for Morton, and not for Henry Moorman as Blaize and others have supposed. Lamennais uses arguments that he has picked up from Bonald, Pascal, Bossuet, Nicolle, and Rousseau, as Maréchal shows, *op. cit.*, pp. 500–512. It is not clear why Maréchal (p. 514) should consider it probable that Morton was converted by Lamennais.

[119] According to Renan, the idea was generally accepted in Brittany in those days that the ecclesiastical state was the only suitable one for those who intended to devote their lives 'aux travaux de la pensée'. See Spuller, *Lamennais*, p 80.

[120] See de Courcy, pp. 108, 113.

[121] See Blaize, I, 218; the letter continues as follows: 'Pleine d'amour pour un enfant rebelle, pour le plus indigne des pécheurs, elle (*sc.* Providence) m'arrache à ma patrie, à ma famille, à mes amis, à ce fantôme de repos que je m'épuisais à poursuivre, et m'amène aux pieds de son ministre pour y confesser mes égarements, et m'y déclarer ses volontés. Gloire à Dieu, gloire à son ineffable tendresse, à son incompréhensible bonté, à cet amour adorable qui, entre toutes ses créatures, lui fait choisir la plus indigne, pour en faire un ministre de son Église, pour l'associer au sacerdoce de son Fils! Mais honte, confusion,

Although the Hundred Days were now over, and there was nothing to prevent Lamennais from returning to France, he was so attached to, and dependent on, Carron that he stayed with him in London until November. Then they both reached Paris, where Lamennais took up his residence with Carron, and a small community which was gathered round him, so as to prepare for ordination under his immediate direction. Now that at last Féli had decided to proceed to the priesthood, everyone concerned seems to have felt that it was important to strike while the iron was hot. He was ordained sub-deacon in the church of St Sulpice on 23 December 1815, deacon at St Brieuc on 18 February, and priest at Vannes on 9 March 1816.[122]

The question whether Lamennais ought to have been ordained priest or not is a very involved one and raises a variety of considerations; perhaps it does not admit of a plain answer, but it is so important that it calls for elucidation. I distinguish between the facts of the case which clearly emerge from the correspondence of Lamennais and his friends, and the contradictory interpretations that have been put upon the facts.

As regards the facts—first, there is no doubt that entry into the priesthood was contrary to Lamennais's natural inclination. He procrastinated for years about the decision, and finally accepted it only as made for him by his director, and even then his disposition was that of a victim going to be sacrificed, of a man whom God was calling to bear a heavy cross. Secondly, the priests upon whose advice he depended—Carron, his brother Jean, Teysseyrre, and Bruté[123]—all knew quite well that this was his disposition, and nevertheless encouraged him to proceed, regarding his willingness

humiliation profonde, au misérable qui si longtemps a fui devant son divin Maître, et avec si horrible obstination s'est refusé au bonheur de le servir! Hélas! en ce moment même, je ne le sens que trop, si ma volonté tout entière n'était pas entre les mains de mon père bien-aimé, si ses conseils ne me soutenaient pas, si je n'étais pas complètement résolu à obéir sans hésiter à ses ordres salutaires, oui en ce moment même je retomberais dans mes premières incertitudes, et dans l'ambîme sans fond d'où sa main charitable m'a retiré.' Cp. ibid., I, 221, 228; de Courcy, pp. 122 f.; Ropartz, op. cit., p. 204.

[122] For the dates of Lamennais's ordinations, see Annales de Bretagne, April 1914, pp. 471 ff.; also ibid., January 1914, p. 74. Maréchal (Jeunesse, p. 529) was mistaken in saying that Lamennais was ordained deacon on 9 March and priest on 23 March.

[123] Bruté, who was now a missionary in the U.S.A., had recently been in France, and was keenly concerned about Féli's vocation. See Roussel, Documents, I, 109 ff.

to sacrifice his natural repugnance as a high mark of grace.[124] Thirdly, it is true that directly after taking the fateful step Lamennais for a time suffered from acute depression and blind resignation; he had had similar feelings after taking his earlier steps towards the altar.[125] Fourthly, there is no question but that after his ordination Lamennais was—to judge by the only spiritual and moral standards that men can apply—a model priest, exemplary in devotion,[126] in personal conduct, and in pastoral solicitude.

So far we are on firm, if unfamiliar, ground; but these facts have been interpreted in diametrically opposite ways. On the one hand, it has been said[127] that Lamennais never had a vocation to the priesthood at all, and that his repugnance before his ordination and his distress immediately afterwards plainly show that to have been the case. He ought to have remained a layman, and as a journalist he might never have broken with the church. On this view, the blame for the fatally mistaken step may be attributed in various proportions[128] to Lamennais himself, who ought not to have surrendered his decision into other hands, and to the priests who, knowing his disposition, should not have encouraged and even pressed him to proceed. They were too eager at all costs to secure a powerful apologist for the service of the church.[129]

124 Thus Teysseyrre wrote to Féli on 27 February 1816: 'Vous allez à l'ordination comme une victime au sacrifice. Le saint autel est dépouillé pour vous de ses ornements, le calice enivrant a perdu ses délices et nu vous embrassez et suivez la croix toute nue. . . . Qu'avez-vous donc fait au Père céleste pour qu'il daigne ainsi vous traiter comme son fils bien-aimé?' See Blaize, I, 259.

125 Cp. *Jeunesse*, pp. 533 f. In *Dispute*, p. 110, Maréchal suggests a particular adventitious reason for Lamennais's reaction on this occasion.

126 Unless one takes seriously the view of R. P. Caussette, who attributed Lamennais's 'fall' to the fact that he did not say his breviary: Caussette, *Manrèze du Prêtre* (3rd ed., 1882), I, 85. But in 1819 Lamennais, through the good offices of Lamartine, received from Rome a dispensation from saying the breviary under certain conditions, and a letter he wrote at the time shows that he had a scrupulous regard for the prescribed conditions: see Blaize, I, 390. There seems to be no definite evidence that he did not usually say his breviary: Forgues, II, 209 f., 221, may imply that he was doing so in 1831.

127 For references see Feugère, pp. 216 f., to which should be added *Vitrolles*, p. 8.

128 See Boutard, I, 121 f.

129 See, e.g., Carron's letter to Bruté of 28 October 1815: 'Il (Féli) ne m'échappera point, l'Église aura ce qui lui appartient, telle est ma vive confiance.' De Courcy, p. 124. Of Féli's counsellors Carron has the main responsibility; after him, as Feugère says (p. 209), 'Teysseyrre et Bruté semblent l'avoir poussé au sacerdoce bien plus fortement que Jean-Marie'. Once however the decision had been made, Jean did not scruple to press forward its consequences; cp. de Courcy,

On the other hand, it may be asked whether anyone would now have misgivings about the genuineness of Lamennais's vocation to the priesthood, if it had not been for his later clash with ecclesiastical authority?[130] The period from 1816 to 1833 was that of his most happy and fruitful activity, and it may be that his personal tragedy lay not in his exercise of the priesthood before his rupture with the church but in the prevention of his continued exercise of it afterwards. Henry Bremond said of Lamennais: 'He was a priest to the very marrow of his bones, even when his being so weighed upon him most unbearably—that is clear from the record of his apostolate, and from his letters, and from his writings—that is how the majority of his contemporaries saw him whether they were believers or not.'[131] As M. Foisset, Lacordaire's biographer, observed,[132] many excellent priests have had scruples similar to those of Lamennais at the time of their ordination, so that his repugnance and distress do not necessarily forbid the opinion that he had a vocation to the priesthood.[133] Even the serene and saintly abbé Jean had his moments of depression.[134] There is plenty of sanction in the tradition of ascetic theology for the belief that a man may be called to a state of life that is contrary to his natural inclination, and even that the disposition of a sacrificial victim is to be highly commended.[135]

p. 125. See also Duine in *Annales de Bretagne*, January 1914, pp. 213 f. Teysseyrre's biographer, who did not consider that Lamennais had a vocation to the priesthood, sought to minimize T.'s influence in the matter: see Paguelle de Follenay, *op. cit.*, chap. 14.

[130] Cp. Duine, p. 57; Poulet, *Histoire de l'Église de France: époque contemporaine* p. 235.

[131] Bremond, *Pour le romantisme*, p. 61. Cp. Harispe, *Lamennais, drame de sa vie sacerdotale*, p. 154: 'Prêtre par tempérament, autant et peut-être plus que par vocation, il l'est resté . . . jusqu'à la fin de ses malheureux jours.' It is true that Lamennais is reported in his old age to have told Béranger that he had never been made for the priesthood and that he regretted that he had not married and had children, but this may have been no more than a wistful musing such as may easily escape any elderly and lonely celibate. There is nothing to show that it was his considered opinion, and even if it had been it would not settle the matter. See *Béranger et Lamennais*, p. 261.

[132] *Vie du R. P. Lacordaire* (1870), I, 109.

[133] Cp. Bremond, *op. cit.*, pp. 38 f. See also V. Giraud, *Revue des deux mondes*, 1 March 1919, pp. 125, 127; Paul Dudon on 'La Vocation ecclésiastique de Lamennais' in *Le Recrutement sacerdotale* (Reims), January and March 1912 (an important survey of the whole question of Lamennais's vocation).

[134] E.g. see de Courcy, p. 12. See also what Newman wrote in his private journal at the time of his ordination, Sean O'Faolain, *Newman's Way* (1952), p. 84.

[135] Cp. Duine, p. 55.

I do not consider myself to be either qualified or obliged to decide between these two interpretations of Lamennais's ordination. Indeed, it would be premature to do so at this stage in the unfolding of his career. It may be that the problem should be differently stated. Perhaps the most important question that Lamennais's career as a priest raises is whether it is consistent with the office of priesthood in the Church of Rome—and, maybe, in other churches too—to be an outspoken prophet and an initiator of radical reforms. Or are the docility and submissiveness to authority, that are required in a priest, incompatible with prophetic leadership, at any rate in the case of a man of such strong convictions and of so passionate a temperament as Lamennais? And after all prophets are liable to be like that. There is a problem here which the study of ecclesiastical history must not be expected to solve, but which it may be able to illustrate and explicate.

Chapter Three

NEW APOLOGETICS
1817-1824

I HAVE NOT hitherto been able to claim that either Lamennais or his family were anywhere near the centre of the stage of ecclesiastical history, though I hope that the preceding chapters have provided not only a necessary introduction to what is to follow, but also useful illustrations of the history of the Church of France during the momentous period between the collapse of the *ancien régime* and the restoration of the Bourbon monarchy. However that may be, in this chapter, with the publication of the first volume of the *Essai sur l'indifférence en matière de religion* as our starting-point, Lamennais steps straight into the centre of the stage of French church history, and he will never be far away from it until he makes his final exit nearly twenty years later.

It has been said that the name of Lamennais 'dominates' the history of catholicism in France in the nineteenth century.[1] 'Dominates' may be too strong a word, but it is true that anyone who followed up all the currents of thought that Lamennais originated or popularized, and the controversies that he set in motion, would have fairly fully covered the history of the French Church during the whole century.

The term 'mennaisianism' is a convenient portmanteau word for the whole body of ideas of which Lamennais was the author and to which his disciples were attached. But it is very important to observe not only that the mennaisian body of ideas did not spring full-grown out of its author's mind, but also that there were three distinguishable elements in it. The three distinguishable elements were, first, the philosophical or apologetic; secondly, the ecclesiastical; and thirdly, the political. To be more precise, the mennaisian *apologetic* or philosophy means traditionalism and the philosophy of *sensus communis* in contrast to the cartesian rationalism of the then theological schools; the mennaisian *ecclesiology* means ultramontanism in contrast to

[1] 'Le nom de La Mennais domine l'histoire du catholicisme en France au xixe siècle.'—Ernest Sevrin, *Dom Guéranger et La Mennais* (1933), p. 13.

gallicanism; the mennaisian *politics* means catholic liberalism, especially the liberal doctrine of the separation of church and state, in contrast to the pre-revolutionary assumption of their divinely ordained union or alliance.

Although eventually Lamennais himself held all these three doctrines together and in his own mind they formed a coherent whole, they were not necessarily bound up with one another. One could be a traditionalist without being an ultramontane or a liberal, as was the case with Bonald. One could be a traditionalist and an ultramontane without being a liberal, as was the case with Lamennais himself until 1829. One could be a liberal and an ultramontane without being a traditionalist, as was the case with Lacordaire. It should also be remarked—though this is to anticipate the end at the beginning—that of the three distinguishable elements in mennaisianism only two were condemned by the papacy, and they were condemned at different times. Catholic liberalism was condemned in 1832 in the encyclical *Mirari vos*, and after that many mennaisians continued—as they supposed, quite innocently—to believe in and teach traditionalism and the philosophy of *sensus communis*, until that too was condemned in 1834 in the encyclical *Singulari nos*. As for the third element in mennaisianism—namely, ultramontanism—that was destined not for condemnation but for canonization.

An interesting consequence of the fact that there were these three distinguishable elements in mennaisianism, and that only two of them were condemned, was that disciples of Lamennais who repented of their errors and remained in the church, and their biographers too, were tempted to make out that they had been attached to Lamennais on account of his ultramontanism and not on account of his traditionalism or his liberalism. A striking example of this is the official Benedictine biography of Dom Guéranger (1805–1875), the famous Abbot of Solesmes.[2] A book published in 1933,[3] bearing the *imprimatur*, demonstrated in detail both that Guéranger as a young priest was an all-round mennaisian and that his biographer quite unscrupulously concealed, and indeed denied, that he was.

It is convenient, for purposes of exposition, that Lamennais was chiefly engaged from 1817 to 1824 in working out his apologetic or

2 *Dom Guéranger, abbé de Solesmes,* par un moine bénédictin de la Congrégation de France (1909). The author of the biography was in fact Dom Delatte.
3 Sevrin, *op. cit.* Cp. Aubert, *Le pontificat de Pie IX,* p. 263.

philosophy, whereas from 1825 to 1829 he was principally occupied
with the problem of the church's relation to the state. The division
of interest was, however, only a rough one, for during the first
period he was active in ecclesiastico-political journalism which, as
we shall see, was not without its effect on the reception accorded to
the *Essai sur l'indifférence*, and in the second period he continued to
work on his philosophy.

The bare facts about the *Essai* are that the first volume was published in 1817, the second volume in 1820, and the third and fourth
volumes in 1823. There was to have been a fifth volume, but it was
never completed. In 1821, however, that is between volumes II and
III, Lamennais published *Défense de l'essai sur l'indifférence en matière
de religion*, which is included in the four-volume Garnier edition of
the whole *Essai*, the edition that is now the most accessible.[4] What
is important in the *Essai* is contained in the first two volumes, and
it will not be necessary to say much here about the last two. I may
add that an indifferent English translation of the first volume only,
by Lord Stanley of Alderley, was published in 1895. The transla-
tor's preface is curious both because of the number of erroneous
statements of fact that are packed into it, and also because he appears
to have thought that his production would strike a blow against the
disendowment of the Welsh Church![5]

The publication of the first volume of the *Essai*, which must be
considered by itself, was on any showing a notable event in the
history of the Church of France. It was Lamennais's first major
assault on the minds of his contemporaries and its sensational
success carried him at once from obscurity to fame. The measure of
the book's success surprised everyone, including the author himself,[6]
who did not at all relish the invasions of his privacy to which he
was suddenly and constantly exposed.[7] (He was still living in Paris
under the wing of abbé Carron, the priest who had guided or

---

[4] All references here will be to the Garnier edition.

[5] *Essay on Indifference in matters of Religion* by the abbé F. de Lamennais, translated by Lord Stanley of Alderley, p. xiv. The translation had been made over
thirty years before 1895, when it was deemed seasonable for publication.

[6] Lamennais had written to Bruté on 15 May 1817: 'Pour moi, je ne fais rien
qu'un mauvais livre fort à contre-cœur. Je ne prends jamais la plume pour y
ajouter quelques nouvelles lignes, sans éprouver un dégoût et des angoisses inexprimables.'—De Courcy, p. 135; cp. *ibid.*, pp. 132, 140; Blaize, I, 274, 278 f.,
282, 318, 322, 326, 356.

[7] By 1819 a lithographed portrait of Lamennais was on sale in all the shops of
Paris. See Blaize, I, 388; *Lamennais inconnu*, p. 79.

impelled him into the priesthood.) The first edition was sold out in two months, and three more editions were called for within the year, by which time 13,000 copies had been sold,[8] and the book was being translated into the principal languages of Europe.[9] It made its own way by its own intrinsic appeal. There was no advertising campaign; its ponderously ecclesiastical title was not calculated to attract. The early editions were anonymous, though the identity of the author was quickly noised abroad. The reviewers did not notice the book, till after it had become a best-seller.[10]

Opinions differ about the present readability and the permanent interest of the *Essai*,[11] but there is no doubt that it was alive when it first appeared. Abbé Frayssinous (1765–1841), the leading exponent of the catholic faith in Paris, said that the book would awaken the dead.[12] Indeed, it may be said to have done so. A soldier of Napoleon's Old Guard, who would have held the throne and the altar in an equal contempt, was seen reading this stiff work of catholic apologetic in the café which he frequented; a hardened sceptic confessed that he could not put it down.[13] It became the talk of the fashionable salons. Young men of letters were enchanted by it.[14] 'C'est magnifique,' exclaimed Lamartine, 'pensé comme M. de

---

8 See de Courcy, p. 151.

9 A translation into English was at this time prepared, and its impending publication announced, but there is no evidence that it was actually published. See Blaize, I, 381; de Courcy, pp. 143, 151; *Lamennais inconnu*, p. 75; Maréchal, *Dispute*, p. 66; Duine, *Bibliographie*, no. 955. Lord Stanley's translation belongs to a much later period.

10 See Blaize, I, 328; Duine, p. 59; Maréchal, *Dispute*, pp. 24, 28.

11 Maréchal, (*Dispute*, p. 2) writes: 'Plus d'un siècle a passé; l'ouvrage s'est classé parmi ces grandes œuvres d'apologétique religieuse auxquelles on recourt le plus fréquemment—en se gardant d'ailleurs, non moins souvent, de les citer. On est surpris, quand on le relit, de constater que, dans l'ensemble, si l'on se dégage de certains détails pour s'attacher aux vues générales, il n'a pas vieilli.' Likewise Boutard (I, 146): 'Ce fut ce volume qui fonda la réputation de Lamennais. Il est de tous ses ouvrages un de ceux qu'on lit le plus aujourd'hui, bien qu'il ne soit pas un des plus parfaits.' On the other hand, Duine (p. 66) writes: 'Après avoir joué son rôle, le livre s'est refermé peu à peu. Les jeunes gens du xxe siècle se refusent à l'ouvrir de nouveau. Comme d'autres ouvrages, qui ont mérité des contemporains l'épithète d'immortels, il n'est plus qu'un document du passé, un illustre témoin de la Restauration.' Cp. d'Haussonville (*Cottu*, p. vii): 'L'*Essai sur l'indifférence* trouve aujourd'hui peu de lecteurs. . . . C'est le propre des livres d'apologétique de vieillir vite.'

12 See Roussel, *Documents*, I, 127.

13 See Blaize, I, 319; cp. Maréchal, *Dispute*, pp. 1 f.

14 See Maréchal, *Dispute*, p. 26.

Maistre, écrit comme Rousseau, fort, vrai, élevé, pittoresque, concluant, neuf, enfin tout.'[15]

Lamennais was hailed as another Pascal or Bossuet.[16] The book installed him as the chaplain of the romantic movement. It provoked lively discussion and led to conversions,[17] whereas the effect of Chateaubriand's *Génie du Christianisme* had been dazzling but superficial and temporary.[18] Lamennais was known to practise what he preached and to be deeply in earnest, which is not exactly what would be said of Chateaubriand. Under Louis XVIII the monarchists supported the outward show of catholicism including a galaxy of chaplains and confessors as part of the court,[19] but inwardly their attitude to religion was patronizing or sentimental or cynical or indifferent.[20] 'All these great altar-servers hardly ever approach the altar,' said Paul-Louis Courier, the pamphleteer, and he maliciously added, 'I should very much like to know the name of M. de Chateaubriand's confessor.'[21]

If Lamennais won the attention of the intelligent infidels whom he aimed at addressing, it was because—unlike most christian apologists, then and now—he knew their state of mind from inside and he knew how to speak to it. He had a double advantage. First,

[15] Letter of 8 August 1818 to Virieu, see Maréchal, *Lamennais et Lamartine*, p. 60; cp. H. R. Whitehouse, *The Life of Lamartine*, I, 212.

[16] See Duine, pp. 60 f.; Maréchal, *Dispute*, p. 26.

[17] See Blaize, I, 346, 352, 389, 406, 430; Roussel, *Documents*, I, 244; *Revue des deux mondes*, 15 November 1923, p. 396; Maréchal, *Dispute*, p. 24. Bremond (*Pour le romantisme*, p. 53) writes: 'Les autres [apologistes] prouvaient l'Église, Lamennais [in the *Essai*] la fit aimer, parce que lui-même il l'aimait alors passionément, et que son génie d'écrivain était à la hauteur de ce grand amour.'

[18] 'Après Chateaubriand, il [Lamennais] croyait qu'il restait à montrer que le christianisme est capable, non seulement d'exciter des émotions esthétiques, mais de satisfaire les besoins de la pensée'.—Feugère, p. 187. 'Après la poésie du "Génie du christianisme" qui était venue bercer dans un demi-sommeil l'esprit religieux de la France profondément endormi dans l'athéisme de l'époque révolutionnaire, l'Essai sur l'indifférence vint réveiller la Société de l'époque, combien encore voltairienne.'—Jules Haize in *Annales de la Société Historique et Archéologique de l'arrondissement de Saint-Malo* (1904), p. 119. Cp. Poulet, *Histoire de l'Église de France: époque contemporaine*, p. 150; Maréchal, *Dispute* pp. 5 f. On the personal relations of Lamennais and Chateaubriand, see V. Giraud, *La vie tragique de Lamennais*, pp. 175–185; Y. Le Hir on 'Lamennais et Chateaubriand' in *Nouvelle Revue de Bretagne*, May–June 1948, pp. 182–194.

[19] See *L'Ami de la Religion et du Roi* (1815), III, 298 f.

[20] Cp. d'Haussonville, *Cottu*, pp. viii, xxiii.

[21] Quoted by P. de la Gorce, *Louis XVIII*, p. 312. On Paul-Louis Courier, see Sainte-Beuve, I, 233–276.

in attacking the state of mind which was the legacy of Voltaire, *les philosophes*, and Rousseau, he was attacking himself.[22] He was the natural spokesman of a generation that had been educated in the doctrines of the eighteenth century and then had been horrified by the way in which they had issued in anarchy and despotism during the revolution, and yet a generation that had not abandoned the axioms of its youth, since so far it had found no positive faith with which to replace them. Lamennais had had to struggle hard for a positive faith, but he had found one and he knew just what he wanted to say.

And his second advantage was that he knew how to say it. The lay intellectuals whom he succeeded in addressing would never have come round to reading a work of christian apologetic by a priest, unless it had possessed extraordinary virtues of style, such as they had long ceased to look for in the work of theologians. It was the style of the *Essai* that caused most of the sensation. Seventy-five years had elapsed since the death of Massillon (1663–1742), the last French priest to have had an outstanding literary reputation.[23] The reading public was now amazed to discover a priest who could speak to his age with such eloquence and audacity.

It is hardly possible to do justice to a book like this either by summarizing it or by quoting from it. A summary can give no idea of Lamennais's resourcefulness in argument or fertility in illustration, and in quotations the original loses much of its virtue. But it is necessary here to show what the argument of the *Essai* was, because of the effects it had at the time. There are two prefatory remarks to be made.

First, Lamennais applies the word 'indifference' primarily to doctrines, not to persons. He is talking, that is to say, about intellectual systems according to which the truth of religion or of catholic dogma is a matter of indifference. He is not necessarily accusing the persons who profess these systems of being indifferent in the moral or psychological sense.[24] A man may care very strongly about a doctrine which declares or implies that the truth of religion is a matter of indifference. This is a point that was widely misunderstood at the time, and is liable to be even more so now, in view of the current usage of the word 'indifference'. Although Lamennais's use of the word had been well established in France since the seventeenth

22 Cp. Maréchal, *Jeunesse*, p. 635.
23 See Foisset, *Vie du R. P. Lacordaire*, I, 109.
24 See *Essai*, I, 43 f., II, 26 f.

century,[25] it has been suggested that he would have done better to have entitled his book, *Essai sur l'indifférentisme*.[26] The principal object of his attack is the assumption that there is no necessary dependence of ethics on dogma or of conduct on belief, and if the *Essai* still has life in it, that is because the assumption which it attacks is by no means dead and Lamennais said most of the things that christians are now wont to say against it as well as, if not better than, any subsequent apologist.

The second remark that needs to be made at the outset is that throughout the *Essai* Lamennais is more concerned with the effects of religion on society than on the individual. Thus the first chapter begins with the assertion that the health of a society, its conduct and its culture, depend on the doctrine or faith which it holds. 'Everything', he says, 'proceeds from doctrines: morals, literature, constitutions, laws, the prosperity of states and their calamities, civilization, barbarism, and those terrible crises which destroy whole peoples or renew them.'[27] Therefore systems that treat doctrine as a matter of indifference are fatal not only to the persons who profess them, but to the societies in which they are prevalent. Lamennais's aim was, by insisting on this idea, to attract the attention of men who were already concerned about the future of society but whose interest in religion had to be aroused before they could be expected to face the issue of personal belief. He says that all he is asking people to do in the first instance is to examine the question. 'Nous ne leur disons point: Croyez; mais: Examinez.'[28]

The first half of this volume[29] is an exposition or delineation of three distinct forms of indifference which, Lamennais alleges, were widespread at the time, and he devotes two chapters to each. The first comprehends those who, while atheists themselves, regard religion as politically useful and as necessary for the common people: this was the teaching of *les philosophes*. The second comprehends those who admit the necessity of a religion for all men, but who reject revelation: this was deism, represented by Rousseau. The third comprehends the semi-indifferent who recognize a

25 See *Essai*, II, 27. For particulars of earlier 'essays on indifference', see Maréchal, *Jeunesse*, part IV, chaps. 1 and 2; *Dispute*, pp. 11–14.

26 Feugère, p. 86.

27 *Essai*, I, 30.

28 *Essai*, I, 28; cp. I, 196.

29 The formal division of the volume into two parts was not made till the eighth edition (1825), but it expressed what was the original structure of the work. Cp. Maréchal, *Jeunesse*, p. 635.

revealed religion but hold that only certain fundamental articles need be believed: this was protestantism, of which Jurieu[30] is taken as an example.

When arguing this kind of thesis, Lamennais made use of a great deal of bold and colourful, though often dubious and unconvincing, historical generalization, for example about the Roman Empire or the middle ages or the reformation. But he was very shrewd at spotting logical weaknesses or inconsistencies in his opponents' position. Thus he pointed out that *les philosophes* admitted that the people needed religion to persuade them to those duties without the performance of which society would not hold together. Indeed their theory was that God and morality had been invented by governments for this very reason. Lamennais naturally made play with this fantasy, and also pressed the point that religion must be believed to be true if it is to provide the required sanction for order and morality. But *les philosophes*, while they admitted the necessity of religion, were engaged in disseminating proofs of its falsehood. They were therefore involved in a hopeless contradiction, and they should think again.

It was easy to spot contradictions in the deist position represented by Rousseau, since he is notorious for his inconsistencies. The futility and elusiveness of a 'natural religion' which cannot be identified with any positive religion are brought out.[31] Though deism appears to depend on belief in the existence of God, it makes admissions[32] which imply the possibility of atheism, and turns out to be so incoherent that it resolves itself into dogmatic indifference in the end.

The same can be said of protestantism, of which, according to Lamennais, the cardinal principle is individualism or private judgment. Jurieu had maintained that all christians agreed in accepting certain fundamental articles of faith and that they differed only about subordinate matters. When the catholics asked what these fundamental articles were, no satisfactory answer was forthcoming. Protestants appeal to the Bible, but the Bible knows nothing of the distinction between fundamental and non-fundamental articles of faith.

[30] Pierre Jurieu (1637–1713) perhaps owed his distinction to the fact that Bossuet undertook to refute him. Cp. Boutard, I, 144.

[31] 'C'est un fait remarquable, qu'il n'exista dans aucun temps de peuple déiste.'—*Essai*, I, 112.

[32] ' "Soyez juste, il suffit; le reste est arbitraire." Le *reste*, c'est simplement le culte, la doctrine, l'immortalité de l'âme, les peines et les récompenses futures, l'existence de Dieu, rien que cela.'—*Essai*, I, 126.

When Jesus Christ sends his apostles to proclaim christianity
to the nations, does he say to them: Teach men to distinguish
carefully the fundamental dogmas from those that are not so . . .?
No, Jesus Christ says nothing of the kind. What does he say? 'Go
ye therefore, and make disciples of all the nations . . . teaching
them to observe all things whatsoever I commanded you', everything without exception, *omnia quaecumque*.[33]

According to protestants, the Scriptures are to be interpreted by each
man's reason: 'their principal maxim is to recognize no human
authority in matters of faith'.[34] 'Who does not see that the authority
of Scripture becomes the authority of reason alone . . . everyone
ought to believe what his reason clearly shows him to be true, which
is precisely the principle of the deist and the atheist.'[35]

So far Lamennais may have attacked infidelity and heresy with
more verve and vigour than was customary; he might even be said
to have brought Bossuet up to date; but nothing has emerged which
could be described as 'new apologetics'. It is in the second part of
this first volume, in which he deals with the positive importance of
religion, that he begins to break away from the accepted apologetic
method, although his readers did not perceive how far he had done
so until the second volume of the *Essai* was published in 1820.
The accepted apologetic method was based on the cartesianism of
the theological schools,[36] and the seminary of St Sulpice was its
venerable guardian in the Church of France. The attempt was made
to meet rationalistic unbelievers on their own ground, and to prove
that any individual who used his reasoning powers correctly could
arrive at certitude about the truths of natural religion, which were
the substructure of revealed religion. A sharp distinction, that is to
say, was drawn between reason and revelation and between natural
religion and revealed religion.

The rationalism and individualism of this method of defending
the catholic faith had already been challenged by Bonald, and the
students of St Sulpice had been warned against his teaching. Thus

---

[33] *Essai*, I, 165.

[34] *Essai*, I, 175.

[35] *Essai*, I, 176.

[36] On the cartesianism of the theological schools, see Hocedez, *Histoire de la
Théologie au xixe siècle*, I, 20 f.; de Ladoue, *Mgr Gerbet*, I, 129. Lamennais in the
preface to *Défense* (IV, 151 f.) claims that theology became rationalistic only
after the incursion of Aristotle into the schools and still more after the cartesian
innovations, whereas previously theology had made its appeal to common
consent or to authority.

in a course of lectures in 1809–1810[37] one of the professors, M. Boyer, explained that 'religion is the combination of man's duties towards God. And since these duties are made known by reason and revelation, religion has long been divided into natural religion and supernatural religion.' Boyer went on to say that 'M. de Bonald, one of the most vigorous defenders of the catholic faith, has strongly objected to this division.' Bonald claimed that man could not have acquired the use of language by the use of his own reason, therefore he had received the gift of language by revelation. And with language there had been revealed religion, morality, and reason itself. There was no such thing as a natural law, in the sense of a law discovered by human reason. What had been called the natural law was divinely revealed. Boyer condemned Bonald's teaching because it was novel and broke with tradition, and also because it would make it impossible to meet deists in argument.

Bonald, however, was only a layman, and his manner of writing was dry and ponderous compared with Lamennais's.[38] Lamennais had certainly read Bonald, and he thought very highly of him,[39] but how far he owed his ideas to Bonald or thought them out independently is a moot question.[40] Wilfrid Ward said that 'the most profound thoughts in the *Essai sur l'indifférence* are not Lamennais's but Bonald's; while its exaggerations, which Rome finally condemned, are the work of Lamennais himself.'[41] This both overstates Lamennais's indebtedness to Bonald and with too much confidence exempts Bonald's teaching from Rome's condemnation.[42] Quite different was the opinion of Père Dudon, the jesuit authority

[37] Maréchal, *Jeunesse*, pp. 667 f., quotes from the unpublished MS. of these lectures which is in the Archives of St Sulpice.

[38] As Victor Giraud said: 'C'est une œuvre austère et abrupte que celle de Bonald, et son influence . . . n'est pas de celles qui s'imposent à un très large public.' *Revue des deux mondes*, 1 June 1937, p. 589.

[39] Already in *Réflexions* (O.C., VI, 78) Lamennais had written this about Bonald: 'Déjà un homme de génie a pénétré avec succès dans cette nouvelle route ouverte aux défenseurs du christianisme; et ses ouvrages immortels, que la postérité appréciera, feront un jour révolution dans la philosophie comme dans la politique.' Cp. Maréchal, *Jeunesse*, p. 235.

[40] In *Essai*, II, 127, Lamennais instances one idea among others which he had in common with Bonald but which had occurred to him independently. Cp. Blaize, I, 348. See also Maréchal, *Dispute*, pp. 344–353.

[41] *William George Ward and the Catholic Revival* (1912 edition), p. 93.

[42] See Henri Mouliné, *De Bonald* (1915), pp. 259–267, on 'Bonald et la doctrine traditionaliste condamnée par l'Église'; cp. *ibid.*, pp. 419–425, on 'Bonald et Lamennais'.

on Lamennais. 'It is an exaggeration', he wrote, 'to make Lamennais depend on Bonald. When he read Bonald's books, Lamennais discovered in them not new truths but the expression of his own ideas, so much so that in repeating them he ran the risk of being taken for a plagiarist.'[43] That would appear to be nearer the truth, but, as Père Hocedez points out in the first volume of his *Histoire de la Théologie au xixe siècle*,[44] we still await a critical history of traditionalism and its origins; until we have that, the interrelations between the thought of Bonald, Maistre, and Lamennais should be treated with reserve.

It is certainly misleading to lump all three together as representatives of an uniform school of thought. They do not themselves seem to have realized how much they differed from one another.[45] Hocedez says that Maistre was the precursor of traditionalism, Bonald its father, and Lamennais its herald.[46] 'Herald' is the right word for Lamennais.[47] It was he who first made the public take notice of these new ideas which were in the air, and which can easily have occurred independently to men who pondered deeply on the causes and calamities of the revolutionary period.[48] The principal traditionalist theses were: first, that man is not an isolated individual left to discover what he needs to know by his own unaided reason, but a social being who learns what he needs to know through tradition and must receive it on authority; secondly, that the tradition of the human race originates in a primal revelation by God of the truths which it is needful for man to know, so that revelation is a presupposition of reason, and not an appendix to it. We shall see how Lamennais himself presents these theses in the *Essai*.[49]

---

[43] *Études*, 20 January 1910, p. 221. C. Carcopino said of Lamennais: 'Il fut pour beaucoup un maître, mais on ne peut dire de qui il fut le fidèle disciple.'—*Les doctrines sociales de Lamennais*, p. 13.

[44] *Op. cit.*, I, 104.   [45] E.g. see Mouliné, *op. cit.*, pp. 58 f., 410–419.

[46] *Op. cit.*, I, 105.

[47] E. Spuller well said of Lamennais: 'Il a pris souvent pour des idées, à lui propres et personnelles, des opinions qu'il trouvait chez les autres et qu'il jugeait démontrées, mais il les a présentées, défendues, exaltées, et glorifiées avec une force et un éclat hors de pair.'—*Lamennais*, p. 40.

[48] As Mouliné points out (*op. cit.*, p. 60), the Swiss writer, Charles-Louis de Haller, advocated ideas very similar to those of the other traditionalists, but quite independently of them. On Bonald and Maistre, see also Leflon, *La crise révolutionnaire*, pp. 364–366. On Bonald, H. J. Laski, *Authority in the Modern State*, pp. 123–188; Sainte-Beuve, I, 210–232. On Maistre, Lord Morley, *Biographical Studies*, pp. 131–189; Sainte-Beuve, I, 1–163.

[49] On the ways in which Lamennais differs from Bonald, see also Poisson, *Le romantisme social de Lamennais*, p. 376; Maréchal, *Dispute*, pp. 17–21.

They were certainly in his mind when he wrote the second part of the first volume, which deals with the importance of religion for man whether considered as an individual or in his social relations or in his relation to God. That Lamennais is chiefly concerned with the social effects of Christianity—or with its 'sociological relevance', as we should now say, I suppose—is shown by the fact that he writes about that at much greater length than about the other aspects of the subject.[50] He attacks the unreality and artificiality of the 'social contract' theory of society. Societies are not manufactured by men after some humanly conceived ideal. They are natural; they grow in accordance with those natural laws which express the relations which necessarily exist between men and their Creator. *La philosophie* begins by viewing men as separate and self-contained individuals, who then proceed to form societies. On this disastrous and destructive view, societies depend on a compact of arbitrary and self-interested wills; they have no basis in moral obligation, for the will of a man is not obligatory for himself, let alone for other people. What happens then is that the will of the strongest prevails. There being no authority whom all are morally bound to obey, society falls under the dominion of force. There is an essential difference between force and authority. 'Force is the power to constrain, authority is the right to command. From the right to command results the duty of obeying; from the power to constrain results the necessity of yielding. There is an infinite difference between these two notions.'[51]

Social health and stability depend on order and harmony, and God has made known to men the laws that are favourable to social health and stability; these laws were not invented by men: they belong to the primitive tradition of the race. 'All real legislation emanates from God, who is the eternal principle of order, and the general governor of the society of intelligent beings.'[52] According to christianity, law—whether the law of nations or the civil and criminal law of particular states—is not the expression of the will of the strongest, nor has it for its object the protection of private interests. Its object is the establishment of justice, which is the supreme interest of all, and justice is the order willed by God. Christian kings are bound under oath to observe, and to cause to

[50] In the Garnier edition 113 pages are occupied with the 'importance of religion with respect to society', 39 pages with the 'importance of religion with respect to man', and 34 pages with the 'importance of religion with respect to God'.
[51] *Essai*, I, 267.   [52] *Essai*, I, 290.

be observed, the justice and also the mercy which God has revealed
to be his will.[53] Government is a trust like fatherhood. Obedience
to God and his law on the part of rulers and subjects is society's only
protection against an arbitrary despotism.

Religion, however, does more for society than give government
and law a moral ground in the will of God, and so secure the tranquillity of order which society can never have while it is at the
mercy of the restless wills and conflicting interests of men. Government and law, however good, can reach only men's outward conduct
and can preserve only the framework of society. They can prevent
or punish crime; they cannot infuse virtue or instil morality. This
work religion has reserved to itself. In other words, the negative work
of the state is met and excelled by the positive work of the church.[54]

Christianity does not only hold up to men an abstract idea of
virtue; it offers them virtue itself in the person of the God-man and
the infinite motive of winning heaven and of escaping hell. Religion
founds society in the mutual gift and sacrifice of God to man and of
man to God, and maintains in society ordinances and institutions
which embody and translate into action the principle of love and
self-sacrifice. One of Lamennais's most eloquent passages is this
description of the services rendered to society by the catholic clergy:

> It was certainly a noble idea to place alongside the inexorable
> ministers of the law the sacred ministers of morality and humanity,
> and to make compassion a public function. Make your way into
> the heart of families, question their members, and they will tell
> you what they owe to this wonderful institution. How many
> quarrels it has made up, how many husbands and wives, relations
> and fellow-citizens it has reconciled, how many victims it has
> snatched from the jaws of vice, how many wrongs have been
> righted, how many crimes prevented, how many burdens light-
> ened, how many secret miseries eased! Do you know what a
> priest is, you who are provoked by the very word or who smile
> with contempt when you hear it? I will tell you. It is the duty of a

[53] It should be noted that Lamennais's royalism, which anyhow receives little
emphasis in the *Essai*, was always thus conditioned.

[54] 'Les bonnes mœurs achèvent l'ouvrage des bonnes lois. *Quid leges sine moribus
vanae proficiunt*? disoient les païens mêmes. À quoi sert d'écrire l'ordre dans un
code, si la Religion n'en grave l'amour dans les cœurs? Les lois d'ailleurs se
bornent à proscrire certains délits; elles ne commandent aucune vertu. La
Religion s'est réservé à elle seule cette sublime partie de la législation, qui règle
tout dans l'homme, jusqu'à ses désirs les plus secrets et ses affections les plus
fugitives.'—*Essai*, I, 343 f.

priest to be the friend, the living Providence of all the unfortunate, the comforter of the afflicted, the protector of anyone who is without protection, the support of the widow, the father of the orphan; it is for him to redress all the disorders and all the evils which your passions and baleful doctrines bring forth. His whole life is nothing but a long and heroic self-sacrifice for the welfare of his fellows. Which of you would be willing to exchange like him the joys of home, all the pleasures of life, all the good things that men so eagerly seek, for obscure labours, painful duties, heart-breaking and repulsive offices, to receive in return often nothing but derision, ingratitude and insult? While you are still fast asleep, this man of charity has already anticipated the dawn and has begun again his round of beneficent works. He has relieved the poor, visited the sick, dried the tears of the miserable, or drawn tears of repentance, instructed the ignorant, strengthened the weak, and confirmed in the path of virtue souls troubled by the storms of passion. After a day filled up with such good works, evening at last arrives, but no respite for him. At the hour when you are going to the theatre or to a party, a messenger arrives in haste for the priest; a christian is approaching his last moments; he is about to die, perhaps of an infectious disease; no matter; the good shepherd will not let his sheep expire without easing their agony, without surrounding them with the consolations of hope and faith, without praying at their side to the God who died for them, and who gives them at that very moment, in the sacrament of love, a certain pledge of immortality.[55]

Having thus extolled the beneficent influence of religion on society, with a variety of historical illustrations which cannot be reproduced here, Lamennais claims that apathetic indifference to the doctrines of religion is inexcusable. It is not however by reasoning, he says, that men find out the truth of religion, but by faith which is the will to accept testimony. Thus God respects man's freedom: for whereas evidence constrains the reason, testimony leaves the will free to accept or reject it.[56] We do not come to know

[55] *Essai*, I, 365 f.
[56] 'La volonté est toujours libre d'*écouter* ou non un *témoignage*, de l'admettre ou de le rejeter: et c'est même ainsi qu'en croyant, sans y être forcé par une évidence intrinsèque et invincible, l'homme rend volontairement à Dieu un hommage digne de lui; véritable *adoration en esprit et en vérité*, qui consiste à reconnoître, par une soumission parfaite à sa parole, la dépendance infinie où notre raison est de la raison divine.'—*Essai*, I, 384 f.

other people—that they exist or what they think—by reason, but by their communicating themselves by speech, i.e. by revelation. It is pride that causes men to set their individual reason against the testimony that God bears to himself in his church—atheism, deism, and protestantism are different degrees of this pride. Men are so constituted that they must have some object of worship. If they do not choose to serve the true God who has revealed himself, they will serve their own passions, or will worship idols of their own reason, or will fall down before tyrants.

All Lamennais claimed to have done in this first volume of the *Essai* was to have shown that, if there is a true religion, it is of infinite importance. That there is a true religion, and that it can be easily distinguished from false religions, he undertook to prove in the subsequent volumes.

The reviewers of the first volume[57] failed to detect the hidden explosives it contained—philosophical, theological, and political, and so were quite unprepared for the argument of the second volume. The royalist periodicals reviewed the first volume with flattering approval, since they supposed that Lamennais belonged to their camp—but quite superficially. They praised the style and the eloquence without noticing what was new in it. They failed to observe how subdued Lamennais's royalism was. They took his association in journalism with the ultra-royalists to mean that he was as much attached to the throne as to the altar. A discerning reader might have seen that he valued the throne not so much for its own sake as for the services he expected it to render to the altar.[58] If the restored monarchy did not set the church free to do its regenerative work in society—if instead of supporting the church it hindered it—there was nothing to prevent Lamennais from throwing over the traditional alliance of church and state.

Reviewers in the liberal camp, when the mounting success of the book made it incumbent on them to notice it, attacked it violently as a matter of course. But their attacks were for the most part[59] based on a misunderstanding of what Lamennais had said, or at any rate of what he had meant. They too were misled by his association

---

[57] For a full and elaborate account of the way in which the *Essai* was received and of the controversies it started, see Maréchal, *Dispute*.

[58] Cp. Maréchal, *Dispute*, p. 18.

[59] They made some quite justified criticisms of Lamennais's historical generalizations. E.g. see Maréchal, *Dispute*, p. 53.

with the ultra-royalists. They took it for granted that he wanted, like the ultras, to revive the *ancien régime* and to use the church as a buttress of the monarchy and its temporal interests. Overlooking the fact that he had drawn a clear distinction between the claims of authority and the use of force, as well as between personal and dogmatic indifference, they represented his argument for the necessity of an authority morally entitled to obedience as a plea for coercion in matters of belief and for the revival of persecution. They failed to see that he wanted order for the sake of true liberty.[60] In the preface to the second volume this calumny is indignantly repudiated.[61]

Three parties can roughly be distinguished in France at this time[62]: (1) the ultras, who wanted the king without the constitutional charter, (2) the liberals, who wanted the charter without the king, and (3) the comparatively small group of *doctrinaires* who wanted the charter and the king, i.e. a constitutional and progressive monarchy. The most perceptive comments on the first volume of the *Essai* came from one or two reviewers in this group, particularly from Charles Loyson (1791–1820), a young poet who died prematurely, uncle of Père Hyacinthe Loyson who became well known later in the century.[63]

Loyson agreed with Lamennais that there could be no society without morality and no morality without religion, and that government is a divine ordinance, not the outcome of a social contract. But he goes on to say that God has also ordained constitutional liberties to prevent government from becoming despotic or arbitrary. Both the sovereignty of government and the liberty of the people 'subsist essentially, not in virtue of some paltry pact imagined by certain philosophers, but in virtue of an eternal pact, written by

---

60 'Plus le droit, le pouvoir et la loi sont parfaits, c'est à dire plus l'ordre est complet, plus la liberté est grande; car la liberté consiste dans l'exclusion des bornes arbitraires mises à la volonté; et quand elle n'est bornée que par des volontés obligatoires ou légitimes, l'homme alors jouit du plus haut degré de liberté possible.'—*Essai*, II, 165. The experience of the revolution had taught Lamennais that liberty understood as independence—the freedom of *la philosophie*—leads to anarchy and despotism; therefore he distinguished between true and false liberty. Cp., *Essai*, I, 326 ff. See also Maréchal, *Jeunesse*, pp. 682 f. 685, 687.

61 See *Essai*, II, 28.

62 Cp. Maréchal, *Dispute*, p. 57. For a fuller classification of political parties and groups, see G. Weill, *La France sous la monarchie constitutionelle*, pp. 13–20; P. Thureau-Dangin, *Royalistes et Républicains* and *Le Parti libéral sous la Restauration*.

63 See Albert Houtin, *Le Père Hyacinthe*, 3 vols. (1920–1924).

Nature's own hand, and of which human constitutions are, so to speak, only copies.'[64] Here was a line of thought calculated to appeal to Lamennais, and we know from a letter written at the time[65] that it made an impression on him. Loyson concluded his review with words which are a first pointer to that marriage of liberalism with catholicism of which the author of the *Essai* was in due course to become the prophet: 'It will be a happy day for christianity, for governments, for peoples, and for our beloved France, when we all come to understand that there is nothing more liberal than religion and nothing more religious than liberalism.'

The fact, however, that on the whole the reviewers of the first volume of the *Essai*, whether friendly or hostile, had failed to appreciate the new ideas with which it was pregnant meant that they, and those who depended on them for enlightenment, were quite unprepared to understand the second volume which was at length published on 7 July 1820. An unfavourable reception awaited it for another reason too. Between 1814 and 1820 Lamennais had been becoming increasingly incisive and provocative as a journalist.[66] Unable to found a journal of his own, he had had *faute de mieux* to collaborate with gallican and royalist journals with which he was far from being in complete sympathy. But he had taken an independent line, and had launched attacks in whatever direction he had considered that the liberty of the church was threatened or obstructed. Moreover, his friends had not scrupled to enlist his talents, where he would not himself have taken an initiative, in partisan manœuvres against powerful personalities. The consequence was that by 1820 Lamennais had alienated many of his original friends, e.g. in St Sulpice, and had prepared for himself a large number of actual or potential enemies—in the University, on the government Board of Censors, and in both the gallican and liberal camps—enemies who were ready to avenge themselves on this gadfly whenever an opportunity arose, or who at least were not likely to approach anything he wrote in a sympathetic frame of mind. This background of animosity must not be forgotten, for it was a heavily contributing factor to the violent reactions with which the second volume of the *Essai* was received.

[64] See the account of this article, which appeared in *Le Spectateur politique et littéraire* (1818), given by Maréchal, *Dispute*, pp. 33–41.

[65] See Blaize, I, 360.

[66] See Maréchal, *Dispute*, part II, for an account of Lamennais's journalistic activities during this period.

Soon after the first volume had been published, Lamennais had told Bruté in a letter that the second volume would be the most important, and that in it he would 'develop a new system of defending christianity against all the unbelievers and heretics'.[67] He expended more labour on this than on the first volume, and its argument is more closely knit. Only a summary of the most important stages in the argument can be attempted here.

Lamennais has undertaken to show that there is only one true religion, and that there is a sure and easy way of distinguishing it from false religions.

He begins by considering how men can arrive at certitude about anything, and this is the hub of his whole thesis. His opening chapter might have been headed (to borrow a title from Paul Elmer More) 'The Sceptical Approach to Religion'. For, pressing the cartesian method of doubt to its logical conclusion, he contends that it leads to universal scepticism. The individual man has no rational[68] ground for being certain of anything.

> It is a fact that our senses, our intuitions[69] and our reason often deceive us, and that we have within ourselves no means of knowing when we are mistaken, no infallible rule by which we may know what is true. Indeed, we cannot rigorously affirm anything, not even our own existence. Nothing is proven, because the proofs themselves would need other proofs, and so on *ad infinitum*.[70]

Nevertheless, although we are not rationally justified in being certain about anything, yet in point of fact we are certain about all sorts of things. Without such certitude it would be impossible for either individuals or societies to exist. 'The universal, absolute doubt, to which a severe logic condemns us, is impossible to men. . . . All men, without exception, believe invincibly thousands of truths which are the necessary bond of society and the foundation of human life.'[71] There must then be a ground for certitude elsewhere than in the

[67] Letter of 22 February 1818: de Courcy, p. 140; cp. *ibid.*, p. 150; Forgues, I, 158.
[68] Lamennais distinguished two senses of 'reason': the faculty of knowing or the apprehension of truth, and ratiocination or the discursive understanding which passes from premises to conclusions; his question is whether certitude is rational in the latter sense. Cp. A. Viatte, *Le catholicisme chez les romantiques*, p. 116.
[69] 'Le sentiment intérieur'. For the meaning that Lamennais attaches to 'sentiment' —a word that it is difficult to translate satisfactorily into English—see *Essai*, IV, 244 f.; cp. *Discussions critiques*, pp. 77 f.
[70] *Essai*, II, 93.   [71] *Essai*, II, 93.

reason of the isolated individual. Indeed, there is. The things of which we are certain are the things about which everyone agrees, as that the sun will rise tomorrow. Certitude is grounded in the general reason of the human race, common consent, *sensus communis*. 'Madness consists in preferring one's own reason, one's individual authority, to the general authority or to common consent.'[72] We have certitude about matters of every-day life because we have faith in the testimony of the human race, and not because we have each rationally demonstrated them for ourselves.

That that is so must be granted, Lamennais says, but by what right does common consent produce certitude in us? At this stage of the argument, he observes that the common consent of mankind affirms with virtual unanimity the existence of God, for he maintains that even atheists implicitly believe in God. It is indeed a truth that is much more certain than our own existence, since it rests on a much larger volume of testimony. Now, once the existence of God is acknowledged as a fact, all other facts appear in a new light. For God is by definition Necessary Being; he and he alone contains his *raison d'être* within himself; he is the Eternal Reason. All other facts are contingent. If we consider them only by themselves, we never can attain to certitude concerning them, since they do not contain the reason for their existence in themselves. God is the source of all existence and the creator of all things; in him alone there is certitude about all that is. Therefore truths, which God has revealed or attested, *are* certain.

Next, Lamennais lays it down that, when God bestowed life on mankind, he must also have bestowed knowledge of those truths that are necessary for the realization of life—the personal life of the individual, the life of men one with another in society, and life in communion with himself; otherwise God would have stultified his purpose from the outset.[73] These truths comprise the law of nature, which is God's primal revelation to mankind. It is the law of nature, not in the sense that it can be known by reason independently of revelation, but in the sense that it is the law that corresponds to the true nature of man.

---

[72] *Essai*, II, 94.
[73] 'Il existe . . . nécessairement, pour toutes les intelligences, un ordre de vérités ou de connoissances primitivement révélées, c'est-à-dire reçues originairement de Dieu comme les conditions de la vie, ou plutôt comme la vie même; et ces vérités de foi sont le fond immuable de tous les esprits, le lien de leur société, et la raison de leur existence.'—*Essai*, II, 137.

God's primal revelation of the necessary conditions of human life and thought was originally made by his Word (the Divine Reason), and it has been communicated to successive generations by the testimony of the human race or by tradition.[74] It is by means of what they receive and accept from society that men come to know the truth, not by each individual's making the vain attempt to discover it for himself. Without faith in the testimony of the human race it is impossible for men to perform the simplest actions of daily life, such as eating. Likewise science, art, and commerce demand faith as their pre-condition.[75] If we waited for rational demonstrations, we should be paralysed.[76]

Because tradition is ultimately derived from the testimony of God or from revelation, it provides firm ground for human certitude. The primal revelation has 'an infinite certitude'[77] and is 'infallible',[78] since it is the testimony of God himself. Unlike the individual

---

[74] Lamennais adopts Bonald's theory of the origin of language (see Mouliné, *De Bonald*, part II, chap. 4, 'La théorie de langage'). According to this, it is impossible that man invented language (as naturalism supposed), because it would require the pre-existence of thought, and there cannot be thought without language which is the indispensable means of articulating and communicating thought (see *Essai*, II, 191). The birth of thought and language was therefore miraculous, a direct simultaneous gift of God. Human speech is the medium which the Divine Word uses to communicate with our intelligence. Lamennais accepted the historical character of the Genesis narratives, but he says that the Word of God who addressed Adam also addresses each individual man. Whether we go back to the origin of the human race or consider each individual apart, the Word is veritably and in all senses 'the light that lighteth every man coming into the world' (John 1: 9) and 'the breath of life which animates his intelligence' (Genesis 2:7). See *Essai*, II, 141 f.

[75] Scientific theories, for instance, depend on conventional assumptions which can never be logically demonstrated. See *Essai*, II, 90, 208.

[76] Lamennais points out that the necessity of faith in this sense was clearly recognized and stated by the Fathers. See *Essai*, II, 147. When in the *Essai* he speaks of 'faith' he usually means the alogical presuppositions of thought and action, though he may tend sometimes to confound this sense of 'faith' with the 'saving faith' of the Bible and of christian theology. See *Essai*, IV, 248, where he writes: 'Il ne s'agit point ici de la foi qui est une grâce surnaturelle dans l'ordre du salut. Nous entendons par ce mot une croyance que ne détermine aucune preuve rationelle.' In a letter of August 1821, he writes: 'Il n'est question dans mon ouvrage de la foi *divine*: évidemment je ne pouvais en parler aux incrédules, parmi lesquels il en est qui n'admettent pas même l'existence de Dieu. D'ailleurs, on dit tous les jours en français: *j'ai foi dans vos paroles, dans votre jugement, etc.*'—Blaize, I, 402.

[77] *Essai*, II, 149.

[78] *Essai*, II, 150.

reason, the general reason or the *sensus communis* cannot err. 'Fallible men and infallible society' might seem to be the formula for Lamennais's doctrine of certitude. He does not, however, say or mean that the tradition of any and every society is infallibly true, for it is part of his doctrine that particular societies, as well as individuals, because of original sin can pervert and falsify the *sensus communis* of the race, and he proposes criteria by which what is true and false in tradition may be distinguished.

Having now, as he supposes, established the way by which men attain to certitude in general, Lamennais says that it will be easy to find how they can attain to certitude about *the true religion*. And he proceeds to show how it is done.

He defines religion as the expression of the relations between God and men. He sees God, man, and the world as a vast complex of relationships. 'Nothing is independent, nothing is isolated, in the creation. Since they are an expression . . . of a magnificent thought of God's, beings are thereby bound to beings, and worlds to worlds, as words are joined to one another in speech.'[79] In God himself there are three persons bound together in immutable relations. In the secret depth of his being God himself is an eternal society, and man has been adopted into that society.[80] Since the nature of God and the nature of man are constant, and do not vary from place to place or from time to time, and religion is the expression of the relations between them, there can be only one true religion in the nature of things.

But is there a sure and easy way by which men can distinguish the true religion? It is absurd, Lamennais says, to suppose that God, who has enabled the animals to know and obey instinctively the laws appropriate to their nature, would have withheld from intelligent beings the laws appropriate to their nature, and then have threatened to punish them for disobeying them. The human race testifies that it has not been treated like that.

> All peoples have had a religion which they regarded as true; therefore all peoples have believed that one could know the true religion. . . . There is no force in the objection that there has been a multitude of different religions, for that would be like objecting that it is impossible to arrive at certain truths because of

[79] *Essai*, II, 166.
[80] 'Il faut se représenter l'homme, non comme un être isolé, mais comme un chaînon de la vaste hiérarchie des êtres, comme un membre de l'éternelle société des intelligences.'—*Essai*, II, 181.

the multitude of different opinions. The diversity of religions proves only that men can neglect the means which God has given them of recognizing the true religion. . . . This diversity . . . is evidence of the ignorance and passions of man, the weakness of his spirit, when he substitutes his own thoughts for the ancient traditions; it proves the need for serious examination, and nothing else.[81]

Men can recognize the true religion by the same means as they recognize all other truths, namely authority, tradition, the testimony of the human race, which derives from God's primal revelation. Included in the primal revelation were the following truths: the existence of one God, immaterial, eternal, infinite, almighty, the creator of the universe; the necessity of worship, prayer, and sacrifice; the moral law; the existence of good and evil spirits; the fall of man and the need for redemption and a redeemer; the immortality of the soul and the eternity of future rewards and punishments.[82] Lamennais maintains that all the religions of mankind agree in testifying more or less plainly to these truths, and differ from one another only where they depart from them and have corrupted the original revelation.

In the third and fourth volumes of the *Essai* he seeks to demonstrate with a monotonous wealth of historical evidence that the essential religion of mankind, to which the *sensus communis* testifies, bears the marks of unity, universality, perpetuity, and holiness, whereas the falsehoods in idolatrous religions had the opposite characteristics.[83] Idolatry and the diversity of religions were the result of the fall. Because of the spread of idolatry among the nations, God gave a second revelation, namely the mosaic revelation to Israel, which contained a clearer and more developed knowledge of the primitive revelation, a system of positive law that was a safeguard against idolatry, and more definite promises of the Mediator to

---

[81] *Essai*, II, 182 f.   [82] See *Essai*, II, 282 f., 306, 394.

[83] 'Il suffit d'avoir montré que tout ce qu'il y a d'universel dans l'idolâtrie est vrai, et fondé sur une tradition qui remonte à l'origine du genre humain; que dans ce qu'elle a de faux, elle manque et a toujours manqué des caractères essentiels de la véritable Religion, d'unité, d'universalité, de perpétuité, de sainteté.'—*Essai*, II, 385.

Lamennais's view differs from the deistic theory of natural religion, e.g. Rousseau's, in that (1) the true religion is revealed by God, not discovered by the unaided reason of men, and (2) the medium by which it comes to be known is tradition or the authority of society, not the individual conscience of each separate man.

come, the desire of all nations, who was to be born of Israel. The second revelation like the first was preserved and continued by means of tradition.

The first and second revelation, Lamennais says, made known all that was necessary for men's physical, moral, and spiritual *existence*: the third revelation—the coming of the God-man—made known all that was necessary for human *perfection*. When Christ came, he came not to destroy but to fulfil. The third revelation, which is continued in the tradition of the catholic church, fulfils all the previous hopes and prophecies of a universal Redeemer who would gather together in one communion all the dispersed children of God. Whatever was true in all religions was implicitly christian, and the faithful in all religions are saved by implicit faith in Christ.

> Since Jesus Christ, what authority dare anyone compare to that of the catholic church, the heir of all the primordial traditions, of the first revelation and the mosaic revelation, of all the truths known in antiquity of which its teaching is only the development? Going back as it does to the origin of the world, it reunites in its authority all the authorities.[84]

> When we speak of christianity, we ought not to restrict our thought to the times that have elapsed since the incarnation of the Divine Word, but we must include the entire history of religion, before as well as after Jesus Christ. Whether he had come or was still to come, he has always been the foundation of true faith, the unique Mediator, the supreme head of the spiritual society of the righteous, and never have men been saved except in view of his infinite merits and by virtue of his blood.[85]

To this perfect religion the testimony of the human race bears witness, and of this testimony the catholic church, by its unity, universality, perpetuity, and holiness, is manifestly the infallible organ. It is simple and easy for all men, by accepting its authority, to come to the knowledge of the truth.[86] Lamennais had intended to develop the ultramontane corollary of the *Essai* in a fifth volume,[87] which was never written, i.e. that the pope is the infallible organ of the testimony of the human race to the one true religion. It is plainly

[84] *Essai*, II, 283; cp. III, 266 f.
[85] *Essai*, II, 287; cp. II, 406-416, where Lamennais cites the testimony of the Fathers to the salvation of faithful men in all religions by implicit faith in Christ.
[86] See *Essai*, IV, 136 f.
[87] See *O.C.*, VII, 122; cp. *Lamennais inconnu*, pp. 216 f.

enough set forth in the second part of his book, *De la religion considérée dans ses rapports avec l'ordre politique et civil.*

It remains to be said that, having rested his apologetic on the ground of authority and *sensus communis*, Lamennais finished the fourth volume of the *Essai* with an exposition of the conventional arguments of the theological schools for the truth of Christianity, —the arguments from prophecy, miracles, etc. The inclusion of these arguments was incongruous,[88] and they seem to have been added in order to disarm those who were frightened by the novelty of his apologetic. It was complementary to, and not exclusive of, the arguments to which they were accustomed.[89]

The second volume of the *Essai* had a very different reception from the first volume. That had been received by catholics with almost universal acclamation. The fact that a radical departure from the church's accepted method of apologetic was implicit in it had not been noticed. The second volume left no room for mistake about that. It confounded and alienated many of Lamennais's admirers, and set in motion a bitter and protracted controversy.

Among the Jesuits, for example, who had shared the general enthusiasm for the first volume, a reaction set in when the second appeared, though many younger Jesuits in France, as well as in Rome, became ardent advocates of the *sensus communis* philosophy. In order to prevent quarrels in the Society and to preserve uniformity in its teaching, the General sent a secret directive to the French Provincial setting out seven propositions that were drawn from the second volume of the *Essai* and that were not to be taught in jesuit colleges. When Lamennais heard a report of this, he wrote and asked the Provincial whether it was true. The Provincial at first tried to avoid the question, and then said that he was bound to secrecy in the matter. Lamennais's hostility to the Jesuits dates from this period.[90]

The attacks on the second volume of the *Essai*, as has been pointed

---

88 Cp. Dudon, *L. et le S.S.*, pp. 12 f.: 'Il (Lamennais) a recours aux prophéties et aux miracles pour établir la divinité du Christianisme, mais c'est par oubli ou par précaution. La preuve à ses yeux décisive, le critérium par lequel on distingue la vérité de notre religion, aussi facilement que son existence, c'est qu'elle est attestée par l'universalité du genre humain.'

89 Cp. his promise at the end of the *Défense* (IV, 314) to show that his doctrine, 'so far from derogating from the ordinary proofs of religion, completes and fortifies them.' See also Boutard, I, 221 f.

90 For the foregoing paragraph, see Dudon's articles in *Études*, 5 June 1908, pp. 598–627, and 20 October 1909, pp. 206–223.

out, [91] were not entirely motivated by a disinterested concern for truth. But even if there had not been victims of Lamennais's irony waiting to take their revenge, it is to be remembered that the sceptical approach to religion usually strikes rationalists as perverse if not as ridiculous.[92] It is also very easy to misrepresent, and Lamennais, who was always inclined to overstate his case, invited misrepresentation.

For instance, it could be represented as absurd that after demolishing the powers of the individual reason, he should glorify the general reason, since it is only by the exercise of his own reason that a man concludes that the general reason shall be authoritative for him. But Lamennais pointed out that what he denied was that we can find *in* our own reason the foundation for rational certitude; he did not deny that it is *by* our own reason that we recognize its true foundation in the general reason.[93] Nevertheless, he invited misunderstanding because practically all his emphasis was on the former point.[94] In denying the power of the individual reason, Lamennais may not have intended to go further, but he certainly seems to go further, than Coleridge, who said: 'The imperfect human understanding can be effectually exerted only in *subordination* to, and in a dependent *alliance* with, the means and aidance supplied by the all-perfect and supreme Reason.'[95]

Again, most of Lamennais's critics at first took his argument that the individual man, who depends on his own reason alone, is incapable of finding rational grounds for certitude concerning what in practice he has to treat as certain, to mean that he was himself a complete sceptic. They failed to perceive that what he was saying was that atheists, i.e. those who carry dogmatic indifference to its logical conclusion, had on their own assumptions no rational ground for certitude about anything. The fact that they inevitably had to live on the basis of practical certitude about many things showed that implicitly they accepted the authority of the general reason, which is the human refraction of the Divine Reason.

The older theologians, e.g. at St Sulpice, saw no need for a new

[91] See p. 84, *supra*.
[92] Cp. the eminent British theologian who is reported to have said that A. J. Balfour's book *The Foundations of Belief* should have been called *The Foundations of Unbelief*. See Francis W. Hirst, *In the Golden Days* (1947), p. 63.
[93] See *Essai*, IV, 249.
[94] Moreover, he was not consistent in avoiding the expression 'par sa raison': e.g. see *Essai*, IV, 295.
[95] *Aids to Reflection*, LXXXIX, 13.

apologetic. They did not realize the extent to which the powers of reason (in the cartesian sense) had been riddled by the criticism of philosophers such as Hume. From their point of view, there was no call for an apologetic that would reckon with the force of thorough-going scepticism. Lamennais's originality lay in his determination to do precisely that. His design was to heal the schism in the post-cartesian mind, the cleavage between rationalism in philosophy and science, on the one hand, and authoritarianism in theology, on the other.[96] He proposed to heal it not, as the deists had done, by sub-mitting theology to the dominion of natural reason, but by showing that philosophy and science as well as theology were necessarily authoritarian. For the older theologians, who had been trained in cartesianism, this idea involved so radical a break with their way of thinking that they could scarcely understand what Lamennais was talking about. Thus, whether his new apologetic was true or false, which is not here the question, it was bound to be viewed with suspicion and hostility by the official representatives of theological orthodoxy.

On the other hand, it was welcomed—doubtless too uncritically—by those who felt the need for a new apologetic. It won many enthusiastic adherents among the younger clergy. It attracted to Lamennais a growing following of ardent disciples, not least among teachers in theological seminaries,[97] but among the laity also. The nature of its appeal to young intellectuals is well brought out in the following passage:

> Lamennais's party was composed, first and foremost, of the younger generation of catholics which in 1823 was considerable in numbers. Whether they were priests or laymen, the young members of this party were looking in their religious studies for more movement and life, above all for a new spirit. They were indignant that the French clergy seemed to be only muttering in their sleep and repeating the centuries-old arguments and formulas of the ancient apologetic. So they were enraptured by a doc-trine that opened up new horizons for their minds. Eager and enthusiastic, they had no other ambition than to range the whole of France, and then Europe, behind the banner of *la raison traditionnelle*, and they would doubtless have succeeded, if all

[96] Cp. Maréchal, *Dispute*, p. 357.
[97] For an example of the enthusiasm that was engendered in a seminary, see Albert Houtin, *Un Dernier Gallican, Henri Bernier* (2nd ed., 1904), p. 17.

that had been needed for that had been activity, ardour, and talent.[98]

Many dioceses from now onwards were torn with dissension about the respective merits of the cartesian philosophy and the philosophy of common consent, and a violent war of pamphlets was engaged. Lamennais soon had friends and supporters at Rome, and as early as 1822 the mennaisians were claiming that the holy see was on their side. The only tangible evidence of official approval for the new apologetic, to which they could point, was the *imprimatur* that had been given to the Italian translation of the *Défense de l'essai sur l'indifférence*. They were entitled to derive encouragement from this, because Lamennais's opponents had tried to get the *imprimatur* refused, and it had been accorded only after an examination of, and favourable reports on, the book by three Italian theologians.[99]

But this did not formally commit the holy see, and the campaign against Lamennais continued to gather momentum. His moods oscillated between extreme exhilaration and extreme melancholy. At times the misunderstanding, hostility, and intrigue by which he felt himself surrounded made him want to retire altogether from public activity; but a sense of mission was growing upon him. In November 1820 he had written to abbé Carron who had—probably at the instigation of St Sulpice—besought him to consult safe and reliable guides before publishing any further works[100]: 'If the judgment of Rome is favourable to me, I shall rejoice for the sake of religion; if it is unfavourable, I shall be enchanted for my own sake. In that case I am decided to write nothing further, and I shall be the happiest man in the world; for then I shall be able with a good conscience to enjoy a little repose, which to my mind is the only good here below.'[101] This sentiment recurs like a refrain in Lamennais's correspondence.

To settle his course, he looked for a more signal mark of approbation from Rome. His first journey to Rome, in 1824, does not seem

---

[98] M. Deschamps, Lecture on 'Souvenirs Universitaires' in *Mémoires de l'Académie des sciences, inscriptions, et belles-lettres de Toulouse*, 1893, p. 35. Cp. 'Les Mennaisiens Franc-Comtois' by Louis Boiteux, in Bulletin of *Académie des sciences, belles-lettres et arts de Besançon*, 1928, pp. 65–94; ibid., 1936, pp. 73–93.

[99] The reports are printed in the original Italian in Blaize, *Essai biographique*, pp. 65–68, and in a French translation in Blaize, I, 413 f. See also Boutard, I, 381–385; Roussel, *Documents*, I, 158 ff.; Dudon, *L. et le S.S.*, pp. 11 f.

[100] See Forgues, I, 29.

[101] See Forgues, I, 159. Abbé Carron died in 1821.

however to have been prompted by the desire to force the issue there, but by the quest for distraction. He found no sufficient escape from the controversies, by which he was surrounded, in translating *The Imitation of Jesus Christ* into French. He was engaged on this task early in 1824, and subsequently added comments or reflections to each chapter.[102] Incidentally, it was a notable success and proved to be Lamennais's most reliable source of income till the end of his life.[103] But it did not set his mind at ease,[104] and he decided on a period of foreign travel.

He arrived in Geneva early in April 1824 and stayed with the curé, his friend abbé Vuarin (1769–1844),[105] till early in June when he accompanied Vuarin to Turin and Genoa and finally to Rome. Although they were warmly received and hospitality was provided for them by the pope, Lamennais's first wish was to return at once to France.[106] He could never be happy for long away from France.[107] However, except for a visit to Naples at the end of July,[108] he stayed in Rome for nearly three months.

He was treated by the Vatican authorities as a distinguished visitor. He was twice received in audience by Leo XII with much cordiality, and the pope accepted his portrait. It has often been added[109] that, together with a picture of the Blessed Virgin, it became the sole

[102] In the latter part of the nineteenth century there was a very involved controversy about whether Lamennais really did translate *The Imitation* and whether the reflections attributed to him were really his work. For particulars of this controversy and reasons for holding to the authenticity of Lamennais's work on *The Imitation*, see Dudon on 'Les Trois Éditions de l'*Imitation* dues à Lamennais' in *Études*, 20 March 1912, pp. 745–769. See also Roussel, *Documents*, I, 212–216; Laveille, *J.-M. de La Mennais*, I, 388 ff.

[103] In fact it retained its popularity after his death and despite his rupture with the church, e.g. there were new editions in 1914 and 1916. Of Lamennais's translation Louis Barthou wrote: 'La traduction de Lamennais, augmentée des *Réflexions* admirables qu'il y ajouta dans l'édition de 1828, est la meilleure que l'on ait faite du livre unique."—*Revue des deux mondes*, 1 November 1923, p. 167.

[104] See *Cottu*, p. 154.

[105] On Vuarin and his relations with Lamennais, see Roussel, *Correspondants*, pp. 235–389; V. Giraud on 'Une correspondance inédite de Lamennais. Lettres à M. Vuarin' in *Revue des deux mondes*, 15 October and 1 November 1905.

[106] See Blaize, II, 15; Dudon, *L. et le S.S.*, pp. 20 f.; Boutard, I, 260.

[107] Cp. *Cottu*, p. xxxv.

[108] See Dudon, *L. et le S.S.*, p. 28; Boutard, I, 269 f.

[109] See e.g. Laveille, *J.-M. de La Mennais*, I, 422; Boutard, I, 268. Lamennais himself credited the story: see Forgues, II, 49; *Lamennais inconnu*, p. 234.

ornament of the pope's study, but alas! this story is inadequately attested.[110] Lamennais derived encouragement from the way in which the pope received him and allowed him to unfold his ideas.[111] Remarks that Leo XII is reported to have made suggest that he had formed a just opinion of Lamennais's character and knew how to handle him. To abbé Vuarin he said that Lamennais was 'a man whom one must lead with one's hand on his heart'.[112] And according to a confidential report made in September 1824 by the French minister to the holy see, the pope said of Lamennais to one of the cardinals: 'This Frenchman is a distinguished man; he has talents and learning; I believe him to be in good faith; but he is one of these lovers of perfection who, if one let them have their way, would turn the world upside down.'[113]

Leo XII's benevolence to Lamennais upon this occasion and later has sometimes been exaggerated because of the story, to which Cardinal Wiseman lent his authority[114] and which Lamennais himself credited,[115] that the pope had intended to make him a cardinal. It seems that at a consistory on 2 October 1826 Leo XII designated one or more cardinals *in petto*, but who they were has been regarded as uncertain.[116] The claims of the English historian, Lingard, as well as of Lamennais have been canvassed.[117] Père Dudon, who had searched the Vatican Archives, maintained that there was no evidence

---

[110] See Dudon, *L. et le S.S.*, p. 29.

[111] Cp. the long memorandum 'Sur l'état de l'Église de France' which Lamennais afterwards submitted to the pope. Blaize, II, 311–340. Its full text is reproduced from the Vatican Archives by Dudon in *Recherches de Science Religieuse* (1910), pp. 476–485.

[112] 'C'est un homme qu'il faut conduire avec la main dans le cœur.' See *Revue des deux mondes*, 15 October 1905, p. 799.

[113] See Dudon, *L. et le S.S.*, pp. 31 f.; Boutard, I, 265.

[114] *Recollections of the Last Four Popes*, p. 335.

[115] Lamennais believed that written evidence of Leo XII's intention had been found among his papers after his death: see his letter of 22 January 1830 to the Countess de Senfft in Forgues, II, 110 f. In *Béranger et Lamennais* (p. 157) there is a report of Lamennais's having said that the pope had indirectly offered him a cardinal's hat, but the pope there in question is Gregory XVI.

[116] See however Schmidlin, II, 113, who gives the names of six cardinals reserved *in petto* at this consistory.

[117] E.g. see art. on 'Dr Lingard's Alleged Cardinalate' in *The Rambler*, November 1859, pp. 75–83, and W. J. Hegarty on 'Was Lingard a Cardinal?' in *The Irish Ecclesiastical Record*, February 1953, pp. 81–93. *The Rambler* concludes that Leo XII made both Lingard and Lamennais cardinals *in petto*; Hegarty concludes in favour of Lamennais and against Lingard. Wiseman also, *loc. cit.*, discusses the question.

that Lamennais had been so designated,[118] but he allows that in 1824 Leo XII would have liked him to have settled in Rome and would have made him a bishop *in partibus*, had not the French government objected.[119] Dudon is probably right in supposing that whatever intention Leo XII had of attaching Lamennais to the curia in Rome should be interpreted as signifying not that the teaching of the *Essai sur l'indifférence* met with papal approval, but that it was deemed prudent to try to attract a writer at once so talented, so excitable, and so extravagant into an environment which would moderate his enthusiasm and check his dangerous excursions into polemics.[120] However that may be, Lamennais returned to France satisfied that he had the pope's confidence and goodwill, though not the formal approbation for which he hoped, and for which he would hope still more when he had crowned—or complicated—his new apologetics with a new politics.

I have not attempted in this chapter, nor shall I attempt in this book, to pronounce upon the cogency or fallaciousness of the argument or arguments of the *Essai*. That would be a task proper to a philosopher or a theologian, not to an historian. I may, however, point out that Lamennais looked upon the *Essai sur l'indifférence* as only a *first essay* in a new apologetic method, and that after its publication he set to work on a more systematic, constructive, and comprehensive *Essai d'un système de philosophie catholique*,[121] at which

118 So in *L. et le S.S.*, p. 30. V. Giraud in *Revue des deux mondes*, 1 March 1919, pp. 133 f., argued that there was more to be said for the view that Lamennais had been designated a cardinal than Dudon allowed. For Dudon's reply to Giraud, see *Études*, 5 January 1932, pp. 94 ff. He maintained that there was still no reliable evidence.

119 See Dudon, *L. et le S.S.*, pp. 30 f. The government appears to have been under the entirely false impression that Lamennais had gone to Rome in 1824 as an agent of the ultras. See Boutard, I, 262 f.

 On the question whether Lamennais was to have been made a cardinal see also Forgues, I, 53, 269 f., 298.

120 Dudon, *L. et le S.S.*, pp. 31 f.

121 Maréchal (*Essai d'un système de philosophie catholique par F. de La Mennais*, pp. xvi f.) shows that from 1822 onwards Lamennais recognized the necessity of following up the *Essai sur l'indifférence* with 'une nouvelle philosophie' which would set forth the essential and constitutive laws of the social order, and he gradually conceived the idea of doing it himself.

 It would serve as a counterpart to the *Essai*. For example, whereas in the *Essai* Lamennais had denigrated the powers of reason, he designed in his future work, as he wrote to Victor Cousin on 30 June 1825, to show that 'la foi catholique qu'on accuse d'étouffer la raison ou de la réduire à un état purement

he continued to labour until his break with the church.[122] The
manuscript was never published and until recently was supposed to
have disappeared.[123] Happily, it has now come to light, and is being
prepared for publication.[124] Any final assessment of Lamennais's
philosophical and theological teaching would have to take it into
account, not to mention the *Esquisse d'une philosophie* which belongs
to the period after his rupture with catholicism.

From an historian's point of view the importance of the *Essai sur
l'indifférence* lies not in the truth or falsehood of its arguments, but
(1) in the fact that it was the first striking post-cartesian and post-
revolutionary essay in a new method of attacking infidelity and of
approaching and presenting the truth of catholicism, and (2) in the
fact that in the *Essai* Lamennais called attention to a number of
aspects of the catholic faith and elements in its faithful presentation,
which had been either long neglected or never clearly perceived,
and which have been discovered and developed in the work of
subsequent theologians, quite apart from the mennaisian system.

As regards (1), it may suffice to recall Paul Janet's testimony that
Lamennais did what neither Maistre nor Bonald, any more than the
apologists of the eighteenth century, had done: he tackled modern
scepticism at its root, and so replied to Descartes across two centuries.[125] Or, if this was to overestimate the philosophical originality

> passif, l'excite au contraire et la féconde, en même temps qu'elle guide son
> activité. J'aime toutes les connaissances, lorsque l'homme ne les tourne pas
> contre lui-même; j'aime tous les efforts de l'esprit, lorsqu'ils ont un but
> honorable, et qu'ils ne tendent pas à renverser toute espèce d'ordre sur la terre;
> car la science qui nuit est une fausse science, et fût-elle véritable, la vertu vaut
> encore mieux.'—See Feugère, pp. 302 f.

[122] It was then transformed into his *Esquisse d'une philosophie*.

[123] In 1906 Maréchal (*op. cit.*, p. vi) wrote: 'Il faut perdre tout espoir de jamais,
retrouver le manuscrit original et autographe de l'*Essai d'un système de philosophie catholique*.' Maréchal's reconstruction of his work was based on notes
taken by some of those who heard Lamennais lecture on the subject.

[124] By Professor Yves Le Hir, who has kindly communicated this information
to the present writer.

[125] See Janet's judicious consideration of the *Essai* in his *La philosophie de Lamennais*
(1890). 'Lorsque Descartes proposa comme méthode en philosophie l'examen
personnel et le doute universel jusqu'à ce que l'on ait rencontré l'évidence, il est
remarquable que personne ne parut deviner la gravité de cette proposition et
n'en vit les conséquences. . . . L'originalité de l'abbé de Lamennais fut de voir
ce que n'avaient vu ni de Maistre, ni de Bonald, ni les apologistes du xviiie
siècle, à savoir que, si l'on voulait sauver l'autorité de l'Église, il fallait remonter
à la source du scepticisme moderne, c'est-à-dire au principe du libre examen, à
la règle de l'évidence, à l'autorité de la raison individuelle. . . . La philosophie

or profundity of the *Essai*, one may take the view of Maude Petre that it is 'a startling instance of the effect produced by the breaking of a long silence with a loud cry. . . . It was a cry to the deaf; an appeal to the blind. It was the living utterance of a living mind, that felt within itself the need it exposed in others; that sought while proclaiming; that experienced itself the hunger which it endeavoured to excite in others.'[126]

As regards (2), Lamennais brought to light aspects of the relation between revelation and reason and between authority and freedom that had fallen out of sight; he fastened on the weighty part that tradition plays in religion; he recognized the dependence of ethics on dogma, the impossibility of making the mind a *tabula rasa*, and the necessity of presuppositions in science as in every other field of thought; he emphasized the social character of the catholic faith and the errors that flow from individualism, the fact of development in religious history, and the universal scope of Christ's work as the regenerator of mankind. It need hardly be said that on none of these topics did Lamennais say the last word, but on most, if not all, of them he said a first word or a fresh word. If the *Essai* has little to say to contemporary theologians that they will not find more adequately said elsewhere, that may be because Lamennais had a certain prophetic awareness of the directions in which theological thought would move in the coming generations; in so moving it has naturally left him behind.

The success of the *Essai* and its extraordinary influence in its own time were due to its being a genuine and imaginative attempt to meet the demands of a new age and of a new intellectual climate. My final illustration of this point is part of a letter that Lamennais wrote to Joseph de Maistre shortly before his death in 1821. It indicates what Lamennais aimed at doing and why, and what many believed that he had done. He is speaking about the kind of books that Roman theologians were then producing.

> To judge by the books that reach us from Rome, I should be inclined to say that they are a bit behind the times. They give you the impression that nothing has changed in the world for half a

de l'abbé de Lamennais répond à celle de Descartes à travers deux siècles.'— *Op. cit.*, pp. 26 ff. 'Le système de Lamennais, tout paradoxal qu'il est en réalité, n'en a pas moins mis en lumière une vérité notable, et nous a obligés utilement à serrer d'un peu plus près le problème difficile de la certitude.' *Ibid.*, p. 37.
126 M. D. Petre in an article on the 'Essai sur l'Indifférence' in *The Modern Church-man*, February 1930, p. 642.

century. They defend religion as they would have defended it forty years ago. They always seem to be talking to people who would grant certain fundamental principles and facts, which unfortunately are very far from being taken for granted today. Moreover, proofs of this kind make no impression nowadays on people's minds, as I am daily in a position to observe. Indeed I know several people who used to be christian but have become unbelievers through reading apologias for religion. I do not mean to deny that these apologias are very weighty: they were excellent for the time when they appeared, when everything was stable, and there were universally accepted ideas; but in another state of society they do not answer the questions that reason puts to them or they give inadequate answers. They ought to realize at Rome that their traditional method, according to which everything is proved by facts and authorities, is no doubt admirable in itself, and one neither can nor need abandon it; but it is insufficient, because it is no longer understood. Since reason has proclaimed itself sovereign, one must go straight to it, seize it on its throne, and compel it, under pain of death, to prostrate itself before the reason of God.[127]

[127] See *Lettres et opuscules inédits du comte J. de Maistre* (5th ed., 1869), pp. 120 f.

Chapter Four

NEW POLITICS
1825-1829

LAMENNAIS's governing idea or ideal was the social regeneration of France, and indeed of Europe, through a renaissance of
catholicism. The diseased state of society had been revealed in
the revolution and in the anarchy and despotism that had been its
outcome. It was equally clear that the church had been in no condition to arrest the causes of the crisis, and was in no condition yet
to accomplish its social mission. If there was to be a renaissance of
catholicism a many-sided strategy was required.

In the first place, the catholic faith must be so presented as to win
the attention and command the intellectual respect of men in whom
the acids of philosophical scepticism had done their work, and it
must be so presented that its universal scope and its bearing on every
area of human life were displayed. Lamennais believed that he had
at least adumbrated such a presentation of the faith in the *Essai sur
l'indifférence*. Certainly, what had impelled him to write the *Essai*
had been not an interest in metaphysical or theological speculation
but an urgent concern for the recovery of a society and a civilization
that seemed to him to be threatened with dissolution.[1] He had sown
the seeds of a new apologetic appropriate to the nineteenth century,
out of which there could grow not only a revival of theology but
also a new christian culture.

In the second place, a catholic renaissance would come about
only if the church was free to put forth its latent powers. Its ministers
must be free to confer, and to decide what measures of reform and
of discipline were needed. A priesthood, trained to meet the demands
of the new age, must be forthcoming. There must be liberty for the
church to educate the people. This meant that the church must be
liberated from its dependence on, and subservience to, civil governments, which had for too long used the church for their own temporal interests. There must be a new settlement of the relations

[1] Cp. Boutard, I 19,2 f.

between church and state, which would include in its provisions allowing free course to the divinely ordained leadership of Christ's vicar on earth.

In the third place, if there was to be a catholic renaissance, Christ's vicar would of course have to give to the church and to the world the leadership and direction that he was providentially appointed and equipped to give. We have seen Lamennais leaving Rome, at the end of his first visit in 1824, not indeed with the pope's formal approbation of his program in his pocket, but under the impression that Leo XII was very well disposed not only towards him personally but towards his ideals for the church.

During the years 1825–1829 the various elements in the mennaisian strategy were being clarified and developed, and a movement was taking shape which would be ready in 1830 to break out in the campaign of the *Avenir*. The most remarkable features of the present period were the rapid evolution of Lamennais's thought about the relations of church and state, the shedding of his last illusions about what was to be expected of the royalist or restoration régime in France, and his embracing of the idea of a union between catholics and liberals or of a liberal catholicism. But there were other important developments of the mennaisian movement during these years, of which we must take note if we are to have a full picture of its assets and of its striking force.

I begin with a significant little incident that occurred when Lamennais arrived in Paris on his return from Rome at the end of September 1824. It is significant both of the suspicion with which the authorities in France already viewed him and of the spirit in which he intended to set about them. He had intended to stay in Paris for a few days in the apartment which had been occupied by his brother, abbé Jean, in his capacity of vicar-general to the Grand Almoner of France.[2] Abbé Jean had in fact just relinquished this appointment which he had held since 1822, but he still had the use of his apartment in the Grand Almonry though he had himself already left Paris. The Grand Almoner at this time was the Prince de Croÿ (1773–1844),[3] who was an aristocratic prelate, a strong gallican and a

[2] See Laveille, *J.-M. de La Mennais*, 1, chap. 20, 'La Grande Aumônerie de France.' The Grand Almoner's most important function had to do with the nomination of bishops, until in August 1824 this was transferred to the newly created Ministry of Ecclesiastical Affairs.

[3] Subsequently Archbishop of Rouen and a cardinal.

faithful servant of the royal government. On hearing of Lamennais's arrival, he let him know through a mutual friend, Count de Senfft, that he wished him to quit. In reply Lamennais wrote the following note:

1 October 1824

Monseigneur,

Count de Senfft has sent on to me the letter which you wrote to him on 29 September.

In alighting, upon my return from Rome, at a house which my brother's relatives and servants will be occupying for some days yet, I thought I was accepting his hospitality, and not yours. You inform me that I made a mistake. Within an hour I shall have left a lodging which you invite me to 'quit promptly'.

Three weeks ago, the Sovereign Pontiff urged me to accept an apartment in the Vatican. I am grateful to you for enabling me to realize so quickly how men and countries differ from one another.[4]

A fortnight before this interchange of civilities, the death of Louis XVIII had taken place (16 September 1824), and he had been succeeded by his brother, Charles X. This was a turning-point in the fortunes of the restored Bourbons. Louis XVIII,[5] despite his age and indolence and lack of previous political experience, had been a shrewd and effective king and a good judge of men and measures. At the time of his death France seemed to be well on the way to recovery from the ravages of the revolution, the collapse of the Empire, and the set-back of the Hundred Days. The occupation of France by foreign troops had been brought to an end in 1818, the finances of the country had been made good, and the rival parties and factions were more united in loyalty to the régime than they had been before. In particular, France's successful military intervention in Spain in 1823 had restored the nation's self-confidence and sense of counting in international affairs; it had had the even more important effect of rallying to the throne[6] the army, in which napoleonic nostalgia had been most rife.

Charles X was about as different as possible from Louis XVIII. Louis was of too phlegmatic a disposition ever to have evoked the

4 See Blaize, II, 24; Laveille, op. cit., I, 421 f.

5 See P. de la Gorce, La Restauration: Louis XVIII (1926); G. Weill, La France sous la Monarchie constitutionelle (1902); Émile Bourgeois, Modern France 1815-1913 (1919).

6 The army which invaded Spain had been commanded by the Duke of Angoulême who became heir to the throne upon the accession of his father, Charles X.

enthusiastic devotion of his people, though he was able to instil respect. Charles, on the other hand, had the temperament and style and personal attractiveness which, other things being equal, might have made him a popular monarch. But other things were not equal. The government of France at such a time required wisdom above all things. Louis had studied the ways of political moderation, and he had realized that the restored dynasty could survive only if it complied with the spirit and terms of the constitutional charter[7] which—characteristically—he had affected to concede spontaneously though in fact it had been forced upon him. Charles's aim was the restoration of the *ancien régime* and no compromise with the ideas of the revolution. He had neither the strength nor the resourcefulness that would have been necessary for the successful pursuit of such an enterprise. He was able to revive the traditional ceremonies of coronation at Reims, but not the powers of the kings who had been crowned there before the revolution.

Again, Louis XVIII had been a voltairian sceptic and at the same time a realist. His support of the church had been based on grounds not of personal faith but of political expediency. Charles X after a libertine youth had become fanatically devout. Too much personal piety may be a source of grave weakness in a statesman. Charles was an idealist of the altar as well as of the throne, and he stirred up all the scarcely dormant fears of (what later came to be called) clericalism. The rumour went round that he was a Jesuit in disguise and that he had secretly been consecrated a bishop; he was caricatured celebrating mass in his private apartments.[8] He was more responsible than anyone else for the hostility to the church which characterized the revolution of July 1830—in contrast to 1789 and 1848.

The survival of the restoration régime depended on the main-

---

[7] 'La Charte.' Cp. de la Gorce, *op. cit.*, chap. 1. For an English translation of the charter see Lamartine, *The History of the Restoration of Monarchy in France* (1891), I, 445–451.

[8] For instance, he scandalized the liberal intelligentsia by taking part on foot in religious processions in the streets of Paris. See Weill, *op. cit.*, p. 10; cp. Lucas-Dubreton, *La Restauration et la Monarchie de juillet* (1926), p. 100. P. Thureau-Dangin, *Le Parti libéral*, pp. 353 f., wrote: 'On eût pardonner à Charles X d'avoir des maîtresses et de les promener dans Paris. On était choqué de le voir marcher à la suite du clergé, dans les processions. . . . Le roi ayant, à cause d'un deuil, porté dans une de ces cérémonies un costume violet, le bruit se répandait parmi le peuple que, engagé secrètement dans les ordres sacrés et promu évêque, il remplissait les conditions imposées à cette faveur singulière. . . . La rumeur présentait le prince comme un affilié secret des jésuites auxquels, pour prix du ciel, il avait livré son royaume.'

tenance of a practical compromise both between contradictory principles—the divine right of legitimate kings and the sovereignty of
the people—and between parties that were fundamentally opposed
to one another in their interests as well as in their opinions—the
returned émigrés, on the one hand, and the natural heirs of the
revolution, on the other. A king without the art of compromise, or
even the readiness for it, was not likely to last very long.

Lamennais was a thorn in the side of the royalist party because,
though he was still generally supposed to be an ultra-royalist, he was
not concerned about the material interests of the returned émigrés
nor with the struggle for political power. Moreover, he ridiculed the
notion of reviving the pre-revolutionary order, and in particular he
attacked the gallican liberties which were as much prized by the
royal government as by the ecclesiastical hierarchy. He insisted on
raising the most embarrassing questions and on pressing principles
to their logical conclusion.

He did all these things at once in his next book *De la religion
considérée dans ses rapports avec l'ordre politique et civil*.[9] This book was
published in two parts: the first part in May 1825, and the second
part in February 1826. The first part might be compared with
Gladstone's book *The State in its relations with the Church* (1838).[10]
Both Lamennais and Gladstone, in analogous circumstances, were
trying to think out afresh the fundamental reasons for the traditional
relationship between church and state, in the light of the challenge
to that relationship that was presented by the arrival of states with a
liberal constitution, that is, states which recognized more than one
religion or which tolerated all religions. Both Lamennais and Gladstone argued that the state was a 'moral person'[11] and ought to
recognize the church—the Church of Rome or the Church of
England, as the case might be—on the ground of the truth of its
teaching, and not merely because it was the religion of the majority
of the citizens. Both Lamennais and Gladstone argued that the state
was bound to translate its recognition of the church's authority into
consistent legislative effect, and was never justified in adopting an
attitude of religious neutrality, though they had both abandoned
the idea of persecuting or penalizing dissenters. Both Lamennais and

9 See *O.C.*, VII.

10 See my book, *The Orb and the Cross: a normative study of the relations of church
and state with reference to Gladstone's early writings* (1945).

11 I.e. a being able, and therefore morally bound, to discern the truth and to do
the right. See *O.C.*, VII, 39, cp. VII, 241 f.; *The Orb and the Cross*, chap. 4.

Gladstone—Lamennais more swiftly than Gladstone—awoke to the fact that they were arguing for a theory which could not be put into practice—political realities being what they were; and both, in consequence, became converts to the political liberalism which they had begun by regarding as one of the principal errors of the age.

Lamennais's contention was that the restored Bourbon monarchy in France, although it used the traditional christian language about itself, was very far from being a christian monarchy in the traditional sense. 'The king is a venerable memento of the past, like the inscription of an ancient temple which has been placed on the façade of an entirely different building.'[12] For France was now a democracy, and the doctrine of the sovereignty of the people was atheistic. It meant that the people, through its representatives in parliament, had the right to do anything it liked. It could change or modify the religion of the country, as it pleased. Either God was presumed not to exist, or his law was regarded as a matter of indifference. Not the will of God but the will of the people was assumed to be the supreme arbiter of what was lawful and just.

It was an illusion to suppose that the napoleonic concordat had made France once more a christian state. It put a stop to the persecution of the church, and it allowed to individuals freedom of worship, but the state as such remained atheist and it had continued to be so under the Restoration. Since according to the terms of the constitutional charter the state accorded an equal protection and support to contradictory forms of religion, it was evident that the state itself professed no faith and was therefore atheist. When the state was christian it recognized a law superior to itself to which the spiritual authority bore an independent and perpetual witness. The endowed place secured to the church in the constitution of the realm was evidence of that. But now the relation between the state and the church was a purely budgetary matter that could be changed from year to year. It no longer signified that in the political order the church was acknowledged as the permanent witness to the truth and law of God.

Democratic states are founded on the doctrine of the sovereignty of the people, and are thereby in inescapable conflict with christianity which proclaims the sovereignty of God. But a democratic state does not necessarily make an open and frontal attack on the church. It may seek to make the church a docile instrument of civil government, by restraining and controlling its activities and by preventing reforms that would lead to a fuller deployment of its forces. This is

[12] O.C., VII, 17.

the policy of intimidating and seducing the church, and it is a graver menace than was the unconcealed opposition of the revolutionary Convention and Directory.

Present conditions, Lamennais says, are unlike any that have existed before.[13] The new kind of state, unlike a christian monarchy, acknowledges neither God nor his commandments nor truth nor moral obligations. It recognizes no authority superior to itself. If it accords a kind of establishment to the church, it is no more than a concession to the obstinate prejudices of some millions of Frenchmen. The church is tolerated, supported, and regulated like art-galleries, theatres, and stud-farms. In this way christianity in France is being steadily and indefatigably destroyed by the establishment of a national church that will be entirely submissive to the government.[14] On that note Lamennais paused, and published the first part of his new tract for the times.

Before considering the second and positive part of the book, we also may pause to remark that Lamennais's allegation that the France of 1825 was an atheistic state and that Charles X and his ministers were governing on atheistic principles was on the face of it paradoxical and perverse.[15] The royal government was used to having precisely the opposite accusation levelled against it by the liberals, namely that it was identified with the *parti-prêtre* and was much too favourable to religious fanaticism. And this accusation was plausible enough, since the watch-word of the royalists was the interdependence of the altar and the throne, and the government had handsomely helped the church in a variety of ways.[16]

It is obvious that Lamennais put his case provocatively, if not extravagantly, for when he meant 'neutral' he said 'atheistic'. But of

---

[13] 'Ce qui est ne ressemble à rien de ce qui fut; et l'idée contraire est la source d'une multitude d'erreurs qui, à force d'être répétées, passent enfin pour des vérités établies.'—O.C., VII, 76; cp. VII, 269.

[14] The last paragraph of Part I reads as follows: 'Nous le répétons, l'anéantissement du christianisme en France par l'établissement d'une Église nationale, soumise de tout point á l'administration, voilà ce qu'on prépare avec une infatigable activité; voilà où mèneroit infailliblement le système suivi jusqu'ici, voilà enfin ce que veut la révolution: l'obtiendra-t-elle? L'avenir répondra.'— O.C., VII, 80.

[15] Cp. Dudon, L. et le S.S., p. 33: 'Pour beaucoup de fidèles qui avaient assisté avec émotion au *Te Deum* chanté à Notre-Dame devant Charles X, le 25 septembre 1824, pour célébrer son joyeux et chrétien avènement, les révélations de Lamennais durent paraître quelque peu paradoxales.'

[16] Cp. Dudon, L. et le S.S., p. 34.

course he never said that the king and his ministers were personally atheists. He was considering not the faith of individuals but the assumptions underlying the French constitution and the government's administration of it. He had argued that the law of sacrilege,[17] for example, or the government's attitude to education[18] showed that the state was now neutral or indifferent in matters of religion, and his contention was that religious neutrality or indifference on the part of the state ends in its complete secularization and is equivalent to practical atheism. Perhaps his prophecy that France was in process of becoming an atheistic state may seem to us more far-sighted than far-fetched, since after oscillation and equivocation liberal democracy in France did eventually and overtly issue in the état laïque.

But what was Lamennais's remedy—in 1826—for the evils that he had diagnosed? His remedy, set forth in the second part of De la religion considérée dans ses rapports avec l'ordre politique et civil,[19] was the substitution of the ultramontane for the gallican doctrine of the relation between the spiritual and temporal powers.

The christian religion, he says, affirms that power is entrusted by God to civil governments as well as to the church, but governments

[17] The law of 1824–1825 presupposed that sacrilege was a crime not against God but against the beliefs or sentiments of the people. The fact that the law applied equally to all forms of religion meant that the state regarded all forms of religion as equally true or equally false, i.e. that the state was dogmatically indifferent or atheistic. Yet the law against sacrilege involved the state in inconsistency, for it was monstrous to punish as sacrilege the desecration of the eucharistic host if, so far as the state was concerned, it might be no more than a piece of bread. See O.C., VII, 35–46.

[18] Before the revolution public education had been universally acknowledged to be the exclusive prerogative and responsibility of the church, and of the episcopate in particular. But it had now been taken over by the government whose policy was officially atheistic. When in a college alongside the catholic chapel there was established a calvinistic meeting-house, was it surprising that the pupils ridiculed religion and refused to take it seriously? See O.C., VII, 62–68.

Lamennais had previously (in August 1823), in an open letter to the Grand Master of the University, Mgr Frayssinous, made specific allegations about scandalous happenings in colleges under the control of the University. For instance, at one college thirty of the pupils who went to receive holy communion were said to have kept the consecrated hosts and used them for sealing letters to their parents. The fact that a bishop was the present head of the University increased the evil by blinding simple people to the fact that atheism was being placed under the protection of religion. See O.C., VIII, 355–361. Cp. Maréchal, La Mennais au Drapeau Blanc, chap. 7.

[19] As has been said, the second part was published in February 1826.

try to nullify the independent authority of the church and to make religion merely a branch of the civil service. He specifies a number of ways in which the French government was doing this. It made a working system of ecclesiastical discipline impossible by preventing the establishment of a series of church courts with a final appeal to Rome. It would not allow national or provincial synods to be held, at a time when more than ever before the church needed to be able to make its voice heard throughout the land.[20] 'Il faut parler au peuple dans les démocraties.'[21] Not only had public education been taken out of the hands of the church but the government by its prohibitions handicapped the training of the clergy and even laid down the law about the teaching that was to be given in seminaries. It also interfered with the administration of the rites of the church, e.g. by ordering christian burial to be given to suicides and duellists. The government had suppressed a bishop's pastoral letter, and had tried to have all pastoral letters submitted to its censorship before publication. Moreover, the government restricted communication between the episcopate and its head, 'the centre and bond of unity, from which, as is well known, the bishops draw all their strength'.[22] Finally, the government claimed a right of veto over the decrees of the pope, and so set itself up as the supreme authority in spiritual matters. In all these ways[23] the church was in bondage to the civil power, and it was all done in the name of the so-called gallican liberties. The time has come to examine them afresh.

Lamennais challenges the use of the word 'liberties' in this connexion. If the gallican church enjoyed 'liberties', the implication would be that the rest of the church was in some kind of bondage, or that there was something defective in the common laws and customs of the church. All that the expression 'gallican liberties' properly signifies is such privileges as the holy see has conceded to certain dioceses, e.g. special liturgical uses. As for the four principles asserted in the Declaration of 1682,[24] they were not 'liberties' but

---

20 'Représentez-vous, au contraire, l'épiscopat entier élevant sa voix, et ses gémissemens, et ses lamentations prophétiques au milieu de la France, rappelant à la souveraineté temporelle, avec une sainte et respectueuse liberté, ses devoirs envers Dieu, envers la religion, envers la société humaine qui, séparée de son principe de vie, se dissout comme un cadavre.'—O.C., VII, 90.

21 *Ibid.*   22 *O.C.*, VII, 97.

23 Lamennais gives other examples, see *O.C.*, VII, 269-291.

24 For this famous Declaration and its attendant circumstances, see W. J. Sparrow Simpson, *A Study of Bossuet* (1937), chaps. 7 and 8. The four Articles, which were almost certainly drawn up by Bossuet, were: (i) that the pope's jurisdiction

grievous errors. They can be reduced to two propositions: (1) that temporal sovereignty according to divine institution is completely independent of the spiritual power, and (2) that a general council is superior to the pope.

With regard to the relation between the temporal and the spiritual powers, Lamennais's teaching is that both are divine in their origin, and obedience to each is due in its proper sphere. The temporal power, however, is subordinate to the spiritual as the body is to the soul and, in cases of doubt about what belongs to Caesar and what to God, it is for the higher, i.e. the spiritual, authority to decide. Politics separated from religion is no more than 'force directed by interest'.[25] The temporal power is ordained by God to administer his law and to exercise his authority for the good of human society. Its sovereignty is not its own nor the people's, but God's. It is therefore itself subject to the law of God. The spiritual power, i.e. the pope (whom God had appointed as the supreme and infallible interpreter of his law[26]) while he fully respects the temporal power as such, and cannot for instance dispose of kingdoms as he likes, has a 'directive and ordinative'[27] or 'coercitive'[28] office towards temporal rulers. If these transgress the law of God which it is their task to administer—'la loi divine, source primitive et base nécessaire de toutes les lois humaines'[29]—the pope can bring spiritual sanctions to bear against them. He can absolve the subjects of an apostate or tyrannical or unrighteous king from their oath of allegiance. Citizens

is in things spiritual and not in things temporal, and therefore kings are not subject to ecclesiastical authority in such matters; (ii) that the authority of a general council is superior to that of the holy see; (iii) that the pope's authority is limited by the rules, customs and institutions of the universal church, and therefore the institutions of the Church of France remain inviolable; and (iv) that the judgment of the pope in matters of faith is not irreversible until it has been confirmed by the consent of the church. For the full text, see Sparrow Simpson, *op. cit.*, pp. 75 ff.

25 *O.C.*, VII, 116.

26 Lamennais regarded it as axiomatic that if any society worthy of the name was to exist there must be a supreme authority that has the right to command. According to whether the supreme authority is held to reside in all the members or several members or one member of the society, its constitution is democratic, aristocratic, or monarchic. He adduced the obvious, though controvertible, texts from Scripture and tradition to prove that Jesus Christ endowed his church with a monarchical constitution and appointed the pope to be the sovereign authority. The authority of the pope is the principle of the church's existence as a society, and so to overthrow his authority is to destroy the church. See *O.C.*, VII, 122–132.

27 *O.C.*, VII, 174.   28 *O.C.*, VII, 181 f.   29 *O.C.*, VII, 240.

have a right of resistance to governments which defy the law of God, since to carry out his law is what governments are for.

The spiritual power is the 'supreme defender of justice and of the rights of humanity'[30] and if the temporal power were not subject to this check there would be nothing to prevent the rulers of this world from becoming absolute tyrants. The gallican doctrine, which makes temporal sovereignty completely independent of the spiritual power, would, so Lamennais concludes, render the peoples of the world liable to

> a despotism without any limits, since it would release sovereigns from their obligation to any rule or law *exterior* to themselves, and would declare that neither tyranny nor godlessness nor persecution, to whatever excess they should be carried, affect the rights of sovereignty, according to the order established by God . . . and that subjects, whatever injustice they meet with from the prince, have neither the right to resist nor the right to have recourse to any other power, and that God actually commands an eternal obedience to an eternal oppression.[31]

With regard to the other principal gallican proposition, viz. that a general council is superior to the pope, it would mean that supreme power or sovereignty in the church is vested in the council and not in the pope, and the church would then be an 'aristocratic republic'[32] and not a monarchy. It would mean that the episcopate, and not the papacy, is the centre of unity, which would be equivalent to saying that there is no centre of unity except when a general council is assembled. It would mean that there is no perpetual organ of infallibility in the church, since general councils meet only occasionally. Moreover, they can assemble only with the permission of princes, who can also, according to the gallicans, prevent the decrees of a general council from acquiring force in their dominions.[33] Thus the spiritual power is made subordinate to, and dependent on, the temporal power. These consequences are by common consent heretical, therefore the Declaration of 1682 was heretical. Or is it to be supposed that 'when Jesus Christ said to Peter, Feed my sheep, he made an exception of the gallican church!'?[34]

[30] *O.C.*, VII, 255.   [31] *O.C.*, VII, 190.   [32] *O.C.*, VII, 201, 231.
[33] 'Est-il assez clair maintenant que, lorsqu'on déclaroit le concile supérieur au pape, c'étoit pour se mettre soi-même au-dessus du concile, pour asservir aux rois de la terre l'épouse du Roi des cieux?'—*O.C.*, VII, 228.
[34] *O.C.*, VII, 226.

Lamennais's summary of the ultramontane doctrine is:

No pope, no church;
No church, no christianity;
No christianity, no religion (at least for any people that has once
    been christian);
No religion, no society.

If there has not yet been complete social disintegration in those
European countries where the catholic religion has ceased to be
dominant, that is owing to the residual christianity that has remained
after the papacy has been rejected. Otherwise, Europe would already
have sunk into barbarism. Pre-christian societies, according to
Lamennais, were able to exist without depending on the authority
of the pope, because they had the primordial religion, which was
preserved by tradition in the family, to guide and sustain them, but
there was little stability in their governments, since there was no
supreme authority to arbitrate between government and subjects.[35]

The work of the church is to moralize human relations and to
establish and maintain unity among mankind. What binds people
together, more than anything else, is a common faith, a common
cultus, and common moral standards, whereas diversity of religion
is the greatest source of conflict among nations as well as within
nations. If the Church of France became a national church, separated
from the centre of unity and spiritual authority in Rome—which
would be the logical consequence of the gallican maxims—it would be
a political as well as a religious disaster. The state needs not a national
church which it can control and dominate, but the universal church
to move and enable it to do its proper work. For the proper work
of the state, rightly understood, is not concerned only with material
interests.

Never was a state founded for the satisfaction of physical needs.
The increase of riches and the accumulation of possessions create
no real bonds between men, and a bazaar is not at all the same thing

[35] 'Le principe de la vie sociale étant fixé dans la famille par la première institution
    du genre humain, il en résultoit que la famille soutenoit seule l'ordre politique,
    qui, ne s'appuyant que sur elle, ne pouvoit s'élever à un état plus parfait que la
    constitution domestique; et il en résultoit encore que les lois qui règlent le
    pouvoir, et qui sont le fondement de son droit, n'avoient d'autre interprète que
    la famille ou le peuple, ni d'autre garantie que sa force: c'est la véritable cause
    du peu de stabilité des gouvernemens anciens. Nul juge, nul conciliateur entre le
    pouvoir et les sujets: se touchant par tous les points, avec des intérêts divers, il
    y avoit entre eux une guerre continuelle.'—O.C., VII, 293.

as a city. To try to reduce to relations of that kind the relationships that constitute a nation is to look for the laws of human nature and of society in what man has in common with the animals.[36]

Intelligence and morality are distinctive of human society, and the state makes a fatal mistake if it is indifferent to the beliefs and moral standards of its citizens. Instead of thwarting and cramping the activity of the church, as the French government was doing, it ought to provide the fullest possible scope for the church to do what the church alone is capable of doing, and what the state itself in the nature of the case is incapable of doing.

Before he finished this book, Lamennais seems to have understood that his message was hopelessly unrealistic and that it would not be heeded. He ends on a gloomy and prophetic note. Christendom would not be reborn in his time, but only after a long period of social disorder and upheaval.

> If order is to revive, it will not be in our time. . . . The whole attitude (*esprit*) of peoples cannot be changed in a few years; and until there has been a fundamental change of attitude, it is impossible for Christendom to be reborn. It is the fruit not of violence, but of conviction; its basis is the faith, and not the sword.[37]

And anticipating a separation between religion and politics or between church and state, which ostensibly he has been writing to condemn, but to which ineluctably he will be led, Lamennais exclaims already:

> The true dignity, the real strength, of bishops as of priests depends today on their detachment from public affairs; there is enough for them in the work of the church. The future of religion is assured; it will not perish, its foundations are unshakable. Separate it then from what is collapsing. Why try to combine things that do not belong together?[38]

I pause again to remark that, while Lamennais's social doctrine at this phase of its evolution is commonly described as 'theocratic', it would better be described as 'papocratic'. He certainly held—what is a familiar christian assertion of our own time—that, if earthly rulers do not realize their subordination to the rule of God, they are likely to become absolute tyrants. But what was distinctive of his doctrine was not that assertion, but his locating the rule of God or the

---

[36] *O.C.*, VII, 241.   [37] *O.C.*, VII, 298 f.; cp. VII, 301.   [38] *O.C.*, VII, 280.

divine authority in the holy see. He argued that national churches are prone to identify themselves with purely national interests and are inevitably subservient to the civil power. Only a church that depends on the supernational authority of the papacy is able both to bear an effective witness to the universality of Christ's kingdom and to keep national rulers in their place. There was force in this papocratic argument, and I apprehend that its validity could be illustrated from subsequent history. But it might also be suggested that the unity of the universal church really resides in the Holy Ghost rather than in the papacy, and that what really keeps earthly rulers in their place is not the fear of the pope but the fear of God. It may be that national churches, without reference to the papacy, can bear as powerful a witness as the papacy itself to the authority of a living God. This suggestion also might be illustrated from subsequent history.

In any case, Émile Bourgeois was quite mistaken when in his *History of Modern France* he said of Lamennais at this period that he was 'carried away by his zeal for theocracy . . . and preached furiously in favour of crushing all freedom, both in Church and in State'.[39] Lamennais always loathed, dreaded, and denounced tyranny.[40] The reason why he wanted the spiritual and moral authority of the papacy made effective was his belief that that was the only way of *preventing* civil governments from 'crushing all freedom, both in church and in state'. He never ceased to point the contrast between tyranny, which is based on the arbitrary use of force, and order, which springs from willing obedience to an authority morally entitled to obedience. The tradition of his family, his own experiences during the revolution and the Empire, and his own extremely independent disposition, which had made him so reluctant to submit to the bonds of priesthood—all these had combined to make him prize freedom—personal freedom as well as political freedom and the freedom of the church. Where Lamennais changed was not in the valuation he put upon liberty, but in his understanding of the way in which liberty could best be secured in the conditions of the nineteenth century.

It was apparent before his latest book was published—and, if there were any doubt about it, it was made more than apparent immediately afterwards—that there was no prospect whatever of the ultramontane doctrine of the relation between the spiritual and

[39] *Op. cit.*, I, 82.
[40] Cp. Duine, p. 108; Carcopino, *Les doctrines sociales de Lamennais*, p. 39.

temporal powers being accepted in France; and therefore he had to look for some other way by which the freedom of the church to accomplish its mission could be won. This was one factor that moved him eventually to combine his ultramontanism with the liberal doctrine of the relations of church and state. The other factor, which was more positive and more persuasive, was his discovery that in Belgium a combination of liberalism in politics with ultramontanism in religion was already proving to be not only workable but full of exciting promise.

Before proceeding with the course of events, it may be well to remark upon the different senses that the words 'liberal' and 'liberalism' bore in France in 1826. These terms have indeed carried many different meanings and associations in different countries.[41] It is said[42] that the term 'liberal' as a political label was first introduced in France after 18 Brumaire to describe the ideas of Bonaparte and his assistants. If so, it shows how the title 'liberal' can be used by parties and individuals whose aim is the destruction of liberty, as well as by those who believe in free institutions and are determined to achieve them. This ambiguity was illustrated in France at the time which we have now reached by the difference between the majority of so-called liberals who, being voltairian sceptics, were anti-clerical and anxious to restrict and reduce the influence of the church in every way possible, and a small group of young liberal writers who were responsible for the journal, Le Globe.[43] This group was sincerely in favour of allowing complete liberty to catholics, including ultramontanes, as well of course as to the opponents of catholicism, since they believed that out of the free conflict of ideas the truth would prevail. Whereas the older liberals stood by the so-called gallican 'liberties' in which they saw a means of hampering and controlling the church, the younger liberals, although they themselves had little sympathy with catholicism, appreciated the force of Lamennais's objections to the gallican doctrines.

As for the meaning—or successive meanings—that liberalism will come to bear for Lamennais himself, these will become clear as we proceed.

41 Cp. Leflon, La crise révolutionnaire, p. 431.   42 See Haag, p. 150.
43 Founded in 1824 by P. F. Dubois (1793–1874), who continued to edit it till 1830, when it passed into the hands of the saint-simonians. Le Globe was against a state religion and supported religious liberty. See Paul Janet on 'Le Globe et la Restauration' in Revue des deux mondes, 1 August 1879, pp. 481–512; Boutard, I, 328–331; Duine, pp. 106 f.; Thureau-Dangin, Le Parti libéral, pp. 217–264.

Lamennais's new book was about as unfortunate in the time of its appearance as two of his earlier books—*Réflexions*[44] and *Tradition*[45]—had been. For, just about the same time, another book appeared by a certain Count Montlosier (1760–1838), which purported to disclose a vast underground conspiracy in France to overthrow the existing order in both church and state. Montlosier was a somewhat bizarre character with a keen sense of his own importance: Baron d'Eckstein described him as 'a feudal Quixotic figure'.[46] He was not anti-christian, but represented himself as a plain, sensible layman. 'Je ne prétends pas être théologien; je suis un simple chrétien. En cette qualité je vais quelquefois à la messe de ma paroisse', he wrote in his book, which was entitled *Mémoire à consulter sur un système religieux et politique, tendant à renverser la religion, la société et le trône*.[47] The four parties to the conspiracy that he had unearthed were alleged to be the 'Congregation', the Jesuits, the ultramontanes, and the *parti-prêtre*.

There was just sufficient substance in this piece of anti-clerical McCarthyism to make its skilfully presented[48] 'revelations' plausible and explosive.[49] The 'Congregation' was the name of an association that had been founded in the time of the Empire by a former Jesuit, Père Bourdier-Delpuits (1736–1811), in order to fortify catholics, chiefly of the upper classes, in a devout way of life and in works of charity. It was popularly confused with another association the 'Chevaliers de la Foi', which did wield considerable political influence, and which the liberals and even some royalists regarded as all the more sinister because of the mystery surrounding its existence.[50]

---

[44] See p. 49, *supra*.   [45] See p. 58, *supra*.

[46] See *The Rambler*, 1 May 1859, p. 56.

[47] *Op. cit.*, p. 183. It is dated February 1826, and was published on 1 March 1826 (see Foisset, *Vie du R. P. Lacordaire*, i, 122). Eight editions were published in one week. The Cambridge University Library has a copy of the fourth edition. Montlosier followed up his *Mémoire* with further publications of the same kind. Cp. Lavisse et Rambaud, x, 130 f; Thureau-Dangin, *Le Parti libéral*, pp. 386–392.

[48] Here is one specimen of his style. He is speaking about the 'Congregation'. 'Son objet n'est pas moins difficile à déterminer que sa nature; ce sera, quand il le faudra, de simples réunions pieuses: vous aurez là des anges. Ce sera aussi quand on voudra un sénat, une assemblée délibérante; vous aurez là des sages; enfin ce sera, quand les circonstances le demanderont, un bon foyer d'intrigue, d'espionnage et de délation: vous aurez là des démons.'—*Op. cit.*, p. 18.

[49] Cp. Foisset, *op. cit.*, i, 124 ff.

[50] Catholic historians have denied and anti-clerical historians have affirmed the political influence of the 'Congregation': see e.g. Geoffroy de Grandmaison,

The Jesuits had made their reappearance in France, and the legacy of suspicion which they brought with them could easily be fanned into flame. Lamennais and the school of young disciples which was gathering round him and which now had a monthly journal, Le Mémorial catholique, as its regular organ of expression, provided adequate pretext for fears of ultramontanism. The parti-prêtre was a term that covered the clergy as a political interest and various forms of aggressive clerical activity—for instance, the much advertised missions of the Restoration period and the zealous attempts of curés and others to intervene and gain influence in public administration and affairs.[51]

Montlosier's revelations were taken very seriously by the public, and caused an immense sensation. The whole episode was a kind of cross between our English popish plot in the seventeenth century and papal aggression of the mid-nineteenth century. The Journal des Débats described Montlosier as the 'Torch of France'.[52] Although he was a catholic[53] and a royalist, he was taken up with enthusiasm by the liberal press, with the exception of Le Globe, and was treated as a national hero. It was in the midst of this state of wild alarm throughout the country that Lamennais's book appeared, and added fuel to the flames.

Gallicans and liberals, normally at daggers drawn, united to denounce it, and clamoured for action by the government. The government, though not anxious to get involved in theological controversy, felt that it must do something,[54] as governments usually do in such circumstances. At one point, in the hope of appeasing all parties, it thought of taking legal proceedings against both Montlosier and Lamennais, but it soon realized that Montlosier

La Congrégation (1889), and Debidour, pp. 366 ff., 391. It was not possible to do justice to both sides of the truth until the confusion between the 'Congregation' and the 'Chevaliers de la Foi' was cleared up by G. de Bertier de Sauvigny in his book Le comte Ferdinand de Bertier (1782-1864) et l'énigme de la Congrégation (1948), see especially pp. 402-407.

51 See Pasquier, Mémoires, VI, 46.   52 'Flambeau de la France.' Boutard, I, 327.

53 After the publication of his book it is said that Montlosier suddenly began to display an unwonted piety. 'Il affecta tout à coup de se rendre à la grand'messe du dimanche, à laquelle il allait fort rarement auparavant; il assistait dévotement à tous les offices; il vint se confesser en grande pompe; il conviait le clergé à bénir solennellement sa ferme en Rondane, ses moissons et ses champs!' Grandmaison, La Congrégation, p. 321.

54 According to Lucas-Dubreton (La Restauration et la Monarchie de juillet, p. 102), government newspapers in Paris at this time had only 12,580 subscribers, whereas the anti-government newspapers of the right and left had 44,000 subscribers.

was much too popular. It decided therefore to proceed against Lamennais alone, and in order to strengthen its hands Mgr Frayssinous, now Minister of Ecclesiastical Affairs, called upon members of the hierarchy to subscribe a gallican declaration which deplored attacks on the 'maxims received in the Church of France'.[55]

This declaration, although it received fewer signatures than the government had hoped for, was presented to the king on 10 April 1826, and on 20 April Lamennais was charged in a civil court with having attacked the rights of the king and with having incited people to disobey the laws of the realm. He was defended by the famous lawyer Berryer (1790–1868), who took the line that the court was incompetent to deal with the substance of the charge, which involved questions of high theology. He justified Lamennais on purely juridical grounds, e.g. that the Declaration of 1682 had never had the force of law, and he maintained that the constitutional charter guaranteed to all Frenchmen the right to discuss freely the questions with which Lamennais had dealt in his book. After Berryer's speech, which is said to have been one of his most effective, Lamennais himself made a short statement to the court in which he said that he remained inviolably attached to the principles he had affirmed in his book and that he would continue to profess and defend them until his last breath.[56] Though he was condemned to a fine of thirty francs with costs and to the suppression of his book, the judgment[57] was framed in very moderate terms and showed great deference to his person and character; he was acquitted on the charge of having attacked the rights of the king, so that altogether he came out of the affair with more credit than his opponents.[58]

The incident had revealed the inveterate gallicanism of the royal government, and intensified Lamennais's impatience with it. Moreover, that was far from being the end of the matter. The controversy between gallicans and ultramontanes went on, and as it did so Lamennais became more and more desperate about the monarchical régime in France, until, as we shall see, in 1829 he produced his next manifesto which registered a notable change in his political outlook. It was not only events in France, however, that gave a new turn to

[55] On this affair, see Boutard, I, 334–337; Duine, pp. 105 f.; Dudon, *L. et le S.S.*, pp. 37 f.; Schmidlin, II, 49.

[56] See his own exact report of what he said in Forgues, I, 247.

[57] For the full text of the judgment, see Blaize, II, 35 f.

[58] 'Cette condamnation solennelle et ridicule ne diminua pas l'écrivain devant l'opinion, pas plus qu'elle ne grandit le parti qui l'avait cité en justice.'— Garnier, *Frayssinous*, p. 424.

his thinking, but what was happening in Belgium at this time and the friends he made there. So it is to a brief survey of the Belgian contribution to the mennaisian movement that I now turn.[59]

Belgium, which in 1789 had unsuccessfully attempted to achieve its independence of Austria, became to all intents and purposes a part of France by the treaty of Campio Formio in 1797. In 1815 the Congress of Vienna, with a view to creating a strong state to the north of France, joined Belgium to Holland and placed it under William of Nassau (1772–1844), the first king of the Netherlands.[60] To have made the union of the two countries viable, great political skill would have been required, since their economic interests clashed, and they were opposed in religion.

William made the mistake from the outset of treating Belgium not as an equal partner in the united kingdom, but as a territory that had been added to Holland. Thus the seat of government was almost entirely in Holland, and Dutchmen were in a vast majority in the composition of the ministry and of the civil service. The king, like other sovereigns of the time, aspired after the absolute monarchical powers of the *ancien régime* and in practice, so far as Belgium was concerned, combined a generally oppressive policy[61] with occasional concessions. In his dealings with the catholic church, while in 1827 he made a surprisingly accommodating concordat with the papacy, he sought on the whole, in spite of the fact that he was a protestant, to exercise the same sort of control over the church in Belgium as had been exercised by Joseph II (1741–1790)[62]—which had provoked the insurrection of 1789. A Belgian catholic writing to Lamennais in 1829 said of the king of the Netherlands that he 'combined the hatred of a heretic and the malice of a calvinist with the guile of a jansenist, an extraordinary degree of theological knowledge, and a remarkable talent for splitting hairs'.[63]

---

59 Some important books on the origins of liberal catholicism in Belgium have been published during the past twenty-five years. See F. J. J. Vrijmoed (Père Clémentin, O.F.M.), *Lamennais avant sa défection et la Néerlande catholique* (1930); A. Simon, *L'Église catholique et les débuts de la Belgique indépendante* (1949); Henri Haag, *Les Origines du Catholicisme libéral en Belgique, 1789–1839* (1950).

60 See Lavisse et Rambaud, x, chap. 9.

61 For the disabilities under which the Belgian catholics laboured, see Haag, pp. 100, 115; Goyau, *Portefeuille*, p. 77.

62 After whom the error that catholics know as 'josephism' was named. Cp. L. Sturzo, *Church and State* (1939), pp. 358, 360; A. Latreille, *L'Église catholique et la Révolution française*, I, 45 ff.   63 Goyau, *Portefeuille*, p. 78.

Obviously, all these conditions were likely to cause dissatisfaction and unrest in Belgium, and to revive the desire for national independence. The Belgians, however, had one source of weakness, apart from their lack of experience in self-government; they were divided into two hostile parties, the catholics (conservatives) and the liberals. If the king had been wiser, he would have kept these parties divided, and played them off against each other. But his policy was so ill-judged that he succeeded only in bringing the catholics and the liberals together to sink their differences for the time being in a united determination to secure the freedom of their country. Without this union—the alliance of the catholics with the liberals was known as 'unionism'—the Belgian revolution of 1830 could hardly have taken place; at any rate it would not have issued so swiftly and smoothly as it did in the establishment of an independent state.

From 1815 to 1830 the catholic church in Belgium was quite differently circumstanced from the Church of France, and had no inclination to desire the restoration of an *ancien régime*. The way the Belgian catholics had been treated in the eighteenth century by Joseph II had predisposed them not to gallicanism but to ultramontanism, and when in 1815 they were placed under a protestant king they had less inducement then ever to depend on the civil power for the free exercise of their religion or to prop the altar against the throne. Further, they were fortunate in having at this time not only wise and strong clerical leaders,[64] but also a number of distinguished laymen who took an active part in public life and who were capable of thinking out a new christian politics.[65]

Of these laymen I take particular note of Henri de Merode (1782–1847) and Ernest de Beauffort (1782–1858), since they entered into closest association with Lamennais. When I say that they were

[64] In particular Cardinal Sterckx who was Archbishop of Malines from 1832–1867 and who as vicar-general had been the power behind the preceding primate. See A. Simon, *Le Cardinal Sterckx et son temps, 1792–1867* (1950).

[65] For a fully documented account of the thinking of this group and of its relations with Lamennais, see Haag, *op. cit.* Vrijmoed, *op. cit.*, traces in great detail the influence of Lamennais on the journalist J. G. Le Sage Ten Broek (1775–1847) and more summarily on the following: the poet Jean Wap (1806–1880); the notable preacher Père Bernard Hafkenscheid (1807–1865); Père Roothaan (1785–1853), a Dutchman by origin who became General of the Society of Jesus; C. van Bommel (1790–1852) who translated the first two volumes of the *Essai sur l'indifférence* into Dutch and was later Bishop of Liège; and C. Broere (1813–1860), philosopher, theologian, and poet.

capable of thinking out a new christian politics, I do not mean that
they were themselves original political philosophers, but rather that
they were alive to the fact that christians needed new ideas, and
that they were enterprising in assimilating all that they could find and
in interpreting it to meet the circumstances of the church in their
country. They revived the attack on the assumptions of the *Auf-
klärung* and of the revolution that had been carried on towards the end
of the eighteenth century by the Belgian apologist F. X. de Feller
(d. 1802),[66] who had himself been influenced by Burke. In particular,
like Lamennais but independently of him, they fastened on Bonald's
traditionalism, though, as we shall see, they did not become blind
followers of Bonald. The teaching of the German romantics also
made its impact on Merode and Beauffort, so that they drew on
many fresh currents in European thought.[67]

These Belgian catholics were conservative in the sense that they
made their own the traditionalist theses about the nature of society
and political constitutions—theses which are neatly summed up in
Haag's words: 'Ne pas imaginer des cités d'Utopie, mais retrouver
les lois de la société pour mieux s'y conformer, telle est la sagesse
politique.'[68] But unlike Bonald they did not tie their traditionalism

[66] See Haag, pp. 43-48.
[67] The following passage from H. Lichtenberger's *Qu'est-ce le romantisme?* (1937),
pp. 354 f., gives a useful impression of the range of ideas with which the
traditionalists worked:

'Dans le secteur politique et historique, les romantiques opposent avec
Fichte au cosmopolitisme du xviiie siècle l'enthousiasme patriotique. À la
conception individualiste qui fait de l'État une simple entreprise de sécurité publique garantissant les citoyens contre les invasions du dehors et les usurpations
de leurs concitoyens, ils substituent une conception "sociale" d'après laquelle
l'homme, incapable d'atteindre à la liberté en tant qu'individu, ne la réalise
que dans la société par l'intermédiaire de l'État. Rendus sceptiques par l'exemple
de la France révolutionnaire sur les capacités organisatrices de la raison, ils
insistent sur l'importance et les droits de l'Histoire et de la tradition. Ils pro-
fessent le plus grand respect pour les institutions qui se sont lentement dévelop-
pées au cours des siècles, comme la constitution anglaise: elles auraient, à les
en croire, une valeur intrinsèque de par leur antiquité même et surpasseraient
infiniment les institutions sorties du cerveau d'un législateur ou des débats d'une
Constituante. Ils réhabilitent dès lors le moyen âge décrié par les rationalistes
comme l'ère de l'obscurantisme et de la barbarie. Ils vantent ses institutions, sa
civilisation, sa littérature, ses arts. Ils présentent avec Hugo et Savigny le droit,
non point comme le résultat d'un acte de volonté consciente, d'un contrat
social, mais comme un acte inconscient et nécessaire de l'âme nationale, du
Volksgeist, qui vit et palpite dans tous les individus faisant partie d'une même
collectivité.' Quoted by Haag, pp. 58 f.
[68] Haag, p. 63.

up with an attachment to the pre-revolutionary form of government in France. On the contrary, they regarded the despotism of Louis XIV and his successor as one of the principal and just causes of the revolution. The post-reformation dynasties with their unqualified doctrine of the divine right of kings (which was a departure from previous christian teaching) had tyrannized over the church and over the peoples. Gallicanism represented the unpardonable treachery of churches which had failed in their duty to withstand, in the name of a higher authority, earthly monarchs who abused their power. The authentic christian tradition was to be found not in gallicanism, febronianism, or josephism, but in the doctrine of the christian middle ages which provided safeguards against despotism in its emphasis upon the subordination of earthly rulers to the law of God and the vicar of Christ and also in its teaching about the importance of balanced political constitutions.

On 6 January 1817 Henri de Merode had written a long letter[69] in this sense to Bonald himself. He said that he understood Bonald to be dissatisfied with the existing form of government in France (i.e. the constitutional monarchy of Louis XVIII), because his principles required a return to the régime of Louis XVI and Louis XV. Merode then stated vigorously why he could not agree with Bonald and why he was prepared to welcome representative government. He made the interesting suggestion that absolute monarchy in France had been a reflection in the social order of deism. There was everything to be said against attempting to restore it. What was needed now was a distribution of the attributes of sovereignty—'un souverain collectif et la monarchie mixte'.[70]

This means that in 1817 Merode was further advanced towards a liberal catholicism than Lamennais was in 1826. In 1817 Lamennais had still been hand-in-glove with the ultra-royalists in France, though even then he had got beyond looking for a return of the ancien régime. But it also means that there were catholics in Belgium ready to welcome and applaud his successive moves in a liberal direction. The Essai sur l'indifférence had established his fame in Belgium as an apologist, especially among the clergy; indeed it was soon being used as a text-book in Belgian theological seminaries, and the mennaisian philosophy had nowhere a stronger following.[71]

There do not appear, however, to have been any personal communications between Lamennais and the Belgian catholics before

[69] The full text of this letter is published by Haag, pp. 263 ff.
[70] Haag, p. 265.   [71] See Haag, p. 111.

1826, i.e. until after the publication of the second part of *La Religion considérée*. Characteristic of the enthusiasm with which this attack on gallicanism was received in Belgium is the following letter from Beauffort to one of his friends, written on 15 March 1826:

> If you haven't read abbé Lamennais's book, read it! If you have read it, read it again! If you have read it and re-read it, make it the subject of your meditations! Learn it by heart! That is what I shall say to every sensible man. Are we agreed?[72]

Lamennais's new book proved indeed to Beauffort and Merode that the mind of the brilliant French writer was moving in the same direction as theirs, and they lost no time in getting into touch with him. Within a month or two both of them had been to visit him in Paris, and they had put before him certain considerations (concerning the relation of the temporal and spiritual powers) which were the fruit of their reflection on their experience in Belgium, and which they hoped would influence the future course of his thinking.[73] While the Belgian catholics had no need of Lamennais to win them to ultramontanism, they were fortified by the knowledge that henceforth their cause had an advocate and a leader of such passionate faith, of such rare endowments, and of such firm resolution.[74]

Lamennais on his side, as will appear in his next book, did not fail to profit from the considerations that were submitted to him by his Belgian friends.[75] But what impressed him most of all was the union between catholics and liberals in Belgium—their agreement to sink their differences for the time being in order to achieve the freedom of their country. This agreement was an accomplished fact by the end of 1828,[76] i.e. before the publication in February 1829 of *Des Progrès de la révolution et de la guerre contre l'Église*.[77] There is no

---

72 See Haag, p. 86.
73 See letter from Merode and Beauffort to Lamennais in Haag, pp. 266 ff.
74 See Haag, p. 89; cp. Forgues, II, 67 f.
75 See Haag, book II, chap. 2.
76 The union had first been proposed in December 1825 by E. C. Gerlach (1785–1870), leader of the catholics in the upper house of the Netherlands parliament, but the liberals at that time doubted the sincerity of what seemed to be a *volte-face* on the part of the catholics, i.e. a willingness for free institutions. A second overture was made in March 1827, this time from the liberal side, and gradually the idea of unionism gained ground till it was fully realized in the autumn of 1828. See Haag, pp. 100–110.
77 Lamennais was still working on the manuscript of the last chapter on 12 December 1828; see Forgues, I, 488. The book was published in the middle of February 1829; see *Cottu*, p. 201.

doubt that the Belgian example hastened the birth in Lamennais's mind of an analogous strategy for French catholics.

I return now to the course of events in France itself, which led up to the publication of *Des Progrès*. Throughout 1827 the position of Villèle, who had been prime minister since 1822, had become increasingly insecure. J.-B. Villèle (1773–1854) had originally belonged to the extreme right and Charles X was greatly attached to him, but experience had taught him the expediency of moderation. He had however constantly tried to appease the ultra-royalists, but was always doing so too late. Thus in the end he had the worst of both worlds, and had to reckon with an opposition of the extreme right as well as with that of the liberals. As his popularity waned and his hold on power became precarious, he resorted to arbitrary and violent measures,[78] and the two oppositions combined at last to bring about his fall.

There was a general election in November 1827 as a result of which only 170 ministerial candidates were returned against 180 of the left and 70 of the extreme right. Villèle was succeeded (4 January 1828) by J.-B. de Martignac (1778–1832), a moderate royalist, who sought to form a centre party by following a constitutional policy and adopting some liberal measures. Liberalism anyhow was now in the ascendant, and, since the king had no idea of becoming a constitutional monarch, there were evidently political storms ahead. It was likely that liberals would insist that the power of the church should be curbed and the ambitions of the *parti-prêtre* countered, and it is at this point that we may pick up Lamennais's reactions.

At the beginning of 1828, sending his best wishes for the new year to one of his friends, he wrote from La Chesnaie: 'It will appear later on . . . whether in publishing my last book (*sc. La Religion considérée*) I was taken up with false alarms. Perhaps the time is not far off when I shall have to speak out again.'[79] A day or two later he wrote to another friend:

We are approaching great events. I should not be surprised if the war against the church started at once; anyhow it cannot be long delayed. They will ask of us declarations, signatures, oaths,

[78] Censorship, dissolution of the garde nationale for having after a review cried 'À bas Villèle', creation of over sixty new peers to strengthen his following in the upper house. See Lavisse et Rambaud, x, 131–135.

[79] Letter of 5 January 1828 to Countess de Senfft. Forgues, I, 395 f.

what have you?—and all with a view to their being refused. After that it will be declared that the 'Roman religion' is incompatible with the Charter and with the public liberties, and they will set about forming a national or gallican clergy. To it they will hand over the bishoprics, the churches, the presbyteries, the seminaries, the schools. . . .[80]

And a fortnight later, with the prescience that he often seemed to possess, he wrote: 'It is certain that great events are on the way. All the same we are not yet at the crisis. They will begin this year by attacking the clergy, particularly in the field of education. The rest will follow in due course.'[81]

As a matter of fact, on the following day (22 January 1828) it was announced that the government was appointing a commission to consider what measures might be necessary to see that the laws of the realm were carried out in the ecclesiastical secondary schools. This was the first move in the involved politico-ecclesiastical campaign of 1828, and its background needs to be explained before its sequels are unfolded.[82]

When the Bourbons returned, the napoleonic system of national education, which was based on control by the University, had with minor modifications been maintained. Secondary and higher education was the almost exclusive preserve of the University. In the field of primary education, which had been grossly neglected under the Empire, there was much more freedom for local and ecclesiastical enterprise.[83] An ordinance of Louis XVIII (8 April 1824) indeed conferred on the clergy a dominant place in the control of primary schools.[84] Consequently, the education of the children of the poor was under the direction of the clergy. But the state was determined

[80] Letter of 7 January 1828 to Coriolis. Forgues, I, 399.
[81] Letter of 21 January 1828 to Mlle de Lucinière. Forgues, I, 408. On 11 March 1828 he will write to Countess de Senfft: 'Les choses vont plus vite que je n'aurais cru, et je ne serais pas surpris qu'avant deux ans tout fût terminé. . . . Je compte . . . beaucoup sur la fermeté du clergé, pourvu que *la question soit claire.* On parle du mariage des prêtres, et cela est bon. Je voudrais qu'on proposât de leur faire prendre deux femmes'(!)—Forgues, I, 447 f.
[82] All previous accounts of the events which preceded and followed the ordinances of 16 June 1828 were superseded by Adrien Garnier's book, *Les Ordonnances du 16 juin 1828 d'après des documents inédits tirés des Archives du Vatican et des Archives nationales* (1929). Except where otherwise stated, in what follows in the text to p. 134 I depend on Garnier's record.
[83] See Garnier, *Frayssinous,* book IV, 'L'instruction primaire'.
[84] See Debidour, p. 377.

that the children of the upper and middle classes should grow up
under its own care and that secondary schools should be under the
direction of the University, and in this it was continuing what had
been Napoleon's intention.[85] The only exception made was in
favour of the diocesan *petits séminaires* by means of which clergy
were recruited, chiefly from the poorer classes in country districts:
these were allowed to be independent of the University (ordinance
of 5 October 1814).

From 1822 when the royalists were in undisputed power, the
government was more easy-going, and the bishops were permitted
to open, alongside their *petits séminaires*, a number of schools which,
although they served a different purpose, were also virtually independent of the University. In order to save appearances, they were
called *écoles ecclésiastiques*, but they were in fact the counterpart of
what in England are known as the 'public schools'. The nobility
and the bourgeoisie started sending their children to these schools,
some of which became very prosperous. This was a development,
however, that was regarded with extreme disfavour by the liberals,
who saw in it a device by which catholicism would re-establish
its domination over society by the hold it would get on the upper
classes. Moreover, in some cases (actually, in eight cases) the bishops
had put these schools under the direction of the Jesuits, who were
looked upon with especial suspicion as mysterious agents of the
counter-revolution.[86]

The government of M. Martignac was not itself hostile to the
church, but it had to offer some gage to the liberals who were
now the most powerful party and were demanding measures against
the clericalist and jesuit conspiracy that Montlosier had 'unmasked'.

[85] Cp. what Roger Soltau says about Napoleon's reasons for instituting the
University: 'Napoleon acted upon the principle that education of some sort
was sufficiently demanded for its refusal to be virtually impossible. The question
was as to who would give it, and what it would be like; and to this question he
declared that education could be given only by the State, if not directly at least
only under its close supervision; only thus could it be certain that the schools
would not become the tools of its enemies. This reasoning . . . applied in
practice solely to higher and secondary education. What happened in the ele-
mentary school mattered less. . . . What mattered to Napoleon was the training
of the *élite*, officers, Civil Servants, lawyers, those who were to carry out
Imperial policy: this training he proposed to make a rigid State monopoly.'
—*French Political Thought in the Nineteenth Century* (1931), p. 67.

[86] See Garnier, *Frayssinous*, for a documented account of these developments,
especially chap. 13, 'Petits séminaires et Université', and chap. 14, 'Jésuites et
petits séminaires'.

Realizing how thorny the problem was, the government hoped to screen itself behind the report of the commission which it appointed on 22 January 1828. At the beginning of February Frayssinous, as Minister of Ecclesiastical Affairs, sent out a questionary to all the bishops about the number of pupils in their seminaries, whether they paid fees or not, whether they wore the soutane or not, whether they were taught music, dancing, and fencing(!), and whether the masters were laymen or priests, seculars or religious, etc. The answers to these questions were intended to supply information for the commission. The bishops, who naturally were not eager to supply ammunition for their opponents, objected to the questionary, and were very dilatory in sending in the required information—though eventually most of them did so.

When Lamennais had heard of the appointment of the commission, he had interpreted it as the government's first step towards the nationalization of the church, which he now regarded as the logical outcome and equal design of liberalism and gallicanism. On 28 January 1828, in the course of a long letter to Berryer, he wrote:

We are not seeing anything . . . that was not to be expected, and we are seeing only the beginning. I have said so to you many times, and I can never say it too often. The great object of liberalism is less to change the dynasty than to change our religion. . . . I have not doubted for a moment that they would begin by attacking ecclesiastical education with a view to proceeding further afterwards. You ask me what I think of the declaration of war against the church signed *Portalis*, and lower down CHARLES.[87] Here is a little commentary on the first paragraph of this declaration. . . .

'The necessity of ensuring, in all the ecclesiastical secondary schools, the execution of the laws of the realm, is generally recognized.'

I ask myself first, as a general question of right, what have the laws of the realm to do with the ecclesiastical schools, whether secondary or otherwise? If the state is catholic, it must along with all catholics recognize, as a point of faith, the absolute independence of the church in the education of its ministers, which cannot be put under the civil magistrate without a sacrilegious usurpation.

[87] The ordinance appointing the commission had been signed by Portalis as Minister of Justice and by the king. On 22 January Berryer had sent Lamennais a copy of the ordinance and asked him what he thought of it. See Goyau, *Portefeuille*, p. 71.

He has the right to intervene only if it is necessary to deal with public scandals, just as he can and ought to prevent disorders in churches during the celebration of divine service.

If the state is not catholic, its claim to regulate by legislation ecclesiastical education is an even more frightful enormity. It is a beginning of persecution, and the king of the Netherlands, who attempted it recently, has been obliged to withdraw by the rightful opposition of his catholic subjects. . . .

The real intention of the Minister may be expressed thus: 'We accuse you of having violated the laws, in order to have a pretext for making a law against you, because, in pursuance of our design to establish a church of which we shall be masters, we must first of all be masters of its teaching.'—That is what will become clearer shortly.[88]

Lamennais did not always[89] distinguish between the conscious intentions of the government and unspoken presuppositions of its policy or historic forces of which it was the unwitting agent. There is no reason to suppose that the government of Charles X desired or intended that the Church of France should fall entirely under its control or should break altogether with the papacy. On the other hand, Lamennais rightly discerned that forces were at work in France which would not only prove fatal to the restored Bourbon dynasty but which also threatened the foundations of a church that continued in a position of dependence on the state. He was also right in anticipating that the government—despite his exaggeration of its persecutive designs—would soon go further in restricting the liberties or privileges of the church.

This did not become immediately apparent, for the commission that had been appointed on 22 January 1828 was unable to report promptly owing to the reluctance of the bishops to supply the information, for which they had been asked, about their ecclesiastical secondary schools. Towards the end of February indeed Lamennais was saying that the commission had adjourned for six months.[90] That was not so. It made its report, as we shall see, at the end of May. Before this, however, on 21 April, the Minister of Education had issued an ordinance which removed the control of primary schools from the bishops and transferred it to the University. These schools were in future to be under the direction of local committees

[88] See Forgues, I, 416 ff.
[89] Though he did so clearly enough when he wanted to; see e.g. O.C., IX, 76, 98.
[90] See Forgues, I, 439.

of nine members, of which the bishop was entitled to nominate only three.

The main question in Lamennais's mind was when and in what form he should publish another ultramontane manifesto. On 7 March 1828 he had written to his brother, abbé Jean:

I am watching things closely, on the look out for the right time to speak. The moment has not come yet. I could only discourse vaguely, and repeat what I have said before. . . . The government has not yet come down on one side or the other. . . . This indecision will not last; but . . . so long as the point and moment of attack (sc. on the church) have been fixed by no clear act or words, one could speak only for the sake of speaking, which would be a huge mistake.[91]

On 21 March after he had had an opportunity of talking things over with abbé Jean, he wrote to Countess de Senfft:

I was thinking of publishing a brochure on the Present Dangers of the Church; but Jean and I agree that the moment has not yet come. It is better to let the government do something which must be resisted and which will make the question clear for everyone: that will happen soon enough.[92]

When the ordinance of 21 April 1828, dealing with the primary schools, appeared Lamennais was in Paris, about to set out on a long-projected visit to his friends the Senffts at Turin.[93] He did not change his plans and evidently did not consider that this ordinance brought the issue to a head. He was thus absent from the scene of action when the commission at last made its report on 28 May. The report falls into two parts. The first part, which was adopted unanimously, made a number of recommendations which were designed to put an end to the irregularities that had grown up in the ecclesiastical schools, and to restrict them to the training of boys who had a vocation to the priesthood. The second part of the report dealt with the Jesuits, and by five votes to four the commission recommended that there was no need to prohibit them from teaching in the *petits séminaires*. It seems, however, that the government had already decided to proceed against the Jesuits,[94] and in any case there was such

---

91 See Blaize, ii, 72.   92 See Forgues, i, 450. Cp. *Lamennais inconnu*, p. 214.
93 See *Lamennais inconnu*, p. 216; Forgues, i, 451 ff. Lamennais left Paris with Baron de Vitrolles with whom he stayed for a time on his way to Turin.
94 The report of the commission was not published in the *Moniteur* until 21 June, i.e. after the ordinances had been promulgated.

a furious outcry on the part of the liberals that, in order to avert worse measures, the king was persuaded to sign the ordinances of 16 June.

The first ordinance decreed that from 1 October following the eight ecclesiastical secondary schools, which were under the direction of the Jesuits, should be brought within the régime of the University, and that no one should be allowed to teach in them who had not affirmed in writing that he did not belong to a religious order not legally established in France.

The second ordinance made a number of regulations about the rest of the ecclesiastical secondary schools, with which the bishops would have to comply if they were to retain control of them.[95]

On 6 July 1828 Lamennais was on his way back to Paris, where his friends were anxious for his presence. He spent a couple of nights with the Archbishop of Lyons (de Pins[96]) who, he was delighted to find, was determined to oppose the ordinances even if others favoured compliance. From Lyons Lamennais wrote to Count de Senfft, giving him this good news. 'If only thirty bishops stand firm,' he added, 'they will embarrass the persecutors tremendously.'[97]

In the event not only thirty bishops but practically the whole hierarchy[98] united in addressing a long and firmly worded *non possumus* to the king. This document—entitled *Mémoire présenté au roi par les évêques de France au sujet des ordonnances du 16 juin 1828, relatives aux écoles secondaires ecclésiastiques*, and dated 1 August 1828[99]—was drawn up chiefly by Mgr de Quélen, Archbishop of

[95] E.g. the number of pupils in these schools was not to exceed 20,000; the number and location of the schools must be approved by the government; only boarders to be admitted to them; the superiors to be approved by the government, etc. For the full text of the ordinances, see Garnier, *Ordonnances*, pp. 74–77.

[96] De Pins was in fact administrator of the see, and an archbishop *in partibus*. The titular Archbishop of Lyons was Cardinal Fesch who resided in Rome.

[97] Letter of 6 July 1828, see Forgues, I, 454 f. Two days later he wrote to Mme Champy: 'Je reçois, chaque courrier, des lettres qui me pressent de revenir à Paris. . . . Il est presque impossible que je n'aie pas, prochainement, de grands devoirs à remplir.' *Ibid.*, I, 455 f.

[98] Among the few who did not sign were de Pins (of Lyons) who wanted stronger wording, and of course Feutrier, Bishop of Beauvais, who had earlier in the year succeeded Frayssinous as Minister of Ecclesiastical Affairs and who, as minister responsible for the issue of the ordinances, was regarded as the villain of the piece.

[99] For the complete text, see *Le Mémorial catholique*, August 1828, X, 74–88; *O.C.*, IX, 237–258. The declaration contains these words: 'Ils (i.e. the members of the episcopate) se contentent de dire avec respect, comme les apôtres, *Non possumus*, nous ne pouvons pas.'

Paris; it was signed by Cardinal de Clermont-Tonnerre, Archbishop of Toulouse, doyen of the French episcopate. The *Mémoire* was meant to be kept secret, and it was hoped that the king would so modify the ordinances that in consequence the bishops would be able to say *nunc possumus* instead of *non possumus*. But within a week or two the *Mémoire* became public property and aroused great excitement.[100]

The grounds on which the bishops' protest was based were perfectly consistent with the gallican principles which most of them held.[101] They acknowledged that the prince had authority not only in temporal, but also in spiritual, matters.[102] They claimed however that the ordinances contravened the authority which the bishops properly had over the training of the clergy, and that they constituted such an interference of the civil power with the responsibilities of the ecclesiastical hierarchy as had no warrant in traditional teaching about the relations of church and state nor in the tradition of the Church of France in particular.

Lamennais had not expected such unity and firmness on the part

[100] The subsequent embarrassment of the bishops was in large part due to the fact that they had, contrary to their intentions, *publicly* committed themselves to a refusal to accept the ordinances. The government had in fact promised concessions, provided the *Mémoire* were kept secret.

[101] Before the document appeared, abbé Jean had enthusiastically anticipated that the bishops were going to make a thoroughly ultramontane protest. On 14 July 1828 he wrote to Count de Senfft: 'Il y a tout lieu d'espérer que nos évêques refuseront unanimement de coopérer à l'exécution des deux ordonnances du 16 juin, et qu'ils prieront le Pape de les diriger par ses conseils et de les affermir par son autorité. Ce sera une belle et grande chose, dont les suites sont incalculables; tous les petits séminaires seront détruits, mais l'unité sera conservée, et les principes catholiques ne recevront pas d'atteinte de la main de ceux qui en sont établis les gardiens et les défenseurs.' See Forgues, I, 456 f.

A copy of the bishops' *Mémoire* was sent to Rome through the nuncio in Paris, but the holy see did not regard it as a formal request for direction. Rome insisted to the last that, except for letters from two or three individual bishops, its ruling had not been asked for by the French hierarchy. There was misunderstanding about this, since the bishops appear to have supposed that the sending of their *Mémoire* to Rome was a request for direction. It is possible that the French government intercepted some correspondence.

[102] 'Que le prince doive avoir, et qu'il ait en effet sur les écoles ecclésiastiques, destinées à perpétuer le sacerdoce, l'inspection et la surveillance nécessaires pour assurer l'ordre public, empêcher la transgression des lois, maintenir les droits et l'honneur de la souveraineté; qu'il puisse exiger, exécuter par lui-même la réforme des abus qui intéressent l'ordre civil; qu'il doive même, en qualité d'*évêque du dehors*, provoquer la réforme des abus dans l'ordre spirituel, et prêter l'appui du bras séculier pour le maintien des règles canoniques, on en convient.'

of the episcopate. He described it as 'une chose tout à fait de Providence'.[103] But he never imagined that it would put a stop to the course of the political revolution, i.e. to the complete liberalizing of the state. He admitted however that it was difficult to calculate what exactly would happen next.[104] What actually did happen was bound to seem topsy-turvy to an ultramontane. For the French government appealed to Rome to induce the hierarchy to withdraw its resistance, and the holy see was obliging enough to tell the bishops that they ought to give way. This appeared to make havoc of the ultramontane thesis. For here was the holy see, instead of standing up to the civil power, conspiring with it to break the spontaneous resistance of a national church to an attack upon its rights and liberties.

At the time there was a good deal of mystery about what actually happened, but it is now possible to reconstruct the course of events. There was only a French chargé d'affaires in Rome at this moment, and the government first showed the urgency of its concern by appointing the Duke of Blacas, a diplomat of great prestige, to present its case to the Vatican, and secondly showed much adroitness in also sending to Rome as a second negotiator a M. Lasagni who was an old friend of Cardinal Bernetti, Leo XII's secretary of state.

On 6 September 1828 Lasagni persuaded Bernetti to write a letter, of which the pope approved, to the French Minister of Foreign Affairs: it was to the effect that the Holy Father saw no need to intervene, and that he would not do so in future without having previously informed the French government of his intentions.[105] Though

---

[103] See Forgues, I, 461; cp. ibid., I, 473.
[104] See Lamennais inconnu, p. 220.
[105] The text of Bernetti's letter was as follows: 'Je suis bien aise de pouvoir assurer Votre Excellence que le Saint-Père est allé au devant du désir de Sa Majesté très Chrétienne, par la conduite qu'Il s'était proposé de suivre relativement à ce qui se passe en France au sujet des Ordonnances du 16 juin et que la mission de M. Lasagni n'a pu que le confirmer dans ses intentions. Sa Sainteté, confiée d'un côté en la haute piété du fils aîné de l'Église, et persuadée, de l'autre, du dévouement sans réserves des évêques de France envers Sa Majesté et de leur tendre amour pour la paix et tout autre véritable intérêt de notre sainte religion, ne sait pas prévoir que des circonstances malheureuses puissent l'obliger à rompre un silence si conforme aux vœux de Sa Majesté très chrétienne. Mais si ce malheur arrivait, j'ose répondre que le Saint-Père ne s'adresserait assurément à personne sans avoir indiqué à Sa Majesté la nouvelle position que son devoir sacré pourrait lui avoir marquée, et Il n'oubliera jamais tout ce qu'Il doit au maintien de l'ordre et de la tranquillité en France et à la dignité du trône de St Louis.' See Garnier, Ordonnances, pp. 154 f.

this letter was skilfully contrived to avoid positively committing the holy see on the subject of the ordinances, it was equivalent to saying—and it was meant to imply—that the bishops ought to submit to them.

Bernetti's letter was not published, and in fact it was treated as so profoundly secret that its very existence was for some a matter of doubt.[106] It was shown only to de Quélen, Archbishop of Paris, and to Cardinal de Latil, Archbishop of Reims—with a view to their persuading the rest of the bishops that they should abandon their resistance to the ordinances. There seems to have been some jealousy and difference of opinion between the two archbishops; anyhow de Latil took the matter into his own hands and on 25 September 1828 sent a circular to the metropolitans and through them to all the bishops, saying that the pope had replied that the bishops should trust in the piety and wisdom of the king, which meant that they should comply with the ordinances.[107]

In view of their much publicized declaration that they could not comply with them, the bishops were placed in a very awkward position. There was a good deal of painful uncertainty about how they could climb down with dignity and integrity. But their resistance at once began to collapse, and eventually all except one of them[108] carried out the ordinances, which when it came to the point the government did not enforce too rigidly. Even the formidable Clermont-Tonnerre, Archbishop of Toulouse, who in September had written to the Minister of Ecclesiastical Affairs a defiant letter that became famous,[109] succumbed, as did also de Pins, who had

---

[106] It was first published in 1846 in Cretineau-Joly's *Histoire de la Compagnie de Jésus* (vi, 260). Garnier's text of the letter is from the Vatican Archives.

[107] The circular read as follows: 'Le roi ayant daigné me faire communiquer les réponses de Rome relatives aux Ordonnances du 16 juin et m'ayant ordonné de vous en donner connaissance, j'ai l'honneur de vous informer que Sa Sainteté, persuadée du dévouement sans réserve des évêques de France envers Sa Majesté, ainsi que de leur amour pour la paix et tous autres véritables intérêts de notre religion, a fait répondre que les évêques devaient se confier en la haute piété et la sagesse du roi, pour l'exécution des Ordonnances et marcher d'accord avec le trône.' See Garnier, *Ordonnances*, p. 156.

[108] The exception was Clausel de Montals, Bishop of Chartres.

[109] 'Monseigneur,—La devise de ma famille, qui lui a été donnée, en 1120, par Caliste II, est celle-ci: *Etiamsi omnes, ego non.* C'est aussi celle de ma conscience.
    J'ai l'honneur d'être, avec la respectueuse considération
           qui est due au ministre du Roi,
               A. J., cardinal, archevêque de Toulouse.'
See Forgues, i, 477.

refused to believe that the pope favoured submission, until he had received a special papal brief to assure him that such was the case. Leo XII, like Pius VIII and Greogry XVI after him, was determined to conciliate civil governments so far as he could, in the hope of keeping the way open to a happier future.[110]

The failure of the holy see to support the catholics of France in their resistance to the government's demands was a bitter blow to Lamennais who, now back at La Chesnaie, was already hard at work on a new manifesto which, instead of being a pamphlet provoked by the immediate circumstances, was developing into a substantial book.[111] In the first flush of his embarrassed disappointment he wrote to Countess de Senfft on 2 October 1828:

> You have seen in the papers how the affair of the ordinances stands. There had been something like a miracle of Providence to bring about a bit of unity among the bishops, and to infuse some strength into their weakness. Clergy, laity, all were rivalling one another in repulsing the first moves towards schism with a courage one could not have hoped for, when behold some sort of a letter from Cardinal Bernetti is announced which engages the bishops 'to have confidence in the piety of the king'—as if in France there was a king, as if he could do anything, as if 'the piety of the king' could prevent the ordinances from being destructive of religion, an attack on the divine rights of the church, tyrannical, impious, etc.; as if it were a question of repressing the excessive zeal of the clergy in a matter of doubtful importance. . . . I don't believe that for centuries anything so scandalous has happened. . . . Rome, Rome, where are you? What has become of that voice which used to sustain the weak, and arouse the indolent? that word which used to traverse the world giving to all in times of great peril strength to fight and to die? At present, all you can say is: 'Yield.' . . . Where on earth are we? If ruin comes to us from the place whence we were looking for deliverance, what remains

[110] Thus Leo XII wrote to de Pins: 'Maintenant, quoique les choses . . . ne soient pas aussi prospères que nous le désirons, elles sont cependant de nature à ne nous pas ôter la ferme confiance de les voir s'améliorer à l'avenir.' See Garnier, *op. cit.*, p. 197.

I have been able to give only the main facts of the story of the ordinances of 16 June 1828. The complete record, as given by Garnier, is of great interest, and a most remarkable illustration of the Vatican's diplomatic skill in handling a delicate and complicated situation.

[111] See Forgues, I, 464 f., 471; *Lamennais inconnu*, p. 221.

to be done except to say with the Prophet: *Elongavi fugiens, et mansi in solitudine*?

I don't know how to write to you about anything else today; my soul is too full of what I see and of what I foresee. Pray, pray for the church! No doubt, she will not perish; no doubt, God, who protects her, is stronger than the weakness of those whom he has charged to defend her. But why does one have to repeat this to oneself so often, and so bitterly?[112]

It should be observed that Lamennais makes no mention of the pope, but seeks to make Cardinal Bernetti, the secretary of state, solely responsible for what had happened. That was how he managed for some years longer to hold up the pope on a solitary pinnacle of infallibility and to keep his ultramontanism intact.[113] His book when it appears will try to cover up Rome's disappointing failure on this occasion to conform to the requirements of the ultramontane thesis by offering an apology based on the habitual patience of the holy see, and by making an appeal to the papacy to give in future the clear and unhesitating lead that was called for by the new times. The indictment of gallicanism, on the other hand, he could now draw in stronger terms than ever, since the abysmal collapse of the bishops' resistance to the civil power after their initial motion of defiance.

It is against this background of events in Belgium and in France that Lamennais's book *Des Progrès de la révolution et de la guerre contre l'Église*, published in February 1829, must be placed. The principal message of the book, which also marks the fresh development in his

---

112 See Forgues, I, 473 ff. Cp. the letter that Lamennais wrote to de Pins when he heard of de Latil's circular to the bishops: 'Monseigneur, qui a de la mémoire, aura lu dans quelque mauvais pamphlet cette phrase, aussi ridicule que triviale, *qu'il faut marcher avec son siècle*, et, par une heureuse imitation, il dit à l'Épiscopat français d'un air d'autorité, *qu'il faut marcher avec le trône*. C'est le trône alors, comme de raison, qui est enseignant, et le corps épiscopal écoutant et suivant. Oh! combien nos Bishops anglais vont être réjouis d'une pareille doctrine; voilà nos prélats à leur niveau; bientôt nous ferons le Roi, comme Georges IV: *Defensorem fidei*.' See Garnier, *op. cit.*, p. 159.

113 Cp. other letters of this period in Forgues. The way in which Lamennais and his friends tried to make out that the pope and the spiritual authority of the holy see were in no way compromised by these proceedings is illustrated by the editorial in the October 1828 number of *Le Mémorial catholique*, x, 229 ff. See also *O.C.*, IX, 128, where Lamennais says that the papal secretary of state has no authority in the church.

political thought, is indicated in the preface. It is obvious, he says, that France and Europe are heading for new revolutions, and it is necessary to take stock of the situation in the light of the eternal laws of society. The time has come to demand that the catholic church shall have accorded to it the liberty promised by the constitutional charter and already enjoyed by the protestants and jews. And by liberty, Lamennais says, he means the liberties which the Belgian catholics were demanding from a persecuting government —liberty of conscience, liberty of the press, liberty of education. This means that Lamennais is accepting—at any rate, for practical or tactical purposes—the liberal idea of the state in place of the traditional idea of a christian polity in which the church had exclusive rights and privileges. He no longer calls upon the state to submit consistently to the law of God and to the authority of the vicar of Christ; he calls upon the state to be consistently liberal and to accord to the church the same freedom as it accords to other groups and individuals.

He starts from the position at which he had left off in his last book. Only after a long period of unsettlement and confusion can one look forward to a new social order such as christians desire—which will include the collaboration of the spiritual and temporal powers or a new alliance of church and state. As things are, it is no good pretending that either peoples or their governments are christian, though the church has less to fear, and more to hope for, from peoples who need her than from princes who want to make use of her. A return to christianity can come about only gradually, since to be genuine and durable it must be the result of personal persuasion and conviction, not of legal attempts to constrain belief and to enforce conformity. Only under conditions of freedom can there be a satisfactory recovery of a common social faith.

In France the liberal or democratic party is sure to triumph over an obsolete royalism and, after all, ought to do so since it has the charter on its side and is asking for no more than the fulfilment of the charter. Everyone is really hoping for a new order to replace the royalist régime and, without avowing it, is calling for a revolution. The revolution will be only another stage in God's providential chastening of the nations who have abandoned his law. The struggle between anarchy and despotism, which has been going on since the time of Louis XIV (as Lamennais has now learned to say, from his Belgian friends) will continue for a long time yet. Errors must work themselves out and show to what they lead. There is no way back to health except through suffering and expiation. While christians will support non-christian civil governments on account of the partial and provisional order that they can maintain, yet christians will not be so dependent on them as to be thrown out of gear by the revolutionary upheavals that are to be expected.

In this revolutionary period, the church must detach itself from the struggle for power, and must cease to be entangled in the interests of political parties and civil governments. Instead, she must concentrate on the renewal and propagation of her own faith, so that her own independent vitality may show the way to the eventual rebirth of a christian social order. In this book Lamennais is as hostile as ever to both liberalism and gallicanism, which he takes to represent the principles of anarchy and despotism respectively. But he distinguishes now between liberals and liberalism, and between gallicans and gallicanism. To liberals he says: What you are really seeking is not an anarchical system in which everyone is supposed to be entitled to think and do whatever he likes, but the true freedom wherewith Christ has made his people free. To gallicans he says: What you are really seeking is not an arbitrary despotism, but an order which is founded on moral authority instead of on mere force. To both he says: You will find that christianity alone secures the conditions of freedom by establishing an order that is based on the true source of authority, God himself and his law.

Thus, although, on the face of it, Lamennais was advocating in this book a christian retreat from politics, he was in effect preparing the ground for the new christian political initiative—the liberal catholic initiative—which he will take as soon as the July revolution has removed the last excuse for the illusion that the pre-revolutionary social system had been, or could be, resuscitated.

Meanwhile, his emphasis was upon the duty of the clergy to rally round the supreme pastor in Rome. He, together with the bishops and priests, must realize that the time for temporizing and compromise is past. There should be no more concessions on the church's part. Clearly and boldly, she should now stand out for the essential liberties, and devote herself to her own proper mission. To the clergy, Lamennais says: 'Do you want to save the faith and to secure to the church her essential independence? Then be bishops, be priests, and nothing more. No dignity, no function in the civil order, is compatible today with the liberty of your ministry.'[114]

If the first duty of the clergy is to liberate the church from bondage

[114] O.C., IX, 188.

to the civil power, their second duty is to carry out the Lord's command 'to teach all nations'. This will entail proclaiming the gospel so as to meet the intellectual and moral needs of the new age. To this end the church must set forward a great renovation of theology and of learning generally, and in a notable passage Lamennais strikes again one of the essential notes of the mennaisian movement.

Do not let us be afraid to acknowledge that theology, which in itself is so grand and attractive and all-embracing, is today—as it is taught in most seminaries—only a degenerate and paltry scholasticism. Its barrenness puts the students off, and gives them no idea of the range of religion nor of its wonderful relations with everything of interest to man and with everything that can be the object of his thought. It was not so conceived by St Thomas who, in his immortal works, made it the centre of all the knowledge of his time. Learn from him his admirable method of co-ordinating and generalizing, and combine with it the profound insights, the lofty contemplations, the warmth and life, that characterize the ancient fathers. Then there will be an end of this awful boredom which extinguishes, in young men destined for the priesthood, the taste and even the talent for study. Remove from your curriculum those futile questions that weary them to no useful effect, and waste valuable time which they might much better employ in learning things that have something to do with the age in which they live and with the world in which they must act. Everything around you has changed. Ideas have taken, and are constantly taking, new directions. Institutions, laws, customs, opinions—none are the same as they were in our fathers' time. What is the use of the liveliest enthusiasm without knowledge of the society in which it has got to be exercised? It is necessary now to learn differently, and to learn more: differently, in order to understand better; more, so as not to be behind those whom you are supposed to lead. It is not at all by what they know that the enemies of christianity are strong; but by what its natural defenders do not know. This kind of inferiority . . . weakens specially the influence of the clergy on the educated classes, and is very prejudicial to religion in an age that prides itself upon its enlightenment. . . .

But it is not enough to improve the training of the clergy; one must look further and have a higher aim. For a long time the church held in her hand the sceptre of the sciences, and this is one cause of the ascendancy she acquired over people's minds. This means of action would be more potent now than at any other period, and in this way men could derive advantage from kinds of knowledge which are in themselves morally indifferent, but which infallibly produce more evil than good if the religious principle does not preside over their development.

During the last thirty years immense works have been set in motion and are being carried on by scholars in all countries. It is time that catholic science began to gather in the rich harvest that has been prepared for it. (Lamennais then runs through the different branches of learning—historical, literary, scientific, moral, and metaphysical—which were rapidly expanding, and he sums up:) The church then—even in the sphere of purely human learning—has a magnificent role before her: it is for her to make the wilderness blossom and for a second time to separate light from darkness.[115]

Within a fortnight of its publication 6,000 copies of Des Progrès are said to have been sold.[116] It is difficult for us to imagine the sense of shock and scandal that was caused by Lamennais's abandoning the claim of the church to a position of exclusive privilege, for we have become accustomed to members of an established church demanding liberation from 'bondage' to the state. Perhaps the nearest parallel in our own history was the conversion—exactly a hundred years later, as it happened[117]—of Bishop Hensley Henson to the cause of disestablishing the Church of England, in apparent contradiction to what he had previously stood for. But English churchmen were much less scandalized by Henson's change of ground than Lamennais's contemporaries were by his.

There were speedy repercussions. Mgr de Quélen, Archbishop of Paris, and other bishops as well, included in the pastoral letters which they issued on the occasion of Pope Leo XII's death (10 February 1829) passages directed against Lamennais's latest manifesto. He was accused of introducing a dangerous division into the church's ranks and of proclaiming without any authority or mission 'doctrines

115 O.C., IX, 192–195. The original French of this passage is for the most part reproduced in Appendix II of my book, The Modernist Movement in the Roman Church.

116 See Foisset, Vie du R. P. Lacordaire, I, 130.

117 See Henson's article 'Disestablishment by Consent' in the January 1929 issue of the Nineteenth Century and After and his second Quadrennial Charge as Bishop of Durham.

subversive of the order which Jesus Christ established on earth',
etc.[118] Lamennais was in no mood to take such rebukes submissively
nor to lose an opportunity of sharpening his attack on gallicanism.
The two open letters which in March and April 1829 he addressed
to the archbishop[119] have been, not unjustly, described as master-
pieces of polemic.[120] I dare say that to 'anglo-catholics' it would
seem to be all in the day's work, but I doubt whether any roman-
catholic priest in good standing has ever publicly attacked his
ecclesiastical superiors with such devastating irony and with such
lofty disdain. It seemed as though—the holy see being vacant—
Lamennais had taken upon himself to be the pope's deputy and to
show how craven and misguided bishops should be dealt with.

There were rumours which Lamennais himself believed,[121] and
which used to be credited by his biographers,[122] to the effect that
the French government instructed its minister in Rome (who was
at this time Chateaubriand) to get *Des Progrès* put on the index, but
Père Dudon has assured us that there is no trace of this proceeding
either in the Vatican Archives or in the Archives of the French
Ministry of Foreign Affairs.[123]

I have been giving the impression that during these years Lamennais was entirely employed in writing books, in journalism, and in
corresponding with his friends.[124] That was very far from being the
case. The reason why in 1830 he emerged as the leader of an impressive movement in the Church of France was that he had done
much more than use his pen to predict and prepare for the collapse
of the Bourbon monarchy. A purely literary leadership would have
led to no concerted action. It was doubtless a great asset to the
mennaisian movement that it could point to Lamennais's books for
the adumbration of the new apologetics and the new politics which
were its guiding ideas. But what made the movement a *movement* was
the fact that Lamennais had with him, first, a company of able and
ardent young disciples, a militant school of thought, and secondly,
a closely knit religious community with an outward-looking and

[118] See *O.C.*, IX, 333 ff.   [119] See *O.C.*, IX, 331–424.
[120] Boutard, II, 54, citing Spuller.   [121] See Forgues, II, 19, 24, 26.
[122] E.g. see Boutard, II, 56.   [123] *L. et le S.S.*, p. 76.
[124] The number and length and quality of Lamennais's letters that have survived
may give rise to mistaken ideas about the place occupied by correspondence
in his daily routine. It has even been said that he must have written fifteen
letters a day; it would probably be nearer the mark to say that he wrote on an
average one letter a day. See Harispe, *Lamennais* (1924), pp. 161 f.

forward-looking ethos, and thirdly, beyond these inner circles, many well-wishers and sympathizers not only among the younger clergy but also among the younger clerisy. In order that our picture of the mennaisian movement shall be tolerably complete, it is necessary that I should say something about each of these, namely, the School of La Chesnaie, the Congregation of St Peter, and the younger clerisy. The relation between the School of La Chesnaie and the Congregation of St Peter was involved and need not be fully unravelled here: they stand for two distinct elements in the mennaisian strategy.

(I) Henri Bremond said that it is at La Chesnaie, and not in the editorial offices of the *Avenir*, 'that one must look for the centre, the home, and the authentic atmosphere, intellectual and religious, of the mennaisian school'.[125] The origin of the School of La Chesnaie[126] can be traced to the association of Lamennais in 1823-1824 with two young priests who were chaplains of the Lycée Henri IV in Paris—abbé de Salinis[127] and abbé Gerbet.[128] Like Lamennais they were dreaming dreams of an intellectual and literary catholic revival in France. In 1824 they founded *Le Mémorial catholique*,[129] a monthly journal, which became the principal organ of the mennaisians till it made way for the *Avenir* in 1830. Salinis and Gerbet had already drawn together in Paris a group of gifted young men who were inspired by their ideals and who met regularly to study and discuss the faith. Many of the catholic writers who made their mark later in the century in literature, in politics, or in theology had been members of this group in their youth.[130]

[125] Bremond, *Gerbet* (1907), pp. 10 f.

[126] See Boutard, I, chap. 22, 'Les commencements de l'École menaisienne'; Ricard, *Lamennais* (1895), chap. 6, 'Fondation et débuts de l'École menaisienne'; Charles Sainte-Foi, *Souvenirs de Jeunesse*, chap. 2, 'L'École menaisienne'. 'Les problèmes de l'École de la Chênaie' by abbé Kerbiriou, which appeared in *La Revue de l'Ouest*, 1935, was a doctorate thesis; it contains little that is original.

[127] De Salinis (1798-1861) became later director of the College de Juilly, professor of theology at Bordeaux, Bishop of Amiens, and finally Archbishop of Auch. See Ricard, *Gerbet et Salinis*.

[128] Philippe-Olympe Gerbet (1798-1864), who became eventually Bishop of Perpignan, was reckoned by Henri Bremond to be, after Lamennais, the greatest French religious writer of the nineteenth century: see his *Gerbet*, pp. v, xi. Cp. Sainte-Beuve, II, 279. See also de Ladoue, *Monseigneur Gerbet; sa vie, ses œuvres et l'école menaisienne* (1872)—Books II, III, and IV of Volume I deal with Gerbet's relations with Lamennais; Charles Sainte-Foi, *Souvenirs de Jeunesse*, pp. 66-69. [129] Cp. Forgues, I, 45 ff.

[130] Boutard, I, 366, mentions the following: Edmond de Cazalès, Louis de Carné, Frantz de Champagny, Bonnetty, E. de La Gournerie, Emmanuel d'Alzon, Foisset, Léon and Eugène Boré, and Melchior du Lac.

When Lamennais was in Paris, he used to attend their gatherings. The intellectual vitality of these young men and their ardent devotion to the cause of the church made such an impression on him that he conceived the idea of forming a similar association on a larger scale which would unite his friends and followers in dedication to a catholic renaissance. Each member of the association would have his own individual contribution to make to the work of the whole—it might be in philosophy, theology, history, literature, the natural sciences, ancient or modern languages. The idea amounted to the production of a new encyclopedia, a catholic encyclopedia, that would efface the memory of the famous encyclopedia of the eighteenth century.[131]

This conception seemed rather too grandiose to the prosaic Salinis, but it captured the imagination of Gerbet who threw in his lot entirely with Lamennais and became his closest and most dependable disciple. They were thoroughly kindred spirits; the disciple was all the more helpful to the master because he was happily free from his turbulence and susceptibility to moods of melancholy. On 16 January 1825 Gerbet who had just arrived at La Chesnaie for the first time wrote to Salinis:

> M. de Lamennais has been thinking over the project for a society of ecclesiastics, which he has often discussed with us, and he considers that a beginning could be made by bringing together four or five with a view to writing and studying. A suitable place could be found in Britanny. The income accruing from the works that this society would produce would go far towards maintaining the establishment. . . .[132]

Lamennais and Gerbet had already had to moderate their first enthusiasm. An attempt to raise a large sum of money to launch the kind of institution they had in view had been fruitless, and in the

---

[131] See Boutard, I, 370. The aim of the mennaisian school was well described by Harispe, *Lamennais*, p. 10, as follows: 'L'école menaisienne . . . n'avait d'autre but que de former, au centre du catholicisme, un foyer de lumière dans toutes les branches des sciences humaines et divines, un foyer d'œuvres de bienfaisance, économiques, sociales et religieuses, pour, de là, les disperser dans le monde comme autant de rayons d'un même soleil qui réchauffent la terre et la fécondent. Elle ne voulait pas que l'Église fut une quémandeuse de science. Elle voulait qu'elle les eut toutes dans son sein, qu'elle ne fut jamais obligée de faire emprunt de savoir à autrui et qu'on lui reprochât son ignorance en quoi que ce fût.'

[132] See de Ladoue, *Mgr Gerbet*, I, 66.

end they decided that La Chesnaie itself, despite the modest size of the house, had best be the centre of their enterprise. Even so, two or three years elapsed—during which period Lamennais underwent a very serious illness—before they were joined by new recruits. The School of La Chesnaie flourished only from 1828 to 1833, but during those years it was as much a burning and a shining light in the Church of France as the tractarian school was in the Church of England when Newman was at the height of his power and influence.

To La Chesnaie came many young men—gifted and gay and aflame with idealism; they stayed for various periods,[133] and went away feeling that they had had a part assigned to them in a great movement of the spirit and that they were disciples of an incomparable master. Not that Lamennais sought to impose himself or his own style or interests upon his disciples. On the contrary, his art was to stimulate and encourage their minds to grow and flower each in the manner appropriate to its native genius.[134] 'We each follow in our studies our natural taste and tendency,' wrote one young man soon after his arrival, 'we all have only one end in view: the science of God, the catholic science; but we are making for it by different routes, thus accomplishing the great law of diversity in unity.'[135]

Many have taken in hand to conjure up in words the quality of the common life of Lamennais and his disciples at La Chesnaie during these most fruitful years. Perhaps, the best description is to be found in the *Souvenirs de Jeunesse* of Éloi Jourdain (1805–1861), but it is

133 When Lacordaire first visited La Chesnaie in 1830, he says there were a dozen young men there with Lamennais and Gerbet. See Foisset, *Vie du R. P. Lacordaire*, I, 144.

134 Cp. Duine, p. 120: 'Pour les jeunes gens, il [Lamennais] était d'un esprit très large dans le choix des lectures. Aussi bien ne cherchait-il pas à les enchaîner dans un règlement qui tyrannisât leur journée entière et les réduisît à être des produits uniformes. Il désirait plutôt permettre à leurs aptitudes diverses de se manifester normalement, et il savait le prix de la liberté pour le développement de l'intelligence et la joie du cœur. Son rôle était essentiellement celui d'un excitateur d'âmes.' For the variety of talents which Lamennais drew out, in different members of the school, see Harispe, *op. cit.*, pp. 10 f. Ricard, *Lamennais*, pp. 121 f., points out that the members of the school came from many different parts of France.

See also Laveille, *J.-M. de La Mennais*, I, 443; Roussel, *Lamennais intime*, pp. 4 f.

135 Maurice de Guérin, letter of 25 December 1832, in his *Correspondance* (ed. B. d'Harcourt), p. 65. See pp. 219 f., *infra*, for further extracts from his letters about the way of life at La Chesnaie and about the impression Lamennais made on him.

much too long for reproduction here. Jourdain, who wrote under the pseudonym of Charles Sainte-Foi, lived at La Chesnaie for some time in 1828–1829, and in his *Souvenirs* (which were not published in full till 1911) he paints a vivid picture of Lamennais and Gerbet, and explains the influence they had on those who were drawn to them.

Although Gerbet in his letter to Salinis, which was quoted above, spoke of 'a society of ecclesiastics' as what Lamennais had projected, in point of fact the members of the School of La Chesnaie were for the most part neither priests nor destined for the priesthood. Lamennais was clearly convinced that laymen as well as priests had an essential part to play in the revival of catholic thought and action.[136] La Chesnaie stood primarily for the lay wing of the mennaisian movement. But the better training of the clergy and a new pattern of priestly and community life had always been one of Lamennais's aims, and we shall now see how it came about that the mennaisian provision for the training of a new kind of clergy was made elsewhere than at La Chesnaie.

(II) In their first book, *Réflexions*, Féli and Jean, as we have seen,[137] had advocated forms of community life for the clergy who were engaged in the ordinary ministry of the church—different, that is, from that of the regular religious orders. They had also urged the foundation of christian schools for the children of the poor. It may well be that this part of *Réflexions* was chiefly the work of abbé Jean and reflected his special *desiderata* for the renewal of the church. Anyhow, in 1819 he had taken an important initiative in the field of christian education by founding the *Frères de l'Instruction Chrétienne*, the community of teaching brothers, which has proved to be the most enduring and valuable outcome of his life's work.[138] The foundation of the *Congrégation de Saint Pierre* in 1828 was his translation into practice of the idea of a community life for the clergy who were engaged in parish, missionary, and educational work.

The opportunity to make a move in this direction came soon after abbé Jean had ceased to be vicar-general to the Grand Almoner of France.[139] About the same time two groups of priests in the diocese

---

[136] Laveille writes in *J.-M. de La Mennais*, I, 442: 'Félicité de la Mennais avait résolu de constituer en France un parti catholique. Pour cela, il se proposait de faire entrer les laïques dans la vie générale de l'Église, et de leur mettre, au besoin, entre les mains des armes de combat. C'était hardi; cela ne s'était pas vu depuis des siècles; raison de plus pour que l'idée fît son chemin.'

[137] See p. 48, *supra*.   [138] Cp. p. 41, *supra*.   [139] See p. 102, *supra*.

of Rennes evinced a desire to form themselves into communities for the better carrying on of their work: one consisted of members of the staff of the diocesan *petit séminaire* at Saint-Méen, the other of the diocesan missioners who had a house in Rennes itself. The bishop approved, and appointed abbé Jean as director; towards the end of 1825 the two communities were united under abbé Jean as superior-general.[140]

In the latter part of 1828, when the company of priests and lay-men around Lamennais at La Chesnaie was increasing, it was agreed by all concerned to start a new foundation to be known as the Congregation of St Peter,[141] which would fuse with the existing community such members of the School of La Chesnaie as desired to make this further commitment, including M. Féli himself. In fact, at the instance of abbé Jean, Féli became superior-general in his stead.[142] It was also decided to concentrate the training of those members of the Congregation[143] who were called to the priest-hood at Malestroit (about forty-five miles from La Chesnaie) where a former conventual building was acquired for the purpose.[144] At first Lamennais intended to move there himself,[145] but as it turned out he appears never to have paid more than one or two occasional visits.[146] But as superior-general of the whole community he took a close interest in all that went on at Malestroit, as did also Gerbet who remained with him at La Chesnaie and who was in effect prior of the community.[147]

140 See Laveille, *op. cit.*, I, 425 ff.
141 So-called of course because of its ultramontane orientation. It was a rule of the community to recite the Roman breviary, a rule that at the time was novel in France. See Laveille, *op. cit.*, I, 449.
142 A document that has only lately come to light suggests that Féli was elected superior because it was thought this would help in obtaining the approbation of the Congregation's constitution at Rome, and that Féli at once delegated the exercise of his powers as superior to Jean. See Y. Le Hir, 'Un document inédit sur Lamennais et la Congrégation de Saint Pierre' in *Annales de Bretagne*, 1949, LVI, 69.
143 Laveille, *op. cit.*, I, 546 f., gives a list of about sixty former students at Malestroit, though not all of these became priests or members of the Congregation of St Peter.
144 See Forgues, I, 465.
145 See his letter of 14 November 1828 to Countess de Senfft in Forgues, I, 485, and other letters of the same period.
146 See Roussel, *Documents*, II, 247.
147 This interest is illustrated by letters that have survived from abbé Blanc, who was superior at Malestroit, to Lamennais and Gerbet: see Roussel, *op. cit.*, I, 227-235.

The constitution of the Congregation of St Peter, which was drawn up by Lamennais and his brother, is of considerable interest.[148] It shows what they meant by the need for a new type of religious community. For example, it was to be more flexible and mobile than the traditional religious orders, less publicly recognizable, and therefore better qualified to go underground, if necessary, and less easily suppressed by civil governments.[149] Lamennais himself was hardly qualified by temperament to be the superior-general of a religious community,[150] despite his extraordinary power of kindling the devotion of young men. Nevertheless, his ideas about religious communities were not the least far-sighted and fertile part of his conception of a catholic renaissance.[151] Père Dudon observed that the founders or restorers of three religious orders in France in the nineteenth century had been disciples of Lamennais, namely Dom Guéranger[152] of the Benedictines, Père Lacordaire[153] of the Dominicans, and Père d'Alzon[154] of the Augustinians, though they aimed at reviving old forms of the religious life, whereas Lamennais aimed at creating a new form.

The training of ordinands at Malestroit was informed by a spirit that was not then, and perhaps is not now, altogether characteristic of ecclesiastical seminaries.[155] The whole household assembled for

[148] See Paul Dudon on 'Lamennais Fondateur d'Ordre' in *Études*, 20 November 1910, pp. 449–473.

[149] The constitution of the Congregation of St Peter contained the following passage: 'À raison des changements nombreux survenus dans la société, dans les lois, les idées, les mœurs, et de l'état de révolution qui doit se prolonger longtemps encore, les ordres anciens rencontreraient des obstacles insurmontables. Trop exposés aux regards, trop aisés à atteindre, ils succomberaient bientôt aux persécutions que l'impiété leur susciterait. Il faut, en ces tristes temps, un ordre à la fois mobile et fort, qu'on ne puisse saisir sous aucune forme rigoureusement déterminée, qui s'applique à tous les genres d'œuvre sans dépendre d'aucune.' See Dudon, *ibid.*, p. 458.

[150] Cp. Boutard, II, 74.

[151] Laveille, *op. cit.*, I, 446 f., points out that the statutes of the Congregation of St Peter anticipated ideas that were later acted upon in the Church of Rome.

[152] On Guéranger, see E. Sevrin, *Dom Guéranger et La Mennais* (1933).

[153] On Lacordaire, see T. Foisset, *Vie du R. P. Lacordaire*, 2 vols (1870).

[154] On Alzon, see Siméon Vailhé, *Vie du P. Emmanuel d'Alzon, 1810–1880*, 2 vols (1926); also G. de Grandmaison, 'Lettres de La Mennais à Emmanuel Alzon' in *Le Mois littéraire et pittoresque*, July–December, 1901.

[155] See A. Laveille on 'Lamennais et les études ecclésiastiques' in *Revue du clergé français*, 1 November 1897, pp. 391–409. Laveille notes that, while Lamennais's *Essai* was naturally much studied at Malestroit, St Thomas Aquinas and St Alphonsus Liguori were also used, contrary to the fashion of the time. 'On

mental prayer and mass in the early morning; apart from that, everyone was left to make such spiritual exercises as seemed good to him at his own times. The bulk of the day was given to study, with intervals for recreation and conversation when there was much exciting and also humorous play of mind. The same comprehensive range of subjects, secular as well as sacred, was studied at Malestroit as at La Chesnaie, and each student was encouraged to specialize according to his aptitudes and attractions. Everyone had to learn at least three languages,[156] so as to have access to as wide a field of culture as possible. There do not appear to have been the conventional courses of lectures, but there were seminars in which all were free to take an active part. Lamennais insisted that everyone should strive not only to think clearly but also to write well. Students even were not discouraged from attempting essays in journalism, but these had to be submitted to severe criticism at La Chesnaie and often never saw the light of day.[157]

Perhaps the most revealing clue to what the Congregation of St Peter aimed at producing is to be found in an underlined expression in a letter from the superior at Malestroit to Lamennais about one of the students there. In spite of some progress this student is reported to be lacking in 'cet élan qui doit être un de nos caractères'.[158] By 1830 Lamennais knew that he had behind him a substantial body of able and devoted young men who possessed just that characteristic, and consequently he was able to launch the campaign of the Avenir with an immoderate degree of hopefulness.

(III) It would be an entire mistake to suppose that the influence or following of the mennaisian school was confined to the groups of professed disciples who had actually been enrolled at La Chesnaie or at Malestroit. There were convinced mennaisians all over France. Men who had never met Lamennais regarded themselves as his disciples equally with those who had stayed with him at La

mettait entre les mains des ordinands saint Thomas pour le dogme et saint Liguori pour la morale. C'était pour le temps une grande hardiesse: ces deux auteurs, dont l'enseignement théologique de nos jours s'inspire à peu près partout, étaient alors bannis des séminaires.' See also Charles Sainte-Foi, *Souvenirs de Jeunesse*, chap. 3, 'À Malestroit'.

[156] At La Chesnaie Lamennais himself taught five or six languages as well as philosophy and theology. See Forgues, I, 492; *Lamennais inconnu*, pp. 224 f., 227.
[157] See Boutard, II, 78-82.
[158] See Roussel, *Documents*, I, 234. Cp. L. Kerbiriou on 'Un Centre intellectue mennaisien: L'École de Malestroit' in *Nouvelle Revue de Bretagne*, January-February 1949, pp. 31-38.

Chesnaie.[159] Moreover, there were others—a significant if heterogeneous group—whom I described as sympathizers with mennaisianism among the younger clerisy. These were men on or beyond the frontiers of the church, who might have been finally drawn inside if they had seen a practical demonstration of the reconciliation of the catholic faith with the liberal, critical, and reforming spirit of the age. They watched with sympathy, and even actively encouraged, Lamennais's attempt to persuade the pope as head of the church to lead a movement towards free political institutions and the regeneration of society. What hopes they had of a catholic renaissance were destroyed by the condemnation of the *Avenir*. But, at the point which we have now reached, they could be counted on as at least marginal collaborators in the campaign that Lamennais was about to launch—collaborators who could give worthy literary expression to any creed that they made their own.[160]

There was Lamartine (1790–1869) who, as we have seen,[161] had been enchanted when in 1818 he read the first volume of the *Essai sur l'indifférence*—who when in the following year he had met its author had exclaimed 'L'abbé de Lamennais: c'est Pascal ressuscité'[162] —and in whose poetry, correspondence, and conversion to catholicism (such as it was) the influence of Lamennais can be definitely traced.[163] Lamartine in fact accompanied Lamennais in the evolution of his political ideas, became in due course a partisan of the pro-

---

[159] E.g. Guéranger, who did not meet Lamennais till 1830, wrote to him on 12 April 1829: 'Veuillez bien, Monsieur l'abbé, me regarder toujours comme votre disciple bien dévoué et bien reconnaissant. . . .'—Sevrin, *Dom Guéranger et La Mennais*, p. 32. Again, writing to Gerbet, whom he had recently met, on 27 October 1829 he spoke of 'notre commun maître' and 'nos communs travaux', *ibid.*, p. 44. See also *ibid.*, p. 55.

[160] When Lamennais had first met Victor Hugo in 1821 he had said of him: 'Il donnera des ailes à la pensée catholique, que nos écrivains pieux traînent souvent sur les pavés et même dans les ruisseaux de la rue.' See Goyau, *Portefeuille*, p. 13.

[161] See pp. 71 f., *supra*.

[162] See Maréchal, *Lamennais et Lamartine*, p. 85. For the influence of Lamennais on the romantic movement, see Amalie Hoiss, *Histoire d'un livre*, chap. 3, 'Lamennais et le romantisme.'

[163] See Maréchal, *Lamennais et Lamartine*, *passim*. Maréchal maintained that Lamartine was no philosopher or thinker himself and simply took over his philosophical ideas from Lamennais. Émile Faguet in an article in *La Revue latine*, 25 November 1907, while acknowledging that Maréchal had demonstrated Lamartine's indebtedness to Lamennais, questioned his assertion that Lamartine was not a philosopher. In the same *Revue*, 25 February 1908, in an article entitled, 'Lamartine est-il philosophe?', Maréchal replied, maintaining what he had previously said.

gram of the *Avenir*, and abandoned catholicism only after the papal encyclical *Mirari vos* had been promulgated.[164]

Then there was Victor Hugo (1802–1885); brought up as a royalist, but as a voltairian sceptic, he had been drawn to catholicism first by Chateaubriand's *Génie du Christianisme*, and then more firmly by Lamennais's *Essai*.[165] In 1821 he was brought into personal touch with Lamennais, to whom he made his first confession. Lamennais continued to be his spiritual director as well as his intellectual guide and close friend for several years.[166] Hugo for his part persuaded the mennaisians, or some of them, to transfer their allegiance from classicism to romanticism in literature.[167]

Hugo went along with Lamennais in the direction of political liberalism. Although when the 1830 revolution occurred they were no longer in close touch and Hugo's faith as a catholic had been seriously shaken,[168] yet early in September he wrote to Lamennais with undiminished ardour and affection, urging him to put himself at the head of a thoroughly liberal catholicism and promising that all the younger generation would follow him.[169] One of Lamennais's

164 Maréchal, *op. cit.*, pp. 259-269, shows this by comparing Lamartine's original manuscript notes for his *Voyage en Orient* with the published version. Subsequently, Lamartine also followed Lamennais in embracing a liberal or social form of christianity that was quite detached from catholic orthodoxy.

165 On the relations of Lamennais and Hugo, see Maréchal, *Lamennais et Victor Hugo* (1906); E. Terrade on 'Lamennais et Victor Hugo; influence du prêtre breton sur la jeunesse et le génie du poète' in *Reflets du passé* (1908), pp. 215-241; and also Pierre Dubois, *Victor Hugo: ses idées religieuses de 1802 à 1825* (1913), especially pp. 340-363. Dubois considers that Maréchal had exaggerated Lamennais's influence on Hugo. But see also Henri Girard on 'La pensée religieuse des romantiques' in *Revue d'histoire littéraire de la France*, 1925, pp. 79-97.

166 See Hugo's letters to Lamennais published in Goyau, *Portefeuille*.

167 Contrast the article, 'Du principe d'autorité dans la littérature' which appeared in the first two numbers of *Le Mémorial catholique* (1824; I, 49-60, 96-101) with those on the same subject which appeared in 1828-1829 (x, 173-184, 377-388; xi, 65-77; xii, 349-356). On Lamennais's own position *vis-à-vis* classicism and romanticism in literature, see Y. Le Hir, *Lamennais écrivain* (1948).

168 Sainte-Beuve's seductive incursion into his life and marriage may have contributed to the shaking of his faith. See Maréchal, *op. cit.*, pp. 121, ff.

169 On 7 September 1830 Hugo wrote to Lamennais: 'Personne, vous le savez, ne contemple avec plus de joie et de bonheur que moi la beauté de votre âme et de votre génie. Voici votre mission que s'agrandit. Je vous bats des mains. Votre voie se rétrécissait de jour en jour, étouffée qu'elle était entre le misérable gallicanisme des vieilles sacristies et les folles vanités d'un clergé de cour et de places. Notre belle révolution d'ordre et de liberté a jeté bas tout ce qui obstruait votre chemin. Maintenant allez! il y a place et large place, il y a route et

first acts, when shortly afterwards he arrived in Paris to launch the *Avenir*, was to call on Victor Hugo.[170] After its condemnation, Hugo became completely estranged from catholicism.[171]

It is less easy to be sure how far Sainte-Beuve (1804–1869) was a sincere mennaisian and whether the 'conversions' to catholicism which took place while he was in personal relations with Lamennais were genuine.[172] There certainly were times during the period of their friendship (1827–1836) when Sainte-Beuve was strongly influenced by Lamennais and appeared to be in earnest about becoming a practising catholic.[173] We shall find him at a critical moment commissioned to act as Lamennais's representative.[174] It was the papal encyclicals *Mirari vos* and *Singulari nos* that determined Sainte-Beuve to break once for all with his catholic past, such as it had been.[175]

Another man of letters, already advanced on the path of fame, who has been discovered in the precincts of the mennaisian temple is Alfred de Vigny (1799–1863).[176] It must be confessed that he was attracted more by Lamennais's than by God's presence within the veil. De Vigny, despite his scepticism and even because of it, was drawn to ultramontane catholicism somewhat as Charles Maurras

large route pour vous, pour votre libre catholicisme, pour vos saines réformes, pour votre alliance de l'Église et de la liberté dans l'avenir. Toute la jeune nation vous aime, vous admire, et sympathise avec vous. Mettez-vous à la tête d'un catholicisme libéral, et tous vous suivront.' See Goyau, *Portefeuille*, p. 95. Hugo had seen Gerbet just before he wrote this letter and had no doubt been apprised of Lamennais's latest intentions. Hugo's enthusiasm for the cause of the *Avenir* is confirmed by Montalembert's journal, see Lallemand, *Montalembert et ses amis dans le romantisme*, pp. 124–135.

[170] See Maréchal, *Lamennais et Victor Hugo*, p. 135.

[171] On 4 December 1832 Montalembert wrote to Lamennais: 'Victor Hugo . . . devient de jour en jour . . . plus étranger à la religion.' See *M. à L.*, p. 24.

[172] On the relations of Lamennais and Sainte-Beuve, see Maréchal, *La Clef de 'Volupté'* (1905); cp. F. Mourret, *Le Mouvement catholique en France, 1830–1850* (1917), p. 40; Sainte-Beuve, II, 321, 323.

[173] See his letters to Lamennais of 24 May and 2 August 1831 in Goyau, *Portefeuille*, pp. 98–102.

[174] See p. 242, *infra*.

[175] See Maréchal, *La Clef de 'Volupté'*, p. 79.

[176] For the influence of Lamennais on de Vigny, see M. Citoleux's article, 'Alfred de Vigny et La Mennais', in *Annales de Bretagne*, July 1916, pp. 301–322. Cp. Goyau, *Portefeuille*, p. 19; Lecanuet, *Montalembert*, I, 146 f.; Paul Vulliaud, *Les 'Paroles d'un Croyant' de Lamennais*, pp. 33 f.; Victor Giraud on 'Catholicisme et romantisme' in *Revue des deux mondes*, 1 July 1937, pp. 146–153, where Lamennais's influence on Lamartine and Hugo is also noted.

was at a later date. In the author of the *Essai sur l'indifférence* he had perceived a priest who was capable of infusing reverence for tradition together with religious warmth and idealism into the hard materialism of the age. It was the apostle of authority, not of democracy, that had appealed to de Vigny, but at his own request he became a collaborator of the *Avenir*.[177]

Mention should also be made of the relations between Lamennais and Auguste Comte (1798–1857).[178] There were natural affinities between their ways of thinking,[179] in particular their common recognition that there could not be a regeneration of society without religion. In 1826–1827 Comte had come to some extent under the influence of Lamennais, whom he even styled his 'confessor'. Once again, it has been demonstrated that Balzac (1799–1850) was considerably influenced by Lamennais and Gerbet, as well as by Maistre and Bonald.[180]

Thus, when the collapse of the Bourbon monarchy at last took place, and the leaders of the church were dismayed by the disappearance of the support on which they had depended, Lamennais was well furnished and prepared not only with clear and definite ideas about what catholics ought now to do, but also with an abundance of young and gifted disciples, and with potential allies and collaborators among the most eminent of the predestined guides of the rising generation. They fortified his conviction that the future was on his side.[181]

[177] He contributed to the *Avenir* on 3 April 1831, and his correspondence with Montalembert bears witness to his interest. Cp. Boutard, II, 220.

[178] See Charles Calippe's article, 'Les relations d'Auguste Comte avec Lamennais', in *Revue du clergé français*, 1 October 1918, pp. 17–28. Cp. Boutard, II, 137; P. Lazerges, *Lamennais: essai sur l'unité de sa pensée* (1895), pp. 53 f.

[179] Cp. Maréchal, *Dispute*, pp. 201, 249.

[180] See Philippe Bertault, *Balzac et la Religion* (1942), pp. 443–485.

[181] On 11 November 1828 Lamennais had written to Vitrolles: 'Quant au peu d'influence qu'exerce la religion sur les mœurs publiques. . . . Le mal est partout, et partout bien grand. L'ignorance du clergé l'augmente encore. Une vaste réforme est indispensable, et elle se fera, à cause de cela même. Il y a un poids immense à soulever; mais, plus heureux qu'Archimède, nous avons un point d'appui. Je consacre à cette œuvre, que le temps accomplira, ce qui me reste de vie. J'ai déjà quelques jeunes gens que Dieu semble avoir faits exprès pour concourir à ce grand dessein.' *Vitrolles*, p. 180. By 1830 he seemed to have good grounds for still greater confidence.

Chapter Five

FOR GOD AND LIBERTY
1830-1832

A. THE CAMPAIGN OF THE 'AVENIR'

B Y THE BEGINNING OF 1830 it was evident that the reign of
Charles X was approaching its crisis. Indeed, that had been
evident since August 1829, when the king had dismissed the
Martignac ministry, which he had never liked on account of its
moderation and willingness to compromise with liberalism, and in
its place had appointed Prince Jules de Polignac (1780–1847) and
other notorious ultra-royalists. The counter-revolution was now in
the saddle, determined to ride rough-shod, if need be, over the
constitutional charter.[1]

On 8 February 1830, not long before the new session of parliament
was due to open, Lamennais wrote from La Chesnaie to Count de
Senfft:

> We await the opening of the session, which must either kill the
> ministry or prolong its agony and that of the royal house a little
> longer. In any case I see no possibility of avoiding a catastrophe.
> If they leave things to take their course, they are heading for ruin;
> if they attempt some strong measure, they will not be able to
> carry it through, since the masses are against them. There can be
> no way out at present, because there is as much error and evil in
> the government party as there is in the opposition. I regret to
> have to say this, but I do say with deep conviction that it is now
> for the peoples to save themselves with the help and support of
> the church.[2]

[1] The government claimed to be acting in accordance with article xiv of the
charter: 'Le roi est le chef suprême de l'État . . . il . . . *fait les règlements et les
ordonnances nécessaires pour l'exécution des lois et la sécurité de l'État.*' This article
had not of course been intended to provide for the suspension of parliament
and for government by order in council, and when the charter was revised at
the beginning of the reign of Louis-Philippe the ambiguity was removed.

[2] See Forgues, II, 115.

Three months later, when parliament had been dissolved because it had called for a change of government, and new elections were impending, Lamennais wrote to another of his friends:

> Speaking for myself, as a catholic, I declare that there is nothing I am more afraid of than despotism, which in this century and with the ideas that are prevalent would be the death of religion. The church is being suffocated beneath the weight of the fetters which the temporal power has put upon it; and liberty which has been called for in the name of atheism must now be demanded in the name of God.[3]

The king made a foolish attempt to influence the elections by a royal proclamation. They went heavily against the government, and so towards the end of July, hoping that the country's attention would be diverted by the successful outcome of a French naval and military expedition against Algeria,[4] Charles took the fatal step of signing ordinances that were equivalent to an abolition of the constitution and to an assertion of arbitrary power. The opposition reacted immediately; there followed the 'Three Glorious Days' (27, 28, and 29 July), and the triumph of the tricolour. Charles X abdicated, and Louis-Philippe was elected 'King of the French', some modifications having been made in the constitutional charter. Among these we should especially note the suppression of the article that declared the catholic religion to be the religion of the state.

The revolution of July 1830 differed from the great revolution in many respects, not least in the speed and ease with which the transition from one régime to another was accomplished. Its resemblance to the English revolution of 1688 was widely noted at the time.[5] 'Here, thank God,' wrote Lamennais from Brittany on

[3] Letter of 9 May 1830 to Coriolis, see Forgues, II, 138.

[4] On 23 July 1830 Lamennais wrote to Vitrolles: 'En province, je vois tout le monde satisfait de la prise d'Alger, mais sans qu'il en résulte aucun sentiment favorable au ministère: on est étonné de voir à quel point il est dépourvu d'appui dans l'opinion; celle qu'on nomme libérale fait chaque jour de tels progrès, que, laissant à part la partie du peuple qui ne s'occupe aucunement de politique, je ne crains pas de dire que les neuf dixièmes de la population appartiennent maintenant au libéralisme.' See Forgues, II, 155.

[5] Indeed the resemblance was much canvassed beforehand and even influenced what happened in France; see Thureau-Dangin, Le Parti libéral, pp. 460–465. On 30 November 1827 Lamennais had written to Berryer: 'Je vois beaucoup de gens s'inquiéter pour les Bourbons: on n'a pas tort; je crois qu'ils auront la destinée des Stuart.' See Forgues, I, 376.

6 August, 'everything has gone off very quietly and, except for the colour of the flag, it might be said that nothing has changed.'[6] What had in fact changed was that political power had been transferred from the aristocracy to the bourgeoisie, and the replacement of the last of the Bourbons by the citizen-king, who despite his bourgeois manner and way of life and his sending his children to the state schools[7] had no intention of being a mere figure-head, was a fitting symbol of what had occurred.

Another conspicuous respect in which the July revolution differed from '89, and also from '48, was in its anti-clerical animus, and in this it seemed to be a striking vindication of Lamennais's warnings to the church to cut itself free from dependence on the civil power. Until the last minute the leaders of the church had continued to identify its interests with those of the monarchy. Prelates and priests threw themselves into the ultra-royalists' desperate electoral campaign in May and June.[8] 'Nos évêques incorrigibles,' wrote Lamennais to Count de Senfft on 16 June, 'se jettent dans la mêlée, leurs ridicules Mandements à la main, et semblent avoir juré d'ensevelir, sous le trône chancelant de la tyrannie qui les écrase, les derniers restes du christianisme en France.'[9]

Mgr de Quélen, Archbishop of Paris, who was known to be not only a devotee of the Bourbon dynasty, but also in close relations with Prince de Polignac, in a pastoral letter which he published ordering thanksgiving services for the French victory in Algeria, wrote: 'It took only three weeks to humiliate and subdue this moslem who not long since was so proud! So may the enemies of our lord the king be treated everywhere and always; so let all those that rise up against him be confounded.'[10] And when on 14 July the king attended the thanksgiving service in the cathedral of Notre Dame, the archbishop received him at the door with these words: 'So may the Almighty help the Most Christian King who entreats his assistance. His hand is with you, Sire. . . . Your trust in the divine succour and in the protection of Mary, Mother of God, will not be in vain. May Your Majesty soon receive another recompense for your trust! May you soon come to

[6] See Forgues, II, 160; cp. *Lamennais inconnu*, pp. 253 ff.
[7] See *A.A.*, IV, 341; Lucas-Dubreton, *La Restauration et la Monarchie de juillet*, pp. 148, 156.
[8] See Leflon, *La crise révolutionnaire*, p. 418.
[9] See Forgues, II, 148.
[10] See Pasquier, *Mémoires*, VI, 238.

thank the Lord for other victories no less gratifying and no less brilliant!'[11] If these words meant anything, they meant giving the church's blessing in advance to the unconstitutional measures which the king was known to be contemplating, and which a week or two afterwards provoked the revolution.

The church had thus asked for trouble, and it got it. In Paris the archbishop's palace was sacked by the crowds at the same time as the Tuileries. The archbishop himself had to go into hiding. Priests could no longer wear clerical dress in the streets without exposing themselves to abuse. The churches had to be kept shut during the week and were opened only for Sunday services and then not without risk. There were similar outbreaks in the provinces, and some bishops decided to emigrate. The calvaries decorated with fleurs-de-lis, that had been erected during the missions which were a prominent feature of church activity under the Restoration,[12] were in many places destroyed. The church was violently attacked in the press and on the stage. Christianity was represented as moribund.[13]

These popular manifestations of anti-clericalism were tolerated or weakly connived at by the new government, whose primary object was to consolidate its position; but this connivance did not mean that it was bent upon persecuting the church. It is true, as has been said, that in the new constitutional charter catholicism was no longer declared to be the religion of the state; nevertheless, it was declared to be the religion of the majority of Frenchmen, and ministers both of the catholic church and of other denominations were to be paid by the state. The government did not regard the traditional alliance between church and state as having been

11 See Pasquier, *ibid.*; Leflon, *op. cit.*, p. 418; Debidour, p. 412. It was Quélen who, in the hearing of Montalembert, once made the following declaration in the pulpit of Notre Dame: 'Non seulement Jésus-Christ était Fils de Dieu, mais encore il était de très bonne maison du côté de sa mère et il y a d'excellentes raisons de voir en lui l'*héritier légitime* du trône de Judée.' See Lecanuet, *Montalembert*, II, 3.

12 The Bourbons had been referred to in many of the hymns that were used during these missions. The refrain of one of the best-known was as follows:

Vive la France!
Vive le roi!
Toujours en France
Les Bourbons et la foi!

See Thureau-Dangin, *Le Parti libéral*, p. 364.

13 For the foregoing paragraph, see Thureau-Dangin, *L'Église et l'État sous la Monarchie de juillet*, pp. 2–5. Cp. Lecanuet, *Montalembert*, I, 127 ff.; Boutard, II, 111 f., who gives relevant references to the *Avenir*.

terminated; at any rate, it had no intention of abandoning its right to nominate bishops and the other traditional rights of the kings of France.[14]

The new régime at once presented some delicate problems not only to the French hierarchy but to the holy see.[15] We are in a better position to know how delicate they were, since a book was published in 1949 which made use of unpublished documents in the Vatican and other archives.[16]

First, there was the question whether or when the holy see should recognize the government of Louis-Philippe, the stability of which was at first regarded as very uncertain. At the end of August, following the custom of christian monarchs upon their accession, Louis-Philippe addressed a letter to the pope (Pius VIII), but the letter was brief and cavalier in tone and entirely lacking in the unction that usually characterizes pontifical correspondence.[17] The reception of this letter caused some embarrassment at Rome, since a decision had to be made not only about the recognition of the new king of the French, but also about the manner in which he should be addressed. Should he be addressed in the same style as his predecessors or not? As regards the former question, hurried inquiries were set in motion in order to discover the intentions of other European courts. It soon became obvious that the new régime would have to be recognized, so that the real problem was: how should it be done? If Louis-Philippe were recognized in the traditional style, all the legitimists in France as well as their sympathizers elsewhere would be scandalized. If however the customary formulas of recognition were withheld, Louis-Philippe would be offended and would probably make things more difficult for the church.

In the second place, directly after the July revolution a whole crop of difficult questions, requiring a speedy answer, arose in the

---

[14] E.g. when later in the year there was a papal election consequent upon the death of Pius VIII, Louis-Philippe sent a special ambassador to the conclave to claim the traditional rights of the kings of France. See Martin, *La Nonciature de Paris*, pp. 57 f.; cp. *A.A.*, II, 220 f.

[15] See C. Vidal on 'La Monarchie de juillet et le Saint-Siège au lendemain de la Révolution de 1830' in *Revue d'histoire diplomatique*, October–December 1932, pp. 497–517.

[16] Jacques Paul Martin, *La Nonciature de Paris et les affaires ecclésiastiques de France sous le règne de Louis Philippe (1830–1848): contribution à l'histoire de la diplomatie pontificale au xixe siècle, d'après les correspondances diplomatiques et divers documents inédits des Archives Secrètes Vaticanes* (1949).

[17] See Martin, *op. cit.*, p. 16.

Church of France. These were referred to the holy see by the papal nuncio in Paris.[18] 'A thousand questions of conscience have already arisen,' he wrote on 14 August to the cardinal secretary of state (Albani). 'And everyone wants to know what may and what may not be done.'[19] For example, an archbishop asked whether it was lawful to take the oath of fidelity to the new régime and to pray publicly for the king. A bishop was uncertain whether it was in order to celebrate the *Te Deum* for the Glorious Days of July, for which the government had called. Others asked whether the order of the government to place the tricolour in churches should be obeyed.[20]

Pius VIII in principle gave the answer to all these questions when in a brief of 29 September 1830 he directed the French catholics to rally to the new régime.[21] He himself, instead of waiting upon the decision of other governments and despite strong opposition in the sacred college,[22] set the pace both by recognizing the government of Louis-Philippe and by insisting on addressing him in the traditional style: *Carissimo in Christo Filio Nostro Ludovico-Philippo Francorum Regi Christianissimo.*[23] The use of the term 'Most Christian' must have been singularly gratifying to this sceptical monarch, to whom it was a notable advantage, in his relations with foreign powers, to be treated as the heir of the Bourbons.[24] In his letter to the king the pope expressed his confidence that previous agreements between the holy see and the French government would remain in force and would be faithfully observed.[25]

This implied, as it was intended to do, that Rome regarded as

---

[18] Luigi Lambruschini (1776–1854). He was nuncio in Paris from 1827 to 1831. Previously he had been Archbishop of Genoa and had adopted a very friendly attitude to Lamennais. But in Paris he became a strong partisan of Charles X and of the ultra-royalists, in the success of whose cause he expressed confidence up to the last. His position in France after the July revolution was therefore awkward, and he was replaced in 1831. Later, from 1836 to 1846, he was secretary of state to Gregory XVI.

[19] Martin, *op. cit.*, p. 26.   [20] Martin, *op. cit.*, pp. 26 f., 34–47.

[21] See Thureau-Dangin, *L'Église et l'État*, p. 73.

[22] See C. Vidal, *op. cit.*, pp. 501 ff.

[23] Martin, *op. cit.*, pp. 20 ff.

[24] See Leflon, *La crise révolutionnaire*, p. 421; cp. Lecanuet, *Montalembert*, I, 128. Though Louis-Philippe is generally supposed to have been as sceptical as Louis XVIII, he also attended mass regularly; see *A.A.*, v, 397.

[25] Martin, *op. cit.*, pp. 20 f. Lambruschini was much distressed by the pope's decision, see his letter of 16 October 1830 to the cardinal secretary of state quoted *ibid.*, pp. 54 f. Cp. C. Vidal, *op. cit.*, pp. 499 ff.

still in force the existing concordat, which in practice meant the
concordat of 1801 since the concordat of 1817, designed to supersede
that of 1801, had never come into operation owing to the refusal of
the French parliament to ratify it.[26] The working arrangement between the holy see and the French government, which had held
under Louis XVIII and Charles X, was therefore, deliberately and
by tacit agreement, continued,[27] despite objections in France from
the legitimists as well as from the liberal catholics. In a message to
the Archbishop of Paris, a die-hard legitimist, Pius VIII explained
that, in what was certainly a very unfortunate situation for the
church, he was determined to follow a friendly and conciliatory
policy, provided religion was not attacked.[28]

Thus, though this was not publicly known at the time, both the
papacy and the July monarchy had each decided that the most
prudent course was to maintain and to make the best of the existing
church–state relationship. It follows that an agitation for a radical
disturbance of that relationship, or for the separation of church and
state, would be viewed with equal disfavour by the holy see and by
the French government. Moreover, it goes without saying that the
gallican bishops, most of whom fondly imagined that the new
régime could not last, would not take at all kindly to so revolutionary an idea. It is perhaps fortunate that Lamennais and his friends who
launched the *Avenir* did not realize how heavy were the obstacles in
the way of the success of their campaign: otherwise, their idea of
a liberal catholicism, instead of being an infant prodigy, might have
been still-born.

We can now return to the mennaisian reactions to the July
revolution. The way the wind was blowing at La Chesnaie can be
inferred from the following letters which Lamennais wrote early in
September 1830 to members of the Senfft family, who had been
alarmed by rumours of new mennaisian moves that had reached
them in Italy.

There is no need for you to worry about me: my doctrines
have not changed, and they will not change; but their application
changes, and must change with events. There are many things
which you cannot see or judge at such a distance. Generally speaking, everything boils down to the following points:

[26] See Debidour, pp. 348–357.
[27] See Martin, *op. cit.*, pp. 27–34.
[28] See Thureau-Dangin, *L'Église et l'État*, pp. 73 f.

Everywhere the church is oppressed by governments; it would perish if this state of affairs should continue. Therefore the church must be set free, which can be done only by totally separating it from the state. . . .

As regards France, I have no doubt that we have got to go through awful and difficult times: there is nothing I have said on that score that I do not still hold to. But every situation prescribes its own duties, and all the duties of our present situation are, to my mind, concentrated in one, namely to arrest the anarchy which threatens us, and consequently to uphold without hesitation the existing civil power, so long as, in defending itself, it defends us from the furies of jacobinism. And what will jacobinism do, if it triumphs? It will persecute religion, it will abolish all christian education, it will violently attack persons, property, and all rights. What then must we demand? Religious liberty, liberty of education, liberty of persons and property, that is to say the enjoyment of those rights without which society cannot even be said to exist; in other words, precisely what I have never stopped calling for during the last fifteen years. And how can one continue to call for these things without liberty of the press? Destroy that, and there is nothing left to do but to bow the head beneath all the tyrannies.

There is no way of salvation then either in the future or in the present except with liberty and by liberty.[29]

A few days later, Lamennais wrote to another member of the same family:

Broadly speaking, there are today three parties in France: the jacobin party which is strong because of its violence and drive. . . . The royalist party, which is as stupid and absurd as it always has been; all it can do is to raise scares, to disunite and to dissolve . . . it makes for anarchy much more dangerously than the jacobins themselves. Finally, there is the party, incomparably the most numerous, of those men who are disposed to unite for the maintenance of order, on a wide basis of liberty. What they lack is something to draw them together, an organization with which they have not yet been able to provide themselves, and which is held back by the remains of old prejudices and suspicions: it is to this last party that all the clergy, with the exception of some incorrigible gallicans, will soon belong.[30]

[29] Letter of 5 September 1830 to Mlle Louise de Senfft. See Forgues, II, 169 f.
[30] Letter of 13 September 1830 to Countess de Senfft. See Forgues, II, 171.

In the same letter Lamennais said that he was leaving La Chesnaie on the following day (14 September 1830) for Paris where he expected to stay for four or five weeks. In point of fact, he was going to try to give the liberals the leadership, the organ, and the organization, which he considered that they needed if they were to preserve France from the perils of despotism and anarchy; in doing so, he would be acting on his own precept: 'On tremble devant le libéralisme: eh bien, catholicisez-le, et la Société renaîtra.'[31]

The author of the idea of founding a new daily newspaper as the organ of liberal catholicism was a man about whom little seems to be known: Harel du Tancrel.[32] He first approached Gerbet who was in Paris at the time of the July revolution, and through Gerbet Lamennais's co-operation was secured. By the beginning of September arrangements for the publication of the *Avenir* had been decided on,[33] and the capital required was being subscribed by 'des hommes honorables de divers partis'.[34] Though Lamennais was from the outset the best-known and most influential member of the editorial staff he was not himself the actual editor-in-chief, at least not at first.[35]

---

[31] See Forgues, II, 106.

[32] F. Mourret, *Le Mouvement catholique en France de 1830 à 1850* (1917), pp. 75 f., writes: ' Le nom de celui qui avait pris l'initiative de cette fondation (*sc.* the *Avenir*) et recueilli, pour la réaliser, un modeste capital, est aujourd'hui universellement oublié. Il s'appelait Harel du Tancrel. C'est lui qui eut le titre de rédacteur en chef, mais son prestige devait bientôt s'effacer devant le prestige grandissant de ses collaborateurs. Il eut alors le mérite très appréciable de ne point s'en aigrir et de rentrer sans bruit dans l'ombre modeste d'où il était sorti.' See also Foisset, *Vie du R. P. Lacordaire*, I, 154; Duine, p. 138. Harel du Tancrel disappears from the editorial staff in the course of the year, and he is not even mentioned among those specified in the memorandum presented to the pope in February 1832: see *A.R.*, p. 80. There is a reference to his death (in unhappy circumstances, apparently) in a letter of 1 May 1833 from Lamennais to Montalembert: see *L. à M.*, p. 115.

[33] See the previously unpublished letter of 16 August 1830 from Lamennais to Gerbet in Trannoy, pp. 509 f. Cp. *Lamennais inconnu*, pp. 254 f.

[34] See *Lamennais inconnu*, p. 255.

[35] C. S. Phillips, *The Church in France 1789–1848*, p. 236, said that 'the editor in chief was of course Lamennais himself'. But apart from the fact that during the first few months Harel du Tancrel was stated to be 'le rédacteur en chef' (e.g. see *A.A.*, I, 328), it is to be observed that on 14 January 1831 Lamennais wrote to Coriolis from Juilly: 'Je suis tout à fait en dehors de la partie administrative, et je ne puis même habituellement m'occuper de la rédaction, vu mon éloignement de Paris': see Forgues, II, 194. On the other hand, on 5 May 1831 the *Avenir* said of 'le comité de rédaction' that 'M. l'abbé de La Mennais le préside et n'a point cessé un seul instant de le présider': see *A.A.*, IV, 190. To begin

Gerbet wrote the prospectus,[36] which was ready for distribution on 20 August 1830.[37] Taking some words of Louis de Potter (1786–1859), the leader of the Belgian liberals, as its text, the prospectus says that there are now two liberalisms. The old liberalism, 'inheritor of the destructive doctrines of the philosophy of the eighteenth century, and in particular of its hatred of christianity . . . exhales intolerance and oppression', whereas the young liberalism, 'which is growing and which will finish by supplanting the other, confines itself, in regard to religion, to demanding the separation of church and state, which is necessary for the liberty of the church, and which all enlightened catholics equally desire'. It is plainly indicated that the *Avenir*—witness its title—will stand for a *rapprochement* and unity of action between the young liberals and the enlightened catholics, and that its cause will be that of liberty for all—witness its motto: *Dieu et la liberté.*

But before we become absorbed in the story of the *Avenir*, I ought to point out that, when in the middle of September 1830 Lamennais travelled from La Chesnaie to Paris, he was drawn there not only by the desire to be at the centre of action in this new adventure, nor only by the need to face one of the periodic crises in his financial affairs (into the details of which we need not enter); he had also been invited to transplant both himself and the Congregation of St Peter to the College de Juilly, where he would be within easy reach of Paris.[38] This college is one of the most illustrious educational establishments in France. Before the revolution it had been the glory of the French Oratory. It had since then fallen on evil days, and in July 1828 Salinis, whom we have already met in company with Gerbet, got possession of it, and was able to give it a fresh start as a college by receiving pupils for whom, as a result of the ordinances of 16 June 1828, the jesuit colleges were no longer available.[39]

with, the members of the editorial staff in addition to H. du Tancrel and Lamennais were Gerbet, Rohrbacher, Lacordaire, Ad. Bartels, C. de Coux, and A. Daguerre: see *A.A.*, I, 328. Cp. Boutard, II, 121 f. who points out that other active collaborators included d'Ault-Dumesnil, Baron d'Eckstein, Joseph d'Ortigues, de Potter, Baader, and Count de Merode. Montalembert took a leading part in the editorial work, but he joined the staff later than the rest.

[36] See Trannoy, p. 138. There is a reproduction of the original prospectus in Harispe, *Lamennais et Gerbet*, p. 97.

[37] See Foisset, *Vie du R. P. Lacordaire*, I, 157.

[38] See F. Duine on 'La Mennais à Juilly' in *Revue de Bretagne*, December 1903, pp. 542–552.

[39] For an account and prospectus of the college in 1831, see *A.A.*, VI, 114–124.

In October 1830 Lamennais settled at Juilly, and the members of the Congregation of St Peter either joined him there or were established in a house in Paris, where he also stayed on his frequent visits to the city. But Juilly was his normal place of residence until August 1831.[40] Here he wrote most of his articles for the *Avenir*. Here too, between December 1830 and April 1831, he unfolded his catholic philosophy in a course of lectures, which made a deep impression on Sainte-Beuve among others.[41] These lectures were based on Lamennais's *Essai d'un système de philosophie catholique*, which was still in process of composition, and to which reference has been made in a previous chapter.[42] His purpose was to give a coherent account of the presuppositions which were the starting-point of the whole mennaisian movement, and the implications of which the members of the mennaisian school were going to work out in various fields of thought and action. But these lectures were known only to a small inner circle of Lamennais's disciples; they had no direct or observable effect on the campaign of the *Avenir* and its sequels.

It is upon the *Avenir* that we must now fix our attention. It was published as a daily newspaper from 16 October 1830 to 15 November 1831, and it claimed to be the first daily paper founded in Europe in the interests of catholicism.[43] I propose in this chapter, first, to outline the principal themes or doctrines of the *Avenir*; and secondly, to take some examples, of varying importance, of how the paper applied its principles, including the activities of the *Agence générale*, which was the association through which it worked. The range of the *Avenir's* support and the reasons for the opposition it aroused will be considered in the following chapter, in connexion with the decision to suspend its publication and to appeal to Rome.

[40] See *Cottu*, p. 224. On 27 August 1831 Lamennais wrote to abbé Jean that there was no future for the Congregation at Juilly which was hopelessly mismanaged, and that he now concentrated his hopes on the house in Paris: see Blaize, II, 83 f.

[41] See Sainte-Beuve, II, 25 f. Cp. Montalembert's impressions reproduced from his journal in Lallemand, *Montalembert et ses amis* (1927), pp. 147 f.

[42] See pp. 97 f., *supra*.

[43] See *A.R.*, p. 79. At first the paper was entitled: *L'Avenir: journal politique, scientifique et littéraire*. The sub-title was dropped from 2 December 1830 onwards. It was a four-page newspaper in small type with the usual features of the period—home and foreign news, court circular, parliamentary and legal reports, exchange rates, reviews of books, plays, etc. There were supplements when specially extensive reports had to be included.

THE DOCTRINES OF THE 'AVENIR'

The *Avenir*[44] claimed to be integrally catholic and sincerely liberal; integrally catholic in its unshakable attachment and submission to the centre of unity in Rome; sincerely liberal in its determination to defend the liberties of all individuals and communities within the state whatever their opinions, for 'true liberalism . . . understands that liberty must be equal for all or it is secure for no one'.[45]

While it was axiomatic that a common faith—the catholic faith—was the essential condition of social stability and health,[46] in a revolutionary epoch such as the French revolution had ushered in no normal stability could be expected, nor was the recovery of a common faith possible except after a long period, a period that would doubtless last for centuries.[47] During this period rival beliefs should be allowed to contend with one another freely, so that the truth might in the end prevail.[48] The function of government was not to favour any form of belief but to respect and secure the conditions of liberty for all. The *Avenir* maintained that the government of Louis-Philippe was committed to this course by the constitutional charter, however much it might fail to act in accordance with it. Catholicism had been declared to be no longer the religion of the state: what had in fact been the case before had now been openly proclaimed, namely that the state was indifferent in matters of religion. Very well, let it be consistently so, and refrain from interfering with the free exercise of every form of belief that was not dangerous to public order. The defence of an orderly liberty for all was in the common interest of all,[49] and the *Avenir* aimed at uniting behind this purpose all who wanted a genuinely liberal régime, whatever their creed or party.[50]

As this theme was developed with ever-increasing enthusiasm, it

---

[44] References here are for the most part to *Articles de l'Avenir* (*A.A.*), Louvain, 1831–1832: 7 volumes in which the principal articles were reprinted, and which are more accessible and easier to handle than the files of the paper itself. I have however been through the latter too, and where I need to refer to articles or reports which were not reprinted in *A.A.*, I give a reference to the date of issue of the *Avenir*. In the case of articles by Lamennais himself, I add a reference to *O.C.*, x, which is the volume of the *Œuvres complètes*, 1836–1837, in which his *Avenir* articles were collected.

[45] *A.A.*, I, 3; *O.C.*, x, 134.

[46] *A.A.*, I, 23 f.; *O.C.*, x, 149 f.

[47] *A.A.*, I, 57.

[48] *A.A.*, I, 4; *O.C.*, x, 136.

[49] *A.A.*, I, 161; *O.C.*, x, 175.

[50] *A.A.*, I, 154; *O.C.*, x 169.

was carried to further lengths. Less and less was said, particularly by Lamennais himself,[51] about the hope of an eventual return to a christian society in which church and state would once again work in close alliance. A liberal régime began to be extolled for its own sake, as the proper and even final[52] outcome of christian progress, and as what was permanently desirable. That is to say, Lamennais's liberalism ceased to be a strategy for an age of revolution, and became a fundamental element in his faith as a catholic. Political freedom became for him part of the liberty wherewith Christ had come to make all men free.[53] In terms that came to be used in this connexion later in the nineteenth century, the 'hypothesis' took the place of the 'thesis'.[54] However, this was not perhaps more than a change of emphasis, and in practice it made no difference to policy since from the outset the *Avenir* assumed that generations, not to say centuries, must elapse before a christian state, in the traditional sense, could be realized again.

The policy of the *Avenir*—the original liberal catholic program for translating doctrine into action—was summarized by Lamennais himself under six heads,[55] to which I will add some detailed references.

(i) *Complete religious liberty.*[56] No form of belief was to be either privileged or penalized, and in consequence there would be a total separation between church and state.[57] This would entail the suppression of the ecclesiastical budget, i.e. of the payment of the clergy by the state,[58] and the state would have no right in future to interfere

---

[51] See his articles 'De l'avenir de la société' and 'Ce que sera le catholicisme dans la société nouvelle', 28, 29, and 30 June 1831. *A.A.*, v, 160–166, 169–179, 182–190; *O.C.*, x, 315–350.

[52] *A.A.*, v, 169; *O.C.*, x, 324.

[53] It is clear from *M. à L.*, p. 124, that both Lamennais and Montalembert came to regard the separation of church and state not as a transitory measure but as a normal and fundamental law of society.

[54] The distinction between 'thesis' and 'hypothesis' was first formulated in these terms in the *Civiltà cattolica*, 17 October 1863: see Aubert, *Le pontificat de Pie IX*, p. 252.

[55] See his article 'Des doctrines de l'Avenir': *A.A.*, i, 382–389; *O.C.*, x, 196–205.

[56] See 'Éclaircissemens sur la liberté de conscience', *A.A.*, v, 205–212.

[57] Cp. Lamennais's article, 'De la séparation de l'Église et de l'État': *A.A.*, i, 23–30; *O.C.*, x, 149–159.

[58] 'De la suppression du budget du clergé' (Lacordaire), *A.A.*, i, 124–127, 155–158, 179–183, 197–200; 'Le clergé doit-il renoncer à sa dotation? le peut-il?', *A.A.*, i, 250–254.

in the affairs of the church, e.g. in the nomination of bishops (see below). Concordats should be abolished.[59]

(ii) *Educational liberty.*[60] The University's monopoly, a legacy from Napoleon, should be abandoned, and the natural right of parents to have their children educated as they desire should be recognized. Any laws that restricted the freedom of schools and colleges, such as the ordinances of 1828, should be repealed; in any case they no longer had legal force since they were in contradiction to the constitutional charter.

(iii) *Liberty of the press.*[61] Freedom of speech should be accompanied by freedom of communication in print, and by the removal of all obstacles in the way of the expression of ideas, including censorship of stage plays.[62]

(iv) *Liberty of association.*[63] This is a natural right, and especially important in a democratic society. Liberty can be preserved only if groups and parties as well as individuals are free to express themselves and voice their interests in combat with one another. Otherwise a despotism easily establishes itself.

(v) *Universal suffrage.*[64] The vote should not be the right of only a financially privileged class. Government should be in the interest of all and to this end all should have a voice in its election.

(vi) *Decentralization.*[65] Centralization plays into the hands of would-be tyrants. There should be the largest possible measure of local autonomy and self-government, which would enable different

---

59 'De l'abolition des concordats', *A.A.*, II, 43–47, 235–241.

60 'De la liberté d'enseignement' (Lacordaire), *A.A.*, I, 14–18, 31–34, 112–116; cp. III, 210–214, VI, 132–135, *et passim.*

61 'De la liberté de la presse', *A.A.*, I, 226–228, IV, 505–509; 'Encore de la liberté de la presse', *A.A.*, V, 146–152. The *Avenir* argued that the censorship of publications by the state was quite a different thing from the church's putting books on the Index. See 'Différence entre la censure de l'Église et celle de l'État', *A.A.*, V, 145 f.; 'Propositions prétendues contradictoires', *A.A.*, V, 241–244.

62 'D'un projet de censure théâtrale', *A.A.*, IV, 80 f.

63 'Des associations patriotiques' (de Coux), *A.A.*, III, 324–329.

64 'Du cens électoral selon M. Decazes' (de Coux), *A.A.*, III, 397–399; 'Du cens électoral dans l'intérêt des classes ouvrières' (de Coux), *A.A.*, III, 425–429; 'Du cens électoral suivant M. Casimir Périer', *A.A.*, III, 435–438; 'Du suffrage universel' (d'Eckstein), *A.A.*, IV, 496–499; 'Sur le suffrage universel', *A.A.*, V, 142 f. Cp. *O.C.*, X, 277 f.

65 'Du régime administratif en France et des abus de la centralisation', *A.A.*, II, 65–72; 'De la centralisation dans ses rapports avec la liberté de la presse', *A.A.*, III, 330–335; 'De l'organisation communale et départmentale' (de Coux), *A.A.*, VI, 493–517, VII, 111–117; 'La centralisation,—Ses conséquences.—Ce qu'elle coûte annuellement à la France', *Avenir*, 13 March 1831; 'De la centralisation

parts of the country to manage their own affairs with due respect to local conditions and traditions. The vital unity of a nation is a unity in diversity, not the imposition of a uniformity from above.

THE DOCTRINES ILLUSTRATED

I proceed now to take some examples, of varying importance, of how the *Avenir* applied its principles and sought to extend their influence.

A. Prayer for the King

It was the custom in France at the end of the chief mass in parish churches on Sunday for prayers to be chanted for the king.[66] Three times the whole congregation sang: 'Domine, salvum fac Regem et exaudi nos in die qua invocaverimus te'; and then the officiating priest alone intoned a collect in which the reigning monarch was named.[67] Many catholics, especially among the clergy, refused at first to continue this practice after the July revolution, since they regarded Louis-Philippe as an usurper.[68] With rare exceptions, the bishops maintained silence on the subject, a circumstance which was significant of their attitude to the new régime.[69]

dans ses rapports avec les intérêts matériels de la France', *Avenir*, 7 July and 13 October 1831; 'La centralisation jugée par M. d'Argout', *Avenir*, 20 and 21 October 1831. See also O.C., x, 241 f.

[66] Article 8 of the concordat of 1801 read as follows: 'La formule de prière suivante sera récitée à la fin de l'office divin, dans toutes les églises de France:

'Domine, salvam fac Rempublicam;
'Domine, salvos fac Consules.'

See Constant, *L'Église de France sous le Consulat et l'Empire*, p. 347.

[67] See A.A., III, 180, 478 f.; cp. I, 338.

[68] An extreme case was that of Cardinal de Latil, Archbishop of Reims, who went with Charles X into exile, and persisted in his refusal to have anything to do with the new régime. As late as 1836 he wrote to Lambruschini, then papal secretary of state: 'Demander à Dieu par des prières publiques de faire triompher un usurpateur *serait au-dessus de mes forces*.' See Martin, *op. cit.*, p. 46.

[69] Belmas, the (ex-constitutional) Bishop of Cambrai, was exceptional in rallying immediately to Louis-Philippe and in seeking to persuade his clergy to do likewise. See L. Mahieu, *Mgr Louis Belmas* (1934), II, 314, 318–321.

De Quélen, Archbishop of Paris, stayed at his post and continued to administer his diocese, but he refused until his death in 1840 to recognize Louis-Philippe as lawful king, despite persistent efforts on the part of the pope himself to persuade him to do so. See Martin, *op. cit.*, pp. 85–109.

On 1 April 1831 a correspondent informed the *Avenir* that the refusal of the Bishop of Mans to allow his clergy to add the name of the king to the *Domine*,

The question was still a burning one when the *Avenir* began publication in the middle of October. In its first issue it welcomed the pope's recognition of Louis-Philippe, and before the month was out it had at some length declared its mind on the subject of prayer for the king. Two articles, 'De la prière pour le roi', appeared on 24 and 28 October 1830.[70] They were written by abbé Prosper Guéranger.[71] In these articles, which are somewhat diffuse and less forceful than most that appeared in the *Avenir*, Guéranger made three points.

First, both Scripture and tradition plainly enjoin that the church shall pray for civil governments. Secondly, the obligation is to pray for the existing rulers whoever they may be, that they may so preserve peace and order that the church is free to fulfil its divine mission. The church does not identify itself with any particular dynasty, nor do prayers for governments signify support for them in the party sense. Thirdly, princes had, especially since Louis XIV, arrogated to themselves the right to issue orders about what prayers should be said in church. This practice was never justified, even in the time of christian monarchies; there is no excuse whatever for its continuance now that the state has declared itself to be purely secular.

Two days after the appearance of the second of Guéranger's articles, Lacordaire reported in the *Avenir* that the prefect of the Jura had threatened the priests in his department with the forfeiture of their stipends if they refused to pray for the king. Lacordaire apostrophized them as follows:

salvum fac Regem had led to scandalous scenes in many churches. 'Un grand nombre de maires, d'adjoints, ou d'autres individus, se sont permis de faire eux-mêmes cette innovation: ils n'ont été arrêtés ni par leur ignorance du chant ou même du latin, ni par leur inaptitude à chanter à l'église, ni par le scandale qu'ils devaient donner, ni par le ridicule dont ils ne pouvaient manquer de se couvrir aux yeux du public. . . . M. l'évêque ne parait pas disposé à céder, pour éviter ces abus révoltans. Il aime mieux faire cesser les offices publics dans les églises où les curés cesseront d'être les maîtres.' *A.A.*, III, 430.

70 *A.A.*, I, 104–112, 133–142.

71 As has been pointed out, Guéranger was at this time a thorough-going mennaisian (see p. 69, *supra*), despite the attempt of his official biographer to conceal the fact. These were the only articles that Guéranger contributed to the *Avenir*, and the biographer tried to make out that this was because of his incomplete sympathy with the aims of the paper, but Sevrin (*Dom Guéranger et La Mennais*, part II) has proved that Guéranger wanted to contribute more articles, and was discouraged from doing so by Lamennais who had very reasonable misgivings about his literary style.

Very well, catholic priests of the Jura! we on our part address a proclamation to you, to all our brethren, to all men who offer heartfelt prayers to God, and we say this to them: 'Pray for the king, pray for his family, for the peace of his reign and the tranquillity of the world, not for the sake of your prefect, but for the sake of God who commands you. . . .'[72]

Lacordaire returned to the subject in the *Avenir* of 5 March 1831 when he attacked a circular which the Minister of Public Worship had addressed to the bishops of France, directing them to add the name of Louis-Philippe to that part of the prayer for the king in which the whole congregation joined. Since the civil authorities knew that many catholics were still carlists or legitimists, they naturally wanted to remove the possibility of their joining in the prayer with an ambiguous intention.[73]

B. Nomination of Bishops

The concordat of 1801 (articles 5 and 17) had provided that the First Consul and his successors should nominate to vacant bishoprics in France, though, if any of his successors should not be a catholic, it was agreed that a new convention would have to be made. The French bishops continued to be nominated according to this provision throughout the nineteenth century. At the beginning of the reign of Louis-Philippe, however, there were serious misgivings about it among gallicans as well as among ultramontanes.[74] Though the head of the state happened still in private life to be a professing catholic, he was no longer bound to be so, and the outbreaks and outrages against the church, with which the new régime was ushered in and which the government appeared to approve, augured ill for the use to which the right of nominating bishops would be put. Moreover, it was at first expected that Louis-Philippe himself would be a mere figure-head and that his ministers, who might be extremely hostile to the church, would wield all the power.

Indeed, however laudable its intentions might be, the new govern-

---

[72] *A.A.*, I, 155 f.

[73] *A.A.*, III, 179–184. Similarly, when on 18 July 1831 the king directed the bishops to see that there were memorial services in all churches for those who had lost their lives during the three days of the revolution in July 1830, the *Avenir* protested against the government's issuing such an order, while at the same time it approved of the prayers' being offered: *A.A.*, V, 390–393. See also *Avenir*, 20 February 1831, and 25 April 1831.

[74] See Martin, *op. cit.*, pp. 116 f.

ment was confronted at the beginning by formidable difficulties in the way of making good nominations. On the one hand, nearly all the natural *episcopabiles* had been legitimists; they were, to say the least, distrustful of the new government, and would have been unlikely to accept preferment from so dubious a source. On the other hand, the government was besieged with requests for preferment from the least desirable type of ecclesiastic. On 18 September 1831 the Archbishop of Toulouse wrote to Rome: 'If it were only a question of seeing one or two undeserving candidates raised to the episcopate as the result of a passing intrigue, the thing would be tolerable; but it is terrible to contemplate the probability that nearly all the candidates chosen will be of that sort.'[75]

The nominations to vacant sees made by Louis-Philippe during the first year or two of his reign were, in fact, of such a kind as to cause grave and just disquiet both to the French hierarchy and to the papacy.[76] In November 1830 the king decided to translate Belmas, Bishop of Cambrai, an ex-constitutional who had refused to retract, to the see of Avignon,[77] and to nominate a certain abbé Labouderie, a priest of very latitudinarian views who had been under ecclesiastical discipline, to the see of Cambrai, and abbé Guillon, a cultivated but worldly divine, to the see of Beauvais. All three had shown their sympathy with the new régime, a circumstance to which obviously they owed their promotion. As soon as the papal nuncio in Paris (Lambruschini) heard that these nominations were impending he hurriedly and strongly protested to the king that the pope would never be able to authorize the institution of the first two, at any rate. Louis-Philippe gave way, though reluctantly, in the case of Belmas, and Labouderie also was dropped, but he persisted in nominating Guillon, who was chaplain to the queen. The Vatican played for time and had an excuse for doing so, since Pius VIII died on 30 November 1830 and many months elapsed before the new pope (Gregory XVI) was obliged to decide whether or not to accept the nomination of Guillon.

He had not done so, when in May 1831 Guillon queered his own pitch by ministering on his death-bed to Henri Grégoire (1750–1831), the most famous and most impenitent of the constitutional bishops, in spite of a prohibition from the Archbishop of Paris.[78]

[75] See Martin, *op. cit.*, pp. 120 f.; cp. *ibid.*, p. 139.
[76] *Ibid.*, pp. 119–135.
[77] See Mahieu, *Mgr Louis Belmas*, II, 322–325.
[78] See Martin, *op. cit.*, pp. 64 f.

In July and August, before the pope's decision about Guillon was known, two hardly less objectionable episcopal nominations were made. Abbé Rey was nominated on 9 July to the see of Dijon and abbé d'Humières on 1 August to Avignon.[79] While objection could not be taken to either of these on grounds of faith or morals, Rey is said to have been ambitious, contentious, and an intriguer (he did in fact cause a lot of trouble in his diocese, and in 1838 was prevailed upon to resign). D'Humières was almost an octogenarian, weak in body and mind, who owed his preferment to his friendship with Casimir Périer (he died a year after his consecration).[80] Towards the end of August 1831 the pope refused to institute Guillon, and he had to withdraw.[81]

This was so far as things had moved when the *Avenir* ceased publication in November 1831. We need not follow here the subsequent history of Louis-Philippe's episcopal nominations.[82] All that needs to be said is that, from the church's point of view, the July monarchy made an excellent recovery from its bad start, and from this time onwards the bishops it nominated were, with one or two exceptions,[83] consistently acceptable. Those responsible for the *Avenir* had of course no means of anticipating this remarkable change,[84] for which Mgr Garibaldi, who in 1832 replaced Lambruschini as the Vatican's representative at the French court, was largely responsible.

As it was, the *Avenir* appeared to have in Louis-Philippe's early episcopal nominations a most impressive argument in favour of the separation of church and state, and it exploited it to the full. No sooner did the first nominations that Louis-Philippe proposed to make become public knowledge than Lacordaire and Lamennais pro-

---

[79] See *A.A.*, VI, 13, 22–27, 65.

[80] See Martin, *loc. cit.* Lamennais in *Affaires de Rome*, p. 61, writes as though Guillon, Rey, and d'Humières were all nominated at the same time, and is followed by Boutard, II, 216. Trannoy, p. 155, makes the same mistake.

[81] Gregory XVI tried to soften the blow by writing personal letters to both the king and the queen of the French to say how sorry he was not to be able to comply with their wishes, and in December 1832 he made reparation by appointing Guillon to the bishopric of Morocco *in partibus infidelium*. See Martin, *op. cit.*, pp. 127, 134.

[82] The subsequent history is dealt with by Martin, *op. cit.*, pp. 135–190.

[83] See *ibid.*, pp. 185 f.

[84] On 10 October 1831 the *Avenir* said confidently but, as it turned out, mistakenly: 'Trois évêques, jusqu'à ce jour, ont été nommés, et *par ces nominations on peut juger de ce que seraient les autres.*'—*A.A.*, VI, 410 (italics mine). Cp. 'De la servitude où tombe insensiblement le clergé catholique', *A.A.*, VII, 72–75.

ceeded to write highly provocative articles on the subject, which appeared on 25 and 26 November 1830.

Lacordaire entitled his article 'Aux Évêques de France'.

> The government has shown its hand [he began]: it has just told the catholics what is in store for you: it is testing you to see how far it can go. . . . Do not suppose it will call a halt. The catholic religion is no longer its own. . . . The nomination of your colleagues in the episcopate is henceforth without any legislative or moral sanction. It is given over as a prey to the ministries that will rapidly succeed one another. . . .
>
> Since the catholic religion is no longer the religion of the country, the ministers of the state are and ought to be legally indifferent with regard to us. . . . They are laymen, they can be protestants, jews, or atheists. . . .[85]

And so on, with plenty of rhetorical amplitude. The *Avenir*'s case was put more concisely and forcefully by Lamennais whose article was entitled 'Oppression des Catholiques'.

> The selection of your chief pastors [he wrote] is in the hands of men who are only too justly suspect of designing the ruin of your faith; and the nominations of which we hear . . . are of a kind to heighten our sense of alarm. Estimate how many years would elapse before the renewed episcopate would consist only of men picked out from the French clergy by the government to carry out its designs. Consider what the teaching in the seminaries would become bit by bit under their influence. You can see schism taking shape within this corruption, and the hideous sight of a national church all of a sudden making its appearance. You cannot take precautions too soon against so threatening a future. Join your voices to ours; let us urge, let us beseech those whom the common father of christians has appointed to rule the Church of France to avert from us and from our descendants the evils which we foresee. They alone with their head, the vicar of Christ, can save us. They will no doubt recognize that the only remedy is the entire and absolute separation of church and state, and that any sacrifice is worth while to bring this about. The principle is laid down in the charter; all that is needed is to implement it. Just because there does not exist and can no more exist a state religion, the intervention of the government in religious matters is altogether absurd

[85] *A.A.*, I, 311, 313.

and illegal; and consequently the concordat is implicitly abolished together with all the laws and regulations that followed from it. When the bishops have explained to the sovereign pontiff the situation of our church, when they have told him of their desires with that accent of conviction, disinterestedness, and charity which will move his paternal heart, then all the difficulties which arise from previous undertakings will promptly be removed. . . .[86]

The issues of the paper containing these articles were seized by the police, and the writers were summoned to answer in the law courts for what they had said. This they did on 31 January 1831 amid scenes of enthusiasm. Lacordaire, who had been a lawyer before he became a priest, conducted his own defence. Both Lamennais and Lacordaire were acquitted, and the incident was calculated to encourage the mennaisians to carry on with their campaign all the more boldly.[87] Certainly, throughout its short but intense career, the *Avenir* continued its attacks on the nomination of bishops by the government, telling both the French hierarchy and the papacy what ought to be done about it.[88] In addition, Guéranger published in June 1831 a book entitled *De l'élection et de la nomination des évêques*, which aimed at providing an historical basis for the contentions that the *Avenir* was making.[89]

C. The *Agence Générale*, Liberty of Association, and Educational Liberty

No one realized better than Lamennais that, if the new ideas which the *Avenir* was advocating were to become a power in the church and in the world, they must not only be written and talked about but acted upon, and acted upon not by isolated individuals here and there but by men mobilized and organized in association. Liberal catholicism would be no more than a fantasy if it did not become incarnate in a social movement that could inspire and hold men's loyalty and impart to them the sense of being engaged in a common mission. At the same time, with his deep distrust of the centralization of power (except in the case of the papacy!) Lamennais saw that the

[86] *A.A.*, I, 318 f.; *O.C.*, X, 193 f.
[87] A complete account of the proceedings was published by the *Agence générale*, entitled *Procès de l'Avenir* (1831). They were also fully reported in the *Avenir* itself: see *A.A.*, II, 361–419, 425–433, 445 f., 494–512.
[88] See *A.A.*, I, 381, II, 240, III, 245–248, 393–396, 434 f., IV, 116, 363 f., V, 4–12, 28 ff., 44–51, 205, 263 f., VI, 13, 22–27, 65, 186 f., 224–228, 365–368, 372–376, 410, VII, 124, 147.
[89] See Sevrin, *Dom Guéranger et La Mennais*, chaps. 6, 7, and 8.

kind of association needed must grow from local roots and allow scope for the greatest possible measure of local initiative and autonomy.

The *Agence générale pour la défense de la liberté religieuse*, which was founded in December 1830 with Lamennais as its president, met all these conditions. It was one of his most constructive and far-sighted projects, a consequence of his perception that in the new age of secularism and democracy christians would have to exert themselves in new ways and shed their nostalgia for the *ancien régime* and its secure privileges. Associations like 'Catholic Action', 'Christian Action', and dozens of others, in which laymen combine to bring their faith to bear on the life of society, are now so familiar that it is not easy to imagine the novelty and strangeness of what Lamennais set on foot in 1830. Catholics in France were then accustomed to regard their christian duties as done if they complied with the precepts of the church.[90] They had supposed that it was for the clergy and for the government of the 'Most Christian King' to safeguard christian interests and the rights of the church. In view of the hostility with which the religious orders, especially the Jesuits, and pious confraternities, such as the Congregation,[91] were regarded by the majority of citizens, there was a natural fear that, if catholics formed new kinds of public association for the defence and propagation of their faith, the only effect would be to arouse more suspicion and to invite more determined persecution. It was safer to continue in the accustomed ways.

In 1828 Lamennais had experimented with an *Association pour la défense de la religion catholique*,[92] but despite aristocratic patronage it had proved abortive.[93] Its aims had been more restricted and more conservative than what he contemplated now. During November 1830 Lamennais and his colleagues had already been canvassing the question of founding a new association,[94] but without reaching a decision. What convinced them that the time was ripe for going ahead was the response to the appeal made by the editors of the *Avenir* on 28 November 1830 for subscriptions towards the defence

[90] Cp. Boutard, II, 170 f.
[91] See p. 116, *supra*.
[92] See *Le Mémorial catholique*, May 1828, IX, 275–284. Cp. Foisset, *Vie du R. P. Lacordaire*, I, 134 f.; Laurentie, *Souvenirs inédits*, chap. 9.
[93] See Boutard, II, 172–176.
[94] When Montalembert visited Lamennais for the first time on 5 November 1830, Lamennais spoke about a project for 'une association catholique': see Lallemand, *Montalembert et ses amis*, p. 141. See also Trannoy, pp. 162 f.

of Lamennais and Lacordaire in the legal proceedings that had just been opened against them. The appeal had been addressed to 'all the friends of God and of liberty', and subscriptions had been invited from 5 centimes to 5 francs, the names of all subscribers to be published.[95] The response, not only from individuals but from groups in different localities, was so large[96] as to show that in the course of a few weeks the *Avenir* had made enough impact to warrant a more definite rallying of, and commitment by, its supporters all over the country.

Moreover, the impulse to form regional associations of the kind Lamennais had in mind seems by this time to have been spontaneously at work. The *Avenir* of 13 December 1830, reporting the formation of a new association at Metz to defend and realize the liberties proclaimed in the constitutional charter, makes this editorial comment: 'The need to unite for the defence of our common liberties is showing itself all over France, and perhaps every department will before long have its association to conquer and to protect the rights which the new charter has guaranteed to us.'[97] Thus the formation of local associations appears to have preceded, as well as to have followed, the foundation of the *Agence générale*.

The prospectus of the *Agence* and its articles of association were published in the *Avenir* of 18 December 1830.[98] Its principal objects were defined as follows: (i) The redress of every encroachment on the liberty of the church's ministry by bringing it before the civil courts; (ii) The support of every place of primary, secondary, or higher education against any arbitrary interference with the liberty guaranteed by the charter; (iii) The maintainenance of the right of all Frenchmen to associate for prayer or study or any other legitimate religious, philanthropic, or cultural purpose; (iv) The *Agence générale* to serve as a link between all local associations established to defend religious liberty: while local associations will have their own independent organization, their action will be greatly strengthened by mutual support.

Local associations soon began to multiply,[99] and in order to ensure that their relation to the *Agence générale* was an informed and

[95] See *A.A.*, I, 327 f.

[96] But Boutard, II, 181, goes too far when he says, without citing any authority, that within a few days the amount subscribed reached 20,000 francs, for the *Avenir* of 27 January 1831 (i.e. two months after the appeal had been launched) gives the amount received to date as 9,390 francs from 11,225 persons. See *A.A.*, II, 332.

[97] *A.A.*, I, 415 f.   [98] See *A.A.*, I, 455–458.   [99] See *A.A.*, II, 447, V, 81–85.

personal one, three members of the council—Lacordaire, Montalembert, and de Coux—were appointed to be correspondents or *agens généraux* of the local associations. They divided the country between them into three areas.[100]

Lacordaire we have had occasion to mention before. But it is not until now that Charles de Montalembert (1810–1870),[101] whose name is indelibly associated with that of Lamennais, makes his appearance. They met for the first time only in November 1830, i.e. after the *Avenir* had been launched, and at once became fast friends. Montalembert, a charming, chivalrous, and gifted young aristocrat, had been travelling in Ireland in September 1830 when a friend sent him the prospectus of the *Avenir*. It thrilled him. 'At last!' he wrote to his friend. 'A splendid destiny now opens for catholicism. Disengaged for ever from its alliance with political power, it is going to recover its force, its liberty, and its primal energy. For my part . . . I am determined to consecrate my time and my studies to the defence of this noble cause. If the *Avenir* wants me, I give up everything for it.'[102] That is typical of the idealism that was enlisted in the cause of the *Avenir*. Montalembert wrote from London on 26 October offering his services to Lamennais,[103] and immediately on his return to Paris sought him out. They were enchanted with each other, and were at once devoted not only like master and favourite disciple but like father and son.[104] Montalembert contributed his first article to the *Avenir* on 12 December (on the revolution in Poland), he formally became a member of the 'comité de rédaction' in February 1831,[105] and was henceforth one of the most effective apostles of the gospel of 'Dieu et la liberté'.

Charles de Coux (1787–1864)[106] was responsible for most of the

---

100 For the dioceses assigned to each, see *A.A.*, VII, 302. When Lacordaire and Montalembert left for Rome in November 1831, their places were taken by d'Ault-Dumesnil and Combalot. See *A.A.*, VII, 166.

101 See Lecanuet, *Montalembert*, 3 vols (1910–1912); Lallemand, *Montalembert et ses amis* (1927), which contains much fuller quotations from Montalembert's journal than Lecanuet gives; Trannoy, *Le Romantisme politique de Montalembert avant 1843* (1942).

102 Letter of 10 September 1830 to Lemarcis. See Lecanuet, *op. cit.*, I, 133.

103 See *M. à L.*, pp. 2 ff.

104 See Lallemand, *op. cit.*, chap. 9, 'Montalembert et La Mennais'.

105 See Trannoy, p. 142.

106 No adequate study of his life has yet been made. For such bibliography as there is, see J. B. Duroselle, *Les Débuts du Catholicisme social en France 1822–1870* (1951), p. 40. Charles Périn, *Le Modernisme dans l'Église d'après des lettres inédites de La Mennais* (1881) makes use of Lamennais's letters to de Coux.

excursions of the *Avenir* into christian socialism. He was a political economist, and contributed articles on political and economic subjects.[107]

What did the *Agence générale* and its affiliated associations actually do? It had been in existence less than a year when the *Avenir* which was its principal organ suspended publication, yet its record of activity, if not of successful achievement, is considerable.[108] Wherever liberty of association was interfered with, the *Agence* was on the alert to take the matter up, to give advice about appealing to the courts (it had a special legal committee for this purpose), and to support or to initiate legal proceedings where there were favourable grounds on which to start them. The case that was given most attention in the *Avenir* was the expulsion of the trappists from the Abbey of Melleray in Brittany. Many members of the community were foreigners, and legitimists used to go there for retreats.[109] Though the *Agence* did not succeed in preventing the expulsion of the monks, it made sure that the case received widespread and persistent publicity as a flagrant instance of the government's failure to provide the religious liberty that had been promised in the charter.[110]

The most conspicuous and provocative propaganda, however, which the *Agence* undertook, was for freedom of education. Lacordaire and Montalembert as well as Lamennais had reasons of their own for feeling very strongly on this subject.[111] The *Agence* organized petitions from all parts of the country claiming the liberty that had been promised and the abolition of the University's monopoly.[112] These petitions were presented to both houses of parliament. By 1 February 1832, 379 petitions had been presented containing 18,450 signatures.[113]

Further, in order to impress the claim for educational liberty upon

[107] For an identification of the articles contributed to the *Avenir* by de Coux, see Duroselle, *op. cit.*, p. 41. In 1834 de Coux became professor of political economy at the new Catholic University in Belgium.

[108] See two periodical reports made to all members, *A.A.*, VI, 341–348, VII, 281–308. After the suspension of the *Avenir* bulletins continued to be issued at intervals to subscribers to the *Agence*. Gerbet took charge when Lamennais left for Rome in November 1831.

[109] See Trannoy, p. 175.

[110] See 'Procès de l'Abbaye de Melleray', *A.A.*, VII, 309–421; also VI, 400 ff., *et passim*.

[111] See Trannoy, p. 164.

[112] See *A.A.*, II, 156 f., 241 ff., 449 f., III, 50 f., 168 f., 186 ff., V, 279 ff., VI, 177 f., 204 f., VII, 123.

[113] See *A.A.*, VII, 287.

the public mind and to show how seriously it was being made, the *Agence* decided to open a free school in Paris without asking for the official authorization that was required by law.[114] On 29 April 1831 an announcement was made in the *Avenir* of the intention to open the school, and bills were posted in the streets. On 9 May the school was opened by de Coux, Lacordaire, and Montalembert. The government at once took action to close it, and started legal proceedings against the three masters. These proceedings would in any case have served as a good platform for propaganda, since the three accused were more than capable of using them for that purpose. As it turned out, they got a more magnificent platform than they could have expected. For they had not foreseen that Montalembert's father would die on 21 June 1831. The consequence was that he at once became a member of the upper house of parliament, and was able to demand that the whole case should be tried by his fellow peers. Although the case was lost, this circumstance gave the episode a dramatic quality and a sensational amount of publicity.

Free schools were similarly opened, with the promise of support from the *Agence*, in half a dozen provincial centres.[115] This method of embarrassing the authorities and of compelling public attention would have been extended all over the country if the *Avenir*'s campaign had been able to continue.[116]

D. Liberal Catholic International

So far, what has been said suggests that the *Avenir* and the *Agence* were exclusively occupied with what was going on in France, but this was very far from being the case. Lamennais had all along taken the view that the great revolution had been the signal and earnest of a long-term social and political transformation which would affect the whole of Europe and with which the church in every country would have to make its reckoning. We have traced the stages by which he came at last to the conclusion that religious indifference or neutrality ought to be expected and demanded of civil governments for so long a future as need be taken into account, and that therefore the church, instead of any longer depending on the precarious and dangerous support of states, ought everywhere,

---

[114] For contemporary reporting of this whole episode, see *A.A.*, IV, 111–114, 210 f., 230 ff., 238 ff., 249–255, 268 f., 273–277, 293–296, 431–443, 445–449, V, 51–58, 88–92, 167 f., 179 ff., 250 ff., 315–321, 413 ff., VI, 256 f., 263–337. For further details and references, see Trannoy, pp. 165–174.

[115] *A.A.*, VII, 165.   [116] *A.A.*, VII, 285.

under the spiritual leadership of the papacy, to assert its own independence, and claim, equally with other religious societies, freedom from political control.

The writers of the *Avenir* were convinced that the regeneration of society awaited the church's recovery in every nation of vigorous freedom of action, and that it was the mission of France to spread the gospel of liberal catholicism.[117] They therefore observed with the keenest and most enthusiastic sympathy any attempt that was being made by catholics in other lands to achieve the liberties which the *Avenir* regarded as indispensable.

We have already seen how Lamennais's interest had been engaged in the struggle of the Belgian catholics for their freedom, and how he had been struck by the union between catholics and liberals that was proving so fruitful there.[118] The Belgian insurrection had broken out in August 1830, following closely upon the July revolution in France, and throughout the period when the *Avenir* was being published the new and independent Belgian state was passing through its birth-throes (National Belgian Congress and declaration of independence, November 1830; recognition of Belgian independence and neutrality by London Conference, January 1831; election of Leopold of Saxe-Coburg as king, June 1831; Dutch invasion, August 1831; Treaty of London, November 1831[119]). The *Avenir* dealt at length with each phase of the struggle, regarded the Belgian cause as its own, welcomed the collaboration of its leaders, and nowhere found a more ardent or numerous body of readers.[120]

The career of the *Avenir* also synchronized with one of Poland's periodic attempts to establish its national independence. It has already been remarked that the first article that Montalembert

---

[117] On 28 December 1830 Gerbet wrote in the *Avenir*: 'Comme catholiques, nous possédons nécessairement le principe d'ordre et de stabilité. Mais . . . nous semblions avoir abandonné le principe d'activité et de progrès. Nul appel à l'opinion, à la liberté, à la conscience des peuples: la langue que nous parlions avait oublié tous ces noms qui remuent le monde. Réunissons enfin ces deux forces. Pour la première, nous nous en reposons sur Rome avec une foi imperturbable. Mais elle nous laisse aujourd'hui le soin d'user de la seconde. C'est la grande mission de tous les écrivains catholiques, et surtout des écrivains français. Si Rome est le centre immobile de la foi, la France est le foyer de l'activité intellectuelle de l'Europe.'—*A.A.*, II, 47.

See also 'Mission du peuple français, c'est à dire des catholiques de France', *A.A.*, II, 340–346.

[118] See pp. 119–124, *supra.*

[119] See Lavisse et Rambaud, x, 356–363.

[120] *Articles de l'Avenir* had 5,000 subscribers in Belgium: see *A.R.*, p. 85.

contributed to the *Avenir* (on 12 December 1830) was about the revolution in Poland.[121] The revolution had begun at the end of November, and met with initial success; a provisional government was set up in Warsaw. After that, the fortunes of the Polish arms fluctuated, until in September 1831 resistance to the Russians collapsed and Warsaw fell. The repressive measures taken by the Czar's government were so ruthless and so thorough that not even in 1848—the year of revolutions—would there be any sign of an uprising in Poland. The *Avenir* identified itself with the Polish, as closely as with the Belgian, cause. News of the war was regularly given and commented on. In July 1831 the *Agence* organized a petition to both houses of parliament, urging the French government to support Poland's independence.[122] When in September news of the fall of Warsaw reached Paris, Lamennais published in the *Avenir* a brief but vibrant lamentation and prophecy.[123]

The Irish were another catholic people whose devotion and misfortunes had a large share of the *Avenir's* attention. Montalembert, it will be remembered, had been on a visit to Ireland when he received the prospectus of the *Avenir*. He early contributed a long letter, 'Du catholicisme en Irelande',[124] published in three parts, in which he said that Catholic Emancipation had made no difference to the shocking way in which the catholics were impoverished by the Established Church of Ireland. Nevertheless, the Irish catholics, though poor, were free, and the glowing and self-sacrificing piety of priests and people were evidence of the benefits and blessings brought to a church by its complete separation from the state. It was free to choose its own bishops (subject only to the pope); there was freedom for religious orders; and freedom to educate the people without the intrusion of the government. 1831 was a year in which Ireland was afflicted by one of those appalling famines that seemed

[121] The article, 'Révolution de Pologne', opened with the following sentence, which is eloquent of the *Avenir's* attitude to all such insurrections: 'Enfin elle a jeté son cri de réveil, enfin elle a secoué ses chaînes, et en a menacé la tête de ses barbares oppresseurs, cette fière et généreuse Pologne, tant calomniée, tant opprimée, tant chérie de tous les cœurs libres et catholiques.'—*A.A.*, I, 403 f.

[122] *A.A.*, v, 387–390.

[123] 'Prise de Varsovie', *A.A.*, vi, 240 f. These were its closing words: 'Peuple de héros, peuple de notre amour, repose en paix dans la tombe que le crime des uns et la lâcheté des autres t'ont creusée. Mais ne l'oublie point, cette tombe n'est pas vide d'espérance; sur elle il y a une croix, une croix prophétique, qui dit: Tu revivras!'

[124] *A.A.*, II, 72–81, 135–146, 243–254.

then to be endemic. On 1 June the *Avenir* published an appeal on behalf of the victims of the famine, and opened a subscription list as an expression of catholic solidarity in charity.[125] By the end of August nearly 80,000 francs had been subscribed and forwarded to Ireland.[126] Grateful letters from the Irish hierarchy were received and published in the *Avenir*.

In Belgium, Poland, and Ireland there were catholic peoples who were striving for their faith and freedom against the oppression of non-catholic and alien governments. The *Avenir* was bound by its principles to rejoice at their successes and to deplore their misfortunes.[127] The insurrections that broke out in the papal states in 1831,[128] although like those in Belgium and Poland they were repercussions of the July revolution in France, presented Lamennais and his friends with a dilemma. At least, so it might have been supposed. For here the forces of liberalism and catholicism instead of being allied were in conflict: God and Liberty instead of being on the same side were on opposite sides. The *Avenir*—always starry-eyed where the pope was in the picture, and supported in this case by correspondents in Italy—took wholeheartedly the side of the papal government which it described as 'the most mild, the most pacific, the most legitimate in the whole world'.[129]

It is now generally acknowledged that, whatever may have been the personal benevolence of the popes, the administration of the

[125] *A.A.*, v, 1–4.   [126] *A.A.*, vi, 132.

[127] Likewise, the conditions to which catholics were subjected by other non-catholic governments were closely watched: e.g. see 'Du catholicisme en Suède', *A.A.*, iv, 298–306; 'Oppression de l'enseignement catholique en Prusse', *A.A.*, iv, 151–157; 'État du catholicisme en Hollande', *A.A.*, vi, 414–418. On the other hand, the freedom and progress of catholicism in the U.S.A. were extolled: see *A.A.*, ii, 163 f.

[128] Cardinal Wiseman in his *Recollections of the Last Four Popes*, pp. 426 ff., graphically describes how on the evening of the day on which Gregory XVI was crowned the first report of the insurrection at Bologna reached Rome. For a concise account of the history of these insurrections, see Schmidlin, ii, 197–206. Cp. C. Vidal, *op. cit.*, pp. 506 ff.

[129] See *A.A.*, iii, 253 f.: 'Voilà donc ce que les révolutionnaires d'Italie appellent la liberté! Dépouiller le souverain le plus doux, le plus pacifique, le plus légitime de l'univers, de son autorité bénie des peuples. . . . Autant la cause vraiment catholique des Belges et des Polonais nous inspire de sympathie, autant nous ressentons d'horreur pour ces révolutionnaires des États pontificaux, qui, en précipitant leur pays dans un abîme de désordre et de malheurs, n'ont pas même un seul prétexte à présenter au monde.'

Sainte-Beuve called attention to the *Avenir*'s inconsistency in an article he wrote in 1836: see Sainte-Beuve, ii, 50.

states of the church was at this time about as inefficient and effete as could well be imagined.[130] It could bolster itself up only by invoking the intervention of Austria. The *Avenir*, however, would do no more than admit that a few improvements in the papal administration might be desirable.

> In the papal states, as well as elsewhere, one can legitimately desire certain ameliorations which time has made necessary; but these ameliorations should be wise and gradual—why then convulse the country and overthrow its government, in order to obtain them? The most paternal of sovereigns will not refuse to his children anything for which they ask with justice. And what interest could he have in perpetuating abuses, if there be any? He does not know to whom he will bequeath his power. . . .[131]

The *Avenir* did indeed protest against an edict (14 April 1831) of the pro-secretary of state at Rome which suspended the normal forms of justice in order that the rebels might be summarily punished, but in doing so it reiterated its strong disapproval of the insurrections.[132] The Italian revolutionaries continued to be represented as jacobins and anarchists, who wanted not an orderly liberty but a wild licence.[133]

The *Avenir*'s support of the 'most legitimate' of governments did little, in the eyes of legitimists generally, to redeem its reputation for subversiveness or to mitigate the alarm that was felt in the chancelleries of Europe—not least in Vienna—at its flagrant assaults upon the assumptions of the Holy Alliance. It was the function of established churches to uphold the established political authorities who were the divinely appointed guardians of law and order. It was intolerable that catholics should be called upon to condone, still worse that they should be encouraged to participate in, insurrections and revolutionary movements.

So far from toning down its enthusiasm for the liberal cause, the *Avenir* on the day on which it suspended publication (15 November

---

130 For a contemporary account of the shortcomings of the papal government and the causes of the insurrections, see the document summarized by Schmidlin, II, 198.

131 *A.A.*, III, 424.

132 *A.A.*, IV, 121–125. The *Avenir* thanked God that the edict in question emanated from the pro-secretary of state, that is from the minister of the temporal prince, and not from the Holy Father as head of the church.

133 *A.A.*, V, 349 f.

1831) nailed its colours to the mast more provocatively than ever
before. It published a proposed 'Act of Union'[134] by which catholics
in the first instance, but also other friends of freedom, would pledge
themselves to mutual aid in defending the liberties that were the
basis of every genuinely constitutional government—liberty of
conscience (which implied the separation of church and state),
liberty of the press, liberty of education, and liberty of association.
Such an act of common dedication and commitment, it was declared, would be 'the signal of something great on the earth'.[135]
The catholics, who were citizens of constitutional states, would be
placing themselves 'at the head of the progressive movement of
society'.[136]

Europe was undoubtedly moving towards a system which would
allow the maximum of every kind of liberty that was consistent
with order. It would be for ever glorious that the catholics should
have welcomed this development 'by a great act and by a great
example'.[137] Emphasis was laid upon the duty of raising the material
conditions of the lower classes so that they could have an ever-
increasing share in all social advantages.[138] The proposed Act of
Union was then an incitement to catholics in all countries to take
their place in the vanguard not only of the liberal movement but
also of an incipient christian socialist movement. De Coux, who was
ahead of the other members of the *Avenir*'s staff in perceiving that
economic reform was much more urgently needed than political
reform,[139] had published a few days previously an article in which
he said that the problem of the industrial proletariat put everything
else in the shade.

The debates in our parliament or in the [international] conference [at London], the delimitation of the frontiers of Belgium, the
fall of a dynasty, parliamentary reform—these are questions of
no importance by comparison with the leprosy of *pauperism*
which is ravaging Europe. But like the astrologer who was so
busy looking at the stars that he did not see the abyss that was
open before him, we fix our attention on the lofty regions of the
political world, as if the interests that are canvassed there must have
a permanent influence on the fate of our country. If we want to
know about that, we must look much lower down—into the

---

[134] *A.A.*, VII, 176–185.   [135] *A.A.*, VII, 178.   [136] *A.A.*, VII, 179.
[137] *A.A.*, VII, 181.   [138] *A.A.*, VII, 181.
[139] Duroselle, *Les Débuts du Catholicisme social en France*, regards de Coux as one
of the most important precursors of catholic socialism.

midst of these multitudes who are called 'the people' when they are needed and otherwise 'the populace'. . . .[140]

The proposed Act of Union, which was signed by all the members of the *Avenir*'s editorial board, was the logical outcome of the mission that they had undertaken. It seemed none the less alarming to the *Avenir*'s enemies by its appearance in the last issue before the paper suspended publication in order to make its confident and dramatic appeal to Rome. Governments and hierarchies were kept in a state of fearful suspense by this threat to form a Liberal Catholic International, which would be stirring up trouble everywhere.

[140] 'De la situation actuelle de l'Europe', *A.A.*, VII, 81 f.

Chapter Six

FOR GOD AND LIBERTY
1830-1832

B. APPEALING TO ROME

WHY DID A NEWSPAPER which had speedily won international fame, and which has left more of a mark on history than any of its contemporaries, have to stop publication after little more than a year's existence? It was not suppressed by the government; the editors decided of their own accord to suspend publication. The material reason was that the subscribers to the *Avenir* were falling away so rapidly in the autumn of 1831 that there was no prospect of its being financially viable. But why did it lose subscribers, and why did it not win wider and more enduring support?

The accounts and circulation figures of the *Avenir* do not seem to have survived, but Montalembert assures us that 'the subscribers . . . never amounted to three thousand',[1] and it is doubtful whether they ever numbered more than 1,500 which is the figure given in the paper itself at a time (5 May 1831) when it was probably receiving the maximum of support.[2] Anyhow, the number of subscribers was insufficient, even in those days when newspapers could exist on a very small circulation compared with today.[3] When subscribers dropped off at an alarming rate, a crisis was inevitable. But why *did* the subscribers drop off?

This is a question that must be answered at some length. The intrinsic quality and interest of the *Avenir* were of a high, and indeed of an exciting, order. Its failure as a commercial proposition is to be

[1] Montalembert, *Memoir of the Abbé Lacordaire*, p. 52.

[2] See *A.A.*, IV, 190. Foisset, *Vie du R. P. Lacordaire*, I, 186, writes: 'Les abonnés n'allèrent jamais au delà de douze cents, moitié prêtres, moitié laïques'; but he does not say what his authority was for this statement.

[3] On the *Avenir*'s financial difficulties, see 'Les rédacteurs et les actionnaires de l'Avenir aux catholiques de France': *A.A.*, IV, 185–191; 'Aux catholiques de France et de Belgique': *A.A.*, VI, 141–145. Cp. *Ami de la Religion,* 15 December 1836, p. 516.

accounted for, in the first place, by the absence of any ready-made constituency for a liberal catholic organ,[4] since liberal catholicism was in France an entirely new idea. Therefore the paper had to seek its supporters among liberals and catholics, the great majority of whom were quite unprepared for, and deeply prejudiced against, so unnatural a union. The proponents of this unheard-of marriage needed to do more than display their brilliant talents; they needed, at least as much, to exercise the wise and patient arts of the experienced wooer. Lamennais, as a journalist, had never studied or practised those arts, and he was in no mood to cultivate them now. Nor, consequently, was he in much of a position to restrain the martial ardour of some of his younger disciples, though even he felt that Lacordaire, the most intemperate of them all, went too far and too fast.[5] The *Avenir* writers, instead of trying to woo possible supporters gradually and tactfully, were so enthusiastic and in such a hurry that their shock-tactics aroused powerful hostility in every direction.

As we have seen, the prospectus of the *Avenir* had distinguished between the older and the younger liberals. The older liberals were so inveterately anti-catholic that it was not to be expected that their prejudices would be easily disarmed, but even the younger liberals, who had been represented by *Le Globe*[6] and who were genuinely in favour of liberty for catholicism and of the separation of church and state, were not likely to enlist in force in a movement which, although it professed to demand an equal liberty for all creeds, yet was in reality flamboyantly catholic and seemed to concentrate all its energies on demanding liberty for *catholics*. And even if the *Avenir* and the *Agence* had been more broadly based, and like the Belgian Union had been equally representative of liberals and catholics, liberals might still have been pardoned for not being immediately persuaded that they had found a harbinger of the coming conversion of the Church of France and of the Vatican to the ideals of '89.[7]

As regards the attitude of the government, which was also

---

[4] I.e. in France, with which we are here concerned. The weekly edition of the *Avenir* in Belgium, which reproduced the principal articles and had 5,000 subscribers (see p. 178, *supra*), does not appear to have been a source of financial benefit to the proprietors of the paper in France.

[5] 'Les exagérations de ce garçon-là nous perdront', Lamennais is reported to have said of Lacordaire. See Boutard, II, 123.

[6] See p. 115, *supra*.

[7] For a letter to the *Avenir* from a sympathetic liberal, see *A.A.*, II, 226–229, but it takes more than one swallow to make a summer.

professedly liberal, it might have been expected at first sight to have
looked with favour on the *Avenir* which unlike most catholics had
promptly rallied to the new régime. But apart from the fact that
Lamennais took the line that the new régime was in principle
republican and that monarchy was now a purely ceremonial survival[8]
—which was not at all what Louis-Philippe wished or intended—
the *Avenir* persistently attacked the government for not giving
practical effect to the liberties that had been promised in the constitutional charter. Moreover, the *Avenir*'s advocacy of full-blown
democracy and universal suffrage was not calculated to appeal to a
government determined that power should remain in the hands of
the bourgeoisie. The *Avenir* appeared indeed to the king and his
ministers to be a thoroughly subversive organ, and they did whatever
they could to cripple its influence.[9]

[8] See his article, 'De la République': *A.A.*, III, 225–232; *O.C.*, X, 269–279.

[9] In July 1831 the printer of the *Avenir* applied to the Ministry of the Interior for
authority to install printing-presses in the offices of the newspaper. A civil
servant, reporting on this request, described the *Avenir* as 'l'un des journaux
les plus anarchistes', and the police when consulted said that it was dangerous
to authorize printing-presses 'qui pourraient servir à la production d'ouvrages
hostiles aux institutions de la Révolution de 1830'.—*Archives nationales*: see
Trannoy, p. 147.

An amusing example of the anxiety of the government about the influence
of the *Avenir* in the provinces has been found in the *Archives départmentales de
Rennes*. On 21 May 1831 Casimir Périer, as Minister of the Interior, wrote to
the Prefect of Ille-et-Vilaine to say that a collaborator of the *Avenir* had been
searched at Lille and there had been found in his pocket-book among other
things four letters from 'une dame royaliste' named 'Julie Onfroy', addressed
from Redon (Ille-et-Vilaine). On 30 May the Sub-prefect of Redon wrote to
the Prefect as follows:

'Monsieur le préfet, Mlle Julie Onffroy est une vieille fille de 45 à 50 ans, qui,
après avoir perdu l'espoir de se marier, s'est faite dévote, selon l'usage. Com-
prenant tant bien que mal l'ouvrage de M. de la Mennais (*de l'indifférence en
matière de religion*), elle s'était engouée de l'auteur. Quand il devint journaliste,
elle fut une de ses premières abonnées. Comme elle était très grande royaliste,
elle s'abusa d'abord sur les principes de son journal qui, d'ailleurs, a dévié de sa
primitive direction. La répétition des mêmes idées sans cesse reproduites a
opéré, comme elle fait toujours, surtout chez les âmes ardentes; elle a amené
une conviction, une véritable foi chez Mlle Onffroy, et maintenant elle est
libérale et catholique ultramontaine. Il ne faut que ce trait pour en donner la
preuve: "Comment, Julie, lui disait une de ses tantes, tu lis l'*Avenir*, tu n'es
donc plus royaliste?—Ma tante, avant tout, je suis catholique."

'Mlle Julie ne peut fixer l'attention du Gouvernement. Elle ne fera pas de
partisans à ses principes. Sa position, son existence l'isolent de toute influence. . . .'

See Duine, *Documents ménaisiens* (1919), pp. 32 f.

However, the mennaisians obviously looked for support primarily among the catholics, not among adherents of the government nor even among the younger liberals. It was by the reaction of the catholics and, above all, of the hierarchy that the *Avenir*'s fate was sealed.

It is impossible to say just what proportion of catholics in France, clerical or lay, should be reckoned as having supported the *Avenir* or as having looked with favour upon its campaign. The laity as a whole were inert.[10] Declared supporters were chiefly young priests; during the first few months numerous letters were published from them, which were said to be representative of many more.[11] Letters were also published from some lay supporters, e.g. students.[12] In some parts of the country there was more enthusiasm than others. The *Avenir* had many more supporters than subscribers, and single copies were no doubt passed from hand to hand. It may become possible to be more precise, if more special studies[13] are made of the state of catholic opinion in various regions during the years 1830–1832. What can be said with assurance is that a sufficient proportion of the clergy and seminarists adopted the new ideas to move the hierarchy to resort to drastic measures of repression.

Lecanuet in his life of Montalembert summarized the reaction of the French bishops as follows:

[10] Cp. Foisset, *Vie du R. P. Lacordaire*, I, 179.

[11] Here is just one typical example, published in the *Avenir* on 29 November 1830:

'Clermont-Ferrand, 18 novembre 1830.

'Qu'il nous soit permis de confondre l'hommage de notre admiration dans le concert qui, de tous les points de la France, salue la générosité de vos doctrines. C'en est fait, la moisson est mûre pour la vérité, l'ivraie du gallicanisme sèche sur pied et la génération nouvelle grandit pour l'avenir.

'Un obstacle à rompre et nous sommes libres! Cet obstacle, on l'appelle budget. Quoiqu'en puissent dire ou penser des personnes à vues étroites, nous en voulons la suppression pour mieux travailler au rachat des âmes, et nous repondrons aux craintes de la faiblesse par ces paroles du Sauveur à ses apôtres: *Quand je vous ai envoyés sans sac et sans chaussure, quelque chose vous a-t-il manqué?* Non.

'Agréez, etc. A. B. . . ., *prêtre du diocèse*.'—*A.A.*, I, 342.

[12] See, for example, the letter from five law students at Toulouse, published in the *Avenir* on 19 May 1831: *A.A.*, IV, 297 f. Cp. Roussel, *Documents*, I, 294–296.

[13] Such as the paper by L. Boiteux on 'Lamennais et les Franc-comtois', which supplies evidence both of the enthusiasm of the clergy of Franche-Comté for the ideas of the *Avenir* and of the opposition of the hierarchy. See *Bulletin d'Académie des sciences, belles-lettres et arts de Besançon*, 1936, pp. 257–280.

They verily believed that by its ideas of democracy and separation [sc. between church and state] the *Avenir* was undermining
the church, and they fought it to the death. Some denounced it
in their pastoral letters, others forbade their priests to read it;
seminarists suspected of sympathy with the new doctrines were
not allowed to proceed to holy orders. Professors and parish
priests who read the dangerous newspaper were dismissed. An
endless stream of episcopal letters went out of France beseeching
the pope to censure these revolutionaries, these heretics, these
schismatics who were troubling the church and causing scandal
to souls.[14]

The broad justice of that summary can be accepted, though here too
more special studies of the proceedings of the French hierarchy with
regard to the *Avenir* would be welcome. Its hostility and that of the
senior clergy generally can be accounted for by a number of considerations.

The hierarchy had closely identified itself with the fallen dynasty
and most of the senior clergy were carlists, whereas the *Avenir* not
only accepted, but even applauded, the July revolution. What is
said[15] to have offended the carlists more than anything else was the
attitude of the *Avenir* to the sacking of the church of Saint-Germain-
l'Auxerrois in Paris. On 14 February 1831 a service was held there
in memory of the Duke of Berry—Charles X's son who had been
assassinated on 13 February 1820—and it was made the occasion of
a minor carlist demonstration.[16] A hostile crowd collected, rioting
started, and the church together with other ecclesiastical property
was sacked before the authorities made a serious attempt to restore
order.

The first reports about what had happened were naturally somewhat confused. The report that reached the *Avenir* represented the
royalists as the villains of the piece; they had turned an act of
worship into an act of political provocation. Consequently, on
16 February the paper published an unsigned, strongly worded leading article[17] in which the royalist demonstrators were denounced as
'sacrilegious conspirators'. To make matters worse, two days later,
by which time the proportions of blame for what had occurred
should have been better recognized, there appeared another, shorter
article to the same effect as that published on 16 February. This was

---

[14] Lecanuet, *Montalembert*, I, 271.   [15] E.g. by Boutard, II, 235–239.
[16] For details, see *A.A.*, III, 65, 73–75.   [17] *A.A.*, III, 66–71.

signed by Lamennais himself, and it called upon catholics to separate
themselves for good and all from the royalist cause; the article
concluded thus:

> Catholics, think of your descendants: they will not ask you to
> give account for the monarchy, but for the religion which it is
> your duty to hand on as purely as you received it. There is some-
> thing more precious than royalty, namely the faith: there is
> something greater than a Bourbon, namely God. Break then,
> break for ever with the men whose incorrigible blindness places
> this holy religion in danger, who sacrifice their God to their king,
> and who, if they prevailed, would degrade your altars so that
> they would be no more than a throne.[18]

Lamennais was not in Paris but at Juilly, when he wrote these
words. It transpired afterwards that, when he wrote them, he had
received only the early and inadequate reports of what had happened;
and further that the editors in Paris, who by the time they received
Lamennais's article were aware of the true facts, had not meant to
publish it, so that it appeared in print through an inadvertence.[19]
Nevertheless, the harm was done, and the *Avenir* was henceforth
anathema to all who were still animated by sentiments of loyalty to
the Bourbons.

But in the eyes of the hierarchy worse even than the *Avenir*'s
throwing over the traditional monarchy was its enthusiasm for
liberty, democracy, and the sovereignty of the people. The word
'liberty' reminded older churchmen too much of 1793; they thought
it spelt inevitably licence or anarchy. 'The sovereignty of the people',
likewise, was a fearful doctrine: had not all the crimes and brutalities
of the Terror been perpetrated in its name? It was beyond compre-
hension how catholics could make such ideas their own. It was useless for the *Avenir* to claim, as it did, that it was developing the
principles of the catholic middle ages, when great store was set on
liberty,[20] or to point out that a whole succession of catholic doctors
had taught that the sovereignty of God did not exclude the
sovereignty of the people and that civil government depended on
popular consent.[21]

[18] *A.A.*, III, 78.   [19] See Roussel, *Documents*, I, 272 f.
[20] See 'Qu'il est contradictoire de ne pas être libéral quand on est catholique',
A.A., II, 114–118; 'De la royauté chrétienne', *A.A.*, VI, 165–174.
[21] See 'Le droit divin des rois exclut-il la souveraineté des peuples?'. *A.A.*, I,
423–430; Lamennais's reply to Ventura, *A.A.*, III, 30–43; 'Nouvelles explications
adressées aux catholiques légitimistes', *A.A.*, VI, 349 f., where we read: 'Nous

The strong prejudices of the bishops were not softened by the frequent civil disturbances, anti-clerical outbreaks, and the financial uncertainty which were features of the opening of the reign of Louis-Philippe, at least until Casimir Périer (1772–1832) became premier in March 1831 and began a period of firm government. Even then, industrial unrest and royalist and republican plots continued, so that all who were disposed to regard the new régime as inherently in-capable of providing security and stability had plenty of excuse for their dread of the revolutionary ideas which the *Avenir* tirelessly canvassed.

Then there was the fact that the *Avenir* advocated the separation of church and state and wanted the clergy to refuse the stipends that were paid to them by the government in accordance with the con-cordat of 1801. Here the bishops could not be altogether disinter-ested. If the church were disestablished, they would be likely to lose much of their social prestige and influence; if they refused to accept their stipends from the state, it was not at all evident that they would receive any stipends at all. In any case, they took it for granted that the traditional alliance between church and state should be main-tained so long and so far as it could be, and would they not have been unpardonably irresponsible if they had led the clergy to renounce the modest incomes they were receiving, without knowing how they were in future to be paid? It was all very well for Lamen-nais to say: 'Le catholicisme français rendu à lui-meme, libre de tout ce qui le dénature, *pauvre*, et par là même grand et fort, régénéra le monde',[22] but it was the duty of the bishops to see that the ministry of the church was carried on. Their office required them to curb those who were putting romantic ideas about the virtues of apostolic poverty into the impressionable minds of young priests and seminar-ists. And after all, the stipends of the clergy were not on the same footing as the salaries paid to state officials, but a slight compensation for the endowments of which the church had been deprived.[23]

Moreover, the French bishops considered that responsibility for

refusons au peuple une souveraineté *absolue, exclusive* et *athée* ou indépendante de la loi divine; mais nous admettons avec la plupart des anciens juriconsultes et théologiens catholiques que le peuple est *souverain* en ce sens que Dieu a mis la souveraineté dans le peuple et que par le peuple (au moyen d'un contrat national formel ou tacite) il la communique à la personne ou à la communauté gouvernante.'   [22] See Forgues, II, 177.

[23] The answer of the *Avenir* to this contention was that the government in fact treated the stipends of the clergy as mere salaries. See *A.A.*, IV 115 f.; *A.R.*, pp. 71 f.; Roussel, *Documents*, I, 269 f.

managing the church belonged to themselves, and they were accustomed to governing their dioceses each according to his own lights. They resented the emergence of upstart busybodies—lay as well as clerical—who were taking it upon themselves to declare what the policy of the Church of France ought to be, and who were doing militant propaganda for their unauthorized program. These upstarts might in public pay lip-service to episcopal authority, but they were inciting catholics to think and act for themselves in ecclesiastical affairs instead of leaving the church to be guided by its lawful pastors. And, as if that were not enough, they were further undermining the authority of the bishops by their extravagant exaltation of the authority of the holy see. It must not be forgotten that the *Avenir* was repulsive to the French hierarchy because of its ultramontanism as well as because of its liberalism.

Finally, all administrators are inclined to find disturbers of the peace a nuisance, and the bishops at this time wanted to keep clear of controversy so far as possible, especially political controversy.[24] The *Avenir* stirred up controversy, caused division among the clergy, and unsettled the faithful laity. It was extremely aggressive to those who did not agree with it, accusing them of worldliness, blindness, and cowardice. Naturally, the *odium theologicum* was not inactive on the other side, and all sorts of calumny were in circulation about the *Avenir*[25] and about Lamennais in particular.[26] What could be worse than all this bitter discord in the church at a time of external peril when it was more important than ever that catholics should present a common front and be at peace among themselves? What could the bishops do except try by all means in their power to extirpate the source of the trouble? And as the *Avenir* was always vaunting its loyalty to the holy see, the bishops did not fail to let the Vatican know their view of the matter.

24 The following passage from a letter of the Bishop of Belley to his clergy is typical of the desire of the hierarchy: 'N'oublions jamais l'objet principal de notre ministère: respectons et observons les lois; prenons peu de part aux évènements journaliers qui agitent le monde ... occupons-nous peu de l'avenir de cette vie, mais pensons souvent, pensons beaucoup à l'avenir de l'autre, à cet avenir qui seul est important, puisque seul il est éternel.' See *Avenir*, 4 May 1831.

25 E.g. see 'De l'opposition aux doctrines de l'Avenir', *A.A.*, VII, 1–7. There were persistent rumours going around that the *Avenir* had already been condemned at Rome.

26 For example, a copy of a forged letter was circulated in the south of France in which Lamennais was represented as urging people to join him in order to 'écraser l'épiscopat'. See Forgues, II, 199 f., 202 f. Cp. Boutard, II, 244 f.

The worthiness of these various motives may be differently estimated by different minds. What is beyond dispute is that the hostility of the French bishops to the *Avenir* is perfectly intelligible and that it was the hostility of the bishops that made it impossible for the paper to continue as it was.

The critical condition of the paper's prospects seems to have struck Lamennais and his collaborators somewhat suddenly in the latter part of October 1831. Montalembert's speech in the upper house of parliament on 19 September,[27] when the case about the free school had been tried there, had made him famous, and when immediately afterwards he toured the southern dioceses on behalf of the *Avenir* and the *Agence* he was enthusiastically received nearly everywhere, and he was able to send very encouraging reports to Paris. He was therefore dumbfounded when at the beginning of November he received letters from Lamennais and Lacordaire saying that the *Avenir* would have to stop publication and that the *Agence* would have to be wound up.

> The *Avenir* could go on for two or three months (Lamennais wrote on 29 October); it is probable that we could get together, by a new appeal to our friends, thirty or forty thousand francs so as to prolong our existence by some months. But how could we ask for or accept money the loss of which would be certain in advance? For it will not be in the near future that the bishops will relax their persecution, and every day it deprives us of subscribers: we have lost a hundred of them at the last renewal of subscriptions. The only question to consider therefore was when we should stop. Now it seemed to us that it would be better to retire while we have funds in hand, funds that we might increase by a new appeal: better to retire at a time when we can say: 'If we wished we could continue for four months, or perhaps eight months; but we do not wish to continue—not that we have the least doubt about the truth of our doctrines, nor about the usefulness of the advice we have given, but because passions have prevented people from listening to us; because there is a limit to the injury, insult, and calumny that one can put up with; because there is no more good we can do.'—What we have said has been heard by such men as are free from party-spirit. We have sown seeds in society that

---

[27] Not 'September 29', as C. S. Phillips, *The Church in France 1789–1848*, p. 247, says. On Montalembert's speech, see Lecanuet, *Montalembert*, I, 241–253.

will not be sterile; time will make them grow, and they will grow so much the more quickly as the passions and prejudices against which we have fought bring more calamities.

For the rest, you will doubtless agree with us, that it is impossible to carry on the *Agence* without a journal. We will conclude such business as is in hand, after which the clergy, who have not wanted to be defended, will defend themselves as they like. The incredible oppression which they are going to have to face is perhaps a lesson that Providence in its wisdom has judged to be necessary. As for us, we shall return into silence and wait for the future, and a near future, to justify us. It would be folly to insist on going on talking sense to the frenzied.[28]

Lacordaire's letter to Montalembert was to the same effect. 'Silence is today the only strength of our cause . . .', he wrote. 'It is time for our work to be calmly observed while we ourselves are no longer visible in it. . . . M. de Maistre said that every great work needs the *Sabbath*. . . .'[29]

These letters show clearly that at the end of October both Lamennais and Lacordaire were resigned to the closing down of the *Avenir* and that they had not conceived the idea of merely suspending its publication while they appealed to Rome. This was still the case on 8 November.[30] What brought about the change of plan? For the announcement that was made in the *Avenir* on 15 November said that publication was being suspended while Lamennais, Lacordaire, and Montalembert went to Rome to learn whether or not their enterprise was approved by the pope. If it were approved, as they appeared confidently to anticipate, publication would be resumed as soon as possible; if it were not approved, they bound themselves in advance to a complete submission.

In addition to this announcement, which included a survey of what the *Avenir* had done during the past thirteen months and of the difficulties it had met with, and which was signed by all the members of the editorial staff, Lamennais contributed to the same issue a personal article, entitled, 'Adieux de M. de La Mennais'. In this he wrote:

If we retire for a moment, it is not from weariness, still less from despondency; it is that we may go, as once upon a

[28] *L. à M.*, pp. 6 ff.   [29] See Lecanuet, *op. cit.*, I, 267.
[30] See Lamennais's letters of 6 and 8 November 1831 to abbé Jean in Roussel, *Documents*, I, 288–292.

P.P.—13

time the soldiers of Israel went, *to consult the Lord in Shiloh*. . . .
We leave the field of battle for a moment, in order to fulfil another
duty which is equally pressing.

They were going, he continued, to prostrate themselves at the feet
of the vicar of Jesus Christ, and to say to him:

> O Father, condescend to look down upon some of the least of
> your children, who are accused of being rebels against your
> infallible and mild authority: behold them before you: read what
> is in their minds, there is nothing there that they wish to hide: if
> even a single one of their thoughts deviates from yours, they
> disavow it, they abjure it. You are the rule of what they teach;
> never, no never, have they known any other. . . .[31]

Thus, whereas on 8 November Lamennais seemed to be determined to retire from public activity—presumably to La Chesnaie,
where he could have consolidated the Congregation of St Peter and
have prepared his liberal catholic following for a more favourable
opportunity of action, we find a week later that he had decided to
make a sensational appeal to Rome with a view to resuming his public
campaign after a short interruption. What caused him to change
his mind, and to make what may have been the mistake of his life?

This is what happened, so far as can be ascertained. On November
11,[32] when Montalembert was back in Paris, a formal meeting of
the proprietors of the *Avenir* was held at which it was unanimously
agreed that the paper must stop publication. Early next morning,
however, Lacordaire went to Lamennais's room, and said that they
could not finish like that. They ought to go to Rome to show the
rightness of their intentions, and to submit their thoughts to the holy
see. Whatever happened, this striking step, a proof both of their
sincerity and of their orthodoxy, would be a blessing for them and a
weapon snatched out of the hands of their enemies. 'Yes,' Lamennais replied, 'we must set out for Rome.'[33] Montalembert was called in and
the decision was communicated to him. His first reaction was one of
alarm. 'And what if we are condemned?' he cried. 'It is impossible,
Charles,' Lamennais answered, 'we cannot be condemned.'[34]

[31] *A.A.*, VII, 169 f.

[32] So Trannoy, p. 179, who however says that the *suspension* of the *Avenir* was
decided on 11 November.

[33] See Foisset, *Vie du R. P. Lacordaire*[2] (1873), I, 180 f.

[34] This episode is recounted by Boutard, II, 254, who cites 'Mémoires' as his
authority, but does not say whose 'Mémoires'; also by Lecanuet, *Montalembert*,

This was a grave moment and a grave decision. Lamennais had for years been complaining in private about the silence of the holy see and its failure to rise to the height of the times,[35] but recently he had realized that, if the papacy openly declared itself at all under present conditions, it would declare itself against the whole liberal-ultramontane program for catholicism, and so he had wisely concluded that his only sensible course was to wait quietly for later vindication.[36] Nevertheless, it appears that, when Lacordaire burst out with his imprudent proposition, Lamennais's ultramontane idealism stirred in him and revived. After all, the pope must be able to read the signs of the times! He must be able to see and to seize the opportunity that was before him of leading an immense catholic renaissance—or, at least, he would not refuse to encourage and to bless the enterprise of his most loyal sons and most submissive subjects when they had had an opportunity of explaining their motives and their aims. Anyhow, the die was cast.

The three pilgrims of God and of liberty reached Rome on 30 December 1831.[37] We will first follow the course of events there from their point of view, and afterwards take note of what went on behind the scenes in the Vatican.

Lamennais did not receive so flattering a welcome as he had on his former visit in 1824. No representative of the Holy Father came to greet him. However, he was warmly and hospitably received by his old friend Père Ventura (1792–1861), the General of the Theatine

I, 271 f., who refers to 'Nettement, *Histoire de la Littérature française sous le gouvernement de juillet*, II, 329.' On p. 330 of vol. I of Nettement's work there is an account of the interchange between Montalembert and Lamennais but not of Lacordaire's part in the decision to appeal to Rome. Nettement however gives no reference to a primary source.

Lacordaire had propounded the idea of a pilgrimage to Rome a year before in the peroration to his article 'Aux Évêques de France', see *A.A.*, I, 315.

35 'Oh! si les Papes savient ce qu'ils peuvent! Plus on examine l'état de chaque pays, plus cette réflexion frappe vivement. On voit partout ce qu'il y aurait à faire, et l'on voit partout que rien ne se fait.'—Letter to abbé Jean, 16 May 1824, Blaize, II, 2. Cp. Forgues, I, 474, II, 46, 48, 58, 61, 92, 106, 115, 133, 146.

36 See letter to Countess de Senfft, 8 November 1831, Forgues, II, 227 f.

37 In a letter of 8 January 1832 (Blaize, II, 89) Lamennais said that they had arrived 'après vingt-cinq jours de voyage assez pénible.' This has been taken by some writers to mean that the whole journey from Paris to Rome took twenty-five days (see Ricard, *Lamennais*, p. 218; Lecanuet, *Montalembert*, I, 280), which is certainly wrong. In other letters (Forgues, II, 232; *Vitrolles*, p. 214) Lamennais said that the journey lasted thirty-five days. For entries in Montalembert's journal during this time, see Lallemand, *Montalembert et ses amis*, pp. 150–153.

Order, who, despite a recent disturbance of their friendship,[38] was now a strong partisan of the liberal catholic cause.[39] Later, in *Affaires de Rome* Lamennais wrote a charming account of the journey of the three pilgrims to the Eternal City. No doubt some of these scenes and reflections were retrospectively coloured, but any notion they had that they were approaching the divinely appointed patron and protector of liberty will not have been confirmed by the signs of misery which they saw in the papal states or by the methods by which the recent insurrections were being suppressed. For instance, Lamennais describes how they met the papal police conducting a company of wretched men who were chained together and piteously asking for alms.[40]

Nevertheless, during the first few weeks of their stay they were sanguine about the outcome of their visit. Thus on 12 January 1832 Lamennais wrote to Mlle de Lucinière:

> I have several times seen Cardinal W[eld],[41] and yesterday we dined with him. His attitude to me has been excellent: *he is really a plain dealer man, without politics and ceremonies*.[42] But the French party, that is to say Cardinal de Rohan[43] and the Jesuits,[44] had

[38] In February 1831 Ventura had addressed an open and highly critical letter to the editors of the *Avenir*, which he had first published in another French newspaper (see *A.A.*, III, 4, 6–12). For Lamennais's 'Réponse à la lettre du P. Ventura', see *A.A.*, III, 30–43; *O.C.*, x, 249–268. Lamennais accused Ventura of having completely misunderstood the doctrines of the editors of the *Avenir* and of having travestied their intentions, and he called for a public withdrawal.

[39] 'Le Père Ventura, qui s'est complètement réconcilié avec nous, est notre plus chaud partisan', wrote Montalembert to Cornudet on 3 January 1832. See Trannoy, p. 180.

[40] 'Nous rencontrâmes, conduits par des sbires du pape, une troupe de pauvres misérables enchaînés deux à deux. La figure de plusieurs annonçoit plutôt la souffrance que le crime. Tous se pressoient autour de nous, tendant la main et demandant d'une voix lamentable quelques *bajocchi per carità*. Nous avions sous les yeux les descendants des maîtres du monde.'—*A.R.*, p. 15.

[41] Thomas Weld (1773–1837) was made a cardinal by Pius VIII in 1830. See Wiseman, *Recollections*, etc., pp. 382–390.

[42] The words italicized are in English in the original.

[43] Louis-François-Auguste de Rohan (1791–1833) was the chief of the group of émigrés who had settled in Rome after the July revolution and who were of course bitterly hostile to the *Avenir*. He was a wealthy aristocrat and a pious, if somewhat effeminate, prelate. Cp. Boutard, II, 265; Wiseman, *op. cit.*, pp. 379–382. The nickname of the Romans for de Rohan was *il bambino*. See Lamennais's description of him in *A.R.*, p. 16.

[44] Lamennais regarded the Jesuits as the principal organizers of opposition to the *Avenir*: cp. Blaize, II, 104. He was particularly annoyed at this time with Père

confused his mind a bit about our affair. At present, he is all right. It is untrue that the pope has made any of the remarks that are attributed to him.[45] He has *ordered* Cardinal de Rohan to make it known that he does not want his name mixed up at all with our business. The cardinal said this himself to M. de Montalembert. Our enemies' only object now is to prevent Rome from speaking. As for our doctines, everyone here says that they cannot be attacked. . . . Altogether, I am full of hope about the result of our journey, but I expect to have to wait a long time, for everything here moves very slowly.[46]

A few days before, Lamennais had written in similar terms to Gerbet, and had told him that they were occupied in drawing up a memorandum.[47] The drafting of this long memorandum or *apologia*,[48] which is dated 3 February 1832 and of which the full text is to be found in *Affaires de Rome*, was entrusted to Lacordaire on the ground of his experience and skill as an advocate. It is indeed a very skilful and persuasive statement of the *Avenir*'s position. It surveys the relations of church and state during the Restoration and argues that, after the July revolution, their complete separation was the only tolerable policy for catholics. It tells the story of the *Avenir* and of the *Agence*, and of the opposition that they had encountered in France and that had driven them to appeal to Rome. The conclusion, however, was neither skilful nor persuasive, for it consisted in telling the pope what he ought to do.[49] He was told that it was indispensable that he should make a pronouncement.

Rozaven, S. J., who had published a refutation of the mennaisian philosophy: see e.g. Forgues, II, 236.

As regards Lamennais's relations with the Jesuits, see Paul Dudon, S. J., 'Lamennais et les Jésuites' in *Études*, 5 June 1908, and 'Trois lettres inédites de Lamennais au P. Godinot, Jésuite', *ibid.*, 20 October 1909. Dudon, it should be borne in mind, was strongly pro-Jesuit; as Victor Giraud said, 'Il ne saurait admettre que jamais aucun membre de la Compagnie de Jésus ait pu avoir le moindre tort envers l'auteur de l'*Indifférence*.'—*Revue des deux mondes*, 1 March 1919, p. 116.

[45] I.e. remarks adverse to the *Avenir*, which its opponents in Rome and in France had been alleging that the pope had made.

[46] Forgues, II, 232.   [47] Blaize, II, 89.

[48] 'Mémoire présenté au Souverain Pontife Grégoire XVI par les Rédacteurs de l'AVENIR et les membres du Conseil de l'Agence générale pour la défense de la liberté religieuse.'—*A.R.*, pp. 41–100.

[49] According to an entry that Montalembert made in his journal at this time, when Gregory XVI was told that the aim of the pilgrims of God and liberty was to reinstate the holy see at the head of European civilization, he exclaimed: 'Ah! mon Dieu, ce sera la fin du monde!' See Trannoy, p. 181.

By the time this memorandum had been completed and submitted to the pope through the good offices of Cardinal Pacca (1756–1844), who was dean of the sacred college, Lamennais had experienced a sharp reversal of mood. The inclemency of the weather combined with the spiritual and political atmosphere of Rome to depress him profoundly. On 7 February he wrote to Coriolis an ironical description of the military exploits of the papal forces; the octogenarian Cardinal Albani had just led a martial expedition against another revolt that had broken out in the states of the church.[50] On 10 February Lamennais declared his mind in a letter to Countess de Senfft:

> I hope . . . I shall not have to stay in Rome much longer, and one of the happiest days of my life will be that on which I get out of this great tomb where there are nothing but worms and bones. Oh! how thankful I am for the decision I took, some years ago, to settle elsewhere.[51] . . . In this moral desert I should have led a useless life, wearing myself out in boredom and vexation. This was no place for me. I need air and movement and faith and love and everything that one vainly seeks amid these ancient ruins, over which like filthy reptiles, in the shade and in the silence, the vilest human passions creep. The pope is pious and means well; but he knows nothing about the world or about the state of the church and the state of society; motionless in the thick darkness by which he is surrounded, he weeps and prays; his role, his mission is to prepare and hasten the final convulsions which must precede the regeneration of society; that is why God has delivered him into the hands of the basest kind of men; ambitious, greedy, corrupt; frenzied idiots who call upon the Tartars to re-establish in Europe what they call *order*, and who adore the saviour of the church in the Nero of Poland, in the crowned Robespierre who is carrying through, at this very moment, his imperial 93[52] . . . Another twenty years of this kind of thing, and catholicism would be dead; God will save it through the peoples: what else matters to me? For me, politics means the triumph of Christ, legitimacy

---

[50] See Forgues, II, 234; Boutard, II, 263, 279 (in the footnote, for '1831' read '1832'); Schmidlin, II, 204.

[51] Referring to Leo XII's proposal to Lamennais in 1824 that he should take up his residence in Rome. See p. 97, *supra*.

[52] The allusion is of course to the suppression of the Polish insurrection by the Czar Nicholas I. See p. 179, *supra*.

means his law; my fatherland is the human race which he has redeemed with his blood.[53]

Lamennais went on to say that, all the same, he did not think their journey to Rome would have been a waste of time; there would probably be no public pronouncement in their favour, but there would be a silence which to the discerning would signify consent.

On 25 February 1832 Cardinal Pacca, by the pope's direction, sent them a reply,[54] which Montalembert summarized in his journal on the same day as follows: The Holy Father, while doing justice to our good intentions and to our talents, observes with dissatisfaction that we have stirred up certain controversies that are, to say the least, dangerous: our doctrines will be examined, but, as this examination is likely to take a long time, the pope enjoins us to return to France, where he will let us know in due course what he has decided.[55]

To a letter he was writing to Gerbet on 25 February Lamennais added a report of this reply, and commented: 'That is in line with the pope's decision to institute bishops . . . in order to oblige Louis-Philippe, and with the position he wants to take up with regard to the Powers, and especially to Russia which is destined, so the cardinals and monsignori say, to re-establish order in Europe.'[56] In a postscript added to the same letter on 1 March, Lamennais wrote more cheerfully, saying that the pope's undertaking that their doctrines should be examined was regarded by their friends as a great success: their enemies had been sure that they would be sent away without any reply.[57]

The same post-script of 1 March contains what seems to be the first reference in Lamennais's correspondence to the fact that Lacordaire was about to return to France alone: no reason is given and there is no mention yet of a difference of opinion between them.[58] Not until 10 May did Lamennais explain to Gerbet that

---

[53] Forgues, II, 235 f. Cp. Lamennais's letters to Gerbet of 28 January and 25 February in Blaize, II, 92 f., 97.

[54] For the precise text, see Dudon, *L. et le S.S.*, pp. 154 f.

[55] See Lecanuet, *Montalembert*, II, 285. Montalembert added this comment: 'C'est la ruine de nos espérances; il faut cependant se résigner et attendre notre justification de Dieu et des événements qu'il dirige. Il n'y a rien qui puisse inquiéter notre conscience, rien qui puisse éveiller le moindre remords dans notre âme.'

For Lamennais's reply to Pacca, see Dudon, *L. et le S.S.*, pp. 157 f.

[56] Blaize, II, 99. [57] Blaize, II, 100.

[58] Lacordaire had already decided to return by 23 February, so his decision was not due to Pacca's letter of 25 February. See Foisset, *Vie du R. P. Lacordaire*, I, 206.

Lacordaire's ideas had taken a different direction from his own and from Montalembert's, which had led to a certain coolness in their personal relations.[59] The attachment of Lacordaire to Lamennais had never been so close or affectionate as that of Montalembert, and it seems that he had come to the conclusion that there was nothing to be gained from staying on in Rome where their presence was obviously unwelcome, and that he had better part company from Lamennais and Montalembert.

On 13 March 1832, in response to a request which the three pilgrims had addressed to Bernetti, the cardinal secretary of state,[60] the pope granted them an audience. The fullest contemporary description of this famous audience is that in Montalembert's journal of the same date.[61]

> At last there arrived the day of our audience which we have so impatiently desired. . . . I was overwhelmed by the thought of the important things that might take place . . . and above all by the greatness of the papacy. As always, I was completely disappointed. After we had waited an hour in various ante-rooms at the Vatican, Cardinal de Rohan[62] arrived and led us at once into the small, modest office where the Holy Father was. We made the customary genuflections and kissed the sacred feet. Then we got up and remained standing in face of the pope who also stood: he was wearing a white soutane without any ornament whatever. . . . For a quarter of an hour he talked to us very pleasantly and affably about M. Varin,[63] the curé of Geneva and about Geneva itself, about M. de Lamennais's brother and his schools in Brittany, about the piety of the French catholics. He recalled the saying of

[59] Blaize, II, 109.

[60] See Dudon, *L. et le S.S.*, pp. 158 f.

[61] The account of the audience reproduced from E. Pelletan by Ricard, *Lamennais*, pp. 220 ff., is not to be taken seriously: cp. Boutard, II, 287 f. Gibson, *The Abbé de Lamennais and the Liberal Catholic Movement in France*, pp. 212 f., used it, describing it as 'the traditional account'. See also Roussel, *Lamennais intime*, p. 57.

[62] Though they did not know it, this cardinal's presence was to prevent the mennaisians from putting into circulation a false report of the audience. The Austrian ambassador in Rome wrote to Metternich on 10 March 1832: 'Sa Sainteté les recevra mardi prochain dans la présence du Card. Rohan: Elle craignait que la vanité française et de gazettier aurait pu leur inspirer un bel article flatteur pour eux et leurs adhérents, et c'est pour cette raison que le St Père a voulu d'un témoin à cette audience.' See Ahrens, *Lamennais und Deutschland* (1930), p. 242.

[63] *Sic*. This should be 'Vuarin': cp. p. 95, *supra*.

some cardinal, that the French would all go to hell or to paradise, but there would be no purgatory for them. . . . The pope then went to look for a silver statuette of Moses by Michael Angelo which he wanted to show us; he distributed to us gilt medals of his predecessor Saint Gregory, blessed the rosaries which we presented to him, and dismissed us very graciously, without having uttered a single word that had the least bearing on our mission or on the fortunes of the church.[64]

Lamennais in letters written to abbé Jean, to Gerbet, and to Vitrolles,[65] immediately after the audience, affected to be by no means disappointed. They had been granted all that they had asked for, he said—the examination of their doctrines and an audience of the pope. He was staying on in Rome so as to be available during the doctrinal examination. But there was another reason why he could not return to France at once, even if like Lacordaire he had been disposed to abandon hope of securing some form of papal approbation. As he told Vitrolles, in consequence of some ill-advised and involved financial transactions he was at present liable to be imprisoned if he set foot on French soil.[66] Thus when Lacordaire returned to Paris on 15 March, Lamennais remained in Rome, as the guest now of Père Ventura. Montalembert also stayed behind with him, but spent much of his time in visiting various parts of Italy. On 26 April[67] Lamennais went to stay at Frascati in a kind of hermitage that belonged to the Theatines.

Here, in this solitary place, he brooded on his visions of the death and resurrection of society, and on the part the church and the papacy were destined to play. Here too he continued to write a book which he had begun in Rome[68] and which in its unfinished state was afterwards incorporated in *Affaires de Rome*.[69] He entitled it 'Des maux de l'Église et de la Société et des moyens d'y remédier', and took as his text *Instaurare omnia in Christo* (Ephesians 1:10). If prophecy is an activity directly related to the calling of the church,

[64] See Lecanuet, *Montalembert*, ii, 286.
[65] See Blaize, ii, 100 ff.; *Vitrolles*, p. 216.
[66] See *Vitrolles*, p. 216; cp. Boutard, ii, 298; Blaize, ii, 96, 112 f.; Lecanuet, *Montalembert*, i, 286. For details of the transactions, see Forgues, ii, 243 f.; Blaize, ii, 129–133.
[67] See Roussel, *Documents*, i, 299.
[68] See *A.R.*, p. 117. In a letter of Gerbet on 29 April 1832 Lamennais says that he expected the book would run to about 300 pages; by 10 May this estimate was increased to 400 pages. See Blaize, ii, 107, 110.   [69] *A.R.*, pp. 209–306.

then this is Lamennais's most authentically prophetic piece of writing, and it is appropriate that it was never completed.

It is impregnated with the ideas and language of the Hebrew prophets. The church of Christ is likened to the people of Israel whose vicissitudes are to be interpreted in terms of doom and resurrection. When the church forgets its high calling and instead of rising to new responsibilities sinks into worldliness, God lets loose his chastisements and a spirit of revolt so as to bring about a reformation. Those who guide the church ought to be able to read the signs of the times; if they do not, God himself has to deal directly with the situation.

The French revolution was a sign that the world had reached a day of judgment and a time of divine visitation. Woe unto men who at such a time cry 'Peace, peace' when there is no peace!

I tell you, there is an eye whose look falls from on high like a curse on these sluggards. For what do they suppose they were born? God certainly has not placed man on this earth so that he may make himself comfortably at home here, or hibernate for a period in indolent slumber. Time is not a gentle breeze which as it passes caresses and refreshes his brow, but a wind that by turns scorches and freezes him, a tempest that swiftly carries his frail bark, beneath a stormy sky, through the rocks. He must look out and row and sweat; he must do violence to his nature and bend his will to the immutable order by which it is constantly being bruised and broken. Duty, stern duty, sits by his cradle, rises with him when he leaves it, and accompanies him to the grave. Man is in duty bound to his brethren as well as to himself, he is in duty bound to his country, to humanity, and above all to the church which, rightly understood, is nothing but the universal family, the great city from which the Christ, who is king as well as high priest, rules the world, calling from every part of the universe free creatures to draw together under the eternal laws of wisdom and love.[70]

Judgment must begin at the household of God. It is only through a renewed church that the decadence, fatigue, and passive submission to despotism, which at present mark Europe—and not least the church itself—can be transformed into vigour and rejuvenation. The diseases in society are the result of diseases in the church. Lamennais then surveys the condition of catholicism—first in Italy,

[70] A.R., pp. 225 f.

then in Spain and Portugal, and then in France where he stopped short. The only other part of the book that he drafted out was an epilogue in the style of Ezekiel, which is a foretaste of *Paroles d'un Croyant*.

In these fragments of a book, what Lamennais most deplored was the immobility and silence of the papacy and its dependence on temporal powers, at a time when society never stood in greater need of spiritual guidance and independent leadership.

> Immense questions have been raised in the world, they . . . have produced a ferment in society and are inflaming it like a burning fever: what has she [Rome] said? Nothing. A profound revolution is at work within christianity itself, the excited peoples are discarding their old laws and their ancient institutions, they clamour for a new order and, determined to establish it, they overthrow violently the obstacles in their way: what has she done? Nothing. Her power is both attacked and defended, her teaching is disputed, from all directions voices are lifted up, suppliant voices, catholic voices: Speak, they say, in order that your children may learn from your mouth what they ought to believe. . . . What has she answered? Nothing. . . .[71]

Intellectually, the church had tried to dig itself in behind an arid scholasticism, when it should have been absorbing all the new discoveries which the natural sciences and the study of society were making available. Without a theological renaissance Rome would never be able to influence the nations. Likewise, Lamennais deplored the clerical despotism in the papal states and the absence of responsible government and free institutions there. In Spain, Portugal, and France he condemned the church for clinging to temporal advantages so far as it could, whereas it should have realized that christians have never been stronger than when they have been poor. 'It is not to the rich man in purple but to the Crucified that the nations of the world have been given as his inheritance.'[72]

Catholics had so far failed to distinguish between what was just and what was false in the ideals of the revolutionary movement. Consequently, they had blindly identified themselves with the forces of reaction and had thereby withheld the resources of their faith from the builders of the future. What the peoples of Europe have rejected is not religion itself but the parody of religion that has been presented to them in alliance with political absolutism. Let the church

[71] *A.R.*, pp. 239 f.   [72] *A.R.*, p. 282.

listen to the groans of the suffering masses, which may then become the birth-pangs of a new era for the human race.

As Lamennais thus took up again and developed further the themes of the *Avenir*, his confidence in his own mission and his confidence in the church's calling and opportunity revived. He became eager to resume the campaign that had been suspended in the previous November. 'However it be with others,' he wrote to Gerbet on 10 May 1832, 'I am, for my part, quite determined to continue the work which I began twenty years ago, and which I shall abandon only at the end of my life.'[73] He had also been meditating fresh plans for the Congregation of St Peter.[74] Back in Rome in June he listened more responsively than ever to those of his friends who encouraged all his hopes. On 1 July 1832 he wrote to abbé Jean:

> Our mission here is now completed. The most eminent men look upon our cause as having succeeded with the holy see, since, pressed to condemn us, if we had erred in some point of doctrine, it has kept silence, and these same men urge us to resume our labours without worrying about episcopal opposition, should we have to face that again. I will particularly mention Cardinal Micara[75]—these are his actual words: 'You are in order and perfectly at liberty to do again what you have done, and to say again what you have said. If you had erred, the holy see would certainly have admonished you. It has kept quiet: what more do you ask of it? A formal approbation? It never gives that. Go then, and begin again to defend the church which more than ever needs to be defended. According to the example of the Fathers when they found themselves in similar circumstances, you have spoken forcibly; speak more forcibly still: that is what I should do in your place.'[76]

[73] Blaize, II, III.

[74] See Blaize, II, 91, 98 f., 103, 110 ff. Cp. Boutard, II, 296 f.

[75] Micara seems to have been a black sheep in the sacred college. Lützow, the Austrian ambassador in Rome, wrote to Metternich about him as follows on 7 October 1832: 'Le Cardinal Micara, fils d'un paysan . . ., jadis Capucin . . . a été introduit dans le S. Collège par feu Léon XII au grand chagrin te [de] tous les Cardinaux qui n'ont aucune relation avec ce confrère et desquels il est redouté par sa méchanceté; un Cardinal de mes amis, qui avait été assis au Conclave à côté de lui, me dit qu'il avait "une langue de vipère".' See Ahrens, p. 257.

[76] Blaize, II, 116 f. To de Coux Lamennais wrote that other cardinals shared the sentiments of Micara as did also Olivieri and Mazetti, two of the leading

A month previously, Montalembert had sent equally reassuring reports to Lacordaire.[77]

Lamennais and Montalembert left Rome on 10 July 1832 and began to travel to Munich, by easy stages so as to enable Montalembert to do more sightseeing on the way.[78] Lamennais's letters written during this journey show that he was really expecting to be able to resume publication of the *Avenir* on his return to Paris, as soon as satisfactory financial arrangements had been made.[79] Indeed, he called at the papal nunciature in Florence, and brusquely declared that this was his intention.[80] 'Puisqu'on ne veut pas me juger,' he said, 'je me tiens pour acquitté.'[81] He was not even put out when he heard towards the end of July that the Archbishop of Toulouse and about a dozen other French bishops had sent a document to Rome in which they called for the condemnation of a large number of propositions extracted from his and Gerbet's writings.[82] 'I am charmed by this move,' wrote Féli to Jean on 31 July from Venice, 'and by the publicity that has been given to it. For it is more than probable that these bishops will by no means obtain the

Roman theologians. Mazetti had said: 'Quand vous auriez tous les évêques du monde contre vous, ne vous inquiétez en aucune manière, tandis que le Pape ne vous condamnera pas.'—*Ibid.*, II, 120 f.

[77] See Lecanuet, *Montalembert*, I, 310.

[78] See *ibid.*, I, 314–319.

[79] See Blaize, II, 121–124. At first he had intended to go to Belgium after Munich and to wait there until it was safe for him to re-enter France (see p. 201, *supra*), but when he reached Munich he heard from de Coux on 18 August that the way was clear for him to return direct to France.—Blaize, II, 124. A letter of 24 August from Montalembert to Mgr Foscolo, which was intercepted by Metternich's police, shows that the intention was to restart the *Avenir* 'à la fin de l'hiver au plus tard': see Ahrens, p. 249.

[80] See Dudon, *L. et le S.S.*, pp. 185 f.

[81] See Lecanuet, *Montalembert*, I, 316, where Lecanuet is apparently drawing on Montalembert's journal.

[82] This was the so-called Censure of Toulouse, in which Mgr d'Astros, Archbishop of Toulouse, was the moving spirit and which some theologians at St Sulpice helped to prepare. For the story of this proceeding and the relevant documents, see *Censure de Cinquante-six propositions extraites de divers écrits de M. de la Mennais et de ses disciples par plusieurs Évêques de France, et lettre des mêmes Évêques au souverain pontife Grégoire XVI; le tout précédé d'une préface où l'on donne une notice historique de cette censure, et suivi des pièces justificatives* (Toulouse, 1835). Though dated 23 April 1832 the document was not ready for dispatch to Rome till 15 July. See Dudon, *L. et le S.S.*, pp. 167–171, 243–263; Boutard, II, 318–321; Mourret, *Le Mouvement catholique en France de 1830 à 1850*, pp. 126 ff.; *Dictionnaire de théologie catholique*, VIII, cols. 2510–2513.

condemnation they want, and Rome's silence will be a complete justification for us.'[83]

The travellers reached Munich towards the middle of August. There the *Avenir* had warm friends and admirers especially among the philosophers and artists,[84] and they were delighted to entertain and converse with the French visitors. A.-F. Rio (1798–1874), an authority on art, who had stayed with Lamennais and Montalembert in Rome earlier in the year, was with them also in Munich, and left an interesting account of a confidential interview between Lamennais and Schelling.[85] Lamennais also gave a series of readings from the manuscript of his *Essai d'un système de philosophie catholique*.[86]

On 28 August 1832, to the embarrassment of Lamennais and Montalembert, Lacordaire arrived in Munich. He had not come to rejoin his friends. On the contrary, he had heard that they were on their way back to Paris to restart the *Avenir*, and in order to avoid an awkward encounter he had decided to go into exile. He went to Munich because it was a catholic city and the cost of living was reputed to be cheap. Montalembert happily saved the situation by persuading him to conceal their differences so as not to scandalize their German friends, and it was agreed that instead of restarting the *Avenir* they should found a *Revue catholique*. Thus it came about that the three pilgrims of God and liberty happened to be reunited when the decisive blow fell on 30 August.[87]

Before the blow falls—that is, before the encyclical *Mirari vos* is promulgated—we will go back and take note of what had been happening all this time behind the scenes, especially in the Vatican. It is only in the present century that this knowledge has become available, through access to the Vatican and other archives. Of first importance was the publication in 1911 of *Lamennais et le Saint-*

---

[83] Blaize, II, 124. Since this letter was written from Venice, Dudon (*L. et le S.S.*, p. 251) was mistaken when he said that Lamennais did not hear of the Censure till he reached Munich. It is true that from Munich on 12 August Lamennais wrote to the same effect to Eugéné Bore, and this is what may have misled Dudon: see Roussel, *Lamennais intime*, p. 78.

[84] Charles Sainte-Foi in his *Souvenirs de Jeunesse*, part III, chaps. 2–4, portrays the intellectual and artistic society of Munich at this time. Among the friends of the mennaisians were Baader, Görres, Döllinger, and Schelling.

[85] See Rio, *Épilogue à l'art chrétien* (1870), II, 163–170.

[86] Rio, *ibid.*, II, 171 f.

[87] For the facts in this paragraph, see Lecanuet, *Montalembert*, I, 321 f.; Foisset, *Vie du R.P. Lacordaire*, I, 216 ff.; Lallemand, *Montalembert et ses amis*, pp. 156 f.

Siège 1820–1834 d'après des Documents inédits et les Archives du Vatican
by Paul Dudon. This book has been criticized on account of its
pro-papal bias,[88] which indeed Dudon hardly attempted to conceal,[89]
but this does not alter the fact that his book contains about what led
up to the *Mirari vos* a great deal of information that had not been
published before, even if it failed to damage Lamennais's own
testimony in *Affaires de Rome* as much as Dudon supposed. Other
important documents have since been published,[90] which serve to
check the one-sided impression left by Dudon. In what follows I
accept the authenticity of the documents quoted by Dudon, but not
necessarily his interpretation of them.

The holy see had been warned by its representative in Paris, soon
after the *Avenir* began publication, that its principles were politically
subversive. Lambruschini, at that time the papal nuncio, had reported
to Rome on 1 December 1830 that it was a dangerous journal, and
that Lamennais was surrounded by young editorial collaborators
who were even more 'excessifs' than himself.[91]

Then, the French government for its part, so soon as it learned
in November 1831 that Lamennais was appealing to the holy see,
sent urgent messages to its ambassador in Rome (Sainte-Aulaire)
telling him to make sure that the Vatican was not misled by the
Avenir's ultramontanism into showing any approval of Lamennais—
telling him also to keep a close watch on Lamennais, and to warn
the papal authorities that any encouragement given to him would
have a very adverse effect on the relations of church and state in

88 E.g. Duine wrote in *Annales de Bretagne*, January 1914, p. 197: 'Le volume de
  M. Dudon est une étude *Pro Pontifice et Ecclesia*. . . . La tendance visible de
  l'auteur est de diminuer l'influence des circonstances et des contingences sur
  le Pape pour renforcer la pure inspiration d'En Haut.' Victor Giraud wrote in
  Revue des deux mondes, 1 March 1919, p. 116: Dudon 'ne saurait admettre . . .
  qu'aucun agent du Saint-Siège ait jamais pu commettre à son égard [*sc.* de
  Lamennais] la moindre maladresse. . . . Le P. Dudon a des certitudes,—des
  certitudes *a priori*,—qu'il ne fera pas, j'en ai peur, partager à tout le monde.'
89 Cp. Dudon's account of his presentation of his book to Pius X in June 1911:
  Études, 5 July 1932, p. 86; *ibid.*, 5 February 1935, p. 356.
90 Notably, by Liselotte Ahrens, *Lamennais und Deutschland* (1930), who published the text of letters from the archives of the Austrian Ministry of Foreign
  Affairs, some of which had been utilized in part, but only in part, by Boutard.
  Ahrens, pp. 26–29, criticized Dudon's book. For Dudon's reply, see *Bulletin de
  littérature ecclésiastique*, published by the Institut catholique de Toulouse,
  XXXIII, 1932, pp. 16–34.
    See also G. Charlier, *Revue d'histoire littéraire de la France*, January–March
  1933, p. 114: cp. pp. 233 f., *infra*.
91 See Dudon, *L. et le S.S.*, pp. 89 f.

France. The ambassador replied (6, 8, and 10 December 1831) that he had seen both the cardinal secretary of state (Bernetti) and the pope himself, and that their dispositions left nothing to be desired.[92]

Likewise on 2 December 1831 Metternich wrote to the Austrian ambassador in Rome (Lützow), instructing him to make representations about the dangerous character of Lamennais's campaign; and he was no doubt grateful to receive in reply an assurance that the Holy Father fully shared his ideas on the subject.[93] All this, it will be noted, took place before the representatives of the *Avenir* reached Rome.

Gregory XVI, before deciding how they should be treated on their arrival, consulted at least three Italian theologians whose replies are extant[94]; two of them were known to have had mennaisian sympathies. It was in the light of their advice that the pope decided that the embarrassing pilgrims should be told by Cardinal Pacca that their doctrines would be examined, as they had requested, but that this would take a long time, so that they could go home and await the result there. The Vatican authorities certainly hoped that this communication, together with the refusal of the pope to discuss their business, when on 13 March he gave them an audience, would have convinced them that they had nothing to gain by staying on in Rome.

On 20 March 1832 the French ambassador sent the following report to Paris on the attitude of the holy see: 'The doctrine of abbé de la Mennais is thoroughly unpopular at Rome. It is equally shocking to the good and bad dispositions that are prevalent in this court. There is a sincere desire that religion shall not be exploited in the interests of parties. Still more there is a strong aversion to every kind of innovation and nothing is more foreign to the men of influence here than the spirit of audacity and enterprise.'[95]

Lamennais had no idea at the time—nor afterwards when he wrote *Affaires de Rome*[96]—of the manner in which the doctrines of the *Avenir* were actually examined at Rome. As regards this point, there is no doubt that Dudon was able to correct Lamennais's own testimony. For it is evident from the Vatican Archives that there was

[92] *Ibid.*, pp. 110–113. Several documents cited by Dudon are mistakenly dated in his footnotes. For the correct dates see 'Table des documents inédits' at the end of the book.

[93] *Ibid.*, pp. 116–120.   [94] *Ibid.*, pp. 126–138.   [95] *Ibid.*, p. 163.

[96] See *A.R.*, p. 38: 'Nous avions soumis au Saint-Siège une exposition exacte et nette de nos doctrines. Jamais, que nous sachions, elle n'a été examinée.' Cp. *ibid.*, p. 101.

a regular consultation on the subject, with written reports from a number of theologians. While some were more hostile to the *Avenir* than others, all agreed that the pope must make a pronouncement, since both the French bishops and the mennaisians were pressing for guidance. There was a consensus of opinion that the holy see's pronouncement should be on the lines that were in fact followed in the encyclical *Mirari vos*.[97]

Dudon further claimed that the papal condemnation of the *Avenir* was in no way motivated by political considerations, but his confidence about this, though it was edifying, seems also to have been a little naive. While Lamennais and Montalembert grossly oversimplified the issue when they took the view that the papacy was solely occupied with its temporal interests,[98] and that the condemnation of the *Avenir* was merely an act of complacency towards the European powers, which, as we shall see, *was* the view they took, yet it is not easy to believe that the diplomatic representations or suggestions that were made to the holy see counted for nothing. I do not deny that Gregory XVI may sincerely have supposed that he was concerned only to safeguard the traditional teaching of the church, but I should also say that, if he had consciously been influenced by Metternich or the Czar, he was too good a churchman to let it appear that he had been.

It may be that the naturally adverse reaction of the holy see to any kind of innovation would have been sufficient to account for the condemnation of the *Avenir*,[99] and that Gregory XVI did not need

[97] See Dudon, *L. et le S.S.*, pp. 172–185.

[98] E.g. see Montalembert's letter of 9 February 1832 to Guéranger: 'Notre démarche, si catholique et si simple, a jeté la Cour de Rome dans un embarras qu'elle ne nous a pas pardonné. Uniquement occupés de leurs intérêts matériels qui se trouvent dans la position la plus critique, les cardinaux et les prélats qui entourent le Saint-Père voient avec le plus grand mécontentement les efforts que nous avons faits pour détacher la religion et l'Église de la cause des rois qui sont, à leurs yeux, la Providence vivante de ce monde.'—Sevrin, *Dom Guéranger et La Mennais*, p. 212.

[99] Cp. E. Faguet, *Politiques et Moralistes* (2nd series), p. 123: 'L'Église catholique, abstraction faite de ses dogmes, était la réunion des tempéraments autoritaires. L'homme à nouveautés, le libéral, l'émancipateur, surtout le révolutionnaire, devenait tout naturellement un protestant hétérodoxe quelquefois, un libre penseur souvent, le plus souvent un catholique infidèle n'ayant plus de catholique que le nom.

'À quoi Lamennais conviait donc l'Église catholique, c'était à renoncer d'abord sa tradition historique, ensuite à ce qui était le fort, le vivace, le dévoué et le gros de son troupeau. C'est à quoi une église, pas plus qu'un parti, ne renonce.'

Metternich to tell him that the liberties advocated by the *Avenir* were extremely dangerous. Nevertheless, anyone who reads the correspondence between Metternich and Lützow, which was discovered in the State Archives in Vienna,[100] and who then reflects that the papacy, whose temporal interests were as much threatened by revolutionary movements as those of other powers, depended on foreign powers both for its political independence and for assistance in suppressing insurrections in its own territories, may reasonably come to the conclusion that the truth lies somewhere between the extreme contentions of Lamennais and Montalembert, on the one hand, and of Dudon, on the other.[101] At the same time, it may be granted that the operation of political considerations on the mind of the pope himself may well have been below or above the level of conscious admission. As regards the question whether the personal character and outlook of Gregory XVI were to any extent responsible for the condemnation of the *Avenir*, I shall have something to say about that in the epilogue, when the subsequent facts of the case will also be before us.[102]

This is however the point at which something must be said about Lamennais's allegation, which he reiterated in *Affaires de Rome*,[103] that the papal brief addressed to the Polish bishops on 9 June 1832[104] was the price paid by the holy see for an undertaking by Russia to provide an army that would defend the independence of the papal states.[105] If this allegation were true, it would obviously explain, and perhaps would justify, Lamennais's contention that papal pronouncements at this time were determined by purely political considerations. Indeed, the fact that he certainly believed it to be true does explain his contention.

The papal brief of 9 June 1832 condemned the Polish insurrection of 1830–1831 and called upon the bishops to see that the Polish

[100] See Ahrens, pp. 233–266, where some mennaisian letters intercepted by the Austrian police are also published. Other evidence has come to light of the way in which the Austrian police kept a watch on the movements of Lamennais and Montalembert when they left Rome in July 1832: see *Notes secrètes de la police autrichienne de Venise* (tirées des Archives d'État de Milan) by M. E. Rodocanachi in *Séances et travaux de l'Académie des sciences morales et politiques* (April 1918), pp. 384 f., 391–394.

[101] Cp. Sevrin, *Dom Guéranger et La Mennais*, pp. 213 f.

[102] See pp. 277 f., 282 f., *infra*.

[103] *A.R.*, p. 123.

[104] Not 'January 9, 1832' as C. S. Phillips, *op. cit.*, p. 252, says. For the full text of the brief in Latin and French, see *A.R.*, pp. 344–355.

[105] Cp. Debidour, p. 425.

catholics were in future fully submissive to their legitimate sovereign, i.e. the Czar. Lamennais stated[106] that he had seen a draft of this brief which had been sent in advance for his approbation to the Russian minister in Rome (Prince Gagarine) who had deleted an expression that he did not like. The truth of Lamennais's statements was accepted by abbé Boutard in his biography of Lamennais,[107] and it was impossible to control them until the publication in 1922 of Père Adrien Boudou's *Le Saint-Siège et la Russie: leurs relations diplomatiques au xixe siècle, 1814–1847*. Boudou had access to the Vatican Archives, and chapter 5 of his book, 'La Révolution polonaise de 1831', covers the period with which we are here concerned.

On the one hand, it appears that in the Vatican Archives there is no trace of any undertaking or offer on Russia's part to provide troops for the defence of the papal states, and none of the four drafts of the papal brief that Boudou unearthed bore any marks of alteration by the Russian minister.[108] Lamennais's precise statements must therefore be held to be, at least, non-proven. On the other hand, what Boudou revealed of the papacy's dealings with Russia at this time affords ample warrant for the opinion that the pope (however good his intentions may have been) did in consequence of Russian pressure betray the cause of the Polish catholics, and let himself be tricked by Russian (and Austrian) diplomacy into aiding and abetting the Czar's brutal and ruthless treatment of the Poles. For, before the papal brief was issued, the Czar had begun a series of measures designed to break the Poles' will to resist, measures which were in the same class as those that have been adopted for similar purposes by totalitarian states in the twentieth century. It is true that the pope made some tactful (and entirely ineffective) representations to the Czar about his treatment of the Polish catholics. Lamennais knew nothing about these representations but, if he had, it is questionable whether they would have made him, or ought to have made him, modify his judgment that the papacy had failed to bear a prophetic witness to the divine justice and compassion. Further, while Lamennais may have been at sea in alleging that Prince Gagarine had censored a draft of the papal brief to the Polish bishops, it is quite possible that it was communicated to him before its text was finally

---

[106] *A.R.*, p. 123.   [107] Boutard, II, 313.

[108] One of the drafts has a deletion resembling that which Lamennais claimed to have seen; it is not in Gagarine's, but in Gregory XVI's, handwriting. It must be supposed that somehow or other, perhaps by a backstairs intrigue, Lamennais had seen this draft. See Boudou, *op. cit.*, p. 186.

settled: Boudou himself supplies evidence that other papal moves and letters were subject to approval or alteration by foreign diplomats.[109]

We left Lamennais, Lacordaire, and Montalembert at Munich—in blissful ignorance of the blow that was about to fall on them. On 30 August 1832 Schelling, Görres, and a distinguished company of Bavarian writers and artists gave a farewell banquet to the French visitors.[110] After a sumptuous repast, Lamennais's health was drunk, and then that of union between the catholics of France and Germany. This was followed by the singing of some Bavarian national songs by a young painter, named Schottlauer. Suddenly the door opened and Lamennais disappeared so unobtrusively that Schottlauer noticed nothing and went on singing. A few minutes later Lamennais returned; he appeared to be calm and cheerful, completely master of himself. He asked the singer to be good enough to repeat the verses he had missed. As they left the table, Lamennais took Lacordaire by the arm and whispered to him: 'I have just received an encyclical of the pope against us; we must not hesitate to make our submission.' The whole party then walked to a village outside the city where they took coffee; Lamennais joined in the conversation without betraying the least sign of the calamitous news that had reached him.

It was not until he was alone with his companions (Rio was present as well as Lacordaire and Montalembert) that he read to them the documents he had received—with visible emotion, but without any marks of hostility towards the holy see. First, he read the covering letter from Cardinal Pacca which was designed somewhat to soften the blow that the encyclical would inflict:

> The Holy Father while fulfilling a sacred duty of his apostolic office did not want to forget his affectionate respect for your person, as much on account of your great gifts as of your long-standing services to religion. You will find . . . that in the

[109] E.g., op. cit., p. 196: 'Gagarine connut la note romaine . . . avant son envoi: il n'y trouva rien à redire et l'approuva pleinement.' Ibid., p. 206: 'Le pape refit la lettre . . . Metternich eut la satisfaction de voir ses conseils fidèlement suivis.'

[110] See for what follows Rio, Épilogue à l'art chrétien, II, 173–175, and Lallemand, Montalembert et ses amis, pp. 156 f. (which quotes Montalembert's journal). Harispe, Lamennais et Gerbet, p. 211, and Gibson, The Abbé de Lamennais, etc., p. 217, give a different account of Lamennais's behaviour on this evening, without citing their authorities. Both Rio and Montalembert were actually present.

encyclical your name and even the titles of your writings which contain reprehensible principles have been entirely suppressed.

But since you love the truth, and wish to know it in order that you may follow it, I am going to explain to you candidly and in a few words the main points which, after the examination of the *Avenir*, have most distressed His Holiness. They are as follows:

First, he has been much distressed by the fact that the editors have taken upon themselves to discuss in public and to decide the most delicate questions which belong to the government of the church and its supreme head. The effect has inevitably been to disturb peoples' minds and above all to cause division among the clergy, which is always harmful to the faithful.

The Holy Father also disapproves and indeed reproves the doctrines about *civil* and political liberty which, contrary no doubt to your intentions, tend by their nature to stir up and to propagate everywhere the spirit of sedition and revolt on the part of subjects against their sovereigns. Now this spirit is clearly opposed to the principles of the gospel and of our holy church which, as you well know, preaches obedience to peoples and justice to sovereigns.

The doctrines of the *Avenir* on *liberty of worship* and the *liberty of the press*, which have been treated with such exaggeration and pushed to such lengths by the editors, are at once very reprehensible and in opposition to the teaching, maxims, and practice of the church. They have greatly astonished and distressed the Holy Father; for if in certain circumstances prudence requires that they should be tolerated as a lesser evil, such doctrines can never be put forward by a catholic as good in themselves or as a desirable thing.

Finally, what the Holy Father has felt most bitterly is the *act of union proposed to all who, despite the murder of Poland, the dismemberment of Belgium, and the conduct of governments that call themselves liberal, hope still in the liberty of the world and want to work for it.* . . .[111]

The encyclical *Mirari vos* (dated 15 August 1832) was not so roundly anti-mennaisian as might be inferred from the way in which reference is commonly made to it. It was the first encyclical of Gregory XVI's pontificate, and accordingly much of it is taken up with greetings and exhortations appropriate to such an occasion.

[111] For the complete text of this letter, see *A.R.*, pp. 147–153. The expressions italicized were underlined in the original. The last passage italicized is a quotation from the title of the 'Act of Union' that was proposed in the last issue of the *Avenir*: see p. 182, *supra*.

Its general theme would seem to be lamentation over the evils of the
age. The *Avenir*, though never mentioned, is implicitly censured,
but only in certain passages. These passages do not constitute the
larger part of the document, but it is by reason of them that it has
been remarked upon by historians, as indeed they were what was
chiefly noticed at the time of its publication. The rest of the encyclical, to tell the truth, is conventional material which might find its
place in any papal pronouncement.

The passages upon which Lamennais's attention naturally fastened
were those that made the following points. (1) The idea that, if the
church is to be preserved and increased, it stands in need of restoration and regeneration is characterized as absurd and supremely
insulting.[112] (2) The maxim that liberty of conscience ought to be
assured and guaranteed to everyone is said to be sheer madness and
to be a consequence of 'indifferentism', i.e. of the notion that people
can be saved whatever faith they profess, provided their morals are
respectable; those who say that religion has anything to gain from
this pernicious error are said to be extremely impudent.[113] (3) Liberty
of publication is described as abominable and detestable (*nunquam
satis execranda et detestabilis libertas artis librariae*). Pope Clement XIII's
saying that the only way to deal with erroneous books is to burn
them is quoted with approval.[114] (4) Those who encourage subjects
to revolt against their rulers are unequivocally condemned and
likened to the Waldensians, Wycliffites, and other sons of Belial.[115]
(5) The separation of church and state is disapproved.[116] (6) Associations or unions between catholics and people of other religions are
said to have caused the Holy Father particular distress.[117] (7) 'Our
dearest sons in Jesus Christ, the princes', are said to have been given
their authority not only for temporal government but chiefly for
the defence of the church.[118]

Having read these documents, Lamennais simply remarked: 'It is
the condemnation of liberty and the abandonment of Polish nation-
ality.' Then, after remaining silent for a time, he added: 'God has
spoken: all that remains for me to say is: *Fiat voluntas tua!* and to
serve these two causes by my prayers, since he forbids me by the

---

[112] *A.R.*, pp. 370 f. (References are to the Latin original and the French translation
of the encyclical printed at the end of *Affaires de Rome*. The Latin text will also
be found in Dudon, *L. et le S.S.*, pp. 389–400.)

[113] *A.R.*, pp. 374–379.   [114] *A.R.*, pp. 378–383.

[115] *A.R.*, pp. 382–389.   [116] *A.R.*, pp. 388 f.

[117] *A.R.*, pp. 388–391.   [118] *A.R.*, pp. 392 f.

voice of his vicar on earth to serve them with my pen.'[119] In view of
the abject promises of complete submission to whatever the pope
should decide, which the editors of the *Avenir* had made in advance
and which their extreme ultramontanism required them to have
made, there was no other course that they could consistently adopt.
Then and there Lamennais is said to have drafted an act of submission
on behalf of the editors of the *Avenir* and the council of the *Agence générale*. It is dated 10 September[120] 1832 by which time Lamennais
had returned to Paris and consulted with his colleagues, who all agreed
to sign it. It was published a day or two later.[121] It read as follows:

The undersigned, editors of the *Avenir*, members of the council
of the *Agence* for the defence of religious liberty, being present at
Paris: convinced, after the encyclical letter of the sovereign pontiff Gregory XVI, dated 15 August 1832, that they cannot continue their work without placing themselves in opposition to the
expressed will of him whom God has charged to govern his
church, consider it to be their duty as catholics to declare that,
respectfully obedient to the supreme authority of the vicar of
Jesus Christ, they leave the arena where they have loyally fought
for two years. They earnestly call upon all their friends to give the
same example of christian submission.

In consequence:

1. The *Avenir*, provisionally suspended since 15 November
1831, will appear no more;

2. The *Agence générale* for the defence of religious liberty is
dissolved from today. All the proceedings that have been started
will be stopped, and the accounts will be closed with as little delay
as possible.[122]

---

[119] See Lecanuet, *Montalembert*, I, 325; Rio, *op. cit.*, II, 175.

[120] 'December' in the Garnier edition of *Affaires de Rome* (p. 154) is a misprint.

[121] See Dudon, *L. et le S.S.*, p. 217.

[122] *A.R.*, pp. 153 f. In sending the declaration to Rome, Lamennais accompanied
it with the following brief note to Cardinal Pacca:

'En réponse à la lettre que Votre Éminence m'a fait l'honneur de m'écrire le
16 août dernier, je m'empresse de lui envoyer copie de la déclaration que moi
et mes amis nous venons de rendre publique.

'Je remercie Votre Éminence des choses obligeantes qu'elle a personnellement la bonté de me dire et la prie d'agréer les sentiments respectueux avec
lesquels j'ai l'honneur d'être etc.' See Dudon, *L. et le S.S.*, pp. 215 f.

The contrast between the curtness of this note and the effusiveness of their
previous promise of submission (see p. 194, *supra*) will not escape notice.

The sincerity of this act of submission, so far as it went, may be accepted, but its restricted nature should be observed. The mennaisians undertook to call off their campaign and to keep silence in public, as a matter of ecclesiastical discipline. There was not a word to suggest that they had changed their minds or that they were prepared to make their own the views propounded in the encyclical. In fact, we now know from their published correspondence that they at once started interpreting the encyclical as a purely political act without any doctrinal authority. Thus a few days after the encyclical had been received we find Montalembert writing to a friend:

> [The pope] calls liberty of conscience *sheer madness*, liberty of the press *abominable*, science *impudent*, and proclaims the necessity of the union between church and state, etc., etc. This act, which fortunately in no way obliges our consciences as catholics, does however oblige us to lay down our arms.[123]

There is no reason at all to doubt that Lamennais was as sincere as his colleagues in making this act of submission, nor that they all shared his view of its restricted character.[124] None of the mennaisians (at least none that were of any note) made any further act of public submission until after the pope had promulgated further demands, not even Lacordaire.[125]

Lamennais stayed in Paris for only a week or two. He had no time even to visit Victor Hugo at Aux Roches, who sent him a pressing invitation through Montalembert.[126] By the beginning of October 1832 he had reached the silence and seclusion of La Chesnaie. On 15 October the papal internuncio in Paris (Garibaldi) communicated

---

[123] Letter of 4 September 1832 to Guerrier de Dumast. See Trannoy, p. 184. Cp. other letters of Montalembert to the same effect, quoted *ibid.*, p. 196. Lamennais in a letter of 7 October 1832 to Benoît d'Azy drew a distinction between 'spiritual Rome' and 'political Rome'; they looked upon the encyclical as the work of the latter. See *Lamennais inconnu*, p. 270.

[124] They were encouraged in this attitude by reports received from Rome itself, that the encyclical was regarded there as a deplorable document. See Dudon, *L. et le S.S.*, pp. 221 f.

[125] That is, until after the publication of the papal brief to the Archbishop of Toulouse in July 1833 (see pp. 229 f., *infra*). Cp. Sevrin, *Dom Guéranger et La Mennais*, pp. 291 f. Dudon in *L. et le S.S.*, p. 268, is mistaken in saying that Lacordaire had already 'explained himself'; Dudon misrepresents the letter to which he is adverting. Cp. *L. à M.*, p. 151.

[126] See Lecanuet, *Montalembert*, I, 329; Lallemand, *Montalembert et ses amis*, pp. 135 f. Sainte-Beuve paid a visit to their lodgings in Paris, and saw Lacordaire as well as Lamennais; he noted their different attitudes to the condemnation of the *Avenir*. See Chocarne, *Vie du R. P. Lacordaire* (1873), I, 130.

to de Coux the pope's satisfaction with the act of submission of 10 September; at the same time, he suggested that, if Lamennais would write a letter either to the pope himself or to Cardinal Pacca, he would receive a gratifying reply.[127] When this message was forwarded to Lamennais, he told de Coux that 'from the depths of his inexpressible sadness' there was nothing further he could say to the Holy Father.[128]

Reporting the matter to abbé Jean he wrote on 19 October:

> You will see from the enclosed letter of M. de Coux that the pope is fully satisfied with our submission, and is very far from requiring anything further; it follows that he himself does not regard his encyclical as having any dogmatic character. All the same, I thought it better not to write to him, in case his reply should be conceived in terms that would imply a more extended submission than we have intended to make, and also because his brief-might serve only to place us in an equivocal position.[129]

Again, writing to Guéranger on 30 November, he summed up the attitude of the mennaisians to the encyclical thus:

> We have always regarded the encyclical as an act of diplomacy solicited by the sovereigns [i.e. of the Powers] in order to put a stop to the catholic activity that was alarming them. We were only too well acquainted with the facts to be deceived for a moment, and we were none the less bound as catholics to obey. That is what we have done, and our declaration implies no more than that.[130]

To other and more intimate friends he sometimes wrote more bitterly,[131] but his correspondence during the closing months of 1832 indicates that he intended[132] to remain in retirement and to resume

---

127 See Forgues, II, 249; Blaize, II, 125 f.

128 See Forgues, II, 250. With regard to those who said he ought to make a further act of submission, Lamennais wrote to Coriolis on 13 November 1832: 'L'auteur de la circulaire [sc. the encyclical] nous a fait dire officiellement qu'il était satisfait de notre soumission, et ainsi personne n'a le droit d'exiger de nous rien de plus. . . . Voilà les hommes: après s'être mis en quatre pour vous faire taire, ils se mettent en huit pour vous faire parler; de sorte qu'on ne sait jamais comment les prendre, ni où l'on est avec eux.'—Ibid., II, 253.

129 See Blaize, II, 125. Cp. Vitrolles, pp. 223 f.

130 See Sevrin, Dom Guéranger et La Mennais, p. 270.

131 See his letter of 1 November 1832 to Countess de Senfft: Forgues, II, 251 f. Cp. Cottu, pp. 234 f.

132 His intentions were at first conditioned by uncertainty about whether the legal proceedings consequent upon the financial transactions that have been referred

the communal life at La Chesnaie, where indeed Gerbet, Lacordaire and Rohrbacher were already with him and also some select pupils,[133] and where he was at work again on his *Essai d'un système de philosophie catholique*.[134] In his last letter of the year to his friend Vitrolles, Lamennais wrote on 13 December:

Who would wish to travel a second time through this round of troubles that men call life? Certainly not I. As I approach the end I feel myself drawn more and more towards that mysterious world of which this is only the porch open to all the winds, to the sun and to the rain, as if Providence had wanted to inspire us with a longing to enter the temple.[135]

This melancholy note may have been due in part to Lacordaire's departure two days before. Though he had acted with Lamennais since 30 August, Lacordaire had not been at ease, and on 11 December he made a melodramatic and this time final escape from an association which he wished to break. He disappeared from La Chesnaie without notice, leaving behind him a letter to justify his conduct.[136] He alleged an increasing difference of outlook, specifying Lamennais's republicanism as a primary cause of disagreement. He said that it was a suitable time for him to take his leave, since his departure would do no harm to Lamennais. But his action could be interpreted as the desertion of one whom he had called his father and master, at a time when he had never stood in greater need of friendship and support.[137] Lacordaire afterwards denied that he had

to above (see pp. 201, 205, *supra*) might make it necessary for him to leave France. See *Cottu*, pp. 233 f., 237; *Lamennais inconnu*, p. 277; *Vitrolles*, pp. 218 f.; Laveille, *J.-M. de La Mennais*, I, 487 f.

[133] On 17 December 1832 Lamennais wrote to E. Boré that there were then nine in residence at La Chesnaie. See Roussel, *Lamennais intime*, p. 137.

[134] On 14 November 1832 he wrote to Montalembert: 'Nous continuons ici chacun nos travaux. Il m'est venu beaucoup d'idées sur la philosophie; plus je les approfondis, plus je trouve nos principes féconds.'—*L. à M.*, p. 23. But he did not expect to be able to publish his new *Essai* in the proximate future. To Guéranger, who had inquired about it, Lamennais wrote in the letter of 30 November 1832 that has already been quoted above: 'Je m'occupe, en effet, de l'ouvrage dont vous me parlez, mais sans aucun projet de publication, au moins prochain. S'il me prenait envie, en ce moment, de réimprimer le *Symbole des Apôtres*, il se trouverait renfermer dix ou douze hérésies pour le moins. Or, je ne voudrais pas causer cette mortification aux Apôtres.'—Sevrin, *op. cit.*, p. 270. [135] *Vitrolles*, p. 229. [136] See *L. à M.*, pp. 29 f.

[137] Cp. Duine, p. 175: 'Lacordaire . . . estimant que son chef n'était plus un astre propice à ses desseins, se sépara de lui, le 11 décembre, et sortit de La Chênaie brusquement, comme d'une place assiégée.'

ever regarded Lamennais as his father and master, but there is no doubt that he had used these very words in 1831.[138]

It is pleasant to be able to close the story of this unhappy year with some direct and attractive glimpses of the manner of life that had been resumed at La Chesnaie. They also serve to illustrate Lamennais's undiminished power of influencing young men. Maurice de Guérin (aged twenty-two)[139] arrived in December 1832 to study under Lamennais's supervision with a view to testing his vocation in the Congregation of St Peter. On 18 December he wrote to his sister Eugénie:

M. Féli has plunged me into modern languages, beginning with Italian, and at the same time into catholic philosophy and the history of philosophy. . . . Of the dead languages, I am learning only Greek. . . .

There are now four of us youngsters. Each has his own bedroom; but as there is not a fireplace in them all, we work together in a common room round a good fire. I am becoming used to getting up at 5 o'clock. . . . I am very fond of our little chapel at the bottom of the garden, where we go each morning to hear or serve mass as soon as we are up. It is to wake up in the Lord. Then comes breakfast with butter and bread which we toast in order to make it more appetizing. . . . Dinner, which is very *confortable*, with coffee and liqueurs when there are visitors, is seasoned with a running fire of pleasantries and banter, most of which comes from M. Féli. He says the most delightful things; flashes of wit as vivid, as keen, and as sparkling as you can imagine. . . . His genius goes off like that when he is not working. . . .

M. Féli is in process of writing a book in which he will resume all his philosophy and develop it further. All the beams of his knowledge and genius will be concentrated in it: he has done nothing previously to be compared with this. You must be prepared for mighty wonder and admiration in the world when this work appears. . . .

138 See Boutard, II, 224. At the same time, it may be true to say that as a mennaisian Lacordaire never got beyond the novitiate and had never 'made his profession': see Bremond, *Gerbet*, p. 12. Bremond also said: 'Supprimez Lacordaire, et rien d'essentiel ne sera changé dans la vie intérieure de cette glorieuse école.'—*Ibid.*, p. 5.

139 Cp. pp. 32, 143, *supra.* See Maurice de Guérin, *Journal, Lettres et Poèmes*, edited by G. S. Trébutien with Sainte-Beuve's essay (first published in 1863; 27th ed. 1922); also an article in the *Christian Remembrancer*, January 1864, pp. 1–26.

He loves us like a father; he always calls us 'my son'. . . .
One learns more from his conversation than from books. In a few
words he opens up for you immense perspectives. . . .[140]

A few days later he wrote to another correspondent:

When I first met M. Féli (that is what we call him *en famille*) I
experienced that mysterious sense of awe which seizes one at the
approach of divine things and of great men; but before long this
sense of awe changed into unreserved confidence, and I found that
our imagination gives us quite a false idea of great souls, when it
represents them to us as inaccessible and formidable to ordinary
people; far from it! . . . M. Féli has, so to speak, forced me to
forget his renown by his fatherly kindness. . . . Here I am in his
hands, body and soul, hoping that this great artist will produce a
statue out of a shapeless block of stone. . . .[141]

[140] Maurice de Guérin, *Correspondance*, edited by B. d'Harcourt (1947), pp. 60 ff.
[141] *Ibid.*, pp. 64 f. See also Hippolyte de La Morvonnais's testimony to the impression that Lamennais made upon him at this time: E. Fleury, *Hippolyte de la Morvonnais* (1911), part 1, chap. 5.

Chapter Seven

FAILURE OF A MISSION?
1833-1836

AT THE BEGINNING OF 1833, so far as appearances went, the disturbance that had been caused in the Church of France by the *Avenir* had subsided. Lamennais and his disciples had appealed to Rome, and Rome had, after prolonged deliberation, told them emphatically that they must abandon their campaign. They had promptly undertaken to obey, so proving that they were practitioners as well as preachers of submission to the holy see. The *Avenir* would not appear again; the *Agence générale* was being wound up as rapidly as possible. Lamennais himself had disappeared from the scene of action, and had retired to Brittany. Silence had fallen on the whole mennaisian school. The French bishops might congratulate themselves that, with the pope's somewhat dilatory assistance, they had squashed a dangerous and divisive agitation.

And if they had had access to Lamennais's private correspondence during the first six months of 1833, they would have been pleased to learn that he was insisting to his friends that he would be fully occupied for two years at least in revising and rewriting his philosophy,[1] that he had no intention of returning to Paris[2] or of taking any part in public affairs[3] until this work was completed. The silence

---

[1] On 9 January 1832 he wrote to Montalembert: 'Je voudrais avoir deux bonnes années de loisir pour finir ma philosophie.'—*L. à M.*, p. 39; cp. *ibid.*, pp. 49, 126. The letters to Montalembert, whom Lamennais was now taking into his confidence more than anyone else, are especially important. Except for a visit which Montalembert paid to La Chesnaie in June–July 1833, they never again lived under the same roof.

[2] On 2 May 1833 he wrote to Mlle de Lucinière: 'Quand retournerai-je à Paris? qui le sait? J'aurais besoin de passer encore ici deux ans pour achever certaines choses.'—Forgues, II, 286.

[3] 'Je persiste à penser qu'un silence absolu est ce qui nous convient le mieux.' —*L. à M.* (29 March 1833), p. 98. 'Le silence nous a réussi; continuons de nous taire.'—*Ibid.* (12 April 1833), p. 101. There were indeed moments when it was extremely difficult to maintain this resolution. 'Il y a des instants où le désir du combat bouillonne dans l'âme et y produit des angoisses inexprimables.'—*Ibid.* (2 May 1833), p. 126.

that he designed for himself he equally recommended to his friends.[4]

The bishops would, however, have been much less pleased if they had been able to read his reasons for a policy of silence. During these early months of 1833 he came to some radical conclusions. These did not (at least, in his own mind) raise any question of a rupture with the church or of repudiating the catholic faith; but they did mean that his attitude to the church as it actually existed had undergone a profound change.

Despite the pope's verdict he remained entirely convinced that the program of the *Avenir* had been right. The only way to the new social order for which the peoples were yearning was the way of liberty and emancipation. The church, seeking to preserve its temporal and material interests, had unmistakably identified itself with the old, doomed order. But God would carry through his designs despite the blindness of the ecclesiastical hierarchy. At the same time, schism in the church must at all costs be avoided. To a professor in Mexico, who had written to ask for help in starting a journal analogous to the *Avenir*, Lamennais wrote on 12 March 1833:

> The world is in a great crisis: everywhere it is trying to detach itself from a past out of which the life is gone, and to begin a new era. Nothing will stop this magnificent movement of the human race—it is directed from on high by Providence; but it is being held up by several causes. The welfare of society rests on two principles which, rightly understood, comprise all its laws: 'No liberty without religion' and 'no religion without liberty'. Now, our old Europe is divided into two parties of which one wants liberty without religion and the other religion without liberty, that is to say, both are striving to realize the impossible. The only remedy then is to attach the catholics to the cause of liberty, so as to win back the friends of liberty to catholicism. That is what we attempted in the *Avenir* and I may say with a success that surprised us both by its extent and its rapidity. But the absolute sovereigns, who were alarmed by our progress, sought to stop it: for that purpose they allied themselves with Rome and the episcopate who are unfortunately imbued with the notion that religion would perish without the material support of the powers of the earth and who

---

[4] He gave instructions that when the final report of the *Agence* was sent out nothing should be said about the encyclical or about anything to do with it, but that the report should deal only with finance.—*L. à M.* (12 February 1833), pp. 69 f.

are moreover, on principle (*en théorie*), enemies of liberty. In order not to put ourselves in a false position with regard to catholicism, we have had to suspend our efforts, or at least to modify their form; for it would be an additional and immense calamity to introduce trouble and division into the church. The obstacles which prejudice, passion, and interest put in the way of what is good will disappear in time: God will intervene by means which are unknown to us. Until then we ought, without giving up his work, to avoid everything which would tend to loosen, even for a moment, the sacred bonds of unity. No doubt, there are happening before our eyes strange things . . . which would shake the very elect, if God were not upholding them. But great scandals always announce a great manifestation of Providence: let us then await it with faith, and hasten it by our prayers.[5]

To more intimate correspondents Lamennais was more outspoken and more specific, but he said nothing that necessarily carried him further than the position summarily indicated in the foregoing letter. To Montalembert he described 'the catholicism of our days' as 'the catholicism of the Holy Alliance and of the budget'.[6] That being so, it was useless to try to work for the liberal catholic program in the name of the church. When sufficient time had elapsed to cover their change of ground, they would go to work again for the ideas of the *Avenir* but on a different platform. 'Instead of making ourselves the champions of catholicism, let us leave that in the hands of the hierarchy, and present ourselves simply as the men of liberty and humanity. God alone can fight with success for religion against the clergy.'[7] 'Our first concern must be by degrees to change our position, and it will take time and much prudence to do this. And by changing our position, I mean transposing our action, whatever it may be, outside the church, both by ceasing to occupy ourselves with matters proper to religion (i.e. with ecclesiastical affairs) and by taking care not to treat any question from the theological point of view.'[8] By the beginning of May, he could tell Mlle de Lucinière that what went on in the Roman Curia, now that he had seen how the wires were pulled, interested him as little as 'what goes on in

[5] Forgues, II, 275 f.
[6] *L. à M.* (12 February 1833), p. 70.
[7] *L. à M.* (21 January 1833), p. 45. 'En un mot, nous devons désormais parler comme Français et non comme catholiques' (23 January 1833), *ibid.*, p. 48. Cp. *ibid.*, pp. 43, 63 f.
[8] *L. à M.* (12 February 1833), pp. 64 f.

China, in the great College of mandarins'.[9] (Actually, for some time yet Lamennais would be much more interested in what went on at Rome than he acknowledged.)

What had most strikingly changed was his attitude to the papacy. For years[10] he had been lamenting in private the failure of the popes to rise to the height of times and to fulfil their divinely ordained mission. But now he has given up hope of the church's recovering its health in his lifetime.[11] Gregory XVI's mission, Lamennais now held, was not to lead God's people into a new era, but to complete the church's shame in the old era. To abbé Vuarin, who had been his companion on his visit to Rome in 1824, he wrote on 8 May 1833: 'Providence has sent Gregory XVI to close a long period of crimes and ignominy, to show the world just how low the human part of the divine institution can sink: may he do his work, and do it quickly. *Quod facis, fac citius.*'[12] Lamennais's confidence was fixed now in God, and not in the pope, and he was prepared to wait for God to stretch forth his hand in his own time, as he had done before in Christ's passion.[13]

The doctrine of papal infallibility, which had been the king-pin of his system, had of course to be so modified as to be compatible with his new outlook. He still maintained that there must be an infallible teaching authority at the centre of the church. He explained what he now considered to be the truth of the matter to one of his Polish followers thus:

> If there is not a centre of faith, or . . . if this centre is fallible, it seems to me there is no possibility of unity of faith; I am talking not of internal unity, but of external profession and of teaching. The personal infallibility of the pope in no wise follows from that; it is enough that he be infallible when he speaks in the name of the church . . . when his voice is that of the entire body of which

---

[9] Letter of 2 May 1833, Forgues, II, 287. Cp. *Lamennais inconnu*, p. 294.

[10] E.g.: 'Je ne crois pas que, depuis le monde est monde, il y ait eu un mouvement aussi prodigieux d'idées au milieu du silence de tout ce qui est institué pour parler. Chaque flot a sa voix dans cette vaste mer:—le souverain de l'Océan se tait seul dans sa grotte.'—Letter of 2 March 1828 to Countess de Senfft, Forgues, I, 444. Cp. *ibid.*, I, 226, 239, 243 f., 349, 431 f.; and p. 195, n. 35, *supra*.

[11] *L. à M.*, p. 50: La 'guérison [de L'Église] n'arrivera pas de mon temps. Au contraire, le mal s'accroîtra.'

[12] See V. Giraud, 'Une correspondance inédite de Lamennais', *Revue des deux mondes*, 1 November 1905, p. 193. 'Quod facis, fac citius', was one of Lamennais's favourite sayings: cp. Versluys, p. 16.

[13] See *L. à M.* (15 March 1833), p. 89. Cp. Forgues, II, 280.

he is the organ. As regards that, do you ask how one will distinguish the word of Gregory from the word of the pope? Perhaps not always easily, perhaps not always immediately, but there always comes a time when this discernment is made, with certitude, by a sort of sound sense and general instinct; until then, the duty to obey or to believe remains in suspense.[14]

More remarkable, however, than these changes in Lamennais's views was the deepening of the apocalyptic element in his outlook. Since about 1820 he had often in his correspondence spoken of an approaching world crisis, and had used with regard to it the prophetic and apocalyptic language of the Bible.[15] He never showed any sympathy for crude attempts to predict the date when the world would end, or for literal interpretations of apocalyptic imagery, and he had a horror of the setting up of new sects, to which adventist ideas commonly lead. But what he did do was to take seriously the Bible's prophecies of the last things and to see in them a present relevance. There were the prophecies that pointed to a great catastrophe in which God would judge the corruption of the world; there were the promises that there would be a realization on the plane of history of a new age in which Christ's power as the liberator of all peoples would be made manifest. This he took to be the truth symbolized in the idea of the millennium that would precede the final winding up of the scroll of history and the consummation of God's kingdom in eternity.

Cardinal Wiseman, who got to know Lamennais during his visit to Rome in 1824 and 'held long conversations' with him, left this record of one of them:

> I remember his once describing, in glowing colours, the future prospects of the Church. He had referred to prophecies of Scripture, and fulfilments in history, and had concluded that, not even at the period of Constantine, had perfect accomplishment of

[14] Letter of 5 February 1833 to Count Rzewuski, Forgues, II, 272.

[15] See chapter 2 of the Introduction ('Eschatologie et Messianisme') of Yves Le Hir's edition of *Paroles d'un Croyant* (1949), where quotations are collected. Le Hir suggests that Lamennais's apocalyptic ideas were influenced by those of J. de Maistre, Saint-Simon, and Ballanche.

Towards the end of his life Lamennais testified to the constancy of this kind of expectation in his thought. On 11 September 1848 he wrote to Vitrolles: 'J'ai constamment vu comme prochaine cette dissolution générale d'une société qui doit mourir pour que la vie ne s'éteigne pas dans le monde. C'est la pensée qui, sous toutes les formes, domine dans ce que j'ai écrit depuis trente ans.'—*Vitrolles*, p. 443.

P.P.—15

predictions and types been made: and that, therefore, a more glorious phase yet awaited the Church than any she had yet experienced. And this, he thought, could not be far off.

'And how,' I asked, 'do you think, or see, that this great and wonderful change in her condition will be brought about?'

'I cannot see,' he replied. 'I feel myself like a man placed at one end of a long gallery, at the other extremity of which are brilliant lights, shedding their rays on objects there. I see paintings and sculpture, furniture and persons, clear and distinct; but of what is between me and them I see nothing, the whole interval is dark, and I cannot describe what occupies the space . . .'[16]

Lamennais still has a similar vision of the future, beyond a period of awful upheavals and catastrophes. Previously he had assumed that the church would be preserved intact throughout them, and indeed that the pope would be God's vicegerent in bringing about the fulfilment of his glorious promises. But now he has come to the conclusion that the church itself and the papacy, as at present constituted, belong to what is going to be condemned and destroyed; God is going to raise up—in ways beyond human calculation—a new church fit for a new age, on the analogy of the raising up of the new Israel to take the place of the old Israel. On 25 January 1833 Lamennais wrote to Countess de Senfft:

Today, everything is in a state of flux; nothing has roots; neither thought nor affection is able to attach itself to anything. This is the character of great epochs when everything is changing, when everything is renewing itself. The old foundation, worm-eaten and rotten, crumbles to dust, and one cannot yet see what is going to take its place. Between a past which can no longer stand up and a future which does not yet exist, one can inhabit only formless ruins, into which the rain, the wind, and snow penetrate from all sides. But in the very midst of these ruins, beneath the half-collapsed vault where Providence has provided us with a little shelter, one can in the meantime taste a certain peace as one contemplates these preliminaries of a new creation and . . . this amazing work of God. The world in its old form was used up. Men had abused everything; they had denatured, corrupted everything. That is why the old hierarchies, both political and ecclesiastical, are disappearing together; they are no more than two spectres that embrace one another in a tomb. God, by means

[16] Wiseman, *Recollections of the Last Four Popes*, pp. 338 f.

which to me are unknown, will without doubt regenerate his church: she will not perish; she is immortal, for she is nothing else than the society of mankind under the law of the redemption wrought by Jesus Christ; but in what form will she reappear, when the purifying fire has burned up the dry envelope which hides her today from nearly all eyes? I do not know. One knew no more when the synagogue gave up the ghost or rather when it underwent the transformation that had been predicted.[17]

It was possible for men to do something to set forward the transformation of the political order, but Lamennais was emphatic now that the transformation of the church would be God's work and must wait upon him. It was useless for men to try to accomplish it themselves.[18]

These ideas, which are altogether explicit in his private correspondence of the first six months of 1833, are also presupposed in Lamennais's own apocalypse, *Paroles d'un Croyant*, which was for the most part written in May and June of this year,[19] though, as we shall see, it was not published till the following year. I shall have more to say about it when we reach that point. But what has been said above may explain how Lamennais could regard *Paroles d'un Croyant* as having nothing to do with the church and as lying outside the church's purview, in spite of its being soaked in the thought and language of the Bible and of its having a quasi-liturgical character.

The explanation lies in the sharp distinction he now drew between the transformation of the church (the ecclesiastical institution) and the transformation of society. *Paroles d'un Croyant* had to do only with the transformation of society. He felt it to be a political message to humanity, a message to the poor and suffering about God's impending casting down of their oppressors and the dawn of a new age of peace, justice, and love. It was not a message of his own, but one that had been laid upon him;[20] it was appropriately begun with

17 Forgues, II, 267 f. Cp. *ibid.*, II, 279: 'Il s'agit d'une transformation analogue à celle qui eut lieu il y a dix-huit siècles.'

18 See Forgues, II, 271.   19 See Le Hir, *Paroles d'un Croyant*, pp. 1–4.

20 Le Hir (*op. cit.*, p. 29) rightly, it seems to me, takes some words that Lamennais wrote in 1837 as indicative of the sense of pressure—or inspiration—under which he composed *Paroles d'un Croyant*. On 24 November 1837 he wrote to his friend Marion: 'Il y a en moi une puissance qui me pousse; j'ai une tâche à remplir. Sans cela, sans l'invincible sentiment d'un devoir qui m'est imposé, je serais incapable d'écrire une ligne. Il y a comme une voix qui me parle toujours, et dont je ne suis qu'un faible écho; qu'elle se taise, rendu à moi-même, à moi-seul, il ne me restera plus que le silence.'—*Confidences*, p. 145.

the invocation of the Holy Trinity, although it completely ignores the role of the church. Lamennais's attitude to the church at this time may seem strange, but it is not unintelligible. Pending the transformation of the church, which must wait upon God, it was, he held, the duty of catholics to remain submissive to its existing constitution and to obey its religious discipline, and he intended to do so himself. But he also held that this left him free to work for the transformation of society, outside the ecclesiastical sphere. If we realize that this was where he stood in the middle of 1833—though at the time only a few of his friends had been admitted to his confidence—we shall find it easier to understand the events of the second half of the year.

But first we must note the fact that the silence of the mennaisians during the first six months of 1833 had been broken by one public manifestation. In the middle of May there had appeared a French translation of *Le livre des pèlerins polonais* by Adam Mickiewicz (1798–1855).[21] This book, which resembles and to some extent influenced *Paroles d'un Croyant*,[22] was an apocalypse written to encourage the Polish exiles in their adversities. The gallican paper, *L'Ami de la Religion*, not unreasonably described it as 'un éloge continuel de la révolte et une philippique contre les souverains'.[23] Montalembert, who was responsible for the French translation,[24] contributed a foreword to it which was an enthusiastic defence of the Polish insurrection and an outspoken criticism of the European governments.[25] As an epilogue there were included some verses addressed to Poland[26] which Lamennais had composed during his stay in Rome in the previous year. Neither Montalembert nor Lamennais seems to have regarded this publication as inconsistent with the act of submission to the encyclical *Mirari vos*, which they

[21] See Marie Czapska, *La Vie de Mickiewicz* (1931).

[22] On 16 May 1833 Lamennais wrote to Montalembert: 'Avant d'avoir lu Mickiewicz, j'avais commencé un petit ouvrage d'un genre fort analogue.'—*L. à M.*, p. 133. But the effect of *Le livre des pèlerins polonais* on *Paroles d'un Croyant* has often been exaggerated: see Y. Le Hir on 'Mickiewicz et Lamennais en 1833' in *Annales de Bretagne*, 1948, pp. 47–58.

[23] *Ami de la Religion*, 14 September 1833, p. 307.

[24] Montalembert had only a small part in the actual work of translation since he knew little Polish. See Lallemand, *Montalembert et ses amis*, p. 321; cp. *M. à L.*, p. 34.

[25] See Lallemand, *op. cit.*, pp. 322 ff.

[26] 'À la Pologne', reprinted in *O.C.*, XI, 233–236. The refrain reads: 'Dors, ô ma Pologne, dors en paix, dans ce qu'ils appellent ta tombe: moi, je sais que c'est ton berceau.'

had made in the previous September. But there were others who took it to be signal evidence of the insincerity of that act.

It is indeed improbable that the publication of *Le livre des pèlerins polonais* would by itself have provoked a new crisis. The holy see did not want to have to proceed any further against the mennaisians. That is apparent from the way in which the appeal from the French bishops in the previous year to endorse the Censure of Toulouse[27] had been left unanswered. The Vatican had in fact been so well satisfied with the submission of the mennaisians, or so willing to let sleeping dogs lie, that on 28 February 1833 a Congregation of cardinals had definitely decided that the Censure of Toulouse should receive no endorsement from Rome.[28]

The only formal acknowledgment given to the appeal of the French bishops for a much more comprehensive condemnation of mennaisian doctrines was a papal brief of 8 May 1833 privately addressed to the Archbishop of Toulouse.[29] It commended the French bishops for their vigilance, but studiously declined to add anything to the *Mirari vos* in the way of censure of Lamennais's opinions. The brief did however say that, while the Holy Father had at first been gratified by the completeness of the submission of 'auctores ipsi fautoresque consiliorum, de quibus praecipue quere-bamur', he was now worried by what was being publicly rumoured.

The Holy Father had cause to be disquieted. Not only had reports of what Lamennais was saying in private and in letters to his friends reached Rome, but the Curia—thanks to the indiscretion of Lamennais's friends and the industry of Metternich's police—was in possession of documents which proved that the mennaisians had in no wise abandoned their attachment to the ideas of the *Avenir*. On 22 July 1833 Montalembert reported to this effect in a letter to Lamennais:

> I ought to tell you all that abbé Martin[30] [who had just returned from Rome] has recounted to me. . . . They could not be more worked up against you and us, not only because of the entreaties of the Archbishop of Toulouse and company, but chiefly as a result of the intrigues of the Jesuits who are now masters of everything and especially of the pope. It appears that they know there day by day everything that we do, everything that we say,

27 See p. 205, *supra*.
28 See Dudon, *L. et le S.S.*, pp. 258 f. Lamennais heard of this decision in April, see *Lamennais inconnu*, p. 294; Forgues, II, 288; *M. à L.*, p. 75.
29 For the full text see *A.R.*, pp. 396–401; Dudon, *op. cit.*, pp. 405 f.
30 Martin de Noirlieu (1792–1870), chaplain of the École polytechnique.

everything that we write. Cardinal Bernetti has said: 'These gentle-
men are silent, but they are acting; it is the silence of the Jansenists';
others accuse you of making yourself ultramontane, in order the
better to ruin the church. Finally, what is most serious, there
have been shown to the pope copies of several of your letters
addressed to indiscreet friends, in which you would have expressed
either a formal disapproval of the encyclical or the hope of a
change before long in the church.[31]

There was then disquiet in Rome before *Le livre des pèlerins
polonais* appeared in France; in fact, it was before its publication that
the papal brief to the Archbishop of Toulouse was prepared and
dispatched. The papal brief was however to have remained private.
All we know is that in July—i.e. two months after *Le livre des
pèlerins polonais* had appeared—Rome approved of, or at least connived at, the publication in France of the papal brief which, pointedly
if incidentally, registered the pope's dissatisfaction with the conduct
of the mennaisians. For on 2 July 1833 the Archbishop of Toulouse
wrote to Rome to say that 'he did not think he would be going
against the intentions of His Holiness in letting the brief be published,'[32] and it was actually published in *L'Ami de la Religion* on
20 July.[33]

Montalembert was in Paris at the time, having just returned from
a visit to La Chesnaie, and he called together as many of the leading
mennaisians as were available, but they were not agreed about what
they ought to do. Montalembert himself had no doubt at all about
the right course. As he wrote to Lamennais on 22 July 1833:

> I am for the most absolute silence, first because the document
> [i.e. the papal brief of 8 May 1833] is not addressed directly to us
> so that we are in no wise obliged to reply to it; then, I do not see
> how we could repeat our submission purely and simply, without
> increasing the suspicion of duplicity that lies against us. . . .[34]

[31] *M. à L.*, pp. 99 f.; cp. Lecanuet, *Montalembert*, I, 391.
[32] See Dudon, *L. et le S.S.*, p. 261.
[33] LXXVI, 545–549. It was introduced with the following statement: 'Nous avions
connoissance depuis quelques jours du bref adressé par le saint Père à M.
l'archevêque de Toulouse; mais nous n'avions pas cru devoir en faire usage
dans le journal avant d'en avoir reçu autorisation formelle. Aujourd'hui deux
journaux ayant publié le bref, il n'y a plus, de notre part, de reproche d'indis-
crétion à craindre.' It is possible that more light may yet be shed on this affair.
[34] *M. à L.*, p. 98; Lecanuet, *Montalembert*, I, 391.

On 28 July Lamennais, whose first reaction to the brief had been that the pope's refusal to censure their doctrines was a feather in their cap,[35] replied that he entirely agreed with Montalembert. 'In my opinion it would be a very great mistake to make any new declaration whatever.'[36] Why then a few days later—on 4 August, to be precise—did Lamennais on his own initiative address a new declaration to the pope, using the bishop of the diocese, Mgr Lesquen of Rennes, as his intermediary—a new declaration that could not fail to precipitate a fresh crisis in his relations with the church?

The answer is that just at this moment (not of course accidentally, but as a result of the publication of the papal brief on top of *Le livre des pèlerins polonais*), a storm burst which had been brewing for some time in the diocese of Rennes and in the Congregation of St Peter. It seems to have been a passionate affair in which personalities, politics, and episcopal ineptitude were as much involved as doctrinal principles. Anyhow, it suddenly came to Lamennais's knowledge not only that the Congregation of St Peter was riddled with division on his account,[37] but also that the schools of the Brothers of Christian Instruction, founded by his brother Jean, were in danger of being boycotted by the bishop and many of the clergy of the diocese of Rennes.[38]

In order to pacify the storm and to obviate the threat to his brother's good works, Lamennais without consulting anyone resigned altogether from the Congregation of St Peter,[39] of which he had remained superior until this time,[40] and also wrote a letter to the pope[41] in which he said that, having learned with deep sorrow from the brief to the Archbishop of Toulouse that His Holiness had been led to doubt the reality of his submission, he wished to declare:

First, that for all sorts of reasons, but especially because it is the office of the head of the church to judge what is in her best interests,

35 See his letter of 22 July 1833 to Montalembert: *L. à M.*, pp. 147 ff.

36 *L. à M.*, p. 150.

37 See Laveille, *J.-M. de La Mennais*, I, chap. 24; *Annales de Bretagne*, 1949, LVI, 71 ff.

38 See *L. à M.*, pp. 154 ff., 164, 181; Forgues, II, 317, 319, 347. Cp. *A.R.*, p. 158. The bishop and the older clergy were carlists, and had always been opposed to the *Avenir*.

39 See his letter of 4 August 1833 to Jean: Blaize, II, 137 f. As a corollary of this decision he sent the young men who were with him at La Chesnaie to Malestroit.

40 For evidence of the seriousness with which he still took his responsibilities as superior, see his letter of 15 July 1833 to Rohrbacher in Roussel, *Documents*, I, 333 ff.

41 For the full text of the letter, see Forgues, II, 308 f.; *A.R.*, pp. 158 ff.

I have resolved for the future, in my writings and in my actions, to have nothing to do with matters that affect her [*affaires qui la touchent*].

Secondly, that no one, thank God, is more submissive than I am, from the bottom of my heart and without any reserve, to all the decisions that have emanated or that shall emanate from the holy apostolic see, on the doctrine of faith and morals, as well as to the laws of discipline promulgated by its sovereign authority.

He added that, if these expressions did not satisfy His Holiness, he begged to be told what form of submission would give full satisfaction. Only in his letter to the Bishop of Rennes[42] did Lamennais make the explicit qualification that his complete submission in the religious sphere left him free as regards his conduct and opinions 'in things exclusively relative to the purely temporal order'.

In sending this new declaration to the pope Lamennais had again put the holy see in a position where it could not continue to maintain a silence that it had benevolently been disposed to maintain despite acute provocation. He himself came to realize and acknowledge this mistake.[43] But at first he managed to suppose that his letter to the pope might be the end of the matter. As autumn began, he resumed work on his philosophy,[44] which he had laid aside since the spring, partly because he had been writing *Paroles d'un Croyant* and partly because he had been distracted by a succession of visitors. Though he had been thinking of going to Paris, he now intended to spend another winter and summer at La Chesnaie.

The pope's reply to Lamennais's letter of 4 August 1833 took the form of a brief to the Bishop of Rennes[45] (dated 5 October) in which, amid much unction, he complained of public evidences that

---

[42] The letter is given in Forgues, II, 310, but in a footnote is mistakenly supposed to have been addressed to Mgr de Quélen, Archbishop of Paris.

[43] On 31 December 1833 Lamennais wrote to Countess de Senfft: 'Vous avez grande raison de dire que j'ai commis une faute, une faute très-grave, en écrivant ma première lettre. Je le savais bien; aussi, pour me décider à l'écrire, n'a-t-il fallu rien moins qu'un motif aussi puissant que celui de sauver d'une destruction immédiate des écoles où trente mille enfants reçoivent une éducation chrétienne. J'ai cru devoir m'oublier moi-même pour ne songer qu'à cet immense intérêt.'—Forgues, II, 347. Cp. *L. à M.*, p. 219.

[44] See *L. à M.*, p. 200. Cp. *Vitrolles*, p. 238.

[45] Full text in *A.R.*, pp. 402–411. The pope's letter crossed one sent to Rome on 30 September 1833 by the Bishop of Rennes, in which he asked to be allowed to resign his see on account of his difficulty in dealing with the controversies that had arisen about Lamennais in his diocese. See Dudon, *L. et le S.S.*, pp. 273 ff.

Lamennais was obstinately refusing to accept the judgment of the holy see. These evidences were the publication of *Le livre des pèlerins polonais* which Gregory XVI described as a book 'full of temerity and malice', and one of Lamennais's letters which had been published in a Dutch paper[46] on 22 February 1833 and which clearly showed his determination to maintain the principles that had been condemned. Enough has been said here already about *Le livre des pèlerins polonais*, but on the other piece of evidence there hangs a curious tale.

The letter in question had been addressed to de Potter, the leader of the Belgian liberals, and it contained the following passage:

> I entirely agree with you about the way in which we must act upon the world. It is with the people, the genuine people, that we must identify ourselves; it is to the people alone that we must look, it is they who must be brought to defend their own cause, to will and to act. Any movement less profound than that will have no power for good . . . I am more convinced than ever about this, I also feel more eager than ever to return to the great conflict to which I have consecrated my life. . . . But, in any case, I shall not remain silent, and you can be sure that my words will be to the point. The time has come to say everything.[47]

The papal brief of 5 October 1833 plainly assumed that this letter had been written by Lamennais *after* his submission (of 10 September 1832) to the encyclical *Mirari vos*. Until 1933, biographers of Lamennais took it for granted that that assumption was correct,[48] and indeed that he wrote the letter to de Potter a few days after making the act of submission to the encyclical.[49] If that had been so, the pope would have had a very reasonable ground of complaint, since Lamennais would have been convicted of grave duplicity. In 1933, however, M. Gustave Charlier published an article in the *Revue d'histoire littéraire de la France*[50] in which he showed that the letter from Lamennais to de Potter, to which the papal brief referred,

---

[46] *Journal de la Haye*. It appears that this paper had reproduced the letter from the *Courrier belge*, where it had appeared on 19 February 1833; see Haag, p. 189.

[47] Quoted by Boutard, II, 378.

[48] It is true that in 1906 Feugère, p. 336, treated the date of the letter as questionable.

[49] See Boutard, II, 377 f.; R. Vallery-Radot, *Lamennais ou le prêtre malgré lui* (1931), p. 315; cp. Duine, pp. 178, 181.

[50] January–March 1933, pp. 109–114: article entitled, 'La "Duplicité" de Lamennais'.

was really written on 1 July 1832, i.e. before the encyclical *Mirari vos* had appeared and before Lamennais had left Rome for Munich and at a time when, as we have already seen, he was openly intending to resume publication of the *Avenir*.[51]

What is even more remarkable, it now seems practically certain that a copy of the letter to which the papal brief referred had been communicated to the Vatican by Metternich *in the middle of August 1832*.[52] In that case, the pope and/or his advisers knew, or ought to have known, that in representing the letter as having been written *after* Lamennais's submission of 10 September 1832 they were doing him a serious injustice. Lamennais himself, neither at the time nor afterwards, was able to check the pope's allegation, because, as he said in *Affaires de Rome* (1836), he had been unable to procure a copy of the Dutch paper in which his letter had appeared.[53] Thus, while he knew he was being misjudged by the pope, he was not in a position to defend himself.

On 15 October 1833, shortly before Lamennais received a copy of the papal brief of 5 October, a peculiarly scandalous article, entitled 'Révélation importante', had been reproduced in *L'Ami de la Religion* from a royalist paper, *L'Invariable de Fribourg*, which made scurrilous charges against both the Congregation of St Peter and against the Brothers of Christian Instruction.[54] When therefore his brother arrived at La Chesnaie with the papal brief from the Bishop of Rennes, Lamennais was already in an exasperated mood, and was

---

[51] The letter to de Potter referred to plans for re-starting the *Avenir*. See Forgues, II, 243. The actual letter has recently been discovered among the manuscripts in the *Bibliothèque royale de Bruxelles* [MS. II. 5488, vol. v, no. 117]: see the article on 'Lamennais' by Fr. Ippolito Vittorio in the *Enciclopedia Cattolica (italiana)*, VII, cols. 849–858, published in 1951 in the Vatican City.

[52] On 12 August 1832 Lützow, the Austrian ambassador in Rome, wrote to Metternich from Albano as follows:

'Mon Prince, C'était dans la société (?soirée) d'hier seulement que j'ai eu l'honneur de recevoir la lettre de Votre Altesse du 23 juillet, à laquelle se trouvait annexée la copie d'une lettre de l'abbé de La Mennais à M. de Potter: je le ferai tenir au Pape sans perte de temps; vraiment il ne faut pas d'avantage pour reconnaître dans cet ecclésiastique un véritable énergumène de la révolution: avec d'autres paroles il ne prêche que ce qui a été proclamé en 1793 "Guerre aux palais! paix aux chaumières!"'

See Ahrens, p. 246. In the same letter Lützow told Metternich that the pope was going to promulgate his encyclical on 15 August.

[53] *A.R.*, p. 404.

[54] *L'Ami de la Religion*, LXXVII, 513–518; cp. *ibid.*, pp. 583 f.; LXXVIII, 4 f. See also Roussel, *Documents*, II, 99–107; *M. à L.*, p. 176.

preparing to leave Brittany so as to escape from the controversies that were raging round him there and so as to avoid being the cause of further trouble in the diocese.[55] Before he set out for Paris, he sent this laconic note to the bishop:

> My brother has delivered to me the copy of the brief, which the pope has addressed to you, at the moment when I was preparing to leave for Paris. I shall reply from there, and directly, not having time to do so from here.[56]

The Bishop of Rennes was so piqued by this note that, without waiting for further instructions from Rome, he announced on 4 November in a long circular to his diocese[57] that he had withdrawn Lamennais's authority to exercise his priesthood in the diocese, pending his compliance with the requirements of the papal brief. Lamennais was by this time already in Paris. On 5 November he wrote a letter to the pope in which after giving his complete submission to what the encyclical had laid down as regards the doctrine and discipline of the church he added that, while in the religious order the christian is bound only to listen and to obey, 'he remains, with respect to the spiritual power, entirely free as regards his opinions, his words, and his actions in the purely temporal order.'[58]

That liberty of thought and action for catholics in the purely temporal order was the crucial question now at stake is what Lamennais maintained at the time in letters to his friends and in a memoir which the Archbishop of Paris helped him to prepare, as well as afterwards in *Affaires de Rome*. Thus to Montalembert, who was in Germany, he wrote on 19 November 1833:

> The question now is whether or no there exist two societies, one spiritual, the other temporal, distinct and independent, as tradition has established, and as I established myself in *Progrès de la Révolution* and in my *Lettres à l'Archevêque de Paris*; the question

---

55 See *L. à M.*, pp. 208 f. Cp. *A.R.*, p. 161.

56 See *L'Ami de la Religion*, LXXVIII, 122. Lamennais's reason for wanting to send his reply from Paris through the internuncio was that, if he had sent it through the Bishop of Rennes, it would at once have been made known in the diocese. See Dudon, *L. et le S.S.*, p. 414.

57 Published in full in *L'Ami de la Religion*, 17 and 19 November 1833. The internuncio in Paris (Garibaldi) deplored the bishop's action: see Martin, *La Nonciature de Paris*, p. 344; Dudon, *L. et le S.S.*, p. 281.

58 For the text of this letter, see *A.R.*, pp. 164 ff.; Dudon, *op. cit.*, pp. 410 f.

is whether the catholic, obedient in the first to the authority of the hierarchy, is, so far as the hierarchy is concerned, free in respect of his opinions, his words and his actions in the second;[59] the question is whether, as citizen, as mayor, prefect, deputy, minister, etc., he depends entirely on the curé, on the bishop, on the pope; the question is, in a word, whether the pope is by right the sole sovereign of the universe, in both the spiritual and temporal spheres, and whether absolute theocracy is, according to christians, the only legitimate government.

Furthermore, if one considers the actual state of the world, one sees the peoples carried away by an irresistible and general movement of emancipation, and this movement, which is taking place apart from the principles of order, will produce only an indefinite series of more or less sterile catastrophes, so long as it is not brought under the principles of order which are in actual operation only among christians. If then the christians cannot take part in this movement, we must resign ourselves to endless revolutions, and moreover catholics must resign themselves to undergo for ever the tyranny of men without God and without law. . . . I shall myself stick to the decisive point: perfect submission in the religious order, entire liberty in the temporal order.[60]

Lamennais did not suppose that the holy see would explicitly deny the doctrine of the two societies and claim to be the organ of a complete theocracy.[61] What he sought to show was that that was the implication of its refusal to recognize the liberty of catholics from ecclesiastical control in politics. The holy see could not say, and did not say, that in this respect it held priests to be under restrictions from which laymen were exempt, since it had already singled out a layman, Montalembert, for particular censure.[62] Indeed, the holy see avoided giving any explicit answer to the question on which Lamennais had sought to focus attention in his letter of 5 November to the pope, and he himself failed to press it to a conclusion by reason of his extraordinary gesture of surrender in the

[59] Cp. Forgues, II, 315: 'Catholique, j'écoute la voix du Pasteur suprême, et j'y obéis comme à celle de Dieu; Français, je consulte, sur les choses exclusivement temporelles, ma conscience et ma raison, et je me conduis d'après les conseils qu'elles me dictent' (Letter of August 1833).

[60] L. à M., pp. 216 ff.; cp. ibid., pp. 219-223; Lamennais inconnu, pp. 304 f.; Forgues, II, 330; Confidences, pp. 92 f.

[61] E.g. see L. à M., p. 223.

[62] In the brief of 5 October 1833 to the Bishop of Rennes. See A.R., pp. 404 f.

following month. In the next year it became covered up in what seemed at the time to be the larger and deeper questions in which Lamennais's conflict with Rome culminated.

Soon after Lamennais had arrived in Paris at the beginning of November 1833, the archbishop, Mgr de Quélen, succeeded in establishing very friendly relations with him. Although the archbishop was an impenitent gallican and carlist, and although Lamennais had fiercely attacked him a few years before,[63] they were fellow Bretons. Unfortunately the memorandum,[64] in which with the archbishop's generous help and with the advice of the internuncio[65] Lamennais clearly and temperately explained the meaning of his letter of 5 November to the pope,[66] and which might have made the liberty of catholics in the political order the decisive question, did not affect the course of events because, before the memorandum had reached Rome or even left Paris, another missive that prevented any further discussion was on the way *from* Rome.

What happened was this. The explicative memorandum which Mgr de Quélen undertook to forward to Rome on Lamennais's behalf, together with a covering letter from Lamennais himself,[67] was not ready for signature, and they had not been dispatched,[68] when on 9 December they were rendered otiose by the arrival of a letter written by Cardinal Pacca from Rome on 28 November. In this he said that the pope regarded Lamennais's letter of 5 November as equivocal and that he expected nothing less than 'a simple, absolute, and unlimited' declaration of submission to the doctrine of the encyclical *Mirari vos*.[69]

When the archbishop went to see Lamennais on 11 December

---

[63] See p. 140, *supra*.

[64] For the text of the memorandum, see Forgues, II, 337–341; *A.R.*, pp. 169–176. For the manner in which it was prepared, and for various drafts of it, see Dudon, *L. et le S.S.*, pp. 284 ff., 413–419.

[65] See Martin, *La Nonciature de Paris*, pp. 344 f.

[66] For example, he acknowledged that in the temporal sphere there are mixed questions where the authority of the church extends. 'Assurément l'ordre temporel, en tant qu'il touche, sous une foule de rapports, à la loi divine, est subordonné à l'Église, gardienne et interprète de cette loi. Mais évidemment ce n'est pas là ce que, dans le langage universel, on désigne sous le nom d'ordre *purement* temporel; et M. de La Mennais s'est à dessein servi de cette expression afin de mettre pleinement à l'abri la puissance propre de l'Église.' See. *A.R.* pp. 174 f.

[67] See Forgues, II, 335 f.

[68] See Goyau, *Portefeuille*, p. 121.

[69] See *A.R.*, pp. 176–179; Dudon, *L. et le S.S.*, pp. 411 ff.

1833,[70] he seems to have had no difficulty in persuading him there and then to sign the simple and unqualified act of submission which the pope demanded.[71] Lamennais also communicated his decision to the Bishop of Rennes, apologizing for any lack of respect that he had shown to him.[72] What was the explanation of this sudden collapse of Lamennais's resolution? A number of considerations must be taken into account if it is to be understood and rightly appraised.

First, it was the result of a sudden impulse, not of a process of careful reflection. That this was so is evident both from the speed with which the thing was done,[73] and from his attitude to what he had done as soon as he had had time to reflect on it—to that we shall be coming presently.

Secondly, it must be remembered that Lamennais was never robust in health, and was always subject to nervous strain and sharp fluctuations of mood. He was suffering now from the effects of feverish and sleepless nights.[74]

Thirdly, there was a virulent press campaign going on about him and his affairs; for Lamennais had naturally answered the Bishop of Rennes's publication of his interdict by publishing his own letters to the pope.[75] When one recalls his recurrent and often expressed longing for quiet and seclusion, it is easy to imagine that upon a sudden impulse he would do anything to silence the controversy of which he was the centre.[76]

---

[70] See Goyau, *Portefeuille*, pp. 121 f.; Forgues, II, 343. From *L. à M.*, pp. 226 f., one would infer that this took place on 12 December, but that must be a mistake.

[71] See Forgues, II, 343; *A.R.*, p. 190. [72] See Forgues, II, 343 f.

[73] On the previous day, 10 December, Lamennais had written to Benoît d'Azy reiterating his resolution to stand by his letter to the pope of 5 November: see *Lamennais inconnu*, pp. 306 f.

[74] On 4 December 1833 he had written to Countess de Senfft: 'Mes forces s'en vont; j'ai la fièvre toutes les nuits; peu ou point de sommeil.'—Forgues, II, 333; cp. *ibid.*, II, 331; *L. à M.*, p. 211; *Lamennais inconnu*, p. 307; *Cottu*, p. 253.

[75] See *L'Ami de la Religion*, 19 November 1833, pp. 134 ff., *et passim*; cp. *L. à M.*, p. 216.

[76] On 23 November 1833 he had written to Marion, his faithful friend and neighbour in Brittany: 'Oh! si vous saviez, mon ami, combien je regrette la Chênaie et ces bonnes soirées que nous y aurions passées ensemble! C'était mon seule asile sur la terre, et on me l'a ôté. Je ne songe plus qu'à y faire rapporter mes os. N'oubliez pas cette petite place que je vous ai montrée et que j'ai choisie pour ma sépulture au pied d'un rocher, sous le chêne qui l'ombrage. Je n'aurai de paix que là en ce monde. Qu'importe, pourvu que j'en sorte avec une conscience nette et que j'y laisse un nom qui ne soit pas flétri!' *Confidences*, pp. 93 f. Cp. Forgues, II, 347.

Fourthly, he was at once being taunted by his opponents with failure to act upon his professions of ultramontanism and being besought by his friends, including Montalembert,[77] to follow Christ by a supreme act of self-denial. What was he to do?

Fifthly, Lamennais's life and ideas and emotions had for thirty years been rooted in the catholic church: the prospect of cutting all these roots was horrible. And he had all along been willing to promise complete submission to the church in what he regarded as its proper sphere. True, he was convinced that the outlook of the hierarchy was perverse and that it was blind to the significance of the revolution that was taking place in the world, but all he had asked in the end was that the church should acquiesce in his espousing the cause of the poor and in his trying to prevent his country from falling under the tyranny of ruthless despots.[78] Who that has ever been driven to distraction by the persistent demands of ecclesiastical conformists will fail to understand that a moment may come when the victim inwardly exclaims 'A plague on you all!' and outwardly agrees to sign anything, so that he may be finished with their restless attentions and be left alone in peace? The surrender of abbé Loisy to Pius X in February and March 1904 was in many respects parallel to the surrender of Lamennais to Gregory XVI in December 1833, and not least in this respect.[79]

Finally, Lamennais, as we have seen in his relations with abbé Carron and with pope Leo XII, was along with his love of independence warmly responsive to affection and sympathy, and just now he was feeling very grateful to his extremely kind and considerate compatriot, Mgr de Quélen.[80] What was more natural than that in a moment of desperate exhaustion he should do what the archbishop advised and what would obviously give him great pleasure?

Nevertheless, the bitterness that had entered into Lamennais's soul as a result of this momentary collapse may be inferred from the letter he wrote, two days after signing the act of surrender, to Montalembert, his best beloved and most attached disciple, telling him to remain in Germany and not to think of returning to France to engage in political action.

As for myself [he continued], I too turn my back on practical politics, which have henceforth become impossible so far as we

[77] See M. à L., pp. 155 f.
[78] Cp. Forgues, II, 332; A.R., p. 173.
[79] See my book The Modernist Movement in the Roman Church, pp. 135 ff.
[80] See Lamennais's expression of his confidence in de Quélen: L. à M., pp. 244 f.

are concerned, and on everything without exception that has filled my life hitherto. I shall try, late as it is, to begin a new life. I am not going to tell you any of my ideas about that, because I do not want to involve anyone in my future destiny whatever it may be. . . . We shall rejoin one another hereafter, I hope, but we shall travel by separate paths on earth.[81]

Montalembert was much distressed by this threatened parting and refusal of explanations, and wrote to say so.[82] Thereupon Lamennais relented, and on 1 January 1834 wrote him a long letter in which he recounted just what had happened. He said that while the unqualified submission demanded of him had been invincibly repugnant to his conscience because it implied recognition of the infallibility of the pope as an individual and his virtual deification, yet if he had refused he would have been stigmatized as a rebel and schismatic.[83] This dilemma had led him to some fundamental doubts about the truth of catholicism. The declaration he had signed had been no more than an attempt to secure peace at any price. He would have signed anything, if asked, for instance that 'the pope is God, the great God of heaven and earth, and that he alone is to be worshipped'. At the same time, he added, he had decided to cease from all priestly functions. 'To sum up, I believe that the church cannot remain as it is, that a clear distinction has never been drawn between what is divine and human in her, and that everything is making for her transformation.' He was contemplating going to the Middle East for some years. Lamartine was giving him useful advice about this project.[84]

Montalembert was eager to accompany him,[85] but the project was soon dropped.[86] He could never have settled anywhere but in France.[87] He intended at first to find somewhere to live in the coun-

---

[81] *L. à M.*, pp. 227 f. Cp. his letters to Mme Cottu (*Cottu*, p. 255), to Coriolis (Forgues, II, 345), to Countess de Senfft (Forgues, II, 347), and to Marion (*Confidences*, pp. 94 f.). See also Laurentie, *Souvenirs inédits*, p. 227.

[82] See *M. à L.*, pp. 169–175.

[83] Cp. Forgues, II, 351 f.; 'J'ai voulu montrer que je n'étais pas un homme de schisme, mais un homme de paix' (to Countess de Senfft, 25 January 1834).

[84] *L. à M.*, pp. 229–234. Cp. *Confidences*, pp. 97 f. For some months past Lamennais had been wistfully telling his friends that he would like to get away from Europe and go to the Orient, but that it was impracticable: see Forgues, II, 331, 333; *L. à M.*, p. 186; *Lamennais inconnu*, p. 307.

[85] See *M. à L.*, pp. 180, 182 f.

[86] See *L. à M.*, pp. 237, 239, 244; *Confidences*, p. 99.

[87] On 13 January 1834 he wrote to Countess de Senfft: 'Ma vie, plus que jamais, se concentre en ce pays; et y a-t-il de la vie ailleurs? . . . O ma patrie, terre

try outside Paris but that was more easily said than done,[88] and eventually he decided to return to La Chesnaie and to resume work on his philosophy, in spite of the scandal that might be caused in the locality by his renunciation of his priestly functions.[89] But he stayed on in Paris till after Easter.

He was very soon clear in his own mind that, whatever form his new life might take, he must be free to seize whatever opportunities came to him outside the frontiers of the church of serving his country and of working for a social order in which liberty would be married to justice. In the middle of January 1834 he communicated his intention to the papal internuncio in Paris.[90] Actually, this was his reaction to a brief that Gregory XVI had sent him, congratulating him upon his complete submission,[91] and also urging him to employ his eminent talents and knowledge in persuading others to follow the doctrine of the encyclical.[92] Lamennais's, perhaps pardonable, comment on this request was that it was 'par trop dégoûtant'.[93] Notwithstanding his warm regard for Mgr de Quélen, he firmly resisted his attempts to persuade him to write and thank the pope for the brief.[94] His determination to have nothing more to do with the church was hardened by reports that despite his act of submission his opponents were still intriguing against him and in particular that a plot was on foot to induce him to go to live in Rome.[95]

douce et sacrée! que mes os reposent dans ton sein! De tous mes vœux, c'est là le plus cher, et le seul à peu près que je forme désormais dans ce monde de fantômes et de misères.'—Forgues, II, 349 f.

88 See *Confidences*, p. 100; *L. à M.*, pp. 241, 244.

89 See *Confidences*, pp. 101 f.; Forgues, II, 353.

90 On 15 January he wrote to Montalembert: 'Je dis à Garibaldi que ce que j'avais fait, je l'avais fait pour sauver la paix, irrévocablement décidé, d'ailleurs, à ne m'occuper désormais d'aucune manière de rien de ce qui concerne l'Église et la religion, mais bien résolu à remplir, selon ma conscience et ma raison, mes devoirs envers mon pays, dans toutes les circonstances où je croirais qu'une action quelconque de ma part pourrait lui être utile.'—*L. à M.*, pp. 236 f. Cp. Dudon, *L. et le S.S.*, pp. 294 f.; Martin, *La Nonciature de Paris*, p. 346.

91 For the full text of the brief, see *A.R.*, pp. 412–417; Dudon, *op. cit.*, pp. 420 f.

92 Cp. the message sent by pope Pius X in 1904 to Cardinal Richard for abbé Loisy: 'Vous pourrez ajouter encore que l'Église, loin de lui imposer le silence, sera bien heureuse qu'il puisse manifester la pureté et l'intégrité de ses rétractations en mettant en pratique le précepte donné par saint Rémi à Clovis: *Succende quod adorasti, et adora quod incendisti.*' See Loisy, *Mémoires* (1931), II, 361.

93 *Confidences*, p. 99.

94 See *A.R.*, pp. 191–193.

95 See *A.R.*, p. 192; Forgues, II, 351 f., 355, 358, 361; *Confidences*, p. 100; *L. à M.*, p. 243; *Lamennais inconnu*, pp. 308–311.

As the weeks went on, Lamennais became impatient to give some public and unmistakable sign that his submission to the pope had not meant that he now approved the politics of the Holy Alliance or that he had become indifferent to the cause of popular emancipation. Apart from what was going on in other countries, especially Poland, this spring of 1834 was a time of industrial unrest, insurrection, and violent government measures of suppression in France itself.[96] All the time the manuscript of *Paroles d'un Croyant* was burning in Lamennais's pocket. At last, he could contain himself and it no longer. Before he left Paris for La Chesnaie on 9 April 1834[97] he had arranged with Sainte-Beuve to get it published and to see it through the press.[98] On 29 March 1834, when this decision had already been taken, he wrote to Benoît d'Azy:

> What is going on in France and in Europe, the abominable system of despotism which is developing everywhere with such hateful shamelessness, so revolts me that it has seemed to me that in this situation silence would be almost as infamous on my part as direct approval. Consequently, I have resolved at all costs to save my conscience and my honour, by making a protest with all the force I have. The *Paroles d'un Croyant* are therefore being published. Whatever happens, it does not matter. My own ease of mind comes before everything. I prefer storms without to storms within.[99]

In a letter of 23 March 1834 Lamennais had told Montalembert that he had decided to have *Paroles d'un Croyant* printed.[100] Montalembert, to whom the manuscript had been read when he visited La Chesnaie in June 1833, wrote beseeching him to stop what would be 'an immense scandal'.[101] The Archbishop of Paris, who had heard

---

[96] On the appalling industrial conditions in France at this period, see D. O. Evans, *Social Romanticism in France 1830–1848* (1951), pp. 4–7.

[97] See *Lamennais inconnu*, p. 313.

[98] For Sainte-Beuve's reminiscences of this transaction, see Sainte-Beuve, II, 80–82. They may have been somewhat dramatized: cp. Le Hir, *Paroles d'un Croyant*, p. 6.

[99] *Lamennais inconnu*, p. 308.

[100] *L. à M.*, p. 255.

[101] *M. à L.*, pp. 196 ff. But if Montalembert had wanted to prevent its publication, he ought not to have written in the previous autumn to tell Lamennais how one of the Polish leaders had been 'electrified' when Montalembert had quoted to him from memory so much of *Paroles d'un Croyant* as he could remember. See *M. à L.*, p. 139.

alarming rumours,[102] wrote asking Lamennais to assure him that
they were false, and that he was indeed resolved to maintain an
absolute silence on matters of religion.[103] Lamennais replied that in
future he was going to write only on philosophical, scientific, and
political subjects, and that the little book of which the archbishop
had heard dealt with politics.[104] Though it would speak about Jesus
Christ and the fraternal charity that christianity inculcates, there
would not be a word that applied to any positive or particular
form of christianity nor would the church be so much as mentioned.[105]

At the last minute, Ange Blaize, Lamennais's brother-in-law,
pleaded with him to change his mind. But it was too late. In reply,
Lamennais said that when he had read the manuscript to Gerbet,
abbé Jean,[106] and others, none of them had seen anything in it that
was injurious from the religious point of view. He summarized as
follows the motives that had determined him to publish it:

1. A conscientious conviction that in doing so I am fulfilling a
duty, because I see no deliverance [*salut*] for the world but in a
union of order, right, justice, and liberty; 2. the necessity of defin-
ing my position which, in the eyes of the public, is at present
equivocal and false; 3. to clear my name in the future from the
reproach of having connived at the horrible system of tyranny
which today lies heavily on the peoples everywhere.[107]

---

102 See *A.R.*, p. 194. Sainte-Beuve recorded the following reminiscence: 'Un matin
que je reportais les épreuves, on me prévint que l'imprimeur, M. Plassan,
désirait me parler. "Vous êtes chargé, me dit-il, de l'impression d'un écrit de
M. de La Mennais qui va faire bien de bruit; mes ouvriers eux-mêmes ne peuvent le composer sans être comme soulevés et transportés; l'imprimerie est
toute en l'air".' Sainte-Beuve, II, 81 f.

103 See *A.R.*, pp. 194 ff.

104 Cp. *L. à M.*, p. 261: 'Le petit écrit . . . de quoi s'agit-il? De pure politique?'

105 See *A.R.*, pp. 196–199.

106 Cp. Rohrbacher, *Histoire universelle de l'Église catholique* (1848), XXVIII, 322,
where a last-minute attempt of abbé Jean to prevent the publication of *Paroles
d'un Croyant* is recorded. See also Laveille, *J.-M. de La Mennais*, I, 501 ff. But
Laveille entirely ignores Féli's visit to Paris (November 1833–April 1834),
represents Jean (who was in Brittany at the time) as having persuaded him
to make the final act of submission of '11 *novembre* [*sic*] 1833', and moreover implies that Jean had never heard of *Paroles d'un Croyant* till early in
1834!

107 See letter of 27 April 1834 in Blaize, II, 140 ff. See also Forgues, II, 364, 367;
S. Vailhé, *Vie du R. P. Emmanuel Alzon* (1926), I, 163.

Paroles d'un Croyant was published on 30 April 1834, though
some writers mistakenly give 3 May as the date of publication.[108]
It has often been stated that the first edition appeared anonymously,
but that is not the case.[109] The publication of *Paroles d'un Croyant*
caused an even greater sensation than had been caused by the first
volume of the *Essai sur l'indifférence*.[110] 'Ce fut le plus grand succès
de librairie de l'époque', we are told.[111] People waited in queues at
reading rooms and paid so much an hour to read it; a group of
students in the Jardin de Luxembourg was seen listening with enthusiasm to its being read aloud.[112] Here are some of the epigrams that
were coined at the time to describe it: 'un bonnet rouge planté sur
une croix'; '93 qui fait ses pâques'; 'Robespierre en surplis'; 'l'apocalypse de Satan'; 'un club sous un clocher'. [113] Six weeks after the
book had been published, Montalembert who was travelling in
Austria wrote to Lamennais: 'I never open a newspaper without
seeing your name on the front page.'[114]

Edition followed edition, [115] and the Parisian publisher had to
spend much of his time dashing about the country to stop pirated
editions.[116] The book was soon being translated into the principal
languages of Europe.[117] The first English translation appeared in

[108] E.g. C. Maréchal, *La Clef de 'Volupté'* (1905), p. 73; D. O. Evans, *Social
Romanticism in France 1830–1848* (1951), p. 39. For evidence that 30 April is the
correct date, see *Vitrolles*, pp. 243 f.; Roussel, *Lamennais intime*, p. 259; Harispe,
Lamennais, p. 341. 3 May was the date on which the publication was reported
in the *Journal de la Librairie*; see Le Hir, *P.C.*, p. 16.

[109] E.g. the papal encyclical *Singulari nos* described *P.C.* as anonymous, and Paul
Vulliaud in *Les Paroles d'un Croyant de Lamennais* (p. 20) wrote: 'Très récem-
ment, il a été contesté que la première édition des *Paroles* ait paru anonyme-
ment.' Duine in his *Bibliographie*, p. 6, says that the first edition was anonymous.
They are wrong. *L'Ami de la Religion* pointed out on 3 May 1834 that, although
the author's name did not appear on the title-page, it did appear on the back
of the volume. The author's name would not therefore be apparent if the book
were rebound in cloth. Moreover, Talvart and Place, *Bibliographie*, XI, 169, say
that some exceptional copies of the first edition did appear without the author's
name even on the back. These circumstances explain why there has been so
much confusion about what might be supposed to be a simple matter of fact.

[110] For an interesting and diverting account of the reactions, controversies, and
refutations which followed the publication of *P.C.*, see Paul Vulliaud, *op. cit.*

[111] Le Hir, *P.C.*, p. v.

[112] See *L. à M.*, p. 270.

[113] See Boutard, III, 38 f.; Duine, p. 192; *Vitrolles*, pp. 247 ff.

[114] Montalembert to Lamennais from Töplitz on 9 June 1834: see *M. à L.*, p. 214.

[115] For details see Le Hir, *P.C.*, pp. 16–27; Duine, *Bibliographie*, pp. 6 f.

[116] See Le Hir, *P.C.*, pp. v f.; Goyau, *Portefeuille*, p. 174.

[117] On Belgian editions, see Haag, p. 214.

1834,[118] and there have been many since: the last was published in 1943.[119]

The Times newspaper of 11 June 1834 published the following report from its Paris correspondent which very well illustrates the kind of impression that *Paroles d'un Croyant* upon its first appearance made on a large section of the general public:

The famous Abbé de la Mennais, though but just pardoned by the Holy See, has relapsed! And what a relapse! The *Paroles d'un Croyant* have doubtless already crossed the Channel, and you will have perused this singular work. It is a new book of the prophets, a kind of Alcoran, divided into chapters and verses. It is a book written in the Apocalypse style, and would seem to have arrived from old Jerusalem and to have been inspired on the banks of the Jordan. In the same maledictions the Abbé de la Mennais confounds supreme pontiffs, kings, preachers, and warriors, all powers and privileges, and all social order. There is only, he contends, one legitimate Sovereign, and that Sovereign is Christ. 'Christ alone is great, and La Mennais is his prophet!'

Under the reign of Christ, the earth will be covered with flowers, and the little children will constantly bring nosegays to their mothers. This is a favourite image of this prophet, since he frequently adopts it.

There is no doubt that such a work as this has its ridiculous side; but we must not on that account treat it as altogether without weight. It is admirably written, and on weak and ignorant minds, and youthful imaginations, it can hardly fail to exercise a baneful influence. It will assuredly produce fanatics, and the Abbé de la Mennais will then have his sectarians. This book puts weapons into the hands of the factious of every denomination. It is a fireship launched in the midst of the moral world. I regard its publication as an event. Its editions multiply, and certainly it will be considered in the light of a gospel. The Abbé de la Mennais flatters the lower classes with as much address as perfidy, and his words are calculated to excite that envy which sleeps, but which never ceases to exist in the breasts of those who suffer when they come

118 *The Words of a Believer: and having thus spoken, was eternally damned by the Pope of Rome for having uttered them.* Translated from the French of L'Abbé de La Mennais. London: B. D. Cousins, 18, Duke-street, Lincoln's Inn Fields. 1834.

119 *The People's Prophecy by F. de Lamennais.* Translated by Cuthbert Reavely and published by Andrew Dakers, London (now out of print).

in contact with those who enjoy. This work, of which it grieves me to have to speak, will be spread over the whole of Europe. There is no doubt but that its appearance will provoke the indignation of the church of Rome, and that its thunders will be aimed at the head of the sacrilegious preacher. But it seems he has made up his mind to this, and that persecution will be congenial to his taste, for persecution elevates and glorifies innovators.

There is no book quite like it—no book that has caught to the same extent the spirit and style of the prophetic and apocalyptic writings of the Bible, together with the simplicity of the evangelical parables.[120] No more than the writings that inspired it does it contain a consecutive argument; in order that the flavour of its contents and style may be tasted, two of the shorter chapters are printed here in the Appendix.[121] Professor Le Hir devoted a large section of his book *Lamennais écrivain*, published in 1948, to showing how Lamennais's writings as a whole were influenced by the Bible. 'There can be no doubt', he wrote, 'that Lamennais is in the nineteenth century the writer who best understood the genius of the Hebrew language and who most faithfully conveyed its power and movement.'[122] And in his commentary on *Paroles d'un Croyant* (1949) the same author has demonstrated how this book in particular is dependent on the Bible, chapter by chapter, and almost verse by verse.

The forty-two chapters of *Paroles d'un Croyant* are indeed biblical poems—some naturally more memorable than others—in which the prophetic promises and the apocalyptic judgments of God in the Old and New Testaments were brought to life for the oppressed peoples and the toiling masses of Europe in 1834. As Le Hir has said: 'Like the prophets of the Old Testament Lamennais believed that he had received a mission from heaven; and in order to strike the tyrants, and to cast their insults and blasphemies in their teeth, he shows them, in terrifying visions, their shame and their ruin; to the men who are victims of an atrocious tyranny he unveils the peaceful horizons of the promised Land and the splendours of the new Jerusalem.'[123]

---

[120] On 4 May 1834 Lamennais wrote to Sainte-Beuve: 'J'ai cherché, pour parler aux peuples, les expressions les plus communes et le langage le plus simple. Il me semblait que je devais tâcher, sous ce rapport au moins, de me rapprocher de l'Évangile.' See Feugère, p. 351.   [121] See pp. 285 ff., *infra*.

[122] *Op. cit.*, p. 225. Renan had previously said much the same thing: see Le Hir, *P.C.*, p. vii.   [123] Le Hir, *Lamennais écrivain*, p. 329.

The idea that the Bible's judgments on oppressors and its promises of deliverance to the oppressed could apply respectively to the rulers of the Holy Alliance, and to the peasants and proletariat who were their subjects, took away the breath of the first readers of *Paroles d'un Croyant*. Today the general notion that the Bible's prophecies have a bearing on contemporary affairs is so familiar that it is not easy to realize how shocking the discovery was in 1834. The fact that the *Paroles* were cast in terms of doctrinal orthodoxy made them all the more shocking to orthodox catholics. A protestant or a deist might have been expected so to pervert the word of God, but in the *Paroles* the doctrines of the Trinity, of the divinity of Christ, of the intercession of the Virgin Mary, of original sin and of the atonement, are all explicitly asserted. Moreover, the moral demands of the Bible are maintained in their rigour; there is no declaration of rights apart from duties.

Whether the eschatology of *Paroles d'un Croyant* was or is orthodox, who shall say? There is no doubt romanticism and even utopianism in Lamennais's picture of the future; but he was neither now nor at any time a perfectionist.[124] Nor did he secularize the christian hope of the final, otherworldly destiny that God has prepared for mankind. He did however proclaim that Christ's deliverance of the poor and oppressed is not entirely otherworldly. They might look forward to happier and more just conditions of life in this world and in the proximate future. He encouraged men to combine with, and to fortify, one another in resisting tyrants—he had Poland especially in mind—and he led them to expect that their resistance would not be fruitless. Let it be granted that Lamennais's visions of kings drinking blood out of skulls, etc., may strike us as absurdly bizarre, though they are scarcely more bizarre than some of the visions in the Old Testament prophets or in the Apocalypse of St John; nevertheless, it has not yet been irrevocably decided that the idea of christianity's having a message of amelioration for society is completely heretical.

What public opinion and the judgment of the hierarchy fastened

---

[124] On 23 May 1834, writing to Baroness de Vaux, and speaking of himself, Lamennais said: 'Il n'a jamais rêvé sur la terre le pur règne du droit, un état exempt de crimes ou de désordres, ni le parfait accomplissement des promesses du christianisme, ni la réalisation de cette perfection infinie vers laquelle pousse l'Humanité. Il a simplement montré aux hommes le but vers lequel ils doivent tendre.' See Forgues, II, 370; cp. *ibid.*, II, 378. On 28 February 1835 Lamennais wrote to d'Eckstein: 'Je ne suis pas assez fou pour me permettre quoi que ce soit de parfait sur la terre.' See Feugère, p. 367. Cp. *A.A.*, V, 173.

on at the time, however, was not the question whether or not
Lamennais had over-realized his eschatology, but his identification
of the cause of liberty and emancipation with the name of Christ
and, in particular, his inciting subjects to disobey their rulers if
these transgressed the law of God. If it is true, as an anglican clergy-
man in South Africa was recently reported as saying, that 'it has
been the teaching of the Christian Church throughout the ages that,
when a Government degenerates into a tyranny, its laws are no
longer binding on its subjects',[125] it must be confessed that this
teaching has sometimes been concealed. There is no trace of it in the
encyclicals of Gregory XVI whose emphasis was entirely on the
duty of subjects to obey their rulers and on the monstrous wickedness
of inciting them to do otherwise.

Before leaving *Paroles d'un Croyant*, I will add a few remarks about
some matters of secondary interest. The edition of 1949, edited and
annotated by Professor Yves Le Hir,[126] has superseded all previous
editions, and is the one that should now be used. As I have already
said, Sainte-Beuve saw the first edition through the press; Le Hir
has established that what he handed to the printers was a copy of
Lamennais's manuscript and not the autograph.[127] It is curious that
Lamennais seems never to have carefully checked the proofs of any
of the subsequent editions that appeared during his lifetime.[128] It is
no less curious that no one before Le Hir had taken the trouble to
produce the text of the original manuscript, which is now in the
Bibliothèque Nationale.

It should be noted that the preface 'Au Peuple' was not part of
the original manuscript; it made its first appearance in a popular
edition that was published in 1835. Likewise chapter 10 was not in
the original manuscript but appeared for the first time in the fourth
edition; Lamennais added it in order to remove any pretext for the
suggestion that he was encouraging disorder and lack of respect for
property.[129]

It is more important to note that the passage in chapter 33 which
was directed against Gregory XVI[130] was suppressed in all editions

[125] The Rev. Trevor Huddleston in *The Observer*, 22 February 1953, p. 7.
[126] *Les 'Paroles d'un Croyant' de Lamennais: Texte publié sur le manuscrit autographe
avec des Variantes, une Introduction et un Commentaire.* Librarie Armand Collin,
Paris.
[127] See Le Hir, *P.C.*, p. 13.   [128] *Ibid.*, pp. 25 f.
[129] See *L. à M.*, p. 280; cp. Le Hir, *P.C.*, pp. 16 ff.
[130] Chapter 33 contains a vision in which contemporary kings and emperors are
corrosively depicted, beginning with king William IV of England, though no

until 1837, when Lamennais's break with the church was so complete that there seemed to be no reason why it should not be known. Sainte-Beuve's story of the suppression of this passage is, however, altogether incorrect. Writing in 1861,[131] he said that he had on his own authority suppressed two lines about the pope, and that they had not been restored in any subsequent edition. Not only were considerably more than two lines suppressed but, as has just been said, they were restored in 1837. It is also certain that Lamennais himself was responsible for their suppression.[132]

However much the publication of *Paroles d'un Croyant* agitated other people, its immediate effect upon its author was pacifying. It seemed to remove the burden of guilt which he had felt resting upon him since he had signed the unqualified act of submission on 11 December 1833. He had now made his position clear. He had demonstrated that, while he was willing to submit to the church in

names are mentioned. The passage, referring to Gregory XVI, was as follows:

'Et voilà qu'ayant traversé plusieurs salles désertes, dans une petite chambre, sur un lit qu'éclairoit à peine une lampe pâle, il aperçoit un homme usé par les ans. Autour du chevet étoient sept peurs, quatre d'un côté, trois de l'autre.

Et l'une des peurs posa la main sur le cœur de l'homme âgé, et il tressaillit, et ses membres tremblèrent; et la main resta là tant qu'elle sentit un peu de chaleur.

Et après celle-ci, une autre plus froide fit ce qu'avoit fait la première, et toutes posèrent la main sur le cœur de l'homme âgé.

Et il se passa en lui des choses qu'on ne peut dévoiler.

Il voyoit dans le lointain, vers le pôle, un fantôme horrible qui lui disoit: Tu as froid, donne-toi à moi, et je te réchaufferai de mon haleine.

Et, de ses doigts glacés, l'homme de peur écrivoit un pacte, je ne sais quel pacte, mais chaque mot en étoit comme un râle d'agonie.

Et ce fut la dernière vision. Et le vieillard s'étant réveillé, rendit grâces à la Providençe de la part qu'elle lui avoit faite dans les douleurs de la vie.

Et le pèlerin lui dit: Espérez et priez; la prière obtient tout. Votre fils n'est pas perdu; vos yeux le reverront avant de se fermer. Attendez en paix les jours de Dieu.'

All except the first of these verses was suppressed. The allusion is of course to the pact which Lamennais believed the pope had made with the Czar: see pp. 210 f., *supra*.

131 See Sainte-Beuve, II, 82.

132 This is evident from the fact that in letters of 23 March 1834 to Montalembert (*L. à M.*, p. 255) and of 29 March to Benoît d'Azy (*Lamennais inconnu*, p. 309) Lamennais said he had decided to suppress the passage in question, that is, before he had left Paris on 9 April, and put Sainte-Beuve in charge of the process of publication. Cp. Le Hir, *P.C.*, pp. 21 f.; Maréchal, *La Clef de 'Volupté'*, pp. 72 f.

matters properly ecclesiastical, he was not going to abandon the cause of the poor and oppressed nor silently to connive at the proceedings of the despotic governments that held sway in Europe.[133]

'My intention', Lamennais wrote to de Coux at this time (May 1834), 'is to remain submissive in the church and free outside the church. As regards the church, it seems to me that . . . it is impossible not to admit that she will undergo . . . a necessary transformation; that no one knows in what this transformation will consist, and that consequently no one should believe himself called to carry it through. So then, during this period of waiting for what is to be, one should stay united to the existing institution, adhering sincerely to all that is good and true [in it], separated sincerely from all that is evil and false, without even . . . trying to draw an exact line between what is divine and what is human. . . .'[134]

Lamennais did not consider, so he told de Coux, that there was anything in *Paroles d'un Croyant* that could be condemned on christian, i.e. on doctrinal, grounds, though it was likely enough that the secular powers would successfully press Rome to some form of condemnation.[135] Meanwhile, in the rural seclusion of La Chesnaie he felt more tranquil than he had been for years.[136] He was again absorbed in work on his philosophy.[137] He would even have resumed saying mass, were it not that he did not want to become embroiled again with the Bishop of Rennes.[138]

As the weeks went on, Lamennais came to the conclusion that

[133] Writing to Coriolis on 19 May 1834, Lamennais said: 'Ces gens-là ne savent pas ce que c'est que d'avoir, au fond de la poitrine, une parole qui l'oppresse et demande à sortir. Pouvais-je me taire, entouré, comme nous le sommes, de tant d'iniquités, de tant de tyrannies, de tant de souffrances et de tant de misères? J'ai senti tout cela, et j'ai parlé. Pouvais-je consentir, d'ailleurs, à ce que les générations futures demandassent compte à ma mémoire d'un de ces lâches silences qui ne souillent pas moins, et quelquefois souillent plus, qu'une connivence directe au mal!' See Forgues, II, 369. Cp. *Vitrolles*, p. 246; *Lamennais inconnu*, p. 319.

[134] See Périn, *Le Modernisme dans l'Église*, p. 12. This letter, which Périn dates 21 March 1833, must certainly have been written over a year later, after the publication of *P.C.*, probably on 21 May 1834: see Feugère, pp. 352 f.; Le Hir, *P.C.*, p. 4; Versluys, p. 80.

[135] See Périn, *op. cit.*, pp. 11 f.; cp. Feugère, p. 354; *Vitrolles*, p. 251.

[136] 'Pour moi, au milieu de ces orages, jamais je n'eus l'âme plus tranquille et plus contente.' See Forgues, II, 376; Feugère, p. 363; cp. his letters of this time, *passim.*

[137] See *L. à M.*, p. 266; Roussel, *Documents*, II, 136; *Lamennais inconnu*, p. 314.

[138] Letter of 3 June 1834 to Combalot, cited by Feugère, p. 355, and Boutard, III, 64, from *Nouvelle Revue internationale*, 1899, I, 177.

Rome would take no action[139]—or at least do no more than put *Paroles d'un Croyant* on the 'index politique', i.e. prohibit the entry of the book into the papal states.[140] There are references to a letter written by the pope himself to a correspondent in Paris to the effect that Rome would remain silent, but although one of the young mennaisians claimed to have seen it one cannot be sure that this letter ever existed.[141] Baron de Vitrolles wrote to Lamennais on 21 June that he had dined with the Archbishop of Paris who both desired and hoped that Rome would keep silent.[142] Further, two young disciples of Lamennais, who were resident in Rome at this time (d'Alzon and MacCarthy), wrote assuring him that he need apprehend no act of condemnation.[143]

Thus he was taken by surprise when on 15 July 1834 he heard of the papal encyclical *Singulari nos*[144] in which *Paroles d'un Croyant* was condemned as a book 'small in size but immense in its perversity', especially because its author sought to loosen 'the bonds of fidelity and submission towards princes' and because he reaffirmed the liberties which the *Avenir* had advocated and the encyclical *Mirari vos* had condemned. This was the principal theme of *Singulari nos*, but the pope added a paragraph in which he also condemned a 'fallacious system of philosophy, recently invented', by which, without actually specifying it,[145] he evidently meant the mennaisian philosophy of *sensus communis*. It looked as if Gregory XVI was determined once and for all to have done with the whole mennaisian movement.

It would seem to be improbable that there can have been any real question in the Vatican about condemning *Paroles d'un Croyant*,[146] but as noted above there may have been some hesitation, and the form which the condemnation took does appear to have been

---

[139] See *Lamennais inconnu*, p. 323; Roussel, *Documents*, II, 139; Forgues, II, 385; *L. à M.*, p. 301.

[140] See *L. à M.*, pp. 279, 288; Roussel, *Documents*, II, 137, 139; Forgues, II, 380.

[141] See Roussel, *Documents*, II, 146; *Lamennais intime*, p. 284; *Lamennais inconnu*, p. 324.

[142] See *Portefeuille*, p. 156; cp. Dudon, *L. et le S.S.*, p. 327.

[143] See *Portefeuille*, pp. 147, 151; Roussel, *Documents*, II, 142; *L. à M.*, p. 293.

[144] For the full text of the encyclical which was dated 24 June 1834, see *A.R.*, pp. 418–433; Dudon, *L. et le S.S.*, pp. 427–430.

[145] The indefiniteness of this passage in the encyclical led in Germany to the idea that it was the teaching of Hermes that was in question. See a letter of Rohrbacher to abbé Jean (18 October 1834) in Roussel, *Documents*, II, 172 f.

[146] That there was no real hesitation is the contention of Dudon, *L. et le S.S.* chap. 9.

influenced by the representations of foreign diplomats, especially Metternich.[147] The correspondence that passed on this occasion between Metternich and the Austrian ambassador in Rome, which was published first by Boutard in 1913 and more fully by Ahrens in 1930, is in this connexion suggestive.

On 16 May 1834 Metternich wrote to the ambassador, Lützow, as follows:

> If this atrocious man had not been long since unmasked in the eyes of every impartial observer, he would have been today. Today no other course is open to M. de La Mennais's warmest admirers than to pronounce him mad.
>
> A priest, who abuses the sacred books in order to corrupt the world, who pretends to be inspired and who dispenses what he must himself know to be poison, is an abject being. The Holy Father will take the same view of the matter, and his lofty wisdom will show him what are the most useful measures to adopt with respect to this anarchist. . . . I hardly know what advice to give the pontifical court; to remain silent seems to me impossible, to speak has its drawbacks. Anyhow the head of the church will have to condemn principles which are not christian, which are indeed opposed to every possible religious idea, to all social order, to everything which could ever constitute such an order!
>
> The practice of burning heretics and their works has been abandoned: that is a matter for regret in the present instance. . . . Keep me informed of the course which the Holy Father is going to follow, for it seems to me impossible that he will take no action with regard to a priest who like M. de La Mennais dares to behave so culpably towards the church and the whole of human society.[148]

On 18 May 1834, before he had received the foregoing communication, the ambassador wrote to Metternich:

> I saw the Holy Father on the day before yesterday and made him acquainted with everything that it would be useful for him to know in order to get his judgment right on men and affairs. His Holiness thanked me warmly, and directed me to say, my Prince, that he is always happy to know your opinion which he likes best of all to know and to follow (qu'il aime de préférence à connaître et à suivre).[149]

---

[147] That this was so is argued at length by Harispe, Lamennais, chap. 21; see also Versluys, p. 44.

[148] See Boutard, III, 76; Ahrens, pp. 266 f.   [149] See Boutard, III, 77.

Some days later (31 May 1834) the ambassador wrote again:

> I saw the Holy Father yesterday; I read him the passage from your letter [that is, of 16 May, quoted above]. He listened with the liveliest interest and instructed me to say to your Highness that he entirely shares your opinion; that he looks upon this publication [P.C.] as the work of the most shameful and wild impiety, as the profession of faith of a complete [consommé] revolutionary. . . . The pope instructed me to tell you, my Prince, that you will without delay be informed of the course of action he will adopt with regard to this priest who does everything he can to be considered as a heretic and schismatic. . . .[150]

Similar representations were made on behalf of Prussia and Russia.[151]

Thus Lamennais had some reason for regarding the encyclical *Singulari nos* as having been prompted by diplomatic or political and not doctrinal or theological motives.[152] The French government took the same view.[153] But it is difficult to see how the pope could have refrained from some act of doctrinal condemnation, since the publication of *Paroles d'un Croyant* amounted to a flagrant reassertion on Lamennais's part of that qualification of his submission to the *Mirari vos* which the pope had refused to accept. It is curious that Lamennais should have failed to see at once that he had made his rupture with the church inevitable, unless he were willing to make an even more abject act of submission than that of 11 December 1833, and the possibility of doing that never entered his head.

As it was, he affected to regard the *Singulari nos* with contempt. 'The word that once moved the world would not today move a school of little boys', he wrote to Montalembert.[154] The encyclical had no doctrinal authority; it was merely a political document, by which those elements in the church that anyhow were doomed identified themselves with the interests of absolutist governments.[155] Theologians, said Lamennais, depending on reports from friends in Rome, looked upon the encyclical as 'only the personal opinion of Mauro Capellari, and nothing more'.[156] By publishing *Paroles d'un*

---

150 See Boutard, III, 77; Ahrens, p. 267.   151 See Boutard, III, 77 f.
152 See *L. à M.*, p. 305, 311, 316; *Lamennais inconnu*, p. 327; Forgues, II, 387, 390; Vitrolles, p. 261.   153 See Boutard, III, 79.
154 *L. à M.*, p. 319. For Montalembert's protest against this statement, see *M. à L.*, p. 247.
155 See *L. à M.*, pp. 305, 311; Forgues, II, 399.
156 Forgues, II, 390. As regards the reliability of these reports from Rome, see Vailhé, *Vie du R.P. Emmanuel Alzon*, I, 175 ff.

Croyant, and by following it up with an article, entitled 'De l'Absolutisme et de la Liberté' which appeared in August 1834,[157] he considered that he had won freedom of speech and action for catholics in the political order.[158] It was still his intention to resume saying mass as soon as possible,[159] and he had no idea of leaving the church.[160]

None of Lamennais's disciples took this nonchalant view of the encyclical, nor was he able to hold it for long. The *Singulari nos* finally dispersed the mennaisian school. Gerbet, who was particularly affected since he had been a conspicuous exponent of the philosophy of *sensus communis*, at once made a complete submission,[161] and one after another the leading members of the school followed suit.[162] Montalembert held out longest.[163] He was still travelling abroad when the encyclical was published. His immediate reaction was to write a long and passionate letter to Lamennais, urging him to submit. He anticipated that Lamennais would say that conscientious convictions made it impossible for him to do so. But, Montalembert wrote, the obligation upon a christian to follow his conscience can be exaggerated; the first obligation is to obey like a

---

[157] In *Revue des deux mondes*, 1 August 1834: see also *O.C.*, XI, 163–199. In this article Lamennais argued that two systems, the doctrine of absolute monarchy, which made society dependent on brute force, and the doctrine of liberty, which subordinated force to constitutional right, were contending for the conquest of the world.

The preface which Lamennais contributed in 1835 to *De la Servitude volontaire, par Estienne de La Boétie* (*1548*) is a more readable attack on despotism and on the church's allying itself with tyrannical governments: it is included in *O.C.*, XI, 245–275.

[158] See *L. à M.*, p. 318.

[159] See letter of 2 August 1834 to Mlle de Lucinière: Forgues, II, 395. Vailhé, *op. cit.*, I, 180, cites a document, written by an anonymous visitor to La Chesnaie, which implies that Lamennais was actually saying mass as late as September 1834, but this must be regarded as requiring confirmation.

[160] On 9 September 1834 Lamennais wrote to Lerminier: 'Je n'ai point rompu avec l'Église, je n'ai point imité Luther et je ne l'imiterai point, persuadé que je suis que les schismes ne font que du mal.' See Feugère, p. 363.

[161] See de Ladoue, *Mgr Gerbet*, I, 278 f.

[162] Sevrin (*Dom Guéranger et La Mennais*, p. 316) sums up: 'L'un après l'autre, Gerbet, Salinis, Rohrbacher, Combalot, Jean-Marie de La Mennais, adhérèrent à la deuxième encyclique; les autres, moins connus, restèrent ou rentrèrent peu à peu dans le silence.'

[163] I.e., of the leading and well-known mennaisians. As regards Eugène Boré and a group of young men, who stuck to Lamennais after Montalembert's defection, see Roussel, *Lamennais intime*, p. 314.

little child.[164] Lamennais replied that they must agree to differ.[165] Both wanted to maintain their friendship, and they continued to write to one another at length.

At times, Montalembert was uncertain what to do, and felt torn between his devotion to the cause of liberty and his attachment to the church: should he follow Lamennais who treated the former, or Lacordaire who treated the latter, as the overriding loyalty?[166] However, when it was reported to him that Lamennais had said that 'catholicism was no more than a dead or dying form of the eternal religion',[167] he decided that the time had come when he must publicly take his stand on the side of the church, great as was his distress at renouncing all that the *Avenir* had stood for. On 8 December 1834 therefore he made an unqualified submission to both encyclicals— *Mirari vos* and *Singulari nos*.[168] To Lamennais he gave the following explanation of his action:

> I had to do great violence to my most deeply rooted convictions in order to adhere to an act like the encyclical of 15 August [*sc. Mirari vos*] which conflicts with these convictions in the most formal manner; but I have preferred this violence to the chance of finding myself one day outside the church which alone offers me consolations for those intimate sufferings that no political or intellectual activity could relieve. I feel very deeply the bitter self-contradiction of this course; it is in a way like destroying or denying everything one has loved and defended, everything on which

[164] 'Vous me répondrez, je le sais, que la conscience est invincible, et moi je dirai qu'après avoir bien réfléchi sur ce point, je me suis persuadé que le chrétien ne doit pas obéir exclusivement à *sa* conscience et qu'il y a des cas où il doit avant tout *obéir*! Je ne vois pas que Jésus-Christ ait tant parlé de conscience ni de convictions dans ses divines leçons: je vois au contraire qu'il a toujours parlé de l'obéissance, de la foi des petits enfants, qui n'ont pas de conscience.'— *M. à L.*, p. 234.

[165] See *L. à M.*, p. 312.

[166] On 14 August 1834 Montalembert wrote to Lamennais: 'Que ne donnerais-je pas pour pouvoir sacrifier l'Église à la liberté comme vous, ou la liberté à l'Église comme Lacordaire! Mais je ne puis ni l'un ni l'autre. Je suis un malheureux *homme d'entre-deux*, comme dit Pascal.'—*M. à L.*, p. 244. Cp. his letter of 15 August 1834 to Skrzynecki, quoted by Trannoy, p. 212.

[167] See *M. à L.*, p. 264.

[168] For the full text of the letter which Montalembert sent to Cardinal Pacca, see Dudon, *L. et le S.S.*, pp. 337 f. To E. Boré Lamennais wrote on 31 December 1834: 'Montalembert . . . venait de faire une sottise solennelle, en envoyant, lui laïque, son adhésion aux deux Encycliques que personne ne lui demandait.' See Roussel, *Lamennais intime*, p. 309.

one has founded one's life; but my life has already been so broken by causes quite foreign to my will[169] that it makes very little difference whether or not I give it a new blow with my own hand. What matters to me, I repeat, is that I should keep a refuge from the troubles of the heart, which are after all the sharpest trial of one's life. This refuge exists for me only in catholicism.[170]

After this public parting, Lamennais and Montalembert continued to write affectionately to one another for a year or two,[171] but there were signs of increasing strain and in the middle of 1836 the correspondence simply petered out, and their relations altogether ceased.

Despite the large volume of his private correspondence that has survived, Lamennais is never very revealing about the inner workings of his mind, and during the years 1834–1836, when his break with catholicism was becoming final and he was refounding his religious beliefs, he deliberately avoided discussing with his friends his innermost thoughts. On 15 February 1836 he wrote to Benoît d'Azy: 'It is certain that my convictions have changed on several points; no one however knows on what points or to what extent. I do not have to account to anyone for my inner thoughts, and no one has the right to put his conjectures in the place of my avowals.'[172] Early in 1835 he had told David Richard that his ideas were under-

---

[169] He is referring to an unhappy and protracted love affair as well as to the disappointments of his public life.

[170] *M. à L.* (13 December 1834), p. 265. Père Dudon summarized this letter as follows: 'Le pape se trompe, et ses encycliques risquent de nuire à la société chrétienne; mais le temps et Dieu arrangeront les choses; en attendant, moi qui ne suis point chargé de gouverner l'Église, je me tais sur les doctrines où j'ai mis autrefois ma vie; comme je ne veux pas renoncer aux "consolations" de la religion, je reste pour cela dans l'Église; et voilà comment je me range à la parole du pape.'—*Études*, 5 January 1932, p. 99.

[171] Most of the letters are contained in *L. à M.* and *M. à L.* It appears from *M. à L.*, pp. 280, 287, that they met once more in Paris in May 1835.

[172] *Lamennais inconnu*, p. 349; cp. Forgues, II, 411, 457, 464; *Cottu*, p. 281; *Vitrolles*, p. 266; Feugère, p. 374. Dudon, depending on a passage in a letter of 8 May 1833 from Lamennais to Ventura about changes in his doctrinal views, concluded that Lamennais had really lost his faith by then, and that his subsequent professions of faith (in August, November and December 1833) were mendacious. But apart from the fact that the implications of the passage in the letter to Ventura are obscure, Dudon failed to see that 'loss of faith' is a state of mind that may follow upon a long period of sincere oscillation. See Dudon, 'Lettres inédites de Lamennais à Ventura' in *Études*, 5 June 1910, p. 640; *L. et le S.S.*, pp. 298 ff.

going a gradual transformation but that the new ones were not yet mature in his own mind.[173]

Lamennais was never formally excommunicated, and there is no definite date on which one can say he ceased to be a member of the church.[174] So far as I know, the last date on which he formally asserted that he was still a catholic is 6 October 1834,[175] but as late as August 1836 the Archbishop of Paris was assured that Lamennais was still (or again?) going to mass.[176] He told Baroness Cottu in February 1837 that his ideas had developed and expanded but in no way changed, [177] which suggests that from his point of view there was no one moment when he ceased to be a catholic. There are however three of his published works that register the principal stages or elements in the transposition of his religious beliefs. These are (a) the long preface to *Troisièmes Mélanges* (a collection of his articles in the *Avenir*, etc.—the preface runs to 122 pages), published in February 1835; (b) *Affaires de Rome*, published in November 1836, which he said closed a long period in his life;[178] and (c) *Discussions critiques*, the first edition of which was not published till 1841, and which belongs to the new period of his life, but which consists for the most part of notes that he made while he was writing *Affaires de Rome*.

In the preface to *Troisièmes Mélanges* Lamennais stands, as it were, on the threshold or frontier of the church.[179] There is no certain indication that he means to step right outside. He seems to be designedly enigmatic or quizzical, until his pen runs away with him. The preface falls into three parts: first, Lamennais engages in self-examination about his ideas before 1830; secondly, he offers an apologia for the *Avenir*; and he finishes with one of those slashing attacks on the régime of Louis-Philippe, which he was never tired of making,[180] but which was out of place in this context.

In the first part of the preface, Lamennais does not declaim prophet-wise, but, with an objectivity and inconclusiveness that are

[173] See Roussel and Ingold, *Lamennais et David Richard* (1909), pp. 46, 52 f.

[174] Cp. Duine, p. 265.

[175] In a letter to Ballanche; 'Je suis catholique et je veux l'être sans que cela m'oblige à adopter (la ligne) suivie par les hommes de la hiérarchie ni en général leurs opinions en ce qui ne touche pas la foi.' See Feugère, p. 364.

[176] See Roussel, *Documents*, II, 254.   [177] See *Cottu*, p. 290.

[178] 'Il termine une série d'écrits correspondant à une longue époque de ma vie. Les modifications qui se sont opérées dans mes idées en marquent une seconde époque que caractériseront mes travaux futurs.' Lamennais to Benoît d'Azy on 1 October 1836; *Lamennais inconnu*, p. 356.

[179] Cp. Roussel, *Lamennais intime*, p. 332.

[180] Cp. Versluys, pp. 39 f.

rare in what he wrote for publication, he reflects upon the opinions
that he has previously held and the causes that he has previously
espoused. He readily acknowledges that in the heat of controversy
he was led into exaggeration and one-sidedness. So far from claiming
to have been strictly consistent, he claims credit for the fact that he
learned by experience to see his mistakes and to change his mind.
Only idiots, he says, claim never to have changed their minds.

He then discusses various views of the relation between reason and
revelation or various solutions of the problem of certitude, including
that which he had himself advanced in the *Essai sur l'indifférence*.
He still adheres to his own system, he says, while he has to admit
that it has been rejected by the ecclesiastical authorities. But other
proposed solutions of the problem of certitude remain as open as
ever to fatal objections. That is where matters stand, and that is all
he has to say under that head.

He next surveys the campaign he had conducted on behalf of
ultramontanism and against gallicanism. He still considers that the
idea of the catholic church requires an infallible papacy; otherwise
the church would have no certain centre of unity and authority.
But he now sees difficulties in the dogma of papal infallibility that
he had not seen before. He confesses that the gallicans had a case,
though their position as a whole was intolerable. It must be admitted
that they had stood for safeguards against the abuse of papal power,
which the history of the church had shown to be necessary. It is
difficult to see any satisfactory way both of maintaining papal
infallibility and of preventing it from becoming the ground of a
spiritual despotism. He leaves this problem also unresolved.

He then turns to the relation between the spiritual and temporal
powers or between church and state, which is bound up in his mind
with the relation between the authority that is a necessary condition
of social order and the liberty that is a necessary condition of social
progress. Here again he passes in review various theories that have
been advocated. In fact, the two powers have been in continual
conflict, each seeking to encroach on the province of the other and
to usurp the other's rights. The church no more than the state is
qualified to be the sole judge or final arbiter of where the line
between them must be drawn. Here again the gallicans had been
justified in their criticism of ultramontanism.

Lamennais offers no fresh solution of the relations between church
and state or between authority and liberty, but he points out that
even when he had been advocating too simply the rights of authority

he had always held that the people had imprescriptible rights too, though he had not defined them clearly enough. He had always held tyranny in horror. He had always defended religious liberty and liberty of education. During the Restoration period he had attacked the royalists because they were hostile to liberty, and he had attacked the liberals because they were hostile to religion. He had believed that both christianity and liberty were equally necessary. He had looked back to the great days of the middle ages, when the popes had defended the liberties and rights of the peoples against the might of the emperors, and he had imagined that this glorious past might be renewed. The papacy might now lead the world into a new age in which faith and science, religion and liberty, order and progress would be reconciled. 'We were undoubtedly mistaken,' Lamennais sardonically observes. 'As everyone knows, that has been pointed out to us with sufficient solemnity; but the mistake was perhaps pardonable.'[181]

When he comes to the July revolution and the campaign of the *Avenir* he says that the cause he had advocated had been fatally handicapped by the opposition of the hierarchy and the majority of the clergy, in particular by their unwillingness to forego the salaries which the government paid them, the renunciation of which was an indispensable condition of the church's securing its full liberty. There are two ways of regarding catholic christianity, he says. On the one hand, in its intrinsic nature and in the divine purpose it is the way by which the truth and the love that are mankind's supreme need are actualized in the world, and by which men are delivered from all that enslaves them. On the other hand, it is an external organization which depends inevitably on the protection of civil governments. Catholicism might proclaim to the peoples liberation from the modern slaveries—political servitude and economic exploitation—and if it did so it would be true to its essential nature. But in that case it would have to give up its temporal power; it could no longer depend on the protection of governments or on their external support of religion. The pope and the episcopate, Lamennais says, had decided that catholicism could not afford to forego these advantages and that its preservation depended on the material strength of its organization rather than on its intrinsic moral strength. The decision of the hierarchy must be accepted, he says.[182]

[181] *O.C.*, x, p. lxv.
[182] 'Or, après un mûr examen sans doute, le souverain pontife, en cela pleinement d'accord avec l'épiscopat, a jugé que ce seroit au moins compromettre

In an eloquent passage, which from his point of view contains the
sum of the matter, Lamennais depicts the fatal choice which he
considers the papacy has made:

Catholicism is languishing and tending to die out in Europe.
The peoples are becoming detached from it. Kings either openly
attack it or secretly undermine it. How can it be revived? How
can the vigour which day by day it seems to be losing be restored
to it? Such was the problem to be solved,[183] and there were
two possible solutions.

Full of faith in the truths which fundamentally constitute
christianity . . . one could have broken the bonds that bind the
church to the state, and have liberated it from the dependence that
impedes its action. One could have associated the church with the
social movement which is preparing new destinies for the world—
with liberty so as to unite it with order and to correct its errors;
with science so as to reconcile it, by way of unfettered discussion,
with . . . dogma; with the people so as to pour upon their immense miseries the inexhaustible streams of the divine charity. In a
word, one could have risen above all earthly interests and have embraced the naked cross, the cross of the carpenter who was born
poor and who died poor; the cross of him who lived only for the
love of his brethren and taught them to give themselves for one
another. The cross of Jesus son of God and son of man might
have been set up at the entrance to the ways along which the
human race is now advancing. This could have been done; at least
that is what we believed.

But it was also possible to tighten the ancient alliance with the
absolute powers, to support them against the peoples and against
liberty, in order to obtain from them a tolerance of sorts; to weld
the altar to the throne, to rely upon force, to turn the cross towards

l'existence du catholicisme que de renoncer aux avantages qu'on vient d'énu-
mérer, et que sa conservation, au siècle où nous sommes, dépendoit plutôt de la
force en quelque sorte matérielle de son organisation extérieure, que de la
force intrinsèque et toute morale qu'il puise dans sa nature même. Maintenant
que la hiérarchie a prononcé, nous devons le croire et nous le croyons.'—O.C.,
x, pp. xciv f.

183 Le Hir, *Lamennais écrivain*, p. 425, points out that in the first draft of this
passage Lamennais wrote: 'Le catholicisme languit et *menace* de s'éteindre . . .
tel *est* le problème à résoudre.' But before the manuscript went to the printer
he corrected it to read: 'Le catholicisme languit et *tend* à s'éteindre . . . tel
était le problème à résoudre.' These changes mark a stage in his loss of hope for
catholicism.

the past, to entrust it to the protection of diplomatic protocols, to entrust it to the care of soldiers who have been ordered with fixed bayonets to keep back the trembling nations. Rome has chosen the latter course; she had a right to do so.[184]

Affaires de Rome is like a cool and documented commentary on that passage. Lamennais was able to work on this book at leisure in the seclusion of La Chesnaie, where he continued to live until May 1836.[185] His rupture with catholicism which was latent in the preface to *Troisièmes Mélanges* is openly and finally registered in *Affaires de Rome*.[186] In my view this is Lamennais's most accomplished book and the one that will live longest: W. S. Lilly spoke well of it as 'that fascinating and melancholy book which perhaps reveals him at his greatest as a master of style'.[187] Apart from its historical and theological interest, it contains exquisite descriptions of scenes and experiences during the visit to Rome in 1831–1832. I have often had occasion to refer to it already for Lamennais's account of his relations with the papacy and for the documents that it reproduces.

On the face of it, it is a very restrained and objective record of Rome's reactions to the campaign of the *Avenir*. Lamennais repeatedly claims that he is writing as a simple historian and merely recording facts without seeking to make out a case.[188] Whatever may be thought of that claim, the book is undoubtedly free from the passion and exaggeration that are characteristic of most of his controversial writings, and perhaps in consequence of its restraint and polished irony it is all the more powerful as an indictment.

The conclusion is that the papacy has irrevocably[189] identified

[184] *O.C.*, x, pp. cii f. Lamennais added that he was profoundly convinced that Rome's choice had been determined by Providence. This was now a favourite idea of his: institutions, which have rendered themselves incapable of moving with the times, providentially sign their own death warrants.

[185] Except for a visit to Paris in the early summer of 1835, when he joined with other eminent republicans in trying to assist the defence of the so-called 'accusés d'avril', who had taken part in insurrections at Lyons and elsewhere in April 1834. See Boutard, III, 116–119; *Discussions critiques*, pp. 305–438.

[186] Amalie Hoiss, *Histoire d'un livre: Affaires de Rome par F. de Lamennais (1836): étude critique* (1933) may be consulted, but it contains little that is fresh or distinctive. It does however supply useful quotations from a considerable number of review articles, etc., about Lamennais.

[187] Lilly, *Studies in Religion and Literature* (1904), p. 171.

[188] See e.g., *A.R.*, 161, 189, 316, 320, 322.

[189] 'Comment pourroit-elle [la papauté] renoncer à des doctrines qu'elle a déclarées appartenir à la tradition des Apôtres et des Pères, et par conséquent à la

itself with the absolute powers against the rising tide of political liberty and democracy and the yearnings of the peoples for a fuller life and a more equitable social order. Rome's decision, Lamennais says, has convinced him that he had been mistaken in certain of his fundamental assumptions, and has compelled him to reconsider his whole position. *Affaires de Rome* is to be regarded as closing the series of his writings during the previous twenty-five years.[190]

Catholicism as it at present exists, he has concluded, is bound to die; but he maintains that real christianity, which has inspired all that is best in European history and is at the bottom of the peoples' aspirations after a better way of life, will still be the religion of the future. 'What one rejects is not authentic christianity, but a certain sterile and material system that has taken its name and disgraces it; what is dying is not the divine tree, but the withered bark that covers it.'[191] The future form of christianity will certainly not be protestantism,[192] nor a mere humanism[193]; it will meet and satisfy the universal and the deepest needs of mankind. *Affaires de Rome* closes with an ascription of glory to God: 'GLOIRE À DIEU DANS LES HAUTEURS DES CIEUX, ET PAIX ICI-BAS AUX HOMMES DE BONNE VOLONTÉ!'

And so Lamennais passes out of church history. From now onwards the catholicism, to which he had devoted the best part of his life, was dead so far as he was concerned, and from the point of view of the church he was an apostate. He would continue to look and labour for the regeneration of society—through politics and religion, but no longer through the church. A consideration of his religious

révélation divine? Ce seroit de sa part une apostasie. Diroit-elle qu'elle s'est trompée sur cette révélation, qu'elle l'a mal comprise? Ce seroit abjurer son autorité. . . . La papauté est donc irrévocablement liée au système qu'elle a cru devoir embrasser dans ces derniers temps, et, quoi qu'il arrive, il faut en accepter toutes les conséquences.'—*A.R.*, pp. 328 f.

[190] 'Je regarde . . . et je désire qu'on regarde ce court écrit comme destiné à clore la série de ceux que j'ai publiés depuis vingt-cinq ans. J'ai désormais des devoirs et plus simples et plus clairs.'—*A.R.*, p. 201.

[191] *A.R.*, p. 336.

[192] 'Ce ne sera rien non plus qui ressemble au protestantisme, système bâtard, inconséquent, étroit, qui, sous une apparence trompeuse de liberté, se résout pour les nations dans le despotisme brutal de la force et pour les individus dans l'égoïsme.'—*A.R.*, p. 338.

[193] Cp. what Lamennais wrote to de Potter on 4 February 1836: 'Soyez-en bien sûr, jamais vous ne trouverez de créatures humaines qui disent sincèrement: "Nos frères, qui êtes sur la terre," qu'elles n'aient dit auparavant: "Notre père, qui êtes aux cieux!" '—Blaize, II, 147.

and other beliefs from 1837 onwards would belong to a study of the
last period of his life. It is however in place here to add that in 1841
he published a book, entitled *Discussions critiques et pensées diverses*
that was made up of a variety of notes and jottings on religion,
philosophy, and politics, most of which (so he says in the preface)
he had entered in his private journal during the time when he was
preparing *Affaires de Rome* for publication.

Some of these fragmentary pieces are no more than aphoristic
sentences. 'Il y a des miracles quand on y croit; ils disparaissent quand
on n'y croit plus.'[194] 'Toute philosophie commence et finit dans le
mystère.'[195] Others are pieces of argument. Taken together, they
show how in 1835–1836 Lamennais was brooding sadly and critically
over the creed that he had championed for so many years. He now
felt free, and indeed morally bound, to call in question beliefs that
he had taken for granted as parts of the whole scheme of catholic
orthodoxy, or that he had defended as a matter of course since they
were guaranteed by the infallibility of the pope. The collapse in his
mind of that cardinal doctrine, consequent upon the acts of Gregory
XVI, had driven him to review the several articles of the catholic faith,
in order that he might be sure in what he ought still to believe.[196]

He now seems to submit everything to the test of a reason that
looks very much like the individual reason which he had castigated
so fiercely in the *Essai sur l'indifférence*.[197] In this as in other respects

---

[194] *Op. cit.*, p. 55. References are to the edition of *Discussions critiques* which E. D.
Forgues published, with additional material, after Lamennais's death, in
Mélanges philosophiques et politiques (1856).   [195] *Ibid.*, p. 202.

[196] Lamennais's own account in 1841 of the process and cause of the liquidation of
his former beliefs was as follows: 'Jusqu'à l'époque où Rome exigea de moi un
acte qui, à tort ou à raison, blessait ma conscience, je m'étais appliqué avec le
soin le plus attentif et la sincérité la plus parfaite, à me renfermer dans les bornes de
la plus stricte orthodoxie, ne me permettant, en dehors des doctrines enseignées,
aucun examen dont ces doctrines mêmes ne fussent le dernier critérium. Mais
quand je me vis contraint de renoncer ou à ce critérium, ou à ce que ma conscience me représentait comme un devoir sacré, je dus, pour sortir de l'anxiété
où me jetait cette opposition douloureuse, sonder les bases de l'autorité qui
avait été ma règle jusque-là. Je le fis avec une bonne foi dont on ne m'ôtera pas
le sentiment qui fait ma paix, je le fis par écrit, et mon unique réponse aux
attaques passionnées dont je n'ai cessé d'être l'objet depuis quatre ans, sera de
publier les réflexions écrites pour moi seul originairement [i.e. *Discussions
critiques*].'—From a letter addressed by Lamennais 'au *Semeur*, journal protestant', 26 February 1841: see Duine, *Documents ménaisiens* (1919), p. 21. Cp.
Spuller, *Lamennais*, p. 242.

[197] On 24 April 1836 Lamennais wrote to E. Boré: 'Qu'est-ce le rationalisme?
Qu'est-ce le mysticisme? Je ne suis, pour moi, ni mystique ni rationaliste en un

he can be accused of occupying positions which he had himself
demolished, but he shows no concern to refute directly his own previous arguments.[198] He is altogether less dogmatic now and more
tolerant.[199] He is weary of theological pugnaciousness. He no longer
maintains that the kind of certitude, which in the *Essai* he had
declared to be indispensable, can be attained by man in this world.

> When, on a fine summer's day [he writes], you follow in a
> forest a path covered by branches that form a vault overhead, you
> see along the path, between wide shadows, a shimmering light
> produced by the rays that penetrate the foliage. This path is our
> life, and this flickering and feeble light is our knowledge.[200]

The principal difference in his beliefs, at least so it seemed to
Lamennais himself in 1841, was that he no longer accepted the
hypothesis of a supernatural order.[201] Thus he rejected traditional
notions of an external revelation, of miracles, and of arbitrary divine
interventions. He says nothing in these notes about christology. He
rejects expiatory theories of the atonement, and declares for the
exemplarist view.[202] He still attacks deism, though he himself seems
nearer to deism now than to any form of traditional orthodoxy.

sens exclusif. Je cherche le vrai partout et par toutes les voies, et quand je l'ai
trouvé ou cru l'avoir trouvé, peu m'importe le nom qu'on lui donne.' See
Revue britannique, November 1894, p. 78.

[198] On 28 January 1835 he wrote to Countess de Senfft: 'En relisant bien des choses
que j'ai écrites, je ris de moi-même de bon cœur; cela me met dans une grande
défiance, de mes propres idées d'abord, et puis de celles des autres.' See Forgues,
II, 419. See also Versluys, p. 63.

[199] Cp. Versluys, pp. 45 f.

[200] *Discussions critiques*, p. 266.

[201] Alphonse Chrétien, in *Le Christianisme de Lamennais* (1897), pp. 63 f., remarked
that the supernatural signified for Lamennais the kind of miracles with belief
in which roman catholicism let itself be associated, e.g. those of St Joseph of
Cupertino. In his book Chrétien, an Old Catholic, reviewed in detail Lamennais's theological statements in *Discussions critiques*, and maintained that they
are less negative or heterodox than has been supposed. He concludes: 'Ce n'est
pas la foi chrétienne dans ses principes essentiels qu'il [Lamennais] attaque, c'est
la théologie romaine qu'il veut révolutionner, c'est l'Église catholique de Rome
qu'il veut réformer.'—*Op. cit.*, p. 77.

[202] '*Ecce qui tollit peccata mundi*: rien, certes, de plus vrai. En apprenant à l'homme
à s'oublier lui-même, à ne se préférer à aucun autre homme, à aimer ses frères
d'un amour égal à celui qu'il a pour soi, à se dévouer, à se sacrifier pour eux;
en leur donnant l'exemple de ce sublime sacrifice, Jésus-Christ a vraiment
ôté le péché du monde; car le péché n'est, dans sa source, que l'amour prédomin-
ant, exclusif de soi, la préférence de soi à tout ce qui n'est pas soi.'—*Discussions
critiques*, pp. 128 f.

There does not appear to be in *Discussions critiques* an explicit denial of everlasting punishment in hell—that touchstone of orthodoxy in the nineteenth century; but it must be confessed that, when his old friend Bruté, now a bishop in the U.S.A., visited him at La Chesnaie in 1836, Lamennais not only told him that he did not believe in the eternity of hell but denied that it was a *de fide* dogma of the Church of Rome.[203]

There are some bitter entries in *Discussions critiques*,[204] but most are wistful. The final impression left on the mind by these fragments is of Lamennais's genuine and deep compassion for all suffering and oppressed peoples and of his determination, in God's name, to devote the rest of his life to their well-being. He realized, as scarcely any christians did at the time, that the future of humanity depended on 'cette immense question du *paupérisme*'.[205] All his life he was devoted to the practical, and not merely the theoretical, service of the poor.[206] His very bitterness is provoked by those who oppress them, especially by those who, as he thought, did so under the auspices of religion.

Though Lamennais himself till his death in February 1854 remained entirely detached from the church and refused to have any dealings with the hierarchy, he remained on terms of close friendship with some of his old lay friends who were catholics and even with some who were priests.[207] We shall not be doing him an injustice if we

---

203 See Dudon, *L. et le S.S.*, p. 364. Bruté sent to the pope a résumé of his conversation with Lamennais, which Dudon printed from the Vatican Archives. When Bruté questioned Lamennais about different articles of belief, Lamennais usually replied, 'Ami, je crois cela, mais pas comme vous; si je l'explique, vous ne m'entendrez point.' But when they came to the question of hell, Lamennais was more forthcoming. 'Pour l'enfer, il m'arrêta,' wrote Bruté to the pope. ' "Je ne crois point à l'éternité des peines. Cela n'est point de foi. À Rome (où l'on examine à fond et où on ne se hâte de dire: ceci est ou n'est pas de foi), des hommes instruits, vrais théologiens, sont de mon avis. Si cela eût été décidé, c'eût été à l'époque des conciles tenus lors des affaires de l'origénisme. Je l'ai étudié. Il n'y a eu rien de tel de décidé. L'opinion de l'éternité des peines conduit nécessairement au dualisme." ' See also Laurentie, *Souvenirs inédits*, p. 229.

204 E.g. 'Le besoin de la vie sociale est si grand dans l'homme, qu'une des plus vives souffrances des âmes élevées, à certaines époques, est de ne trouver aucune société à laquelle elles puissent s'attacher pleinement. La société temporelle n'est guère qu'un cloaque, une salle de torture, ou un échafaud. Dans l'Église, la hiérarchie a divorcé avec le Christ, sauveur du genre humain, pour forniquer avec tous ses bourreaux. Le Pape baise au front la Mort, parce qu'elle a un diadème sur son crâne sec, et un glaive à la main. O Dieu! ô Dieu! ils ont fait de ton temple un sépulcre où le prêtre rampe pour disputer aux vers leur pâture immonde.'—*Op. cit.*, p. 194.

205 See Forgues, II, 382.   206 See Versluys, pp. 114 ff.   207 Cp. Versluys, p. 57.

conclude this narrative of his relations with the church by quoting from a letter that he wrote in 1840 to his friend Mme Clément, who had consulted him about whether she should allow her son to receive the first communion.

> I have been thinking about what you wrote concerning Charles's desire to make his first communion. It is quite certain that the absence of religion leaves an immense void in man, and that duty depends on religion for its sanction. So far then there is no difficulty about this grave and important question. But in the present period, when the old faith, enfeebled and almost extinct, is undergoing profound modifications, there is a great need for what society no longer offers us, I mean a faith in harmony with the undying instincts of man, one that speaks to the condition of those minds that are seeking, without having yet found, the teaching which will satisfy them, and the need for which they daily feel more keenly. I have no doubt that it will have its root in christianity, of which it will mark a new phase. But until it emerges, catholicism is, I believe, the christian communion that beyond all comparison has best preserved the essential spirit of the institution of Jesus Christ. I see therefore no solid reason for depriving oneself of the inner satisfaction and the support which can be found by joining in the established religious rites. If then you have in your neighbourhood a truly evangelical priest, who inspires confidence in Charles, and who understands that uprightness of heart is what God looks for above everything else . . . then I should think that Charles not only may do what he desires but that he could not do better. . . . Everything hangs on finding a priest who is sensible and enlightened, good and single-hearted, who relies more on the natural instinct of his conscience as a man and as a christian than on the rules of an absolute theology; but they are few and far between.[208]

We may add that ministers of the church such as Lamennais had been—and might have been to the end?—are also few and far between. Whose fault was it that he was lost to the church? Had he failed in his mission? Or had the pope and hierarchy failed in theirs? It is the office of an historian not to answer those questions but to provide the data on which well-informed answers can be based. But he would be inhuman if he were content to leave without further comment a story that is so provocative of reflection.

[208] See *Revue d'histoire littéraire de la France*, April–June, 1905, p. 318.

EPILOGUE

'La société attend, pour renaître, une nouvelle action du
christianisme, une action grande, élevée comme lui, et ce
n'est pas désormais avec de la diplomatie qu'on sauvera
le monde.'—Lamennais to Ventura, 14 May 1826.

'Si l'on était toujours obligé de s'aligner sur la forme de
pensée théologique, de pratique, de piété ou d'organisation actuellement tenue, il n'y aurait jamais dans l'Église
ni adaptation, ni réforme, ni progrès.'—Congar, *Vraie et
fausse Réforme dans l'Église*, p. 295.

AMONG THE MANY QUESTIONS that rise up out of the subject
of this book, I propose to say something about Lamennais's
changes of front, about the extent of his influence on the
church both in his own time and subsequently, and about the way in
which his conflict with Gregory XVI illustrates the tension that is
perennial in ecclesiastical history between the 'priest' and the
'prophet'.

I shall not attempt any final or comprehensive appraisal of Lamennais's character such as would be called for in a biography; as regards
that, I will do no more than say that the best and most adequately
documented study of his character that is known to me is the work
of a Dutch writer. I refer to a book entitled *Essai sur le caractère de
Lamennais* by Dr J. C. Versluys; it is written in French, though
published in Amsterdam—in 1929. It does not appear to have
received so far the attention it deserves, even in France. Dr Versluys
has provided a just, vivid, and reliable picture of Lamennais as a
man, and has gone further than anyone else to unravel, without
destroying, the fascinating complexities of his personality.

Lamennais's changes of front, even during his career as a catholic
which is all that concerns us here, are at first sight astonishing. He
was a royalist, and then a republican; he was an authoritarian, and
then a libertarian; he was an establishmentarian, and then a dis-
establishmentarian; he was a champion of clericalism, and then a
herald of lay catholic action. The question inevitably asks itself
whether there was any basic consistency beneath these contradictions,

or whether he struck out irresponsibly and at random in opposite
directions as his impulses moved him. It was an easy game, both in
his own lifetime and afterwards, for those who wished to discredit
Lamennais and one or other of the creeds he had professed, to point
to his own unacknowledged self-refutations. That may have been
effective controversy, but it was not very discerning.

It is not difficult for anyone who looks beneath the surface to see
what was the consistent driving force in Lamennais's thought and
action. Few have seen it more clearly than Sainte-Beuve did in 1834,
when he was in much more sympathetic relations with Lamennais
than he was later on. In the article he wrote on the publication of
Paroles d'un Croyant[1] he said that Lamennais's polemical and doctrinal activity could be divided into two distinct periods, during
which he had pursued the same end but by two contrary means. At
the outset he was struck by the spiritual and moral torpor that he
saw around him; society had been depraved and exhausted by the
turmoil and tyranny of the revolutionary and napoleonic periods;
it was like a valley of dry bones. It seemed to Lamennais at first that
breath and life could not be expected to revive in the moribund
social mass unless they were infused authoritatively from above. So
he called upon governments, and beyond governments the holy see,
to mediate the spirit of renewal.

As Sainte-Beuve says, Lamennais never held governments in particularly high esteem, but he began by regarding them as a possible
channel through which regenerating influences might be transmitted
to the whole of society. When by refusing to the church full liberty
of action governments declined to do this work of transmission,
Lamennais denounced them as an obstacle, and invoked the holy see
over and against them. And then he found that the holy see had no
intention of rising to the occasion. Meanwhile, he had looked again
at the social scene, and had detected signs of life in what had previously struck him as an inert mass. It was from that wholesome
ferment, he concluded, that the work of renewal must proceed. Thus
in the end he had recourse directly to society itself, to the people.[2]
He decided that their aspirations towards a new social order, which

[1] See Sainte-Beuve, II, 33 f.

[2] On 22 January 1836 Lamennais wrote to Coriolis: 'Le peuple, le vrai peuple,
qui n'est pas la canaille corrumpue des grandes villes, forme la partie saine de
notre race, si odieuse et si vile à ses deux extrémités qui se rejoignent dans une
commune dégradation.'—Forgues, II, 455. And on 5 April 1836 to the same:
'On se récriera tant qu'on voudra; je soutiens, moi, que le peuple, le pauvre
peuple, travaillant chaque jour, est partout ce qu'il y a de meilleur, et qu'en

were struggling to birth, must be released and allowed to grow. In other words, he substituted the method of liberty for the method of authority as the means of pursuing the end of social regeneration.

The point is that Lamennais's governing aim throughout was the regeneration of society.[3] As early as January 1809 he had set down in a note-book what was to be the guiding object of his life: *Salus populi suprema lex esto*.[4] He wrote the *Essai sur l'indifférence* and laboured at his philosophical system, because he believed that a society cannot recover spiritual and moral health without a sure and well-founded faith in God, the author of all health. He attacked gallicanism and advocated ultramontanism, because he was convinced that churches which let themselves depend on civil governments would never be able to bear an effective witness to the transcendent moral law that is above all states, whereas the papacy, he supposed, was divinely ordained and qualified to do precisely that. At last, he identified the cause of Christ with the cause of liberty and democracy, because he had come to the conclusion that the sources of regeneration were latent within society and needed to be released by the provision of the largest possible measures of freedom. He threw over the papacy and the ecclesiastical hierarchy, when he had inferred that they were irrevocably committed to alliance with the forces that were bent on suppressing the liberal, reforming, and emancipating movements of the age. There was thus a fundamental consistency in Lamennais's action within and upon and against the church, despite its apparently contradictory manifestations.

I need say here only a little about Lamennais's influence on the church in his own time, i.e. before his condemnation at Rome, because that will have become apparent in the foregoing chapters. I will simply sum up by saying that he revivified catholic theology,[5] especially on its apologetic side. He gave a new impetus to clerical

lui seul sont les éléments avec lesquels on peut refaire la société.'—*Ibid.*, II, 465.

It is interesting to note that Jacques Maritain says much the same thing in his book *Christianity and Democracy* (1945), pp. 51 f.; quoted in *The Frontier*, December 1952, pp. 473 f.

[3] Cp. A. Chrétien, *Le Christianisme de Lamennais*, pp. 89 f.; *Vitrolles*, p. 6.

[4] See Duine, p. 375.

[5] Hocedez in his *Histoire de la Théologie au xixe siècle*, I, 123, writes: 'On ne pourra nier, selon nous, que l'école de la Chênaie, non seulement par ses exemples et ses exhortations, mais par les discussions mêmes qu'elle déchaîna, n'ait été un des facteurs, et peut-être le plus efficace à ce moment, d'un renouveau de la spéculation théologique.' Cp. P. F. Dubois in *Revue de Bretagne*, January 1906, pp. 32 f.

studies and devotion. He showed that it was possible for a priest to arouse the interest of men in whom the acids of eighteenth-century philosophy and of the revolution had dissolved the traditional faith of christendom. He did more than anyone else to disturb the complacent gallicanism of the French clergy, to warn them of the consequences of propping the altar against the throne, and to popularize the ultramontane view of the role of the papacy in the economy of the church. For a short and brilliant space, together with the company of young and gifted disciples that he had gathered round him, he actualized the possibility that the church, instead of adhering to a negative and defensive attitude to the liberalizing and reforming spirit of the age, might discriminate between what was good and bad in it, and even take the lead in inaugurating a social order which would both preserve what was of value in the past and also satisfy the aspirations of the peoples of Europe for a fuller and freer way of life than they had ever known before.

It is much more difficult to assess the nature and extent of Lamennais's posthumous influence. Any considerable attempt to do so would carry us far beyond the scope of the present study. I will confine myself to noting some points that would have to be taken into account by anyone who embarked upon such an inquiry.

First, so soon as Lamennais had broken with the church and become an apostate, it became impolitic, to say the least, for those who had been influenced by him, and yet wished to keep a good standing in the church, to acknowledge their indebtedness to him, or if they did acknowledge it they were naturally inclined to minimize it. They were bound strongly to mark their dissociation from him and to join in deploring his fall. Thus although there can be little doubt that later in the nineteenth century the trend towards, and the triumph of, ultramontanism,[6] and also various essays in a more or less liberal catholicism, owed much to Lamennais, we should not expect to discover in the effects confessed or easily observable traces of the cause.

Nowadays when it is comparatively safe and easy for catholic writers to give to Lamennais all the credit that they consider to be

---

[6] Louis Veuillot acknowledged this, and he was in a position to know. On 22 May 1846 he wrote to Désiré Carrière: 'Nous ne pouvons oublier que M. de Lamennais a rendu à la religion d'immenses services: il a eu le premier toutes les idées que nous défendons, il a fait la brèche par où nous essayons de passer. . . .' See Correspondance de Louis Veuillot, edited by François Veuillot (1931), II, 174 f. Cp. Mélanges de Louis Veuillot (1934), V, 240; Boutard, III, 442.

due to him, it may be that some have flown to the other extreme and have exaggerated his posthumous influence and the extent to which his ideas have since found acceptance in the church with which he broke on their account.

For example, is not Claude Carcopino's statement[7] that it would be difficult to find a man of letters or a thinker in the nineteenth century who did not at some point in his life submit to the intellectual domination of Lamennais—an overstatement? And do not the following words of Victor Giraud exaggerate the extent to which Lamennais would have considered that the church after his time adopted his ideas?

> Poor Lamennais! He arrived too soon in a world that was too young. Suppose that he had lived half a century later: he would have seen nearly all his ideas—in a moderate and sober manner— taken up again and applied by Leo XIII, and Rome would not have disappointed his hopes. . . . The genius of our age was so perfectly in him that all the directions of contemporary catholicism originate with him. He is, through Gerbet, who was . . . one of the inspirers of the *Syllabus*, the father of what may be called infallibilist catholicism. Through Lacordaire and Montalembert, he presided over the destinies of liberal catholicism. Social catholicism can claim him as its authentic ancestor. Finally, catholic journalism, as Veuillot was well aware, has to thank him for giving it an orientation and a good example.[8]

Georges Goyau, who was also an authority in this field, made similar assertions about the influence of the *Avenir* on the subsequent development of the church.[9] And Mgr Duchesne, in the course of an address which he gave at St Malo in 1904 when the fiftieth anniversary of Lamennais's death was being observed, said:

[7] Carcopino, *Les Doctrines sociales de Lamennais* (1942), p. 199.

[8] Giraud, *La Vie tragique de Lamennais* (1933), pp. 172 f.

[9] 'Les programmes d'action pratique proposés aux sphères catholiques en l'année 1830—spécialement par les rédacteurs de l'*Avenir*—sont à l'origine du grand mouvement de revendications religieuses qu'illustrèrent Montalembert et Parisis, Dupanloup et Falloux, et qui aboutit, en 1850, à la conquête de la liberté de l'enseignement, puis en 1875, à la conquête de la liberté de l'enseignement supérieur; ils sont à l'origine de cet exercice spontané du droit d'association, qui groupa les Bénédictins de Solesmes, et qui s'affirmait imperturbablement, jusque dans la chaire de Notre-Dame, par le froc blanc où se drapait Lacordaire; et lorsque au bout de cent ans nous revendiquons encore, pour nos religieux, le droit légal de vivre ensemble, nous n'avons qu'à rouvrir l'*Avenir* pour y trouver des arguments auxquels toute puissance civile se réclamant

'I seem to remember having met in certain encyclicals, fifty or sixty years later than that of which he had to complain, ideas which were not without a resemblance to his. People speak nowadays of christian democracy, *et cela sans se signer*. Félicité de Lamennais was speaking of it already in the time of our grandfathers, who called him a blasphemer for doing so.'[10]

There were indeed developments in the church during the pontificates of Pius IX and Leo XIII which at first sight look like vindications of Lamennais's prescience and unspoken admissions that he had been right. I mean the definition of papal infallibility by Pius IX in 1870 and the steps taken or encouraged by Leo XIII towards renovating the church's theology and towards emphasizing the church's social mission, even by making concessions to liberal democracy.[11]

It may however be doubted whether these developments were intended to be in the direction towards which Lamennais had sought to move the church. He had wanted an infallible pope to lead the peoples into a new post-revolutionary christian civilization. He had wanted a pope who would 'ring out the old, ring in the new . . . ring in redress to all mankind', and a pope who in that adventure would call upon the church to cut loose from its temporal interests and its secular attachments. But Leo XIII, despite his reputed liberalism and his larger spirit of diplomatic accommodation, was no more disposed than Pius IX to contemplate so radical a break with Rome's past.

If he was prepared to permit certain concessions that his predecessors had refused, these did not affect his adherence to the received thesis about the relations between the church and society.[12] Because of the hardness of the times, it was impracticable to impose

elle-même des principes de liberté sera toujours embarrassée pour répondre.' Goyau, *L'Épanouissement du Credo* (1931), p. 59. Cp. the passage from Goyau quoted in R. Havard de la Montagne, *Histoire de la Démocratie chrétienne de Lamennais à Georges Bidault* (1948), p. 26; also Goyau on 'L'Église libre dans l'Europe libre' in *Revue des deux mondes*, July 1919, p. 35.

[10] See *Annales de la Société Historique et Archéologique de l'arrondissement de Saint-Malo*, 1904, pp. 84 f.

[11] Cp. Hocedez, *Histoire de la Théologie catholique au xixe siècle*, III, 180: 'Désireux de rendre au catholicisme son influence sur les affaires humaines, il [Léon XIII] traça d'une main ferme, en théologien averti, les distinctions nécessaires entre les exigences de l'immuable vérité et les contingences de son application, et en diplomate avisé fit les concessions compatibles avec la rigueur des principes.'

[12] The quotation in the preceding note from Hocedez follows these words: 'Dès sa première encyclique *Inscrutabili Dei* (1878), il (Léon XIII) renouvelait toutes les condamnations des erreurs modernes portées par Pie IX.'

the norm of the church-state, but when better times came it would be restored in its full rigour. It may be that Leo XIII's policies are reputed to be liberal only because of their contrast to the unbending intransigence of his predecessors and, one may add, of his successor. The question would have to be asked whether the papacy did not continue to be more interested in the rights of the church as an ecclesiastical institution—and, where possible, in its exclusive rights —than in the needs of mankind for fullness of life. To ask that question would not be to impugn the sincerity of Leo's concern for the victims of an unbridled capitalism nor the comparative enlightenment of his social teaching.

It may also be the case that in the twentieth century the writers to whom we have referred and 'christian democrats' generally have been more confident than they should have been that the papacy has now finally and permanently reconciled itself to the intrinsic desirability of liberal constitutions and the liberties for which Lamennais contended—liberty of conscience, liberty of association, liberty of education, liberty of the press. Although Cardinal Pacca, writing to Lamennais on behalf of Gregory XVI, said that such doctrines could never be presented 'comme un bien ou comme une chose désirable',[13] they appear now to have become entirely respectable among catholics in the so-called western democracies—in France, for example, and in the U.S.A. The works of M. Jacques Maritain— *True Humanism,* etc.—are well known far beyond the French-speaking world[14]; and the following statement by the American Jesuit, Father John Courtney Murray, illustrates how ideas with a thoroughly mennaisian ring are now set forth there:

> Democracy today presents itself with all the force of an idea whose time has come. And there are two reasons why it is the present task of Catholics to work towards the purification of the liberal tradition (which is their own real tradition) and of the democratic form of state in which it finds expression, by restoring both the idea and the institutions of democracy to their proper Christian foundations. First, this form of state is presently man's best, and possibly last, hope of human freedom. Secondly, this form of state presently offers to the Church as a spiritual power as good a hope of freedom as she has ever had; it offers to the Church as the Christian people a means, through its free political institutions,

[13] See *A.R.*, p. 151.

[14] See also the important symposium *Tolérance et communauté humaine* (Tournai, 1952).

P.P.—18

of achieving harmony between law and social organization and the demands of their Christian conscience; finally, by reason of its aspirations towards an order of personal and associational freedom, political equality, civic friendship, social justice, and cultural advancement, it offers to the Church the kind of co-operation which she presently needs, and it merits in turn her co-operation in the realization of its own aspirations.[15]

Father Murray ascribes the hostility to democracy of Leo XIII and his predecessors to their preoccupation with the conflict against 'Continental Liberalism' and to the absolutist conceptions of the state with which alone they were familiar. Thus he writes that the 'conception of the state that has been developed in the Anglo-American world, out of the substance of the political and legal ideas of the Middle Ages . . . was . . . foreign to the experience of the Papacy, which by the time of Leo XIII had been standing within the absolutist traditions of nearly four hundred years, and had had little, if any, experience of another political and legal tradition which, paradoxically, had more in common with Catholic ideas than the tradition which had grown up in the historical Catholic nations.'[16] It must be added, however, that these views are by no means undisputed in France[17] and in the U.S.A.[18]

In Spain and in some other countries it is reported that the doctrine of the nineteenth-century popes is still maintained in its integrity, and it would be rash to assume that it has in fact been abandoned by the papacy itself. In view of the probability that the influence of South America on the future of catholicism will not diminish, it is perhaps significant that a few years ago a South American theologian, Jules Meinville, attacked the christian social teaching of Jacques Maritain precisely on the ground that it is a reproduction of the ideas advocated by Lamennais in the *Avenir*, and

[15] Quoted in *Thought: Fordham University Quarterly*, XXVI, no. 102 (1951), p. 447.
[16] See J. C. Murray, S. J., article on 'Leo XIII on Church and State' in *Theological Studies*, XIV, no. 1 (March 1953), p. 21.
[17] E.g. *Histoire de la Démocratie chrétienne de Lamennais à Georges Bidault* (1948) by Robert Havard de la Montagne is a sustained attack on French liberal catholics and christian democrats, especially on the M.R.P., on the ground that they all fly in the face of papal doctrine.
[18] For an account of the attacks that have been made by conservative theologians on Father Murray's teaching, see 'A Church-State Controversy' by Victor R. Yanitelli in *Thought: Fordham University Quarterly*, *loc. cit.*, pp. 443–451; cp. Gustave Weigel on 'The Church and the Democratic State', *ibid.*, XXVII, no. 105 (1952), pp. 165–184.

in contradiction to the doctrine laid down by Gregory XVI and his successors. And when the eminent Roman theologian, Père Garrigou-Lagrange, wrote to Meinville to say that, while he did not himself approve of Maritain's teaching, he wanted to protest against its being identified with that of Lamennais, Meinville stuck to his guns, and proceeded to demonstrate by chapter and verse that Maritain's theses are the same as those of Lamennais in the *Avenir* and that they are, if anything, more in contradiction to papal doctrine.[19] Garrigou-Lagrange thereupon tried to change the subject, and having failed to do that made what may have been the convenient discovery that he had not time to go further into the matter.[20]

It is apparent then that the question of the present acceptance of Lamennais's ideas by the church is far from closed, and there is scope here for much further inquiry.

My final reflection has to do with the way in which the conflict between Lamennais and Gregory XVI illustrates the tension that is perennial in ecclesiastical history between the 'priest' and the 'prophet'. The terms 'priest' and 'prophet' do not of course in all, or most, senses exclude one another. I use them here as symbols. The priest stands for those members of the church who are, or believe themselves to be, responsible for maintaining its traditional doctrine and discipline, and its hierarchical structure and cultus. The prophet stands for those who believe themselves to be charged directly by God with a mission to declare the divine judgment on ecclesiastical corruption, or to promote a more or less radical reformation or the adaptation of the church to a new historical environment.[21] Prophets are sensitive to historic change; they have

---

19 See Jules Meinville, *Correspondance avec le R. P. Garrigou-Lagrange à propos de Lamennais et Maritain* (Buenos Aires, 1947). Meinville pointed out the following coincidences between Lamennais and Maritain: '(1) Le développement historique nécessairement progressif; (2) Qu'en conséquence le régime du Libéralisme qu'a inauguré la Révolution française comporte un progrès par rapport au régime du Moyen Age; (3) Que, par conséquent, l'Église doit s'allier avec le Libéralisme; (4) Que le régime des libertés modernes et en particulier la liberté de professer publiquement n'importe quelle religion est chose nécessaire et conforme à l'esprit de l'Évangile; (5) Que le type d'ordre publico-social chrétien que doivent se proposer les catholiques c'est une cité où catholiques, protestants, agnostiques et athées puissent vivre fraternellement, sans que cette cité, comme telle, doive se déclarer catholique.'—*Op. cit.*, p. 75; see also p. 95.
20 See the letters from Garrigou-Lagrange included in Meinville, *op. cit.*
21 Père Congar wrote: 'Il y a chez tout "prophète" le sentiment d'une œuvre à faire, qui est aussi une mission à remplir; il y a une découverte personnelle,

a gift for reading the signs of the times and for realizing how new occasions teach new duties; they naturally tend to find themselves in conflict with the priests who suppose themselves bound, above all, to preserve what has been handed down and who may be, both by interest and by temperament, inclined to hold on to that which they possess and that to which they are accustomed.[22] The importance of this tension lies in the fact that both the priest and the prophet are indispensable. 'Had there been no prophecy,' said H. L. Goudge, 'we should not care to read the story of Israel. Had there been no priesthood, there would be no story to read.'[23]

The same can be said of the catholic church and of every particular church. For while the relations between the priest and the prophet may become peculiarly acute in the Church of Rome by reason of the nature of its discipline and its centralized authority, a corresponding tension exists in every church that is alive, and it is liable from time to time to become critical. Père Yves Congar has stated with great moderation the character and cause of this tension: 'The prophetic function aims at making understood the meaning of time, of the course of events and of movements that come about in history, principally from the point of view of God and of his purpose. That is an office in which ecclesiastics have sometimes failed, in certain respects. What I mean is that a certain positive understanding of the movement of time, and especially a certain openness to this movement have sometimes been achieved only by advance-guards and by reformers operating on the frontiers.'[24] This tension arises in

tournée en impératif, avec tout ce qu'un tel impératif a de possédant.'—*Vraie et fausse Réforme dans l'Église* (1950), p. 221.

[22] Cp. Congar, *op. cit.*, p. 203; 'Les prophètes de l'Éternel s'opposent à leur temps et le contredisent. Quand leur temps dit: *Je tiens cela*, ils lui disent: *Non, tu ne dois pas*, ou: *Tu vas le perdre*; quand leur temps savoure sa sécurité, ils lui dévoilent des menaces, et quand il se croit perdu, ils lui annoncent le salut.'

[23] Quoted by S. C. Carpenter, *Christianity* (1953), p. 13.

[24] Congar, *op. cit.*, p. 213. Congar's book is a discerning study of the theoretical and practical problems that are involved in the idea of reformation in the church. He brings out the need of both the hierarchic and the prophetic elements in the church, the tension that there is bound to be between them, and the weaknesses and failures to which both are exposed. He has a passage (pp. 562–569) in which he contrasts Lamennais and Lacordaire as would-be reformers, which becomes a panegyric of the latter. Unfortunately, Congar appears to have depended for his information almost solely on a biography of Lacordaire, and to have made no first-hand study of Lamennais. In any case, it would have been much more instructive if he had contrasted Lamennais with Gregory XVI, about whom, despite its wealth of historical illustration, his book is almost silent.

every church; for every church, in order to exist, must have a priesthood (whether or not it uses the term), and every church, in which
prophets are not raised up, especially in periods of historic change,
is doomed to extinction or at least to petrifaction. There may then
be instruction and warning for all churches—for their advance-
guards as well as for their hierarchies—in the encounter between
Lamennais and Gregory XVI, since scarcely any two figures in the
history of the church have exemplified more clearly the distinction
and tension between the prophet and the priest. This was an encounter not between a bad priest and a good prophet, but between a
good priest and a good prophet, who at the same time displayed the
characteristic short-comings of priest and prophet respectively.

Gregory XVI[25] was a good priest. He had the disposition and
personal disinterestedness of a consecrated monk, which is what in
fact he was.[26] He was a man of inflexible industry and, behind an
unengaging exterior, of benevolence too. He was entirely devoted
to the interests of the church as he understood them. He had been
extremely reluctant to accept election as pope, but having been
elected he was far from being a cipher, and indeed imposed his own
very conservative outlook on the whole policy of the holy see
during his pontificate. While it is true that until his election Gregory
had spent most of his life in the cloister,[27] he had already gained
considerable experience of ecclesiastical administration and diplomacy.[28] If he failed to realize the modest hopes that were entertained
when he was elected, and if he left no noteworthy achievement
behind him,[29] that was the result not of innocence nor of inexperi-
ence but of his entirely negative and defensive attitude, in an age of
rapid and inescapable change, to every new current of thought and
to every kind of political reform.

For this good and consecrated and benevolent man also beautifully
embodied the characteristic limitations of the priest. His life-long
aim was exactly expressed in the title of a book he had published in

---

25 For a balanced review of Gregory's pontificate and character, see Schmidlin,
II, 185–409. See also Wiseman, *Recollections of the Last Four Popes*, pp. 415–
532; Dudon, *L. et le S.S.*, pp. 115 f.

26 'Il appartenait à un rameau en partie très vieilli et très affaibli de la très ancienne
et très austère famille bénédictine, qui élevait en effet ses membres dans une
discipline individuelle et une ascèse constantes, mais cherchait à les tenir le
plus possible éloignés de l'engrenage du monde.'—Schmidlin, II, 196.

27 Cp. Wiseman, *op. cit.*, p. 420.

28 See Boudou, *Le Saint-Siège et la Russie*, pp. 171 f.

29 Cp. Wessenberg's remark, quoted by Schmidlin, II, 360.

1799: *The Triumph of the Holy See and of the Church over the attacks of the innovators.*[30] He was resolved to 'hold fast what is good', but it was axiomatic for him that the received ecclesiastical system was good and that whatever threatened to change it was bad and therefore to be resisted.[31] He failed to understand that the French revolution had ushered in a new epoch which was heavy with judgment upon, and opportunity for, the church, and which called for an imaginative and resourceful determination in the leaders of the church to carry through a radical reformation—or at least sympathetically to guide and stedfastly to encourage any elements in the church that were alive to what was needed. When Lamennais qualified his complete submission in ecclesiastical matters with a claim for liberty of action in purely temporal matters, it did not occur to Gregory that he might acquiesce in, or at any rate not disown, even if he could not positively approve, explorations and initiatives on the frontiers of the church. The priest likes to have the prophet under control, and is fearful of allowing him an area of autonomy.

If now we turn to Lamennais, we can hardly fail to see in him both characteristic virtues and characteristic failings of the prophet.[32] He too was personally disinterested. 'Both by taste and reflection', he wrote to Vitrolles in 1820, 'I desire an obscure and tranquil life; it is only the idea of duty that can make me renounce it.'[33] He often said the same thing, and there is no reason to doubt his sincerity. The theory that Lamennais was motivated by an overweening and exceptional pride or ambition—which used to be advanced by catholics in order to account for his 'fall'[34]—has rightly been given up by most catholic writers now[35]; it never fitted the

---

[30] See Schmidlin, II, 194; cp. *ibid.*, pp. 360, 393, 407.

[31] All Gregory's 'reforms' were designed to restore what was traditional. See Charles Pouthas, *L'Église catholique de l'avènement de Pie VII à l'avènement de Pie IX* (Centre de Documentation Universitaire, Paris), pp. 275–284.

[32] On Lamennais's *prophetic* character, see Edward Dowden, *Studies in Literature 1789–1877* (1878), pp. 311 ff.; W. S. Lilly on 'A Nineteenth Century Savonarola' in *Studies in Religion and Literature* (1904), pp. 175 f.

[33] *Vitrolles*, p. 55.

[34] In the present century Père Dudon went on maintaining that Lamennais's 'orgueil' was the simple, sufficient, and final cause of his apostasy. See, e.g., *L. et le S.S.*, p. 378. But he had at last to complain that 'presque tous les ouvrages publiés en France sur Lamennais dans ces dernières années sont un plaidoyer en faveur d'un méconnu.'—*Études*, 5 February 1935, p. 356.

[35] F. J. J. Vrijmoed, *Lamennais avant sa défection et la néerlande catholique*, p. 95, writes: 'Nous ne nions point que *Lamennais* ait participé dans une large mesure au fond d'orgueil qui est le commun patrimonie de l'humanité, mais il ne

facts.[36] Lamennais was as plainly reluctant to undertake the mission which he felt the Lord was laying upon him as Gregory XVI was reluctant to accept election to the papal chair; but having done so he was equally single-minded in doing what he considered to be his duty.

From the time of his first book, *Réflexions*, Lamennais had maintained that a thorough reformation of the church was indispensable if it was to bring healing to the socially diseased condition of France and of Europe. While he remained faithful to this initial insight, he went on reading the signs of the times and was always open to learn from experience and ready to recast his message accordingly, and that was the mark of a good prophet. In 1817 he had written: 'When a revolution is inevitable, the wisest course is to make it yourself, in order to direct it.'[37] He did everything he could to act upon his precept, and to move others to do so. By the time of the *Avenir* he had thought out a coherent policy which, in more favourable circumstances, might have startled and educated catholics into new ways of thinking and new kinds of action, of which the result might have been to prevent the deep and still unhealed division of the French people into the party of the revolution and the party

paraît pas que le sentiment désordonné de sa propre excellence—*inordinatus appetitus propriae excellentiae*, comme disent les théologiens—en quoi consiste ce péché capital, ait prédominé en lui'; and he proceeds to show why he considers that to be so.

See also Carcopino, *op. cit.*, pp. 40 ff.; A. Viatte, *Le catholicisme chez les romantiques* (1922), pp. 138 f.; P.-H. Simon on 'Lamennais entre l'amour et la foi' in *Esprit et Vie*, May 1951, pp. 180 f.

36 For instance, is it reasonable to regard as consumed with pride a man who at the height of his fame could write as follows to a young critic who had just exposed his faults in print? Lamennais wrote to Sainte-Beuve on 30 July 1834 about the picture of himself in *Volupté*: 'Il y a quelques endroits, un surtout, que j'ai pris comme une leçon, comme un avertissement de frère que vous me donniez personnellement, et je vous en remercie. Nous avons tous si grand besoin d'être avertis. Nous glissons si aisément et si vite sur la pente de notre caractère! Il est sûr qu'il y a dans le mien une certaine impétuosité opiniâtre et blâmable que je ne suis pas assez appliqué à réprimer, que mes idées me préoccupent trop, que je les pousse en avant avec trop d'ardeur. Je ferai, mon ami, tous mes efforts pour que vos bons et sages conseils, dont je vous remercie encore une fois, ne soient pas entièrement perdus.' See Maréchal, *La Clef de 'Volupté'*, p. 92.

37 According to Duine, p. 271, this remark which appeared in the first edition of the *Essai sur l'indifférence* was suppressed in subsequent editions at the request of abbé Jean; nevertheless, as Duine says, it continued to be Lamennais's guiding maxim.

of the church.[38] Lamennais was also among the first to proclaim the imperative duty of catholics to bridge the chasms between men of science and men of faith, and also between the workers and the church.[39] He was not mistaken—he was indeed an authentic prophet —in insisting thus upon the fatefulness of the decisions with which the revolution had confronted catholicism.

But in Lamennais we can also see plainly some of the errors and faults into which prophets are prone to fall. He made the mistake of expecting the priest—in this case, the papacy—to assume the role of the prophet. As Baron d'Eckstein said, Lamennais 'would not consider the priest simply as an organ of the Church and the dispenser of the Sacraments; he wanted to make him master of everything, the superior of the state, and the exclusive source of all education and all science among men'.[40] He romanticized the capacities of the papacy,[41] and, as Pierre Harispe pointed out,[42] he failed to allow for the hard fact that the church has to reckon and negotiate with the powers of this world for the defence of its rights and its material interests, and sometimes has to sacrifice its own champions, and even its spiritual interests, to avert greater evils. Lamennais wanted the church, and above all the papacy, to be completely pure from political and diplomatic compromise.[43]

[38] As Professor Butterfield says in *Christianity in European History* (1951), pp. 42 f.: 'From the eighteenth century to the present day Roman Catholicism on the one hand and the more liberal or progressive parties on the other hand have split the French tradition from top to bottom, producing a cleavage which has extended over much of the Continent.' Cp. J. H. Nicholls, *Democracy and the Churches* (1951), p. 49; J. C. Murray, S. J., in *Theological Studies*, March 1953, pp. 9 f.

[39] See Maréchal, *La Mennais au Drapeau Blanc*, pp. 38, 87 ff.; *O.C.*, VIII, 250 ff., 323.

[40] Art. on 'The Abbé de Lamennais' in *The Rambler*, 1 May 1859, p. 65.

[41] Cp. Paul Lazerges, *Lamennais: essai sur l'unité de sa pensée* (1895), p. 51: 'Au lieu de voir la papauté telle qu'elle était, il se l'imaginait telle qu'il l'aurait voulue et qu'elle aurait dû être. Son pape idéal planait sur les sommets, proclamant les vérités éternelles devant les éphémères combats des partis, affirmant une justice supérieure devant les éphémères victoires du mal, père des peuples, arbitre impartial des intérêts de tous, législateur de l'humanité.'

[42] Harispe, *Lamennais*, pp. 226 f.

[43] 'Aussi absolu dans sa foi que dans ses principes, il [Lamennais] considérait l'Église comme une vierge sociale intacte, qui ne devait jamais se commettre avec les combinaisons et les trafics de la politique. Elle devait mettre au-dessus de tous les avantages de la diplomatie son indépendance et ses intérêts supérieurs, spirituels et moraux, dût-elle, pour les conserver, renoncer à toutes ses richesses, à son empire politique, pour remonter à la pauvreté de son divin fondateur, et

Therefore, instead of realizing that the most an institution, conditioned as the papacy was, should be expected to do was to acquiesce in his prophetic campaign, he looked to the pope to come forth as its patron, if not as its leader. He was foolish enough to force an obviously reluctant pope to commit himself, at a time when he could commit himself in only one way.[44] Lamennais should have been grateful if he were treated by Rome with silent indulgence and checked only for his extravagances. But prophets commonly have their vision filled by the one concern that has been laid upon them, whereas priests are responsible for seeing that no aspect of sound doctrine is neglected and no salutary institution is jettisoned. It has been said that Lamennais's creed might almost be summed up in a single article: 'I believe in the social mission of the church.'[45] The priests had to make as sure as they could that there would still be a church to have a social mission.

Then again, he made the common prophetic mistake of being in too much of a hurry and of being too impatient,[46] or at least of forgetting that the prophet is at liberty to speak with more urgency than the priest is at liberty to act. He was not entirely blind to this distinction, for on occasion he would acknowledge it. Thus, Vitrolles once taxed him with writing as if he were a jumper who draws a crowd together and then makes a gigantic leap which no one can follow; the observers are struck with astonishment and admiration, but they remain where they are. To this Lamennais replied that, if he were 'un homme de pouvoir', he would take good care to write quite differently, if indeed he had time to write at all.[47] Likewise, he once wisely observed that, in trying to hasten reforms, men often do more harm than good.[48] But as a rule he gave the impression of

de ses origines apostoliques, et à la simplicité de ses affirmations premières. Aussi toutes les compromissions et intrigues de la chancellerie pontificale lui étaient-elles odieuses.'—Harispe, *op. cit.*, p. 227.

[44] Lamennais's folly in this matter should be contrasted with the wisdom of Cardinal Sterckx, who skilfully avoided pressing the pope for a decision: see Haag, p. 161.

[45] See Boutard, III, 135. Cp. Spuller, *Lamennais*, p. 356.

[46] Cp. Sainte-Beuve, II, 56: 'On peut observer en règle générale que, de même que les livres de M. de La Mennais commencent tous par une parole empressée sur la vitesse des choses et la hâte qu'il faut y mettre, ils finissent tous également par une espèce de prophétie absolue. Cette pensée ardente ne mesure pas le temps à la manière des autres hommes; elle a son rhythme presque fébrile: l'horloge intérieure, qui dans cette tête n'obéit qu'à la mécanique rationnelle, n'est pas d'accord avec l'horloge extérieure du monde.'

[47] See *Vitrolles*, pp. 121, 125.   [48] See *A.A.*, v, 173; *O.C.*, x, 329.

being like a statesman who declares war before he has made the necessary preparations, before he has mobilized public opinion, and before there is a good and easily recognizable *casus belli*.

It was fantastic in 1830–1831 to call upon the French clergy as a whole to renounce their stipends from the state, before there had been a plain and protracted threat to the integrity of the church, which it had proved impossible otherwise to avert. We have seen that, as it turned out, the *Avenir* had raised a false alarm about the nominations to bishoprics that were to be expected from the government of Louis-Philippe [49]; and as regards the relations of church and state, Lamennais ought to have looked upon the campaign of the *Avenir* not as war but as preparation for a probable or possible war —unless divorce would be a more suitable analogy. The campaign of the *Avenir* could have been amply justified as a way of making catholics see the kind of action they must be ready to take, if or when church and state came to breaking-point. Meanwhile, he would have been well advised to make the best, instead of the worst, of the gallican liberties. [50]

Nevertheless, one would probably be carrying historical impartiality to a quixotic length if one pretended that the prophetic shortcomings of Lamennais were as grave as the priestly short-comings of Gregory XVI. And Gregory's simplest, and in this instance most fatal, fault has yet to be noticed; I mean his impersonal and juridical manner of dealing with Lamennais. This too is a not uncommon failing of men who are placed in positions of priestly or other power and who have little aptitude for warm personal relationships. While in 1832 no possible pope would have given positive approval to the doctrines of the *Avenir*, e.g. about the separation of church and state, yet it is possible that another pope might have so handled the affair as to avoid a positive condemnation of Lamennais and his followers. The way in which Leo XII had won Lamennais's affection in 1824, and so secured his confidence without approving his teach-

---

[49] See p. 170 *supra*.

[50] Chateaubriand in some interesting retrospective remarks on Lamennais's career, written in 1841, went so far as to say that 'les évêques se seraient trouvés engagés dans sa cause s'il eût adhéré aux libertés gallicanes, tout en vénérant le successeur de saint Pierre et en défendant l'unité.'—*Mémoires d'Outre-Tombe*, VI, 328 f.

As we have seen, Lamennais himself, when it was too late, came to see that there had been more to be said for gallicanism than he had recognized. See p. 258, *supra*.

ing, is in striking contrast to Gregory XVI's failure to do anything of the kind.

If Gregory had met Lamennais in a frank and friendly confrontation, and had said what he had to say face to face, he might well have persuaded him either greatly to moderate his campaign or to call it off indefinitely. We have Lamennais's own testimony to this effect, and there is no reason to doubt his good faith. In *Affaires de Rome* he writes thus of the way in which he and his fellow-pilgrims were treated when they appealed to the Holy Father to say what he wanted them to do:

> I have often wondered why the pope, instead of keeping us severely at arm's length and leaving us in a mystified and painful state of uncertainty, did not simply say to us: 'You thought you were doing right, but you have made a mistake. Placed as I am at the head of the church, I know better than you do its needs and its interests, and I am the sole judge of them. While I disapprove of the direction in which you have tried to go, I render justice to your intentions. Go now, and in future, before intervening in such delicate matters, take counsel with those whose authority should be your guide.' These few words would have settled everything. None of us would ever have dreamed of continuing what we had already suspended.[51]

I find that my concluding reflection has already been made by a writer upon whose verdict I could not improve: nothing that has come to light since it was given requires that it should be modified.[52]

> A liberal catholicism could win acceptance only by degrees and with the transforming effects of time,—not by a brusque evolution such as captivated the imagination and responded to the ardent passions of abbé de Lamennais. . . .[53]

> If it is true to say that Lamennais had pushed his ideas too far, that he had committed catholicism too much to the path of democracy and revolution, nevertheless his thesis, which urged the reconciliation of the church and liberty, was at bottom wiser,

---

[51] *A. R.*, p. 39.

[52] The quotations that follow are from *La Philosophie de Lamennais* by Paul Janet (1890). My attention was first drawn to them by their appearance in Amalie Hoiss's *Histoire d'un livre: Affaires de Rome* (1933), pp. 106 ff.; but Mlle Hoiss, instead of ascribing them to Janet, failed to indicate where she had found them.

[53] Janet, *op. cit.*, p. 81.

more practical, and indeed more christian than *la politique à outrance* which prevailed in the church . . .[54]

When one recalls the tact, the accommodations, the pliability, the patience which the catholic church employs in its dealings with the powers of this world when it is in conflict with them, one asks oneself whether something of this tenderness and patience could not have been employed with respect to a great genius and a great soul . . .[55]

These conclusions are not calculated to please either the admirers of the prophets or the adherents of the papacy. Neverthelesss, they may be historically just. 'All things human, even the best, have two faces,' said Lamennais. 'Whoever shows only one of them may be an artist, but assuredly he is not an historian.'[56]

[54] Janet, *op. cit.*, p. 89.

[55] *Ibid.*, pp. 90 f. The same writer continues, no less justly: 'Nous sommes loin de blâmer la condescendance de l'église envers les pouvoirs humains, car les choses humaines sont les choses humaines; les affaires sont les affaires. Mais parmi les affaires humaines, ne faut-il pas compter aussi l'état des cœurs? Atteindre un cœur dans ses plus chères convictions, briser une volonté qui ne demande qu'à se soumettre, mais demande aussi à ne pas être accablée, foulée aux pieds, est-ce bien conforme à la mansuétude chrétienne? Ce que l'on demandait à Lamennais, ce n'est pas la soumission, mais une soumission absolue, illimitée, sans aucune réserve. La soumission Lamennais l'avait faite . . .

'Vaincu et humilié, Lamennais se laissa aller, par une réaction facile à comprendre, mais moins facile peut-être à excuser, à un acte de révolte et de colère qui retentit dans le monde entier.'—*Ibid.*, pp. 91, 93.

[56] See *L. à M.*, p. 205.

APPENDIX

(see p. 246, *supra*)

Chapters IX and XXIII of *Paroles d'un Croyant*

IX

Vous êtes dans ce monde comme des étrangers.

Allez au nord et au midi, à l'orient et à l'occident, partout en quelque endroit que vous vous arrêtiez, vous trouverez un homme qui vous en chassera, en disant: Ce champ est à moi.

Et après avoir parcouru tous les pays, vous reviendrez sachant qu'il n'y a nulle part un pauvre petit coin de terre où votre femme en travail puisse enfanter son premier né, où vous puissiez reposer après votre labeur, où, arrivé au dernier terme, vos enfants puissent enfouir vos os, comme dans un lieu qui soit à vous.

C'est là, certes, une grande misère.

Et pourtant, vous ne devez pas vous trop affliger, car il est écrit de celui qui a sauvé la race humaine:

Le renard a sa tanière, les oiseaux du ciel ont leur nid, mais le fils de l'homme n'a pas où reposer sa tête.

Or il s'est fait pauvre, pour vous apprendre à supporter la pauvreté.

Ce n'est pas que la pauvreté vienne de Dieu, mais elle est une suite de la corruption et des mauvaises convoitises des hommes, et c'est pourquoi il y aura toujours des pauvres.

La pauvreté est fille du péché dont le germe est en chaque homme, et de la servitude dont le germe est en chaque société.

Il y aura toujours des pauvres, parce que jamais l'homme ne détruira complètement le péché en soi.

Il y aura toujours moins de pauvres, parce que peu à peu la servitude disparaîtra de la société.

Voulez-vous travailler à détruire la pauvreté, travaillez à détruire le péché, en vous premièrement, puis dans les autres, et la servitude dans la société.

Ce n'est pas en prenant ce qui est à autrui qu'on peut détruire la pauvreté: car comment, en faisant des pauvres, diminueroit-on le nombre des pauvres?

Chacun a droit de conserver ce qu'il a, sans quoi personne ne posséderoit rien.

Mais chacun a droit d'acquérir par son travail ce qu'il n'a pas, sans quoi la pauvreté serait éternelle.

Affranchissez donc votre travail, affranchissez vos bras, et la pauvreté ne sera plus parmi les hommes qu'une exception permise de Dieu pour leur rappeler l'infirmité de leur nature, et le secours mutuel et l'amour qu'ils se doivent les uns aux autres.

XXIII

Seigneur, nous crions vers vous du fond de notre misère.

Comme les animaux qui manquent de pâture pour donner à leurs petits:

Nous crions vers vous, Seigneur.

Comme la brebis à qui on enlève son agneau:

Nous crions vers vous, Seigneur.

Comme la colombe que saisit le vautour:

Nous crions vers vous, Seigneur.

Comme la gazelle sous la griffe du tigre:

Nous crions vers vous, Seigneur.

Comme le taureau épuisé de fatigue et ensanglanté par l'aiguillon:

Nous crions vers vous, Seigneur.

Comme l'oiseau blessé que le chien poursuit:

Nous crions vers vous, Seigneur.

Comme l'hirondelle tombée de lassitude en traversant les mers, et se débattant sur la vague:

Nous crions vers vous, Seigneur.

Comme des voyageurs égarés dans un désert brûlant et sans eau:

Nous crions vers vous, Seigneur.

Comme des naufragés sur une côte stérile:

Nous crions vers vous, Seigneur.

Comme celui qui, à l'heure où la nuit se fait, rencontre près d'un cimetière un spectre hideux:

Nous crions vers vous, Seigneur.

Comme le père à qui on ravit le morceau de pain qu'il portoit à ses enfants affamés:

Nous crions vers vous, Seigneur.

Comme le prisonnier que le Puissant injuste a jeté dans un cachot humide et ténébreux:

Nous crions vers vous, Seigneur.

Comme l'esclave déchiré par le fouet du maître:
Nous crions vers vous, Seigneur.
Comme l'innocent qu'on mène au supplice:
Nous crions vers vous, Seigneur.
Comme le peuple d'Israël dans la terre de servitude:
Nous crions vers vous, Seigneur.
Comme les descendants de Jacob dont le roi d'Egypte faisoit noyer
dans le Nil les fils premiers-nés:
Nous crions vers vous, Seigneur.
Comme les douze tribus dont les oppresseurs augmentoient chaque
jour les travaux, en retranchant chaque jour quelque chose de leur
nourriture:
Nous crions vers vous, Seigneur.
Comme toutes les nations de la terre, avant qu'eût lui l'aurore de
la délivrance:
Nous crions vers vous, Seigneur.
Comme le Christ sur la croix, lors-qu'il dit: Mon Père, mon Père,
pourquoi m'avez-vous délaissé?
Nous crions vers vous, Seigneur.
O Père! vous n'avez point délaissé votre Fils, votre Christ, si ce
n'est en apparence et pour un moment; vous ne délaisserez point
non plus à jamais les frères du Christ. Son divin sang, qui les a
rachetés de l'esclavage du Prince de ce monde, les rachètera aussi de
l'esclavage des ministres du Prince de ce monde. Voyez leurs pieds
et leurs mains percés, leur côté ouvert, leur tête couverte de plaies
sanglantes. Sous la terre que vous leur aviez donnée pour héritage,
on leur a creusé un vaste sépulcre, et on les y a jetés pêle-mêle, et on
en a scellé la pierre d'un sceau sur lequel on a, par moquerie, gravé
votre saint nom. Et ainsi, Seigneur, ils sont là gisants: mais ils n'y
seront pas éternellement. Encore trois jours, et le sceau sacrilège
sera brisé, et la pierre sera brisée, et ceux qui dorment se réveilleront,
et le règne du Christ, qui est justice et charité, et paix et joie dans
l'Esprit saint, commencera. Ainsi soit-il.

BIBLIOGRAPHY

The following books have been used in the preparation of the present study. The abbreviations, by which some of them are referred to, are given in bold type. The fullest existing bibliographies of literature about Lamennais are F. Duine, Essai de Bibliographie de Félicité Robert de La Mennais (1923) and H. Talvart and J. Place, Bibliographie des Auteurs modernes de langue française (1952), XI, 167–229.

AHRENS, LISELOTTE, *Lamennais und Deutschland: Studien zur Geschichte der französischen Restauration* (1930) **[Ahrens]**.

Articles de l'Avenir, 7 vols (1830–1831) **[A.A.]**.

AUBERT, R., *Le pontificat de Pie IX 1846–1878* (1952).

— AND OTHERS, *Tolérance et communauté humaine* (1952).

BAGGE, DOMINIQUE, *Les idées politiques en France sous la Restauration* (1952).

BINDEL, VICTOR, *Le Vatican à Paris, 1809–1814* (1943).

BLAIZE, A., *Essai biographique sur M. F. de La Mennais* (1858).

— *Œuvres inédites de F. Lamennais*, 2 vols (1866) **[Blaize]**.

BOUDOU, ADRIEN, *Le Saint-Siège et la Russie: leurs relations diplomatiques au xixᵉ siècle*, vol. I, 1814–1847 (1922).

BOURGEOIS, ÉMILE, *Modern France*, vol. I, 1815–1852 (1919).

BOURGET, P., and M. SALOMON, *Bonald* (1904).

BOURGOGNE, J. GESLIN DE, and A. DE BARTHÉLEMY, *Études sur la Révolution en Bretagne* (1858).

BOUTARD, CHARLES, *Lamennais: sa vie et ses doctrines*, 3 vols (1905–1913) **[Boutard]**.

BRACHET, VICOMTE DE, *Le Conventionnel J.-B. Le Carpentier, 1759–1829* (1912).

BRÉHAT, RENÉ, *Lamennais le trop chrétien* (1941).

BREMOND, HENRI, *Gerbet* (1907).

— *L'Inquiétude Religieuse*, 2nd series (⁴1921).

— *Pour le romantisme* (1923).

BURNAND, ROBERT, *La Vie quotidienne en France en 1830* (1943).

CARCOPINO, CLAUDE, *Les Doctrines sociales de Lamennais* (1942).

Censure de cinquante-six propositions, extraites de divers écrits de M. de la Mennais et ses disciples, par plusieurs évêques de France, etc. (1835).

CHATEAUBRIAND, *Mémoires d'outre-tombe*, Ed. Pierre Moreau, 6 vols, Garnier.

CHRÉTIEN, ALPHONSE, *Le Christianisme de Lamennais* (1897).

CHURCH, R. W., *Occasional Papers*, vol. I (1897).

COLLIN, SULLIAN, *Dans l'intimité des deux La Mennais* (1935).

CONGAR, YVES M.-J., *Vraie et fausse Réforme dans l'Église* (1950).

CONSTANT, G., *L'Église de France sous le Consulat et l'Empire 1800–1814* (1928).

CZAPSKA, MARIE, *La Vie de Mickiewicz* (1931).

DEBIDOUR, A., *Histoire des rapports de l'Église et de l'État en France de 1789 à 1870* (1898) **[Debidour]**.

DE COURCY, HENRI, *Lettres inédites de J.-M. et F. de La Mennais adressées à Mgr Bruté*, Introduction by E. de la Gournerie (1862) [**De Courcy**].

D'HAUSSONVILLE, *Lettres inédites de Lamennais à la baronne Cottu 1818–1854* (1910) [**Cottu**].

DOWDEN, EDWARD, *Studies in Literature 1789–1877* (1878)

DUBOIS, PIERRE, *Victor Hugo: ses idées religieuses 1802–1825* (1913).

DUBREUIL, LEON, *Le Régime révolutionnaire dans le district de Dinan* (1912).

DUDON, PAUL, *Lamennais et le Saint-Siège 1820–1834 d'après documents inédits et les Archives du Vatican* (1911) [**L. et le S.S.**].

DUINE, FRANÇOIS, *Documents ménaisiens* (1919).

— *La Mennais: sa vie, ses idées, ses ouvrages* (1922) [**Duine**].

DUROSELLE, J. B., *Les Débuts du Catholicisme social en France 1822–1870* (1951).

EVANS, DAVID OWEN, *Social Romanticism in France 1830–1848* (1951).

FAGUET, ÉMILE, *Politiques et Moralistes du xixe siècle*, 2nd series (1898).

FEUGÈRE, ANATOLE, *Lamennais avant l'Essai sur l'indifférence d'après des documents inédits 1782–1817* (1906) [**Feugère**].

FOISSET, J. T., *Vie du R. P. Lacordaire*, 2 vols (1870).

FOLLENAY, PAGUELLE DE, *Monsieur Teysseyrre* (1882).

FORGUES, EUGÈNE, *Correspondance inédite entre Lamennais et le baron de Vitrolles* (1886) [**Vitrolles**].

— *Lettres inédites de Lamennais à Montalembert* (1898) [**L. à M.**].

FORGUES, ÉMILE D., *Lamennais: Correspondance*, 2 vols (1863) [**Forgues**].

FUNCK-BRENTANO, FRANTZ, *The Old Regime in France* (1929).

GARNIER, ADRIEN, *Frayssinous: son rôle dans l'Université sous la Restauration 1822–1828* (1925).

— *Les Ordonnances du 16 juin 1828 d'après documents inédits tirés des Archives du Vatican et des Archives Nationales* (1929).

GIBSON, THE HON. W., *The Abbé de Lamennais and the Liberal Catholic Movement in France* (1896).

GIRAUD, VICTOR, *La Vie tragique de Lamennais* (1933).

GODECHOT, JACQUES, *Les Institutions de la France sous la Révolution et l'Empire* (1951).

GORCE, P. DE LA, *Histoire religieuse de la Révolution française*, vols I–III.

— *Louis XVIII* ([26]1926).

GOYAU, G., *Le Portefeuille de Lamennais 1818–1836* (1930) [**Portefeuille**].

— and P. DE LALLEMAND, *Lettres de Montalembert à La Mennais* (1932) [**M. à L.**].

GRANDMAISON, GEOFFROY DE, *La Congrégation* (1889).

GUÉRIN, MAURICE DE, *Journal, Lettres et Poèmes*, Ed. G. S. Trébutien ([27]1922).

— *Correspondance*, Ed. Bernard d'Harcourt (1947).

HAAG, HENRI, *Les Origines du Catholicisme libéral en Belgique 1789–1839* (1950) [**Haag**].

HARISPE, PIERRE, *Lamennais et Gerbet* (1909).

— *Lamennais: drame de sa vie sacerdotale* (1924).

HAVARD DE LA MONTAGNE, ROBERT, *Histoire de la Démocratie chrétienne de Lamennais à Georges Bidault* (1948).

HERPIN, E., *Saint-Malo sous la Révolution 1789–1800* (1931).

HOCEDEZ, EDGAR, *Histoire de la Théologie au xixᵉ siècle*, 3 vols (1947–1952).
HOISS, AMALIE, *Histoire d'un livre: Affaires de Rome par F. de Lamennais* (1933).
HOUTIN, ALBERT, *Un Dernier Gallican: Henri Bernier* (²1904).

JANET, PAUL, *La Philosophie de Lamennais* (1890).

LADOUE, C. DE, *Monseigneur Gerbet: sa vie, ses œuvres et l'école menaissienne*, vol. 1,
    (1872).
LALLEMAND, P. DE, *Montalembert et ses amis dans le romantisme 1830–1840* (1927).
LAMENNAIS, F., *Œuvres complètes*, 12 vols (1836–1837) [**O.C.**].
— *Tradition de l'Église sur l'institution des évêques*, 3 vols (²1818) [**Tradition**].
— *Essai sur l'indifférence en matière de religion*, 4 vols, Garnier [**Essai**].
— *Essay on Indifference in Matters of Religion*, vol. 1, Trans. Lord Stanley of Alderley
    (1895).
— *Le Guide du premier âge* (²1830).
— *L'Imitation de Jésus-Christ. Traduction nouvelle avec des réflections à la fin de chaque
    chapitre* (1824).
— *The People's Prophecy*, Trans. C. Reavely (1943).
— *Affaires de Rome*, Garnier [**A.R.**].
— *Mélanges philosophiques et politiques*, Ed. E. D. Forgues (1856).
LASKI, H. J., *Authority in the Modern State* (1919).
LATREILLE, A., *L'Église catholique et la Révolution française*, 2 vols (1946–1950).
LATREILLE, C., *Le Marquis de Coriolis: lettres à Lamennais 1825–1837* (1912).
LAURENTIE, *Souvenirs inédits*, Ed. J. Laurentie (1892).
LAVEILLE, AUGUSTE, *Un Lamennais inconnu: lettres inédites de Lamennais à Benoît
    d'Azy* (1898) [**Lamennais inconnu**].
— *Jean-Marie de La Mennais 1780–1860*, 2 vols (1903).
LAVISSE and RAMBAUD, *Les Monarchies constitutionnelles 1815–1847* (vol. X of
    Histoire générale) (1898).
LAZERGES, PAUL, *Lamennais: essai sur l'unité de sa pensée* (1895).
LECANUET, *Montalembert*, 3 vols (1910–1912).
LEFLON, JEAN, *Monsieur Emery*, 2 vols (1944–1946).
— *La crise révolutionnaire 1789–1846* (1949).
LE HIR, YVES, *Lamennais écrivain* (1948).
— *Les 'Paroles d'un Croyant' de Lamennais: texte publié sur le manuscrit autographe*
    (1949) [**P.C.**].
LILLY, W. S., *Studies in Religion and Literature* (1904).
LUCAS-DUBRETON, J., *La Restauration et la Monarchie de juillet* (1926).
— *Louis-Philippe* (1938).

MAHIEU, LÉON, *Mgr Louis Belmas 1757–1841*, 2 vols (1934).
MAISTRE, JOSEPH DE, *The Pope*, Trans. A. McD. Dawson (1850).
MARÉCHAL, CHRISTIAN, *La Famille de La Mennais sous l'ancien régime et la révolution*
    (1913) [**Famille**].
— *La Jeunesse de La Mennais* (1913) [**Jeunesse**].
— *La Clef de 'Volupté'* (1905).
— *Lamennais et Victor Hugo* (1906).
— *Lamennais et Lamartine* (1907).

— *Essai d'un système de philosophie catholique (1830–1831) par F. de La Mennais* (1906).

— *La Mennais: la Dispute de l'Essai sur l'indifférence* (1925) [**Dispute**].

— *La Mennais au Drapeau Blanc* (1946).

MARTIN, J. P., *La Nonciature de Paris et les affaires ecclésiastiques de France sous le règne de Louis-Philippe 1830–1848* (1949).

MENCZER, BELA, *Catholic Political Thought 1789–1848* (1952).

MERCIER, R. P., *Lamennais d'après sa correspondance et les travaux les plus récents* (1895).

MIRECOURT, EUGÈNE DE, *L'Abbé Lamennais* (1854).

MONTALEMBERT, *Memoir of the Abbé Lacordaire* (1863).

MONTLOSIER, R. DE, *Mémoire à consulter sur un système religieux* ([3]1826).

MORLEY, JOHN VISCOUNT, *Biographical Studies* (Edition de luxe, 1921).

— *Voltaire* (Edition de luxe, 1921).

— *Rousseau* (Edition de luxe, 1921).

MOULINÉ, HENRI, *De Bonald* (1915).

MOURRET, FERNAND, *Le Mouvement catholique en France de 1830 à 1850* (1917).

NEWMAN, J. H., *Essays Critical and Historical*, vol. I ([10]1890).

NICHOLS, JAMES HASTINGS, *Democracy and the Churches* (1951).

PASQUIER, CHANCELIER, *Mémoires*, 6 vols ([6]1894).

PEIGNÉ, J. M., *Lamennais: sa vie intime à la Chênaie* (1864).

PÉRIN, CHARLES, *Le Modernisme dans l'Église d'après des lettres inédites de La Mennais* (1881).

[PEYRAT, NAPOLÉON], *Béranger et Lamennais* (1861).

PHILLIPS, C. S., *The Church in France 1789–1848* (1929).

PLAMENATZ, JOHN, *The Revolutionary Movement in France 1815–1871* (1952).

POISSON, JACQUES, *Le Romantisme social de Lamennais* (1932).

POULET, CHARLES, *Histoire de l'Église de France: époque contemporaine* (1949).

Procès de l'Avenir (1831).

QUÉRARD, J. M., *Les Supercheries littéraires dévoilées*, vol. II ([2]1869–1870).

RICARD, A., *Gerbet et Salinis* ([2]1883).

— *Lamennais* ([5]1895).

RIO, A.-F., *Épilogue à l'art chrétien*, vol. II (1870).

ROHRBACHER, *Histoire universelle de l'Église catholique*, vol. XX (1845).

ROPARTZ, *La Vie et les Œuvres de M. Jean-Marie Robert de La Mennais* (1874).

ROUSSEAU, J. J., *Émile ou de l'Éducation*, Garnier.

ROUSSEL, ALFRED, *Lamennais d'après documents inédits*, 2 vols. (1893) [**Documents**].

— *Lamennais intime* (1897).

— *Lamennais à La Chênaie* (1909).

— *Lamennais et ses correspondants inconnus* (1912) [**Correspondants**].

— and INGOLD, *Lamennais et David Richard* (1909).

SAINTE-BEUVE, *Les Grands Écrivains Français: xixᵉ siècle. Philosophes et essayistes*, vols. I–III, Ed. Maurice Allem (1930) [**Sainte-Beuve**].

SAINTE-FOI, CHARLES, *Souvenirs de Jeunesse 1828–1835*, Ed. C. Latreille (1911).

SCHMIDLIN, JOSEPH, *Histoires des papes de l'époque contemporaine 1800–1846*, vol. I, parts I and II (1938–1940) [**Schmidlin**, I and II].

SEVRIN, ERNEST, *Dom Guéranger et La Mennais* (1933).
SIMON, A., *L'Église catholique et les Débuts de la Belgique indépendante* (1949).
SOLTAU, ROGER, *French Political Thought in the Nineteenth Century* (1931).
SPARROW SIMPSON, W. J., *French Catholics in the Nineteenth Century* (1918).
— *A Study of Bossuet* (1937).
SPULLER, E., *Lamennais: étude d'histoire politique et religieuse* (1892).

THOMPSON, J. M., *The French Revolution* (^{2}1944).
— *Leaders of the French Revolution* (^{2}1932).
THUREAU-DANGIN, PAUL, *Royalistes et Républicains* (1874).
— *Le Parti libéral sous la Restauration* (^{2}1888).
— *L'Église et l'État sous la Monarchie de juillet* (1880).
TRANNOY, ANDRÉ, *Le Romantisme politique de Montalembert avant 1843* (1942)
    [**Trannoy**].
TYRRELL, GEORGE, *The Faith of the Millions*, 2nd series (^{2}1902).

VALLERY-RADOT, ROBERT, *Lamennais ou le prêtre malgré lui* (1931).
VERSLUYS, J. C., *Essai sur le Caractère de Lamennais* (1929) [**Versluys**].
VIATTE, A., *Le catholicisme chez les romantiques* (1922).
VILLEFOSSE, LOUIS DE, *Lamennais ou l'occasion manquée* (1945).
VILLERABEL, A. DU B. DE LA, *Confidences de La Mennais: lettres inédites de 1821–1848*
    (1886) [**Confidences**].
VULLIAUD, *Les Paroles d'un Croyant de Lamennais* (1928).

WALSH, H. H., *The Concordat of 1801: a study of the problem of nationalism in the
    relations of church and state* (1933).
WARD, WILFRID, *William George Ward and the Catholic Revival* (1912).
WEILL, GEORGES, *La France sous la Monarchie constitutionnelle 1814–1848* (1902).
— *Histoire du Catholicisme libéral en France 1828–1908* (1909).
WHITEHOUSE, H. R., *The Life of Lamartine*, 2 vols (1918).
WISEMAN, CARDINAL, *Recollections of the Last Four Popes* (1858).
WOODWARD, E. L., *Three Studies in European Conservatism* (1929).

Note.—The periodicals that have been used are included in the index as well as
    specified in the footnotes.

INDEX